CORBA Distributed Objects

Using Orbix

ACM Press Books

This book is published as part of ACM Press Books – a collaboration between the Association for Computing Machinery and Addison Wesley Longman Limited. ACM is the oldest and largest educational and scientific society in the information technology field. Through its high quality publications and services, ACM is a major force in advancing the skills and knowledge of IT professionals throughout the world. For further information about ACM contact:

ACM Member Services
1515 Broadway, 17th Floor
New York NY 10036-5701
Phone: + 1 212 626 0500
Fax: + 1 212 944 1318
e-mail: acmhelp@acm.org

ACM European Service Center
108 Cowley Road
Oxford OX4 1JF
United Kingdom
Phone: 44 1865 382338
Fax: 44 1865 381338
e-mail: acm-europe@acm.org
URL: http://www.acm.org

Selected ACM titles:

Software Requirements and Specifications: A Lexicon of Software Practice, Principles and Prejudices *Michael Jackson*

Bringing Design to Software: Expanding Software Development to Include Design
Terry Winograd, John Bennett, Laura de Young, Bradley Hartfield

The Object Advantage: Business Process Reengineering with Object Technology 2/e
Ivar Jacobson, Maria Ericsson, Agneta Jacobson, Gunnar Magnusson

Software for Use: A Practical Guide to the Models and Methods of Usage Centered Design *Larry L Constantine & Lucy A D Lockwood*

Business Process Implementation, Building Workflow Systems
Michael Jackson & Graham Twaddle

Software Reuse: Architecture, Process and Organization for Business Success
Ivar Jacobson, Martin Griss, Patrik Jonsson

Intelligent Database Systems *Elisa Bertino, Gian Piero Zarri*

Internet Security *Dorothy E Denning & Peter J Denning*

CORBA Distributed Objects

Using Orbix

Seán Baker

IONA Technologies

orbix distributed object technology

ACM Press

Addison-Wesley

Harlow, England • Reading, Massachusetts • Menlo Park, California
New York • Don Mills, Ontario • Amsterdam • Bonn • Sydney • Singapore
Tokyo • Madrid • San Juan • Milan • Mexico City • Seoul • Taipei

Addison Wesley Longman Limited
Edinburgh Gate
Harlow
Essex
CM20 2JE
United Kingdom
and Associated Companies throughout the world.

Cover designed by odB Design & Communication, Reading
and printed by RR Donnelley & Sons Co., USA.
Text design by Sally Grover Castle.
Typeset by 24
Printed and bound in the United States of America by RR Donnelley & Sons Co.

First printed 1997. Reprinted 1997.

ISBN 0-201-92475-7

British Library Cataloguing-in-Publication Data
A catalogue record for this book is available from the British Library.

Library of Congress Cataloging-in-Publication Data
Baker, Seán, 1958–
CORBA distributed objects / Seán Baker.
p. cm.
Includes index.
ISBN 0201-92475-7 (alk.paper)
1. Object-oriented programming (Computer science) 2. CORBA (Computer architecture)
3. Electronic data processing – Distributed processing. I. Title.
OA76.64.B28 1997
005.2'76'0218 - - dc21 97-14386
CIP

To Jane and Sinead

Foreword

Software's next infrastructure

Unless you live under a rock, you will have noticed the emergence of *real* distributed computing, in contrast to the more basic distributed *access* to servers that has been popular up to now.

When networks were new, the relationship of one-application/one-protocol was such a big advance that people did not worry about how limiting it was – files were files, email was email, and if the twain never met, so be it. Those days are long past, and now users need to move beyond integrated email, files and web pages to integrated, distributed applications that use intranets and the Internet as a natural extra dimension.

A touch of history

When I was setting up the Object Management Group (OMG), the major goal was to free the object programmer (as well as the object user) from the intricacies of network programming. In the late 1980s this was met with a resounding 'huh?'. Most programmers were writing standalone multi-user applications. Network applications were alien. Around 1991, the early members of OMG proposed a sensible step, only a few years ahead of its time: suppose, instead of building software as huge monolithic chunks and regarding network connections as unusual features, we designed our software as sets of independent components or objects that could interoperate with other objects regardless of whether they were located locally or remotely from them. In this architecture, network interoperability comes naturally to every component; a big step taken in anticipation of the networked world that lay ahead. Around the world, many researchers, including those at Trinity College, Dublin, were researching this area.

In 1992, OMG defined the standard for an Object Request Broker or ORB, a software component that resides with or near every client and object. An ORB receives invocations from a client, and delivers these to a target object. What if the client and target do not reside on the same machine? In this case, there are two ORBs involved: the client's ORB sends the request over the network to the ORB of the target object, which delivers it to the object itself. Client and object code stay simple, concentrating on core business. Network complexity is dealt with by the ORB – software you bought, not software you built. This is the fundamental idea behind the Common Object Request Broker Architecture (CORBA). It is rapidly becoming the replacement protocol for the World Wide Web. A web of 'interconnected' ORBs will form the basis of how Electronic Commerce and many other applications are conducted over the Internet.

An industry is born

CORBA and IIOP are developments that happened to be in the right place at the right time, and are not prototypes churned out quickly in response to recent 'web time' demands. They were specified and developed by OMG members in an open process, designed by some of the best minds in distributed computing today. From the beginning, they have been designed to meet even the needs of the large, multinational enterprise where robustness, scalability, security and value are evaluated by discerning professionals whenever a new architecture is selected. These characteristics also make CORBA and IIOP the architecture/protocol combination of choice for the World Wide Web.

It will take more than just the core ORB to satisfy all needs, and fortunately a set of layered services are already defined within the CORBA specification. These services are beginning to be deployed rapidly by the suppliers, resulting in services such as Security, Trading, Naming, Transactions, Messaging, and so on. CORBA technology is available off-the-shelf from more than a dozen large and small vendors whose customers use it today in mission-critical systems around the world. IONA Technologies have been instrumental in providing the middleware technology for the fastest growing area of software technology today (1997 revenue of $300 million+), and over the next 5 years ($3 billion by the year 2000).

Seán's book is needed. While many books exist on the subject of distributed objects and programming with CORBA, this book gives a very detailed description of how to use CORBA, IDL, IIOP and the services. It will be required reading for most corporate developers embarking on the road toward distributed objects for the Enterprise or the Internet.

Thanks Seán.

Christopher Stone
CEO, Object Management Group
March 1997

Preface

This book gives a detailed explanation of the CORBA standard, by explaining in full how to use one implementation – the Orbix system from IONA Technologies. I believe that the features and benefits of CORBA cannot be fully understood without looking, in detail, at how to use one implementation. The standard itself, like all standards, is too detailed and abstract to be easily understood.

The book is aimed at designers and analyst/programmers whose applications can run in a distributed, possibly heterogeneous, environment. This heterogeneity may arise because of the use of different programming languages, different operating systems, or different types of networks. Typical users of CORBA will be building either a new system or a system from new and existing components. The book is aimed primarily at programmers who need to have an understanding of CORBA and how it can be used to write component-based software systems.

The choice of Orbix is obvious for a co-founder of IONA, but the choice can easily be justified because Orbix is a complete implementation of the standard, and because it is easy to use and widely adopted. To help readers understand CORBA better, Orbix-specific features are pointed out. Also, there are a number of chapters that are dedicated to explaining Orbix-specifics: these have been included because they give useful insight into the nature of distributed computing, and because they show how other technologies can be integrated with CORBA. Such integrations are very important, because CORBA does not exist in isolation. These technologies and techniques include threading, databases, caching, and monitoring.

C++ is used for programming examples in some parts of the book – to write clients, to implement interfaces, and to write servers. Therefore a basic understanding of C++ is required to get the most from some of the chapters. Readers do not need to be experts on the language, however. Some example code is also shown in Java and in Visual Basic, and the CORBA and OLE integration is also described and illustrated.

A cinema example is used for the coding examples because it could be extended to demonstrate most of the features of CORBA, and because it is a good example of an important rule: that a designer must be careful to allow today's application to act as a component of a larger system tomorrow. It is also an example that can be understood by readers from many different industry domains. This is important because CORBA is being used in telecommunications, manufacturing, finance, realtime, healthcare, embedded systems, defense, education, petrochemical, transport, electronic commerce, and other vertical markets.

I wrote this book because I wanted to give a detailed explanation of the CORBA standard, at the level that IT professionals would appreciate. It is difficult to tread the line between too much detail, which tends to obscure the overall principles, and too little detail, which tends to confuse readers who cannot be happy with a vague understanding. The reader must judge whether or not I have achieved a useful balance, and at the same time shown that the standard is simple and easy to use.

Most of the book can be read without serious study, but in two cases it is likely to go beyond the level of detail that the average reader appreciates: in the two IDL to C++ memory mapping chapters, and in the explanation of the Interface Repository. These chapters require serious study to be fully understood, but the advanced and detailed material has been marked with ✚ at the beginning and end of each of these sections, allowing most readers to read only the introductory material. Some of the marked details will act as a good reference source for advanced users. Chapter 4 covers the most commonly used data types (basic types, strings, and object references), and Chapter 5 discusses the more complex types, such as sequences and unions.

The material in 10 of the 27 chapters started its days as part of the Orbix Programming Guide, but unnecessary details have been removed, advice and comment added, and the examples made more extensive. Naturally, this removal of detail means that this book is not a replacement for a programming guide; nevertheless, sufficient detail is given to fully understand CORBA and to use it – once environment-specific details are understood.

This is a book on CORBA usage, not on how the standard is implemented. Therefore, it does not discuss the internals of Orbix, nor how the communication system is used. For example, the role of the IIOP protocol is explained, but its details are not discussed.

The **core CORBA standard** is covered in depth, including the CORBA Interface Definition Language (IDL), the writing of C++ clients and servers, the Implementation Repository, inheritance, exception handling, the Dynamic Interface Repository (DII), and the Interface Repository. The **CORBAservices**, which extend this core, are also explained in depth, but coding examples are given only for the Naming Service. The other CORBAservices in the current set of 14 are explained in various levels of detail, depending on their importance and complexity. The motivation for each service is given, followed by a technical explanation of how it works and what interfaces it offers its clients. Many of these interfaces are given in whole or in part as reference material in Appendix A.

The **CORBAfacililities** are not covered in any detail because these are still under development, and for the most part are far removed from the *core* aspects of the CORBA standard.

In Jon Siegel's book (Siegel, 1996), of which myself and eight others are co-authors, a Point of Sale example was introduced to demonstrate code from many different implementations of CORBA, for example Orbix and ORB Plus. This example is also used in Chapter 26 of this book, but the IDL definitions are simplified somewhat, and only an outline of the implementation choices is given.

The timing of this book has been a difficult choice, given the rapid pace of development in CORBA and object-oriented middleware in general. As luck would have it, this seems to be a quiet period for new CORBAservices, with only collections and versioning (change management) in the pipeline. A better motivation for waiting a few extra months would be that the CORBA server-side portability rules would then be clear; but this book has been in preparation for too long already, so I believe that the decision to go ahead now is sensible. Therefore, some of the detail of the server-side coding (in particular, the so-called BOAImpl and TIE approaches) will change over the next year, but the overall approach will remain stable. Some change notes will be provided on www.iona.com once the new standardization has been finalized.

Structure

This book is longer than planned – but then there is so much to say:-). Because different readers will need to focus on different aspects of CORBA and Orbix, it has been divided into the following parts:

- Part 1 covers the most important way of using the core CORBA standard – in effect, the aspects that are used day to day by most programmers. Chapter 2, 'Getting started with CORBA,' presents a simple view of how to write clients and servers, and this is expanded on in the subsequent chapters in this part.
- Part 2 discusses the integration of CORBA with the OLE application integration system for Windows. It also gives examples of using CORBA from Visual Basic and Java.
- Part 3 extends the coverage of Part 1 by introducing the remainder of the core CORBA standard. In particular, it covers the *dynamic* aspects of CORBA, which many programmers do not need to use, but which are used extensively by some programmers.
- Part 4 introduces some advanced features of Orbix, which extend the standard and are useful for implementing distributed systems.
- Part 5 gives a detailed explanation of each of the CORBAservices (except the Naming Service, which is covered in Chapter 7, 'Naming and binding'). In each case, the motivation for the

service is explained in detail, and the interface definitions are explained, in whole or in part, depending on the importance and complexity of each individual service. The interface definitions for some of the services are given in Appendix A, 'IDL interfaces for selected CORBAservices.'

- Part 6 presents a revised version of the Point of Sale example that appeared in Siegel (1996).

The introductory pages to each of the parts explain in more detail how they fit into the scope of the CORBA standard, and in some cases also briefly introduce some related topics that are not discussed in depth in the book.

All readers should read Part 1 to get an understanding of the most important way of using the core CORBA standard. Chapters 4 and 5 present the IDL to C++ mapping, and they should initially be read only in overview by most programmers. Only an initial understanding of the mapping is required to understand the rest of the chapters.

Part 2 presents the integration of CORBA and OLE. A basic understanding of this will be useful to all readers, and the example given can be studied by readers who need to have a fuller understanding of the integration. This short part also introduces support for programming languages other than C++.

All readers should have a *basic* understanding of the dynamic aspects of CORBA presented in Part 3, but most will not need to study this part in depth. The material marked as detailed (✚) need be read only by programmers who need to make extensive use of this alternative way of using CORBA.

Part 4 is Orbix-specific, but the material (other than the last few sections of Chapter 19, 'Smart proxies') is easy to read and is aimed at improving the reader's understanding of distributed systems.

Part 5 explains CORBAservices (the Naming Service is presented in Chapter 7, 'Naming and binding'). An outline understanding of the role of each service is useful, but the details need be read only if a particular service is of interest to the reader.

Finally, Part 6 discusses how the Point of Sale example can be implemented in CORBA. It does not present any code, but instead concentrates on showing how the features of CORBA can be used to implement this system. Many of the techniques will have been introduced in previous chapters, but it is useful to bring some of these together in one place, in a simple example.

Seán Baker
Dublin, April 1997

Acknowledgments

Some of my colleagues contributed code segments to this book, in particular coding the C++, Java, and Visual Basic client and server code for the cinema example and the revised point of sale example. My thanks to Dirk Slama, who wrote the C++ and Java code for the cinema, Eamon Walshe and Aidan Hollinshead, who wrote the C++ code for the revised point of sale system, and Paul Tunney, who wrote the Visual Basic client for the cinema.

I have had suggestions for how to improve the book from a number of my colleagues and friends who have seen preliminary versions. Of particular help were the detailed comments made by Michi Henning of DSTC in Australia. His attention to detail and hard work are greatly appreciated. Thanks also for comments and encouragement from Stephen Varey and Jim Watson.

Special thanks to Ann Barry, who has made extensive comments on most of this material and leads the IONA documentation team.

My thanks to Jenny Hughes for a great deal of production assistance; to Ciaran McHale, who wrote summary sheets for the C++ mapping rules for the IONA Professional Services team; to Alan Conway, for helping me to understand the motivation behind some of the parameter passing rules; to Paul O'Neill and Steve Vinoski, for proofreading the IDL to C++ mapping chapters; to Sam Joyce, for his comments on the CORBA–OLE integration, not to mention implementing it; to John Fleming, Paul Tunney, and Andrew Canning for detailed comments; to Andrew Condon, for help with the diagrams, CDs, and Seattle restaurants; to Ronan Geraghty, for help with the DII; to Cormac O Foghlu, for assistance; to John Keeling, for comments on the introduction; to Martin O'Riordan and Andrew Canning, for comments on the DSI; to John Moreau, for comments on OrbixTalk; to Dirk Slama, for comments on the OrbixWeb description; to Terence Cross, for comments on the IFR; to Pierce Hickey, for comments on the CORBA services chapters ; and special thanks to Aidan Hollinshead for checking 'getting started' example.

Special thanks to Jenny and Michael for making all of this possible, for cuppas, and for TLC.

Contents

1 Introduction

The design and implementation of software is a difficult and expensive activity, even where this can be done on a single stable platform using a single operating system and a single programming language. Unfortunately, a considerable amount of the software being written now faces a number of additional complexities:

- It must run on a network of machines, with the overall functionality distributed among these machines. The system's **distributed components** must then cooperate to satisfy the overall aim of the software.
- The machines on the system may run different operating systems, such as UNIX, Windows, MVS, OS/2, Macintosh, and many others; or realtime operating systems such as VxWorks, pSOS, and QNX.
- The components of the system must be integrated easily into new systems, perhaps systems that are not yet planned.
- Legacy systems must be integrated into the system, either to allow the new software to access the legacy data, or to request the legacy code to carry out some processing.
- It may be necessary to use different programming languages for the components of the system, perhaps because of the use of legacy systems or because a particular programming language is a good choice for some subset of the components. For example, Java or Visual Basic may be used at the front end; C++ may be used for core functionality; Smalltalk may be used for rapid prototyping of some components of a system; Ada may be required for contractual reasons; and so on. In addition, a

particular programming language may be forced on a project because some bought-in component can be used from only one or a small number of programming languages.

With these complexities, the cost of writing and maintaining software increases – unless we have a framework that addresses these problems.

The long-term cost of software can also be increased because individual projects produce independent applications that do not interact properly with each other. We then pay twice for software: we pay the cost of developing independent applications, and then we pay again when these applications need to be integrated.

New software needs to be written as a set of interacting components that can communicate across the boundaries of the network, different operating systems, and different programming languages, thus making the task of writing new software significantly easier. We must be able to wrap legacy code to make it act like other components that can easily become part of a system. Once a set of components has been written for one application, it must be possible to construct new applications that use these components – software that was written as part of an application must be able to act as a component of another system. The framework that helps programmers design and implement new applications for heterogeneous environments must encourage them to write components that can be used by new applications.

This book describes the CORBA (Common Object Request Broker Architecture) standard for object management, in which components are **objects** that can communicate with each other across boundaries such as the network, different operating systems, and different programming languages. As we will see in Section 1.4 (p.14), CORBA is defined and controlled by the members of the Object Management Group (OMG).

CORBA has two aims. Firstly, it makes it easier to implement new applications that must place components on different hosts on the network, or use different programming languages. Secondly, it encourages the writing of **open applications**, ones that can be used as components of larger systems. Each application is made up of components, and integration is supported by allowing other applications to communicate directly with these components – subject, of course, to security.

For example, in an electronic trading facility for company shares, it is likely that the investment banks that use the system will need to make independent choices of what operating systems and programming languages to use, rather than having these dictated by the company that provides the trading facility. Some may prefer to use C++ for its efficiency; others may wish to prototype in Smalltalk; others may wish to use Java for its user interface capabilities and because code can be loaded at runtime; and others may wish to use the Visual Basic scripting language built into an Excel spreadsheet. This is trivial to achieve in CORBA, simply by implementing the business objects of the share trading system as CORBA objects, and allowing the investment banks to interact with these objects in order to buy and sell shares. Even though the trading company views the share sales system as an application, the investment banks will treat it as a component of the larger systems that they construct.

There are alternatives, but these are less attractive. For example, the trading company could provide a library that does the low-level messaging required for remote calls, and could then port this to each required programming language and operating system combination.

Enterprise computing with CORBA

CORBA addresses three of the most serious difficulties in large scale – **enterprise level** – computing.

Firstly, it allows each project or department to make some independent decisions that are difficult to centralize, such as which operating systems and programming languages to use.

Secondly, CORBA recognizes that it is an error to make difficulties visible to many programmers who could be isolated from them. At the beginning of the 1980s, the Remote Procedure Call (RPC) concept was introduced as an early example of making some feature of a system **transparent** to most programmers. Some programmers have the time to learn to use low-level facilities for passing messages across a network, but others cannot afford this time, nor the time it takes to perfect their use in any application. Instead, RPC recognizes that all programmers know how to call functions, and so it automatically generates functions that a client can call to request some server on a different machine to carry out some action for it. The details of how messages are sent are hidden from most programmers, and, to some extent, the network is made transparent to them. To a large extent, calling an RPC function is just as simple as calling any other function, except that some extra errors can arise because the network must be used to send messages.

CORBA follows in this direction, but it uses an object-oriented, rather than a procedural, approach. CORBA is available for more operating systems and programming languages, and it addresses one of the weaknesses of RPC, the lack of a strong commercial standard.

Thirdly, without CORBA it has not been possible to use object-oriented design and implementation techniques at the enterprise level. Well-trained programmers can get significant benefits from these techniques within single applications, but these techniques have not been available for larger systems involving many machines and many applications developed by different teams over time. There are many examples of where good use has been made of C++ within a large, individual component, but where ad hoc interfacing has been used between components. These ad hoc interfaces may use a combination of RPC, message queuing, file formats, and so on, and may even be defined in terms of byte-level message formats. Hence, the internals of components may use modern software techniques, but the all-important enterprise level is unclear and poorly defined.

Use of object-oriented interfaces at the enterprise level offers the best benefits of all. Few attempts are made at present to portray object-orientation as a panacea for all software ills, but we know of no better technique for defining interfaces. Inheritance, encapsulation, redefinition, dynamic binding, and delegation are simple and powerful concepts used daily by all programmers using object-oriented languages, and their main contribution is to make it easy to define clear interfaces to objects, allowing their internals to be hidden. This is exactly the enterprise view that we wish to have: where a new application can reuse existing components simply by knowing their interfaces, and not have to worry about details of how or where they are implemented, or how messages are sent to them.

One of the strongest claims for object-oriented software is that it is easier to modify than software written using other techniques. Individual interfaces can be extended, and individual components can be rewritten, without requiring global changes. This property is particularly important at the enterprise level, where any global changes are prohibitively expensive to make.

CORBA enforces an overall object-oriented architecture, and the normal object-oriented facilities are available when designing components. However, the components themselves do not have to be implemented in an object-oriented programming language. This may seem a contradiction, but it must be remembered that once a component has a CORBA object-oriented interface visible to other components, its internal implementation details are hidden and are of no concern to other components. Hence, a component can have a CORBA object-oriented interface, but the majority of its code could be written in C, or some other procedural language.

One of the useful properties of CORBA is that it applies equally across all of the market segments, including manufacturing, telecommunications, finance, realtime, healthcare, embedded systems, defense, education, petrochemical, transport, and electronic commerce. As described in Section 1.3, the CORBA standard has been extended with various services, some of which apply to specific market segments.

1.1 System architecture

A typical system is made up of a set of **client programs** that make use of the objects distributed throughout the system. In most operating systems all processing must take place within some process, so each object must live in a process. In other operating systems, objects can run within threads or within dynamic link libraries. To avoid difficulties with terminology, CORBA states that objects exist within **servers**. (CORBA frequently uses the term *implementation* instead of *server*, but we will use the more commonly accepted term here.) Each object is associated with a single server, and if an object's server is not running when an invocation is made on it, CORBA will automatically activate it. This activation may mean the starting of a process or thread, or the loading of a library, depending on the operating system that the server is registered on. On UNIX, for example, a server may be dormant, and therefore have no process associated with it; or it can be activated, and therefore have a process running its code. In fact, as we will see in later chapters, some servers can have more than one process associated with them.

A server's code includes the code that implements the objects (actually, their types) it contains. It also includes a main function (`main()` in C++) that initializes the server and, normally, creates an initial set of objects. Because objects can be small, a server can contain many CORBA objects. These can all be of the same type, or a server can support objects of different types without any difficulty or special coding. It can also support non-CORBA objects; for example, C++ objects that can only be accessed from within the server. Figure 1.1 shows a client making a call on a CORBA object in a remote server. Another server and its objects are also shown. Note that a server itself cannot be invoked by clients, only its CORBA objects can be.

Even though CORBA uses the terms *client* and *server*, this does not mean that the system must have a star-shaped architecture, where a set of client machines uses a single server machine in the center. Instead, the objects in one server can use the objects in other servers. This is very useful when decomposing a system into components, because it allows a client to invoke on an object in a server, and for that object to invoke on others in order to fulfil the client's request. A server that makes a call to an object remote to it (in another server, on the same or a different machine) is acting as a client for the duration of the call. Note also that the term *remote* is normally used if the call is to another server, even if this is on the same machine as the caller. The first degree of transparency is achieved because the same syntax is used for calls to objects in the same address space, and to objects in different servers on the local and on remote machines.

A set of servers may also cooperate to provide an overall **service** to a client, and in fact there are different ways in which this can be done. In one scheme, each of the servers in the set may provide the same functionality, and a client can use any one of these. A client may choose the one local to it, or if the network is sufficiently fast, it may choose a server that is not heavily loaded. In another scheme, each of the servers in the set can carry out a specialized function: a client might communicate with an object in one of the servers, and this object might use the facilities of the objects in the other servers.

In many cases, each new application added to the system will require the addition of a new client to provide a user interface. It is also likely that some servers

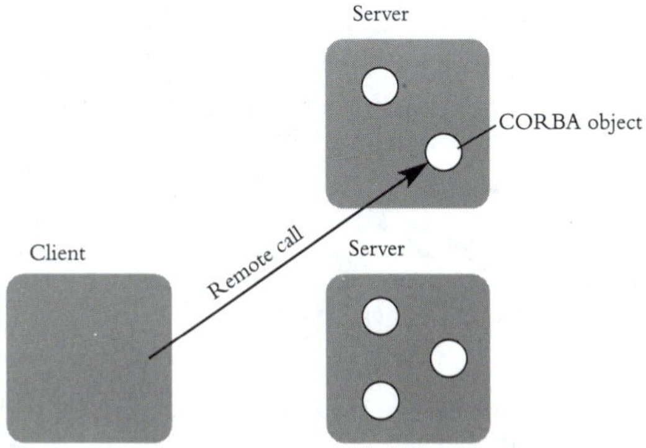

Figure 1.1 *Clients, servers, and objects.*

will need to be added, or some of the existing ones extended. It is important, however, to use as many of the existing objects as possible, so that the network of components can be made use of.

In some implementations of CORBA, client code can also contain CORBA objects. This is very useful because it means that servers can make calls to these objects, perhaps to inform them that some event has occurred, or simply to keep them informed of the current value of some data. The normal way for a server to find an object in a client is for the client to pass a reference to the object to the server as a parameter to some previous call. Object references are easily passed in this way, even between code written in different programming languages.

In most large systems, the speed of the servers has a significant bearing on the overall speed of the system. Whereas all of the users of the system might have their own machine and copy of the client code, the servers are likely to be shared, with either one server shared by all clients, or one server shared by a number of clients. Increasing the efficiency of a server will increase the number of clients that it can support, and therefore reduce the hardware and management costs of the system. Besides using efficient algorithms within each server, another technique is to move processing from the servers to the clients. Many client machines have a large amount of spare processing power, and it is often better to use this than to overload the servers.

Of course, it is sometimes more efficient to process data on a server rather than transferring that data to a client's machine. These decisions can be made based on experience, or by experimentation, but it is always important to allow these choices to be changed at a later time. The transparency provided by CORBA allows designers to address these important efficiency issues, rather than being concerned with low-level interworking and transport details.

By default, calls made by a client are **blocking**; that is, the client is blocked until the call has been transmitted to the target object, the target object's code has been run, and the reply has arrived back at the client. This is a natural choice, because it matches the normal semantics of function calls in programming languages such as C++, Java, and Smalltalk. Other options are available, including **non-blocking** calls, in which the caller is allowed to run in parallel with the request and wait for the reply later; **store-and-forward**, in which the request is stored in a persistent store before being sent to the target object; and **publish-and-subscribe**, in which a message is sent on a specified **topic**, and any object that is interested in that topic can receive messages (provided it has permission, of course).

1.2 The CORBA standard

The number of companies that require an integration framework for their systems, the huge variations in how this could be achieved, and the dangers of proprietary solutions all argue very strongly for a non-proprietary standard. The CORBA standard directly addresses the difficulties that arise from boundaries such as networks, programming languages, and operating systems. CORBA can be viewed as either an environment to support the development of new systems, or an environment for application integration in which new systems can be constructed by combining the features of existing systems and subsystems. The CORBA standard was adopted in October 1991, and the first full implementation was released in July 1993.

An implementation of the standard is known as an Object Request Broker (ORB) – a **middleman** or **go-between** to allow a client to make requests on objects. An ORB must be capable of making requests across a network, between operating systems, and between programming languages. The standard is sufficiently flexible to allow many different implementations; for example, those optimized for realtime or embedded environments, those that integrate into the OLE environment on Windows, those that run on mainframes, and those that can be loaded into a Web browser.

Nevertheless, each implementation must be able to communicate with all others, using a protocol known as the Internet Inter-ORB Protocol (IIOP). IIOP is defined to run on Transmission Control Protocol/Internet Protocol (TCP/IP), which is widely available. (IIOP uses a messaging format called GIOP (General Inter-ORB Protocol); that is, IIOP is the GIOP message format sent over TCP/IP. GIOP can also be layered on other transport protocols. Environment-specific inter-ORB protocols are also allowed for; for example, so that specialized protocols can be introduced for realtime environments.) This means that any CORBA client can communicate with any CORBA object (that it has permission to invoke). IIOP request packets contain the identity of the target object, the name of the operation to be invoked, and the parameters. This information is used automatically at the server side to find the target object, and call the correct function on it. No indirections via other processes are required once a connection has been established between a client and a server. IIOP was adopted during 1996; a secure version, which allows for authorisation and encryption, is now available.

Naturally, a specialized ORB may need to use a different protocol when communicating between two objects running on that same ORB. This specialized protocol may be more suitable than IIOP for some environments, such as on a proprietary network or backplane. However, to be CORBA compliant, an ORB must be able to use IIOP when communicating with objects on other ORBs.

1.2.1 Interface Definition Language (IDL)

The notion of interacting objects is central to CORBA: so too is the notion that each object has an interface defined in a language that is specialized for defining interfaces. This language is Interface Definition Language (IDL), and it can be used only to define interfaces; it has no constructs such as variables, statements, or *if* and *while* loops that could be used to implement an interface. Its syntax is similar to that of C++ and Java, but it is a much simpler language because it need only address a small portion of the concerns of a programming language.

The main construct in IDL is the **interface**. This is the equivalent of a class in C++ or Smalltalk, an interface in Java, or a package in object-oriented Ada95. Each interface defines the *operations* that can be called by clients, but of course no code can be written in IDL to implement them.

An interface defined in IDL can be mapped easily to a definition in any programming language, such as C++, Java, Smalltalk, Ada, Visual Basic, C, and so on. This means that, given an object's IDL interface, this can be translated into, say, Java for a Java-based user of the interface, and, say, C++ so that the interface can be implemented in a server. This is the key to IDL's importance: that an interface can be implemented in one language, and then called from any other. In addition, the ORB runtime must be able to transmit requests from a client across a network to a target object running on another machine, even if the two machines are running different operating systems. This is shown in Figure 1.2.

IDL is pleasantly free from complex constructs such as operators, pure virtual functions, default parameters, and so on. This makes the language easier to learn, and importantly, easier to map to programming languages. Because IDL only captures interfaces, it does not need features such as friendship, redefinition, and private inheritance, which relate to the implementation of an interface (although they appear in C++ class definitions).

IDL includes features such as inheritance of interfaces, exceptions, and basic and compound data types. Its simplicity results in better interfaces, because the interface definer can concentrate on the important application-level issues.

It must be said that use of IDL has advantages and disadvantages when compared to the writing of interfaces in a programming language. One advantage of IDL is that it is independent of the programming language used to implement an interface, which means that it can be used for language interoperability without requiring difficult translations between programming languages; IDL is simple enough that it translates easily into other languages so that these can be used to implement CORBA objects or make calls to them. IDL separates specification from implementation, to the extent that not even the programming language used to implement an object is visible to the users of that object. Another advantage of IDL's simplicity is that there is less tendency to overuse complex language features that distract from the real

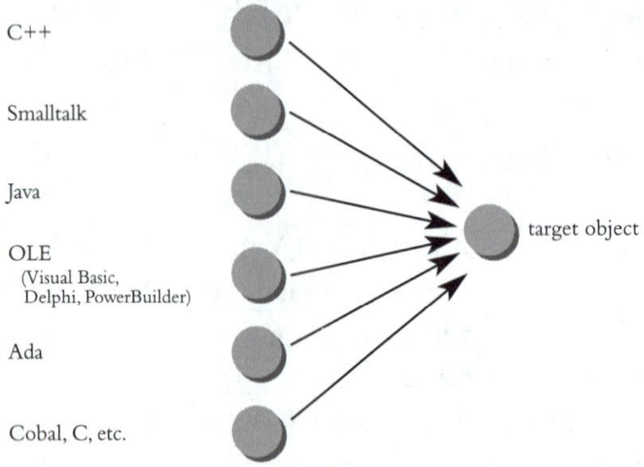

Figure 1.2 *IDL facilitates interworking.*

intention of an interface. The small disadvantage of using IDL is that a new language must be learned and then used in an extra step in system design. However, the learning curve is straightforward because of the simplicity of the language.

CORBA includes IDL because it is felt that the burden of defining IDL interfaces is small compared to the gains. At present, IDL specifications are normally written by hand, but IDL can be generated from commercial object analysis and design tools, or even generated by translating an interface definition written in some programming language – although most programming languages have class definition features (for example, C++ operators) and types (for example, most pointer types in C++) that do not translate into other languages, including IDL.

IDL has been adopted as an ISO (International Organization for Standardization) standard. Currently, IDL maps to C++, C, Smalltalk, Ada, OLE (for languages such as Visual Basic, and systems such as Power Builder and Delphi), and COBOL. The OMG (Object Management Group) is currently defining mappings to Java (due for completion early in 1997), Eiffel, and Objective C.

1.2.2 Relationship to object-oriented analysis and design

Following the requirements stage, the next steps in many projects are to perform an object-oriented analysis and then design of the system that is to be built. The analysis identifies the classes that capture the entities – the business objects – in the system, and the relationships between them. The design stage is used to decide on how these classes are to be implemented and what other, programming-oriented, rather than application-oriented, classes need to be added. All of these stages precede the implementation itself, in which code is written and tested. The details of the techniques differ between the different methods (for example, Object Modeling Technique, Booch, OOram, and so on), but the overall principles are the same.

Such analysis and design is very helpful in a CORBA system because it helps to identify the system's objects and their types. However, it is very unlikely that all of the objects identified should be implemented as CORBA objects; that is, that they should all have IDL interfaces. Consider a electronic shopping application. The analysis of the system is likely to identify classes such as customers, accounts, goods, purchases, images, and so on, and the design stage is likely to add classes such as those required for load balancing. It is likely that some or all of the classes introduced at the analysis stage will need to be defined in IDL, where they model business objects that can be used by clients. These objects will then be available from remote machines, different operating systems, and different programming languages.

On the other hand, it is unlikely that many of the classes introduced at the design level should be available to clients. If these classes are not independent of how the system is to be implemented, then they should not be available to the clients. However, if the system is to be implemented in a number of layers, then some of these layers may be defined in IDL, even though these interfaces will not be available to the ultimate clients.

Making some objects into CORBA objects may also be an opportunity to add some extra functions (**operations**, in CORBA terms) to some classes. Consider a class introduced at the analysis stage with ten attributes that can be accessed by other components of the system. In a system implemented in one address space, it is sensible to require a client to call a function to read each attribute when it needs it, even if all ten attributes are read in this way. In a distributed system, this is unlikely to perform efficiently. Even if the client can afford the time to make the ten remote calls, the server side will have to handle ten calls in rapid succession from just that one client, and this will reduce the number of clients that the server can handle. It is therefore better to add a single operation to retrieve all ten attributes (as a structure), or some subset of the ten that are used together, in one call.

It may also be necessary to modify some operations. For example, if an operation increments a value, then it may make sense to add a parameter that returns the new value to the caller. This should be done if it frequently happens that a change to the value is immediately followed by a request for the current value.

Again, it is important that programmers can address these issues once the first version of their application is working; rather than being distracted by low-level interworking issues. The IDL definitions of the CORBA objects are easy to change, or new interfaces can be added that extend existing ones.

1.3 CORBA architecture

The core of an ORB provides the facilities needed to write distributed systems, to use different programming languages and operating systems, and to integrate applications to give new systems. The following chapters will make the components of Figure 1.3 clear.

Above the core CORBA infrastructure, the OMG has defined the **CORBAservices** and **CORBAfacilities** to extend the built-in support for

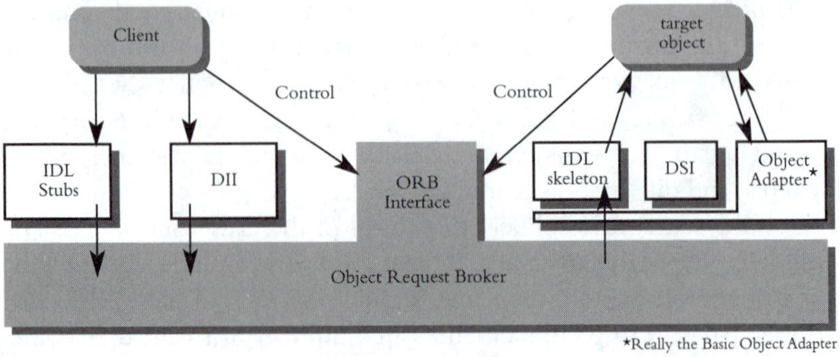

Figure 1.3 *The static and dynamic aspects of the core CORBA standard.*

applications. These three – CORBA, CORBAservices, and CORBAfacilities – make up what is known as the Object Management Architecture (OMA), which is shown in Figure 1.4.

The CORBAservices provide a set of utilities that are useful for objects or distributed applications. In some cases, if these CORBAservices were not defined and implemented by some ORB vendors, the application writers would have to design and implement similar support in each system. Each of the CORBAservices is described in detail in Part 5, but they are listed here to give the reader an initial understanding of what they provide. They have been grouped into categories here to aid discussion later.

(1) Distributed systems-related services:

  (a) Naming Service: allows a client to find an object, given its name. A server can register any of its objects with the Naming Service, giving each a (hierarchical) name that is independent of the name of the server or the host it is running on.
  (b) Event Service: allows a client or server to send a message, or **event**, to any number of receivers. These messages can be stored in the Event Service before being delivered, so that clients and servers can be decoupled.
  (c) Security Service: individual objects or groups of objects can be protected, so that only suitably privileged users can call specified operations on them. Communications across a network can also be encrypted.
  (d) Trading Service: allows a client to find an object given a constraint; for example, to find all schools within a particular region that score sufficiently highly in tests and that take children of a given age range.

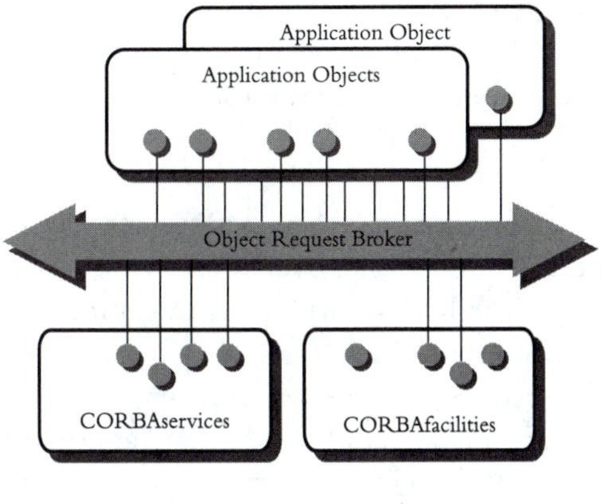

Figure 1.4 *Object Management Architecture (OMA).*

(2) Database-related services:

(a) Concurrency Service: provides a locking mechanism to control the access to an object by concurrent callers.
(b) Property Service: allows properties (name–value pairs) to be associated with any object.
(c) Transaction Service (OTS): controls the commitment and abortion of transactions that span multiple databases, of the same or of different types. That is, it controls a two-phase commit protocol between the databases and a coordinator.
(d) Relationship Service: allows relationships to be constructed and managed between objects.
(e) Query Service: allows queries to be executed against collections of objects. However, a new query language is not specified by this standard, which relies instead on SQL (for relational databases) and the OQL (the object query language for object databases).
(f) Persistent Object Service: defines an abstract framework for how a database and an object should communicate to store and restore the object to and from the database.
(g) Externalization Service: allows an object's data to be converted to and from a stream of bytes, so that it can be copied to another location.

(3) General services:

(a) Life Cycle Service: defines interfaces that allow objects to be created, moved, and copied. However, application-level interfaces for these may sometimes be easier to use and more in keeping with the requirements of the application.
(b) Licensing Service: allows a server to make a call to determine whether or not the machine or network it is to run on has a license to run the software.
(c) Time Service: is used to find the time of day or to obtain an event call after a specified time (or a stream of event calls at a given interval).

These services are not all of equal importance, and their importance will vary from one vertical market to another. The Naming Service, Event Service, Security Service, and Trading Service have general applicability. Similarly, the Licensing Service and the Time Service can be used in many applications.

Some of the database-related services have the disadvantage that they overlap with the facilities of a database management system (DBMS), and applications often find it easier and more efficient to use DBMS facilities directly. These services become applicable only when a DBMS cannot be used for some application-specific reason.

The Transaction Service (normally called the Object Transaction Service) does not suffer from this difficulty, because it relates more closely to the concept of a transaction processing monitor than it does to a DBMS. It works across DBMSs, coordinating the overall commitment of a transaction using the now common two-phase commit protocol. The Externalization Service is also independent of DBMS technology. The Concurrency Service can apply to persistent and non-persistent objects, but in the case of persistent objects, this must be strongly coordinated with the locking facilities of a DBMS.

These remarks may not be clear until the CORBAservices have been individually explained in Part 5, but, for now, remember that these services are optional and should be used only where they make it easier to implement an application. Remember also that an ORB supporting just the core CORBA standard is a useful tool in distributed computing and in application integration; that is, the CORBAservices are optional. Indeed, in some environments, such as for realtime or embedded systems, space or time restrictions may prevent use of any of the CORBAservices.

Whereas the CORBAservices provide utilities for individual objects or groups of objects, the CORBAfacilities provide higher level support for applications. In fact, there are two forms of CORBAfacilities: the **horizontal** CORBAfacilities that can apply to any application domain, and the **vertical** CORBAfacilities that are specialized for individual market segments. The CORBAfacilities are a new area of CORBA, and the specifications are not mature enough to be covered in depth here. This will certainly change rapidly, however, because the core CORBA specification is mature and stable, and the members of the OMG have moved their attention to the next level.

The horizontal CORBAfacilities are planned to address the following areas:

- User interface: presentation of objects and compound documents; help, spelling checking, and grammar checking systems; desktop management; scripting systems. The OpenDoc system for compound documents has been accepted as a CORBAfacility in this area.
- Information management: information modeling; information storage and retrieval; object and compound document encoding and translation; time and calendar support.
- System management: including the management of an ORB and management of CORBA applications. The OMG has chosen another standards group, X/Open, to provide this specification.
- Task management: workflow; agents; rule management.

The OMG has established a set of domain-specific taskforces to provide the specifications for the vertical CORBAfacilities. The current areas are healthcare, telecommunications, financial services, manufacturing, business objects, transport, and electronic commerce. Each group will define interfaces and services that will help application writers in its area to write or manage applications.

It can also be seen that there is no absolute rule for whether a utility should be a CORBAservice or a CORBAfacility. For example, the Licensing Service could have been labeled a CORBAfacility.

Finally, note that each CORBAservice and CORBAfacility must be a specification rather than just a reference implementation, and its interfaces must be defined in IDL.

1.4 The Object Management Group (OMG)

The CORBA standard is written by the members of the OMG, the world's largest information technology consortium. The OMG was founded in April 1989, and the CORBA specification was adopted in October 1991.

As we have seen in Section 1.3, the standard consists of a core – actually the original CORBA – and a growing number of standards, known as CORBAservices and CORBAfacilities, that extend the core. Most of the CORBAservices and CORBAfacilities can be implemented on an ORB, although a small number either must be integrated into the core or require some extensions to it.

The procedure for extending the standard is interesting. After some debate on a proposal for how the standard should be extended, the OMG issues a Request for Proposals, asking its members to submit detailed specifications. Typically, several consortia are formed, each with a small number of OMG members. Each submission must specify how the extension is to be used, normally by defining IDL interfaces, and it must also define any important internal or management interfaces, but it must not define or restrict how the extension is to be implemented. A period of time is then given for each proposer to complete its submission, or merge it with the proposals from another consortium. In nearly all cases, the proposals are in fact merged into one proposal, which is then voted on by the OMG members. In rare cases, the original set of proposals has been merged into two competing proposals, and one has been selected by vote.

Once a standard has been agreed, it can be implemented by any company, without paying any royalty, or even asking permission from the OMG. The OMG continues to maintain the standard by setting up revision committees to improve it, or to change it if this is required by some other standard. Nevertheless, the standards are stable and not subject to frequent changes. The OMG itself does not implement any of its standards, and it stays neutral between the different vendors providing implementations.

The OMG works closely with a number of other standards bodies, including ISO, the Open Group (X/Open), the World Wide Web Consortium, ANSI, IEEE, ITU, POSC, and many others.

1.5 Desirable properties of the object system

For CORBA to support application construction and integration, it must address a large number of challenges:

- Objects must be simple to create, and, in particular, no more difficult to create than normal objects in an object-oriented programming language.
- A CORBA IDL interface must be simple to implement, and require approximately the same amount of programming effort as a normal type implemented in an object-oriented programming language.
- Access to objects must be efficient.
- Objects must be of any size, and, in particular, small objects must be supported without undue overhead.
- Objects must be supported by the current commercial operating systems; that is, they must be supported within processes on UNIX, and dynamic link libraries on Windows, and so on.
- Many programming languages must be supported, using each programming language's normal conventions. Object-oriented languages must be included, and also non-object-oriented languages, such as C. No programming language extensions must be required, although it must also be possible to allow for future languages that add features to cater specially, for example, for distributed systems.
- An object must be accessible from any programming language, and not just the one it is implemented in. Further, this access must use the programming language's normal object access syntax (or some natural syntax in non-object-oriented languages; for example, C function calls).
- Objects must be accessible across a network, with the same syntax as they are accessed within a single machine.

- An object must be accessible from any operating system, not just the one that the object itself is running on.
- Objects must be accessible from Web-based clients, using simple and efficient calls. No indirection, through other processes or script interpreters, must be required.
- The system must be able to work with non-object-oriented systems, such as relational databases.
- The system must interact with other object-oriented systems, such as object databases (OODBMSs), object-oriented analysis and design systems, and Microsoft's OLE.
- Invocations must be secure: for example, unauthorized invocations must be disallowed, and rogue users must not be able to prevent access by authorized users.
- It must be easy to give objects high-level symbolic names. Knowing the name of an object, it must be easy to obtain an object reference to it, and then to make invocations on it (subject, of course, to security checks). These names must be hierarchical so that name clashes can be avoided easily.
- It must also be possible to find an object by giving a description of it (for example, to find a cinema that is showing a particular movie).
- The message details must be hidden – so that a client can make a call on an object in the same way if the connection to the object is direct, if store-and-forward is being used, or if some publish-and-subscribe system is in place.
- Distributed transactions must be supported, so that a series of calls can result in changes to a number of databases, which can be atomically updated.
- If a programmer knows the interface of the object he or she is writing code to communicate with, then (depending on the programming language being used, of course) full compile-time type checking of operation calls must be possible. However, if the types of the objects that must be used cannot be known at compile time, then it must be possible, firstly, to obtain type information at runtime, and, secondly, for a client to make calls to those objects by constructing calls at runtime.
- The system must have wide industrial acceptance, across a large number of vertical markets, including finance,

telecommunications, realtime control systems, manufacturing, petrochemical, office automation, and so on.

- The system must be based on a non-proprietary standard, and not a reference implementation.
- It must be available from multiple suppliers, with more than one supplier on each popular platform.

As explained in the following chapters, CORBA addresses each of these issues, either at the core level or at the service layers specified on top.

1.6 Base requirements and nature of an ORB

Each implementation of the core of CORBA *must* support each of the following:

- The IDL language.
- Mapping of IDL to some programming language or system, such as C++, Java, Visual Basic (or, more exactly, to OLE), Ada, Smalltalk, and so on.
- Runtime support for passing an object request between a caller and a target object. In some environments, this runtime support need not be very sophisticated: for example, two CORBA objects in the same address space may be able to invoke on each other directly, without any indirection into a CORBA layer. As the boundaries between objects become more difficult, the runtime support must become more sophisticated.
- Runtime support for the CORBA application programming interface. Actually, this is not a very complex interface, because the main interfaces used by applications are those defined in IDL by it and other applications.
- The Interface Repository, which gives runtime type information.

The physical incarnation of an ORB is often made up of the following two items:

- A **library** that is linked with client and server code. This allows the clients to send and accept CORBA requests.

- A **daemon process** that sets up communication connections between clients and servers, in particular setting up the TCP/IP connections between processes so that the IIOP protocol can be used. Typically, the daemon process is not involved in the actual communication between a client and target object: there is a direct connection between the two.

Many of the CORBAservices are naturally implemented as servers running on an ORB. However, a small number do require some enhancements to an ORB, or even that some portions be implemented within the ORB. The Security Service is the obvious example of this.

Orbix, from IONA Technologies, is used as the example ORB throughout this book. This is a complete implementation of the standard and has the advantages that it is easy to use, that it runs on many operating systems, and that it can be used from a number of programming languages, including C++, Java, Visual Basic, Smalltalk, Ada, and other Windows systems such as Power Builder and Delphi.

Part one

Basic CORBA Programming

The basic features of CORBA are introduced in this part, where we develop a simple example.

Chapter 2, '**Getting started with CORBA**,' gives a full but simple example of using CORBA to define the interface to a system component and then to code that component and an example client for it. It also introduces the example used throughout this part, firstly using very simple Interface Definition Language (IDL) definitions, and then introducing more complete definitions. The aim of this chapter is simplicity, but the code given is fully functional.

Chapter 3, '**Introduction to CORBA IDL**,' introduces the syntax and semantics of IDL, which is used to define the interfaces of CORBA objects. This language looks like a simple subset of the C++ syntax for defining classes, and it is easy to learn. It allows interfaces to be defined independently of the programming language used to program or use these.

Chapter 4, '**IDL to C++ mapping of simple types**,' and *Chapter 5*, '**IDL to C++ mapping of compound types**,' explain how IDL definitions are translated into C++. Much of this material is for reference, and only an overview of the rules for strings and object references is required on first reading. Basic types, strings, and object references are covered in Chapter 4.

Chapter 6, '**The cinema example**,' shows an outline of the implementation of the complete IDL definitions introduced at the end of Chapter 2. This chapter also goes beyond the level covered in Chapter 2 by introducing some of the choices available at each step.

Chapter 7, '**Naming and binding**,' gives the details on how objects can be named and located in the distributed system. Both a simple binding mechanism and the CORBA Naming Service are introduced.

Chapter 8, '**Registration and activation of servers**,' introduces the details of the CORBA Implementation Repository, which manages the system's servers. The CORBA activation modes are explained by example.

Chapter 9, '**Exception handling**,' explains in more detail how exception handling can be added to the example presented in Chapter 6. Both system- and user-defined IDL exceptions, and how these can be raised and caught, are explained.

Chapter 10, '**Inheritance**,' explains how to use inheritance to define IDL interfaces, and how to implement these interfaces in C++.

2 Getting started with CORBA

We will introduce Orbix by working through a simple example of defining an IDL interface, implementing this in C++, and then writing a client program. We will avoid getting slowed down by unnecessary details at this early stage. Chapter 6, 'The cinema example,' covers details ignored here.

2.1 A simple application

The example is based on the software required by a cinema to manage ticket sales. A simple interface to the **front office** component of this system is defined, an outline of its implementation is given, and a simple client is shown.

The interface to the front office is defined in the CORBA Interface Definition Language (IDL), and this interface is kept simple by defining only sufficient operations to find the price of a given seat and to book a seat. Possible extensions to the definition and implementation of the system are discussed at the end of this chapter. The implications of incorporating the front office into other applications are also discussed.

The interface to the front office component is implemented in C++ and installed in a **server**: a server is an element of the system in which fine-grained Orbix objects execute. Frequently, a server corresponds to a process.

The server and client can be run on different machines in the distributed system, or in different address spaces in the one machine, or indeed within the same address space.

2.2 Programming steps

The following programming steps are typically required to write a distributed client–server system in CORBA and C++:

- Define the interfaces, using the standard IDL.
- Implement these interfaces with C++ classes.
- Write a server main function which creates instances of these classes, and then informs Orbix when initialization has been completed and that the server is ready to accept requests.
- Register the server.
- Write a client main function to connect to the server and to use the server's objects.

We illustrate these steps in the remainder of this chapter.

2.3 The IDL specification

The first step in writing a CORBA program is to define the IDL interfaces to the application's objects/components. The interface to our front office can be defined in IDL as follows:

```
// IDL. In file front.idl.

// Start with some type definitions:
typedef float Price;
struct Place {
      char row;
      unsigned long seat;
};

// Then an IDL interface:
interface FrontOffice {
      readonly attribute string name;
      readonly attribute unsigned long numberOfSeats;

      Price getPrice (in Place chosenPlace);
      boolean bookSingleSeat (in Place chosenPlace,
                  in string creditCard);
};
```

The interface provides two attributes: `name` and `numberOfSeats`. `name` gives the cinema's name as a string, and `numberOfSeats` gives the overall number of seats in the cinema. Both are labeled `readonly`, so that they cannot be directly changed by a client.

There are also two operations:

- `getPrice()`: this returns the price of a place. The place is specified as a structure, which gives the row and seat number.
- `bookSingleSeat()`: this books a chosen seat for a client. A credit card number is passed (as a string) so that the client can be charged for the booking.

The parameters to the operations are labeled as `in`, which means that they are being passed from the client to the server. In other operations, parameters may be labeled as `out` (passed from the server to the client) or `inout` (passed in both directions).

The most serious restriction in the IDL definitions used in this simple example is that the caller of `bookSingleSeat()` cannot specify the date that the booking is required. This, and other restrictions, will be addressed later in this chapter.

2.4 Compiling the IDL interface

The IDL specification must be compiled, both to check the specification and to map it into C++ so that it can be implemented and used.

The IDL compiler can be run as follows on UNIX and Windows respectively (alternatively, a graphical user interface can be used to compile IDL definitions):

```
$ idl -B front.idl
```

The IDL compiler produces three C++ files (the file names differ for various operating systems and compilers; for example, they will be `.hh` and `.cpp` on Windows):

- `front.hh`: A header file to be included into the implementation of the front office and into all clients. This defines the C++ view of the IDL definitions.
- `frontC.C`: A source file to be compiled and included into the clients of the front office. It includes the code required to make remote requests on a `FrontOffice` object. This is referred to as the **stub** code, and its role is to transmit requests, for the interfaces defined in `front.idl`, from a client to a server.

- `frontS.C`: A source file to be compiled and included into the implementation of the front office. It includes the code required to accept remote requests on a `FrontOffice` object. This is referred to as the **skeleton** code, and its role is to accept requests, for the interfaces defined in `front.idl`, from a client.

The role of the stub and skeleton code can be seen in Figure 2.1. If the client and target object are in the same address space, no extra code is required to communicate between them. If they are in different address spaces, on the same or on different hosts, then extra code is required in the client to send the request to the server side, and extra code is required at the server side to accept the request and pass it to the target object.

2.4.1 The C++ produced

The `front.hh` file produced by the IDL compiler contains the following code (for now, types such as `CORBA::Char` should be read simply as being `char`; the details are discussed in Chapter 4, 'IDL to C++ mapping of simple types'):

```
// C++
// Automatically produced (in front.hh)

#include <CORBA.h>

typedef CORBA::Float Price;
struct Place {
      CORBA::Char row;
      CORBA::ULong seat;
};

// Some other definitions not relevant here are omitted.
```

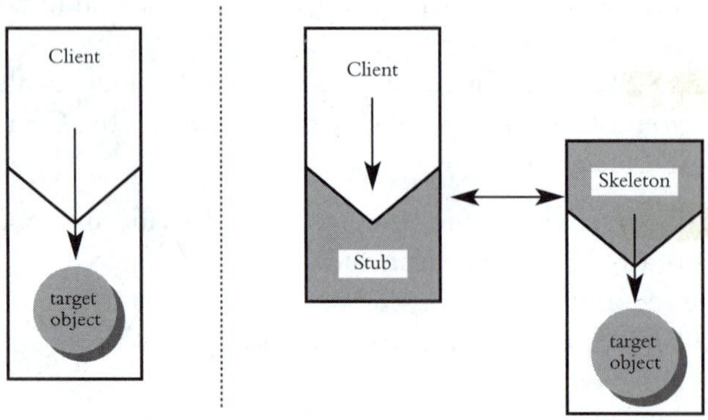

Figure 2.1 *Stub and skeleton code.*

```
class FrontOffice: public virtual CORBA::Object {
    public:
        virtual char* name()
            throw (CORBA::SystemException);

        virtual CORBA::ULong numberOfSeats()
            throw (CORBA::SystemException);

        virtual Price getPrice (
                const Place& chosenPlace)
            throw (CORBA::SystemException);

        virtual CORBA::Boolean bookSingleSeat (
                const Place& chosenPlace,
                const char* creditCard)
            throw (CORBA::SystemException);
    };
```

The Orbix compiler also generates other members for class `FrontOffice`, and some other classes, but these need not concern us here.

Let us first consider the operations, `getPrice()` and `bookSingleSeat()`. The mapping to C++ is very straightforward: each IDL operation is mapped to a C++ function. These C++ functions are labeled as `virtual` so that C++ will use dynamic binding. The parameter types are the natural translations from IDL (structs are passed by reference for efficiency).

Each of these functions is also declared to throw an exception of type `CORBA::SystemException`, and this fact is used in Section 2.9 (p.35) when error handling is discussed. CORBA can also cater for C++ compilers that do not support C++ exceptions, but this will not be covered here.

Note that the IDL basic types `char` and `unsigned long` are mapped to the C++ types `CORBA::Char` and `CORBA::ULong`. The header file `CORBA.h` provides appropriate typedefs to the equivalent basic types. For example, on a 32-bit machine, `CORBA::ULong` would typically be a typedef for the C++ type `unsigned long`.

The two `readonly` attributes have been replaced with functions of the same names. Since the server and client might not be in the same address space, there would be no point in replacing attributes with public member variables.

Finally, class `FrontOffice` inherits from `CORBA::Object`, but this fact need not concern us in this chapter.

2.5 Implementing the interface

When C++ is used to implement the `FrontOffice` interface, the programmer must write a C++ class which provides the functions listed in the previous section. In fact, there are two approaches available for indicating that this C++ class implements the IDL interface, and we will look at one of these in this chapter.

We will call our implementation class `FrontOffice_i` (in files `front_i.h` and `front_i.C`), and we will indicate that it implements interface `FrontOffice` by defining it as follows:

```
// C++
#include "front.hh"

class FrontOffice_i :
        public virtual FrontOfficeBOAImpl {
    // Details shown later.
};
```

Here we have inherited from class `FrontOfficeBOAImpl`, which is automatically produced by the IDL compiler in the front `.hh` header file. The name of this class is the interface name with the string '`BOAImpl`' appended (BOA stands for Basic Object Adapter).

Class `FrontOffice_i` should be written to redefine each of the functions `name()`, `numberOfSeats()`, `getPrice()`, and `bookSingleSeat()`, and to add some member data, a constructor, and a destructor:

```
// C++. In file FrontOffice_i.h.
class FrontOffice_i :
        public virtual FrontOfficeBOAImpl {
    char* m_name;
    CORBA::ULong m_numberOfSeats;
    CORBA::Char m_divide; // Divide between cheap and expensive.
    Price m-highPrice;
    Price m-lowPrice;

    // The seat availability matrix:
    const unsigned short m_rows;
    const unsigned long m_seatsPerRow;
    unsigned char** m_avail; // Availability matrix.

public:

    FrontOffice_i(const char* theName,
        const CORBA::ULong theNumberOfRows,
        const CORBA::ULong theNumberofSeatsPerRow,
        const CORBA::Char theDivide,
        const Price theHighPrice,
        const Price theLowPrice);

    virtual ~FrontOffice_i();

    // Functions corresponding to the two IDL attributes:
    virtual char* name ()
        throw (CORBA::SystemException);
    virtual CORBA::ULong numberOfSeats()
```

```
        throw (CORBA::SystemException);

    // Functions corresponding to the two IDL operations:
        virtual Price getPrice (const Place& chosenPlace)
            throw (CORBA::SystemException);

        virtual CORBA::Boolean bookSingleSeat (
                const Place& chosenPlace,
                const char* creditCard)
            throw (CORBA::SystemException);
    };
```

Class `FrontOffice_i` could also add further functions and constructors. The functions that have been defined can be implemented as follows:

```
// C++. In file front_i.C.
#include "front_i.h"

FrontOffice_i::FrontOffice_i(const char* theName,
            const CORBA::ULong theNumberOfRows,
            const CORBA::ULong theNumberofSeatsPerRow,
            const CORBA::Char theDivide,
            const Price theHighPrice,
            const Price theLowPrice) :
    // Consistency checks are not shown here:
    m_rows(theNumberOfRows),
    m_seatsPerRow(theNumberofSeatsPerRow),
    m_numberOfSeats(m_rows * m_seatsPerRow),
    m_divide(theDivide),
    m_highPrice(theHighPrice),
    m_lowPrice(theLowPrice)
{
    m_name = new char [strlen(theName)+1];
    strcpy(m_name,theName);
    // Now allocate space for the availability matrix:
    unsigned long i,j;
    m_avail = new unsigned char* [m_rows];
    for (i = 0; i < m_rows; i++) {
        m_avail[i] = new unsigned char [m_seatsPerRow];
        for (j = 0; j < m_seatsPerRow; j++)
            m_avail[i][j] = 1; // Initially available.
    }
}

FrontOffice_i::~FrontOffice_i() {
    delete[] m_name;
    // Now free the space for the availability matrix:
    unsigned long i;
    for (i = 0; i < m_rows; i++)
        delete[] m_avail[i];
    delete[] m_avail;
```

```
}

char* FrontOffice_i::name()
            throw (CORBA::SystemException) {
      // Strings that are passed out through a CORBA interface,
      // must be allocated using CORBA functions, such as
      // string_dup():
      return CORBA::string_dup(m_name);
}

CORBA::ULong FrontOffice_i::numberOfSeats()
            throw (CORBA::SystemException) {
      return m_numberOfSeats;
}

Price FrontOffice_i::getPrice (
                  const Place& chosenPlace)
            throw (CORBA::SystemException) {
      if (chosenPlace.row < m_divide)
            return m_lowPrice;
      else
            return m_highPrice;
}

CORBA::Boolean FrontOffice_i::bookSingleSeat (
                  const Place& chosenPlace,
                  const char* creditCard)
            throw (CORBA::SystemException) {
      // Bounds testing not shown here.
      unsigned long rowIndex = chosenPlace.row - 'A';
      if (m_avail[rowIndex][chosenPlace.seat]) {
            // Book that place:
            m_avail[rowIndex][chosenPlace.seat] = 0;
            // Charge the price to the credit card:
            // the code is not shown here.
            return 1;
      }
      else return 0;
}
```

Rather than having `FrontOffice_i` inherit from `FrontOfficeBOAImpl`, a programmer can implement `FrontOffice_i` as a standalone class and **TIE** this class to the `FrontOffice` IDL interface. Some programmers prefer this approach, which is explained in Chapter 6.

The IDL compiler provides a useful switch, `-S`, which produces initial versions of implementation classes. Running the compiler with the `-S` switch as follows:

```
$ idl -B -S front.idl
```

produces two output files: `front.ih` and `front.ic`. The file `front.ih` contains an initial class declaration, including the declaration of each member function that corresponds to an IDL attribute or operation. `front.ic` contains the definition of each of these member functions, each with an empty body. These files can then be renamed appropriately, for example, to `front_i.h` and `front_i.C`, and the details of the implementation can be added.

2.6 Providing a server

Although Orbix can support the collocation of the client and server in the same process address space, we will proceed by keeping them separate in this example.

We need to write a server program in which our `FrontOffice` object will run:

```
// C++. In file Srv_Main.C.
#include "front_i.h"
#include <iostream.h>

int main() {
      // We could create any number of objects
      // here, but we just create one:
      FrontOffice_i myFrontOffice("Royal", 25, 40
                                  'G', 5.00, 3.00);

      // Orbix objects can be explicitly named,
      // but this is not required in this simple example.

      CORBA::Orbix.impl_is_ready("FrontOfficeSrv");
      cout << "Server terminating." << endl;
}
```

(There is a CORBA standard way of communicating with the ORB, but this has not been used in this first example. Instead, for simplicity, the built-in variable `CORBA::Orbix` has been used. See Section 6.5.3, p.149.)

This server program creates a `FrontOffice_i` object. It then indicates to Orbix that the server's initialization has completed, by calling `impl_is_ready()`. The parameter to `impl_is_ready()` is the name of the server as registered in the Implementation Repository (this is explained in Section 2.7). `CORBA::Orbix` is an object that is used to communicate directly with Orbix. As used here, `impl_is_ready()` is a blocking call that returns only when Orbix times-out the idle server. Hence the call to `impl_is_ready()` will not return for some time. While the server is executing in `impl_is_ready()`, Orbix will deliver client calls to its `FrontOffice` object.

We will assume that the server's executable file is called `server` (on UNIX) or `server.exe` (on Windows). These must be linked with the CORBA library.

2.7 Registering the server

The server can be registered so that it will be run automatically when a client uses our `FrontOffice` object. The system maintains a database of servers known as the **Implementation Repository**, which maintains a mapping from a server's name to the name of the executable file that implements that server. In Orbix, the Implementation Repository is implemented by a daemon process (`orbixd`), which must be run on each node that can run servers.

Registration is done as follows, using the `putit` command on your local machine, for UNIX and Windows, respectively:

```
$ putit FrontOfficeSrv <full pathname of server's exec file>
C:\> putit FrontOfficeSrv <full pathname of server's exec file>
```

Again, on Windows this can be done using a graphical user interface.

The first parameter to `putit` is the server's name, which we have chosen as `FrontOfficeSrv`. This was also the name of the server passed to `impl_is_ready()` in Section 2.6. The second parameter is the name of the executable file; an absolute pathname is required.

This registration step is not strictly required, but carrying it out does have the advantage that Orbix will launch a server if it is not running when one of its objects is invoked by a client.

2.8 Writing a client

A client can be written as follows (although it is always better to include error handling, as shown in Section 2.9, p.35):

```
// C++. In file Client.C.
#include "Front.hh"
#include <iostream.h>

int main() {
      FrontOffice_var foVar;

      foVar = FrontOffice::_bind(":FrontOfficeSrv");

      CORBA::String_var itsName = foVar->name();
```

```
    cout << "Name is " << itsName << endl;

    cout << "Number of seats is "
         << foVar->numberOfSeats() << endl;

    Place p = {'B', 27};
    cout << "Price of seat B27 is "
         << foVar->getPrice(p) << endl;
    if (foVar->bookSingleSeat(p,"4531 3458 9487 8120"))
         cout << "Seat B27 booked ok." << endl;
    else
         cout << "Seat B27 cannot be booked." << endl;
}
```

(Note that the variable `itsName` could have been defined to be a `char*`, but use of the type `CORBA::String_var` ensures that the space for the string will be freed automatically when `itsName` goes out of scope.)

The client defines a variable of type `FrontOffice_var`. This type is a C++ helper class automatically generated by the IDL compiler from the `FrontOffice` interface. An instance of `FrontOffice_var` holds a reference to a C++ **proxy** object, that is a C++ object which acts as a representative or stand-in for a remote object.

Hence, the client will have a proxy for the remote `FrontOffice` object that it uses, and its `foVar` variable will hold a pointer to that proxy. This is shown in Figure 2.2. Programmers make normal C++ function calls using `foVar` (using the arrow `->()` operator), and the proxy receives each request and passes it to the remote object. Figure 2.3 shows how the code files generated by the IDL compiler are used by the client and server sides.

Normal operation calls in CORBA are blocking; for example, the client is blocked when it calls `bookSingleSeat()` until the target object has carried out the request. In fact, an application can also make non-blocking calls, as we will see later.

Note that the client is not concerned with the implementation class `FrontOffice_i`, which is only of concern to the server programmer. This ensures that the client does not rely on implementation details within the server.

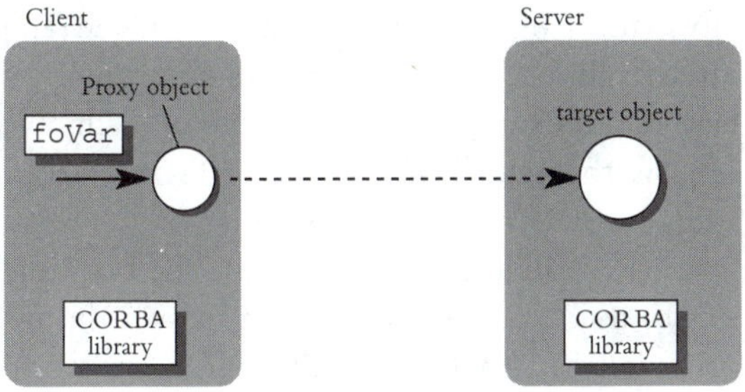

Figure 2.2 *The role of a proxy object.*

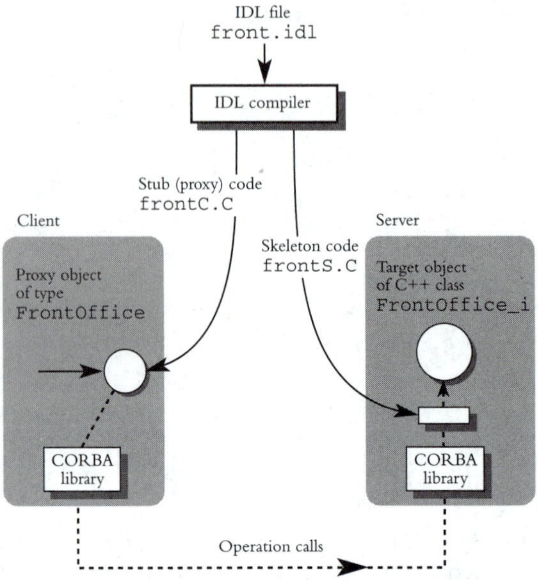

Figure 2.3 *Use of the code generated by the IDL compiler.*

The client and server can normally be run on different hosts, but we will defer until Section 2.10 discussion of any issues that might arise from this.

Finding the `FrontOffice` object

The object reference `foVar` must be bound to an object of type `FrontOffice` (in this case, to a `FrontOffice` object running in the `FrontOfficeSrv` server). This can be done in a number of different ways, but in this client it is done by calling `_bind()`, which is a static member function of class `FrontOffice`).

The first parameter to `_bind()` is a string of the form:

```
"<object name>:<
     server name>"
```

It names the object and the server in which the object is running (see Chapter 7, 'Naming and binding,' for information on naming objects). In the example, the object is not named so Orbix is free to choose *any* `FrontOffice` object in the specified server (`FrontOfficeSrv`). In fact, in our example, there is only one such object. The server name, `FrontOfficeSrv`, is the name of the server as registered in the Implementation Repository (using `putit` or a GUI tool).

Rather than using the `_bind()` function, a client can use the Naming Service to locate the objects that it needs to use. To allow for this, the server should choose a name for the `FrontOffice` that it creates and then call an IDL operation on the Naming Service to make that name and object known to it. Any client that knows the chosen name can call an IDL operation on the Naming Service to resolve the name and obtain a reference to the `FrontOffice` object. The Naming Service is discussed in Chapter 7.

Even this simple example would benefit from use of the Naming Service, but this has not been done because the IDL of the Naming Service would have to be explained and the IDL sequence data type would have to be used. This is too complex for our first example. Nevertheless, once a programmer is familiar with IDL, the Naming Service should be used, it has the following advantages over `_bind()`:

- Servers' names do not have to be specified when locating an object.
- Objects in servers running on remote machines can be located without any extra concerns. Section 2.10 discusses the issues that may arise when using `_bind()`, and in particular that a host name may have to be specified.

Nevertheless, `_bind()` remains easy to use and it is very lightweight: it does not require that the Naming Service is running, and it is efficient at runtime since it communicates directly with the required server.

2.9 Error handling

A full version of the client and server should check for and handle errors. This section shows how to do this, assuming that the C++ compiler supports C++ exceptions, which is the case for the majority of C++ compilers.

2.9.1 Integration with C++ exceptions

The call to `_bind()` or to any operation or attribute could fail, especially if the call is to a remote machine. Such calls should be enclosed within C++ `try` blocks, which will allow any exceptions thrown by functions called within a block to be handled by the subsequent `catch` clauses. Thus, our example client and server could be rewritten as shown below.

Client main function

```
// C++. In file Client.C.
#include "Front.hh"
#include <iostream.h>
#include <stdlib.h>

int main() {
      FrontOffice_var foVar;
```

```
	try {
		foVar = FrontOffice::_bind(":FrontOfficeSrv");
	}
	catch (CORBA::SystemException& se) {
		cerr << "Bind to object failed." << endl;
		cerr << "Unexpected exception: " << endl
			<< se; // Output text of the exception.†
		exit(-1);
	}

	try {
		CORBA::String_var itsName = foVar->name();
		cout << "Name is " << itsName << endl;
		cout << "number of seats is "
			<< foVar->numberOfSeats() << endl;
	}
	catch (CORBA::SystemException& se) {
		cerr << "Call to name or numberOfSeats failed." << endl;
		cerr << "Unexpected exception: " << endl
			<< se; // Output text of the exception.
		exit(-1);
	}

	try {
		Place p = {'B', 27};
		cout << "Price of seat B27 is "
			<< foVar->getPrice(p) << endl;
		if (foVar->bookSingleSeat(p,"4531 3458 9487 8120"))
			cout << "Seat B27 booked ok." << endl;
		else
			cout << "Seat B27 cannot be booked." >> endl;
	}
	catch (CORBA::SystemException& se) {
		cerr << "Call to getPrice or bookSingleSeat failed."
			<< endl;
		cerr << "Unexpected exception: " << endl
			<< se; // Output text of the exception.
		exit(-1);
	}
}
```

Server main function

```
// C++. In file Srv_Main.C.
#include "front_i.h"
#include <iostream.h>

int main() {
	FrontOffice_i myFrontOffice("Royal", 25, 40,
					'G', 5.00, 3.00);
```

† The writing of a system exception using `operator<<()` is Orbix-specific.

```
        try {
              CORBA::Orbix.impl_is_ready("FrontOfficeSrv");
        }
        catch(CORBA::SystemException& se) {
              cerr << "Unexpected Exception during impl_is_ready(): "
                    << endl << se; // Output text of the exception.
        }
        cout << "server terminating." << endl;
}
```

The code in the `catch` clauses outputs details of possible system exceptions raised by Orbix. Chapter 9, 'Exception handling,' explains exception handling in detail and also shows how to define and catch user-defined exceptions.

2.10 Distributing the client and server

The server can be registered on a remote machine by running the `putit` command on that machine. Alternatively, `putit` can be run on your local machine and its `-h` switch can be used to specify a (remote) host name on which the registration is to take place as follows, (alternatively, a GUI can be used):

```
$ putit -h <hostname> FrontOfficeSrv <server's exec file>
```

The client must now be able to find the `FrontOffice` object even though the client and server are not on the same machine. No change would be required to our client if it used the Naming Service to find the objects it needs to use, because the names managed by the Naming Server are independent of host names. However, our client uses the `_bind()` function, and, depending on how the system is configured, it may require some small changes.

In this simple example, we will make a minor change to the client program to specify the host of the server:

```
// C++
int main(int argc, char** argv) {
      FrontOffice_var foVar;
      . . .
      // argv[1] contains the target host:
      foVar = FrontOffice::_bind(":FrontOffice", argv[1]);
      . . .
}
```

The client can then be run by typing, for UNIX and Windows, respectively:

```
$ client <hostname>
```

```
c:\>client <hostname>
```

`<hostname>` is the Internet host name or IP address of the machine on which the server was registered. This first argument (`argv[1]`) is passed as the server's host name to `_bind()`. Note that the client and server applications may be run on machines with different operating systems. For example, a client could be on a UNIX machine and a server on a Windows NT machine, or vice versa.

If the Orbix **Locator** is configured to know the possible location or locations of the `FrontOfficeSrv` server, then the host name can be omitted, and the client code shown in Sections 2.8 and 2.9 remains valid. However, if the Locator has not been configured with this information, then a host name parameter must be passed to `_bind()` if the required server is on another host.

Normally, of course, it is not sensible to build host names into code. Doing so has the serious disadvantage that a server cannot then be moved to another host without recompiling the clients that use it. Some applications, such as those that manage the hosts in a system, must of course use explicit host names, but even these names are likely to be read from configuration files or input by users.

2.11 Summary of programming steps

Having implemented the distributed client – server application in C++, recall the programming steps typically required:

- Define the IDL interfaces.
- Implement these interfaces with C++ classes (passing the `-S` switch to the IDL compiler will produce an initial version of these classes).
- Write a server main function, which creates instances of the classes and then informs Orbix when initialization has been done and the server is ready to accept requests.
- Register the server, using `putit` or a GUI interface.
- Write a client main function to find and use the server's objects. The client can use the `_bind()` function to find the objects it needs, or preferably it should use the Naming Service. Once one or a small number of objects have been found in this way, the client should find other objects by receiving their object references as return values and `out` parameters.

Many more sophisticated architectures can also be supported, such as the use of multiple servers and multiple clients.

2.12 Possible extensions to the example

This section presents a list of possible enhancements to the base example explained previously in this chapter.

Persistent data

The data of a front office object should of course be saved to some file system or database. This topic is discussed in Chapter 22, 'Technology integration.'

Integration with other systems

Initially the front office example can be viewed as a standalone application that remote clients can use with ease. However, one of the advantages of CORBA is that the front office can become a component of larger systems; for example:

(1) The owner of the cinema may need to expand the system to handle a chain of cinemas, with one `FrontOffice` object per cinema. These objects can be created at a central reservations office, or at the geographically distributed cinema locations.

(2) A travel agency may wish to book flights, hotel, and cinema tickets using a single graphical front end. This GUI can communicate with an appropriate `FrontOffice` object, using it as a component of the larger travel agency system.

(3) The financial package used to control the cinema can query the front office system (assuming that we have made the necessary extensions to the IDL interface) to find information such as the number of seats booked at each of the available prices. This communication can be direct from the financial package to the `FrontOffice` object, rather than by the `FrontOffice` exposing its database. If the financial package runs on Windows then it can make calls similar to those shown earlier in this chapter, or it can be written to treat the `FrontOffice` as an OLE object and access it from some OLE scripting language such as Visual Basic – perhaps built into an application such as Excel. (The Orbix transparent interworking between CORBA and Microsoft's OCX / OLE Automation is described in Chapter 22.)

Use of advanced features

A number of extensions can be made to the implementation of the example in order to make it more realistic. These include:

- Allowing the `getPrice()` and `bookSingleSeat()` functions to raise user-defined exceptions, such as an attempt to refer to a non-existent seat.
- An advanced feature of Orbix, smart proxies, could be used to provide a caching facility in clients. For example, the prices of various tickets could be cached for efficiency.

Extending the IDL

The IDL for the cinema example has been kept very simple up to this point. A more complete version follows. Note that some of the data types and operations have been changed substantially in this version, compared to those used earlier in this chapter:

```
typedef float Price;

struct Place {
      char row;
      unsigned long seat;
};
typedef sequence<Place> Places;

typedef string Date; // In format DD.MM.YYYY

struct CreditCard {
      string id;
      Date   expiry;
};


interface Booking {
      readonly attribute Date when;
      readonly attribute Places seats;
      void cancel();
};

interface GroupBooking : Booking {
      readonly attribute string organizer;
      readonly attribute string groupName;
};

interface FrontOffice {

      exception NoSuchPlace { Place where; };
      exception PlaceAlreadyBooked {
                 Place where; Date when; };
      exception InvalidCreditCard  {
                 CreditCard invalidCard; };
      exception InvalidDate { Date when; };
```

```
exception GroupTooSmall {
           unsigned long chosenSize;
           unsigned long minimumSize;
};

// Name of the cinema:
readonly attribute string name;

// The next two attributes give the size of the cinema:
// i) Highest lettered row:
readonly attribute char lastRow;
// ii) Number of seats in each row:
readonly attribute unsigned long seatsPerRow;

// Determine if the cinema is open on a specified date:
boolean checkIfOpen (in Date when,
                     out Date nextAvailableDate)
           raises (InvalidDate);
      // nextAvailableDate is an empty string if cinema
      // is open on the Date when. Otherwise it is the
      // nearest data after when that the cinema is
      // open.

// Find what seats are available on a given date:
Places listAvailablePlaces (in Date when)
           raises (InvalidDate);

// Find the price of a give seat on a given date:
Price getPrice (in Place chosenPlace,
                in Date when)
           raises (NoSuchPlace, InvalidDate);

// Book and pay for a given seat on a given date:
Booking makeBooking ( // See notes later
                      in Places chosenPlaces,
                      in Date when,
                      in CreditCard payment)
           raises (NoSuchPlace,
                   PlaceAlreadyBooked,
                   InvalidCreditCard,
                   InvalidDate);

// Make a group booking by specifying the organization
// making the booking, and the group going to the
// cinema:
GroupBooking makeGroupBooking (
                      in Places     chosenPlaces,
                      in Date       when,
                      in CreditCard payment,
                      in string     organizer,
                      in string     groupName)
```

```
                 raises (NoSuchPlace,
                         PlaceAlreadyBooked,
                            InvalidCreditCard,
                            InvalidDate,
                            GroupTooSmall);
};
```

Figure 2.4 shows an OMT object model for the cinema application.

The features of IDL used in this extended example are presented in Chapter 3, 'Introduction to CORBA IDL.' One particular feature is however worth commenting on here. A second interface type, `Booking`, has been introduced and the return type of operation `makeBooking()` is an object reference of that type. Therefore, a client that calls `makeBooking()` will receive an object reference to an object of type `Booking`, and it can retain this object reference and use it at any later stage to determine the details of the booking, or to cancel it. Therefore, an IDL object reference is a near equivalent of a C++ pointer (although object references do not suffer from the dangers of using pointers). Object references can also be passed as parameters to IDL operations, and to define attributes.

The passing of object references in this way is an important feature of CORBA. It also shows that not all object references are obtained using the Naming Service or `_bind()` function; in fact, the Naming Service and `_bind()` are normally only used to find one or a small number of objects in the system, and normal reference passing is used to obtain most references that a client needs.

The ability to communicate with a front office object and retain a reference to a booking object may be exploited by many applications written in any programming language supported by CORBA. For example, using a Java client,

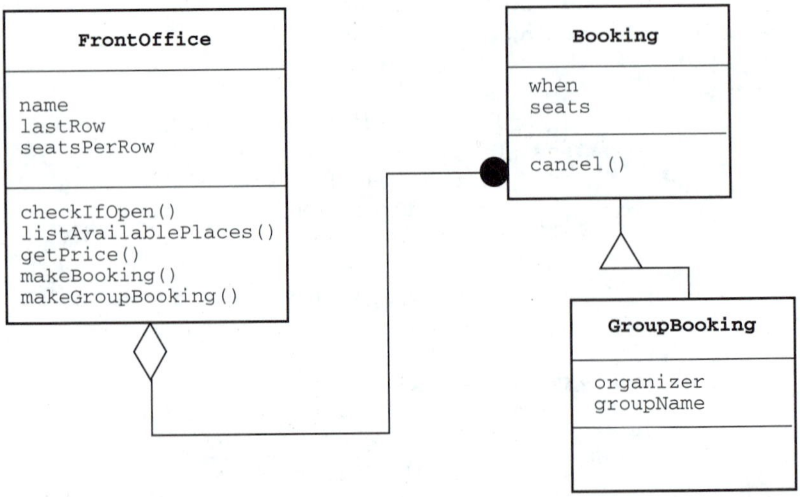

Figure 2.4 *OMT object model for the cinema application.*

access to a `FrontOffice` object can be made over the internet, allowing a simple client running on a home machine to make and manage bookings for a user. The Java code for a client can be loaded on demand across the internet rather than being distributed by normal software distribution channels. A customer may browse the Web site owned by the cinema and from this download the required Java code to interact with the front office object.

3 Introduction to CORBA IDL

This chapter introduces the Interface Definition Language (IDL), which is used to describe the interfaces of objects in CORBA. The language itself is part of the Object Management Group (OMG) CORBA specification, and it is an ISO standard. IDL is not a programming language because it cannot be used to implement the interfaces that are defined in it; its use does not replace the roles of programming languages such as C++, Smalltalk, Java, COBOL, and Ada. An advantage of IDL is that it allows interfaces to be defined independently of the languages used to implement and use these interfaces, and therefore it makes it easy to support language interoperability. IDL is not burdened with many complex features. This makes it easy to learn, and it strongly encourages the writing of clear interfaces.

In this chapter we introduce the commonly used features of IDL, those that will be used in subsequent chapters. The full definition can be found from the OMG (info@omg.org) or from product documentation.

3.1 IDL interfaces

An IDL interface provides a description of the functionality that is provided by an object. An interface definition provides all of the information needed to develop clients that use the interface. An interface typically specifies the attributes and operations belonging to that interface, as well as the parameters of each operation. Defining the interfaces between components is the most important aspect of distributed system design, therefore interfaces are the single most important feature of IDL.

Consider part of the IDL definitions given in Section 2.12 (p.39):

```
// IDL
typedef string Date;
struct Place {
      char row;
      unsigned long seat;
};

interface FrontOffice {

      readonly attribute string name;
      readonly attribute char lastRow;
      readonly attribute unsigned long seatsPerRow;

      boolean checkIfOpen (in Date when,
                           out Date nextAvailableDate);

      Price getPrice (in Place where, in Date when);

      // Rest not shown here.
};
```

The `FrontOffice` interface defines attributes `name`, `lastRow`, and `seatsPerRow`; these are properties of a `FrontOffice` object. The attribute `name` may take values of type `string`, which is one of the basic types of IDL. Attribute `lastRow` is of type `char`, and `seatsPerRow` is of type `unsigned long`. All three attributes are defined to be `readonly`. (An attribute declaration typically maps to two functions in the programming language, one to retrieve the value of the attribute and the other to set the value of the attribute. The `readonly` keyword specifies that there is only a function to retrieve the value. A `readonly` attribute need not be a constant: two reads of an attribute where there is an interleaving operation call can return different values.)

Two operations, `getPrice()` and `checkIfOpen()`, are provided. `getPrice()` takes two parameters: `where` of type `Place`, which is a user-defined structure, and `when` of type `Date`, which is a user-defined alias for `string`. Each parameter must specify the direction in which the parameter is passed, and this **mode** can be one of the following:

- `in`: the parameter is passed from the caller (client) to the called object.
- `out`: the parameter is passed from the called object to the caller.
- `inout`: the parameter is passed in both directions.

In our example, `when` is passed as an `in` parameter. The parameter passing mode must be specified for each parameter, and it is used both to improve the 'self-documentation' of an interface and to help guide the code that IDL is subsequently mapped into.

`checkIfOpen()` takes one `in` and one `out` parameter. If the cinema is not open on the date specified by the parameter `when`, the operation returns false and the `out` parameter `nextAvailableDate` indicates the next day after that when the cinema will be open. If the cinema is open on the specified date, the operation returns true and the `out` parameter will be an empty string. Because IDL has no concept of pointers, it is not legal to pass a null pointer for the `out` parameter, for example if the cinema is open on the specified date.

Comments are written as in C++. The example shows line comments introduced with the characters `//`.

Multiple IDL interfaces may be defined in a single source file, but it is common either to define each interface in its own file, or to define a set of closely related interfaces in a single file.

Note that IDL interface and operation declarations have a very similar form to declarations of classes and functions in C++. There are some differences, however, including the following

- All definitions made in an IDL interface are *public.* There is in fact no concept of *private* or *protected*, since these have to do with the implementation of a C++ interface rather than defining an interface in IDL.

- Member variables cannot be declared. Attributes are different from member variables because they indicate requests that a client can send to an object, and they do not indicate storage that an object must contain. When an IDL interface is implemented as a C++ class, a particular attribute can be represented as one or more member variables, or alternatively the attribute can be calculated from other data in the system. Consider a `readonly` attribute that indicates the number of seats that have been booked in a cinema:

  ```
  interface FrontOffice {
     readonly attribute unsigned long
                        numberSeatsBooked;
     // Rest as before.
  };
  ```

  This attribute can be represented as an integer in a C++ class that implements interface `FrontOffice`. Alternatively, the number of seats that have been booked may be determined by scanning an availability matrix held by the cinema, and hence the attribute would not be represented by any particular member variable.

- The parameter passing mode of each parameter must be specified, as must each parameter's name.

- There are no constructors or destructors. In fact, it would not be a sensible default to allow clients to create objects of a given interface in an arbitrary server in the system. The server itself should decide whether or not this facility should be provided to clients, and a good way to achieve this is for the server to have one or more objects that export object creation operations to clients. `FrontOffice::makeBooking()` is an example of such an operation; it creates objects of type `Booking`. It would not be sensible for interface `Booking` to provide a constructor that any client could call to make a booking.
- Return types must be specified for all operations.

Overloading of operation names is illegal, although it would be a useful feature of the language. Overloading is not allowed because it would cause difficulties when IDL is translated into languages such as C which disallow it.

3.2 One-way operations

Normally the caller of an operation is blocked while the call is being processed by the target object. However, although an IDL operation can be defined to be `oneway`, most implementations of CORBA will not block the caller of a `oneway` operation, but allow the caller to continue in parallel with the processing of the request in the server. For example, we could provide a `oneway` operation on our `FrontOffice` interface to allow customers to send comments on the facilities:

```
// IDL
interface FrontOffice {
      // Other details as before.
      // Send comments on facilities:
      oneway void makeComment(in string comment);
};
```

A `oneway` operation must specify a `void` return type and cannot have `out` or `inout` parameters, and it also cannot have a `raises` clause (see Section 3.4, p.50).

✚ Actually, the CORBA standard does not require `oneway` operations to be non-blocking: it simply states that an ORB is to make an effort to deliver each `oneway` call but no guarantee of delivery is made (this is termed **best-effort** semantics). It does state that each request must be delivered at most once. The CORBA standard has therefore left a great deal of freedom in how an ORB handles `oneway` operations, but the result of this is that applications can never be fully sure of exactly what `oneway` functions guarantee. Overuse of `oneway` operations must therefore be avoided.

Some ORBs do deliver single `oneway` operations reliably because they are delivered on the same connection-oriented protocol (often IIOP; see Chapter 1) as normal operations. Therefore, a single `oneway` call can be made reliably. However, a stream of `oneway` operation calls can swamp a server and therefore block the caller. As an alternative to blocking the caller, some ORBs could discard any `oneway` that cannot fit into the communication buffers between the client and server. In either case, a long stream of rapidly made `oneway` operation calls cannot be handled reliably without blocking the caller. The CORBA Event Service (Section 23.1, p.377) should be used instead when reliability and non-blocking are both required.

A one-way operation differs from a normal operation (one that is not designated as `oneway`) that happens to have no `out` or `inout` parameters and a `void` return type: calls to the normal operation will block until the operation request has been carried out. Note, however, that it is also possible to call a normal operation (one that is not designated as `oneway`) without blocking, and then to block for the reply at some later time, but it is often inconvenient to do this. This is discussed in Chapter 15, 'Dynamic invocation interface'.

A normal two-way interaction can be defined as two `oneway` operation calls, one in each direction. Overuse of this should be avoided since it makes interactions much more difficult to code and understand.

3.3 Modules

An interface can be defined within a module; this allows interfaces and other IDL type definitions to be grouped in logical units. This can be convenient because names defined within a module do not clash with names defined outside the module; that is, a module defines a naming scope. This allows sensible names for interfaces and other definitions to be chosen without clashing with other names.

The following example illustrates the use of a module: the interfaces and other definitions related to our cinema application are defined within a module, `Cinema`:

```
// IDL
module Cinema {
      interface Booking {
              . . . . .
      };
      . . . . .
      interface FrontOffice{
      . . . . .
      };
};
```

The full (or **scoped**) name of `Booking` is then `Cinema::Booking`. Interface `FrontOffice` can refer to interface `Booking` as either `Booking` or `Cinema::Booking`. Definitions outside of module `Cinema` must refer to it as `Cinema::Booking`.

It can be strongly argued that all IDL definitions should be made within a module with a well-chosen name. In this way, only the names of IDL modules can clash, and clients that need to use IDL definitions from different sources can avoid difficulties. Some naming conventions require the name of the orginating company, and possibly the product or project name, to be part of each module's name.

3.4 Exceptions

An IDL operation may raise an exception to indicate that an error has occurred. For example, operation `getPrice()` in interface `FrontOffice` can raise a user-defined exception:

```
// IDL
interface FrontOffice{

      // Rest not shown here.

      exception NoSuchPlace {
            Place where;
      };
      exception InvalidDate{
            Date when;
      };

      Places getPrice(in Place chosenPlace, in Date when)
                  raises (NoSuchPlace,InvalidDate);
};
```

The `getPrice()` operation specifies, using the `raises` expression, that it may raise one of the two exceptions called `NoSuchPlace` and `InvalidDate`, both of which are defined within the `FrontOffice` interface.

The `NoSuchPlace` exception defines a member, `where`, of type `Place`. The `InvalidDate` exception defines a member of type `Date`. These members are used to return the invalid data to the caller of the operation. Adding members in this way can aid debugging in client code, as well as helping client code to provide useful error messages to end users. Nevertheless, exceptions can be defined without any members (that is, without any member definitions between the `{}` characters). Further examples of exceptions are given in Section 3.9.1 (p.58).

As well as user-defined exceptions, a set of standard exceptions is defined by CORBA. These correspond to standard runtime errors which may occur during the execution of a request. All operation and attribute calls can raise any of these standard exceptions.

Exceptions are supported in IDL for a number of good reasons. Given that it is important for any interface to be able to raise errors to its callers, exceptions are probably the cleanest way to achieve this. The alternatives include `boolean` return values, or the returning of structures that hold an error indication and other members that specify why the error occurred. The use of `boolean` is a poor choice because it carries little information. The use of structures suffers from a number of disadvantages. Firstly, it is difficult to separate the normal and error return parameters/values, except by (error prone) documentation. Secondly, it is difficult to specify a set of possible error conditions; certainly more difficult than the way in which operation `getPrice()` was specified to possibly raise exceptions `NoSuchPlace` or `InvalidDate`, earlier in this section. Thirdly, it is important for IDL to have a separate syntax for exceptions, so that they can be cleanly translated into exceptions in programming languages that support them (such as C++ and Ada). IDL exceptions can, of course, be handled when IDL is translated into a programming language, such as C, that does not support exceptions. This is normally handled by adding another parameter to the programming language function that corresponds to each IDL operation.

3.5 Inheritance

Our cinema application also needs to handle booking and group booking objects. These share some attributes and operations, although group bookings require extra members. Before considering the inheritance required to define group bookings, interface `Booking` will first be introduced:

```
interface Booking {
      readonly attribute Date when;
      readonly attribute Places seats;
      void cancel ();
};
```

Using this, operation `makeBooking()` of interface `FrontOffice` can be introduced (its full definition will be given later in this chapter):

```
Booking makeBooking ( /* shown later */ )
          raises ( /* shown later */ );
```

The caller of `makeBooking()` is returned an object reference to a `Booking` object, on which it can call the attributes and operation shown. (The returned object reference can in fact reference any object of type `Booking` or any derived interface of this.)

Interface `GroupBooking` can be defined to extend interface `Booking`, with the addition of two attributes that record the organizer and name of the group:

```
interface GroupBooking : Booking {
      readonly attribute string organizer;
      readonly attribute string groupName;
};
```

Interface `Booking` is called a **base interface** of `GroupBooking`. `GroupBooking` is called a **derived interface** of `Booking`. `GroupBooking` inherits attributes `when` and `seats`, and operation `cancel()`. An implementation of interface `GroupBooking` may provide different code for these attributes and operations than an implementation of interface `Booking`.

If interface `Booking` is used, for example, as the type of an `in` parameter to an operation, then an object reference to a `Booking` object or a `GroupBooking` (or any other interface type that inherits from `Booking`) can be passed to this parameter. Similarly, any object reference of type `Booking` can actually refer to a `GroupBooking` object.

A reference to a `GroupBooking` object is returned by operation `makeGroupBooking()`:

```
GroupBooking makeGroupBooking (
                        /* other parameters shown later */
                        in string organizer,
                        in string groupName)
      raises ( /* other exceptions listed later */,
              GroupTooSmall);
```

Exception `GroupTooSmall` is defined as follows (in interface `FrontOffice`):

```
exception GroupTooSmall {
           unsigned long chosenSize;
           unsigned long minimumSize;
};
```

(The members of this exception show an important pattern: the value of the specified group size, `chosenSize`, is returned, as well as the minimum acceptable size.)

An interface may have more than one direct base interface; that is multiple inheritance is allowed.

✚ If an interface inherits from two interfaces which contain definitions (constant, type, or exception) of the same name, then references to this name in the derived interface will be ambiguous unless the name is qualified by its interface name; that is, unless a scoped name is given (see Section 3.3, p.49). Note that it is illegal to inherit from two interfaces that have a common operation or attribute name.

IDL inheritance differs considerably from C++ inheritance. The latter has variations such as `private`, `protected`, `public`, and `virtual` that are not reflected in IDL, because they concern implementation, not interfaces. `public virtual` inheritance in C++ is similar to IDL inheritance: an instance of a derived interface must behave as an instance of all of its base interfaces; all of the attributes and operations on base interfaces are available on instances of a derived interface. ✚

In addition, since IDL itself has no concept of an operation implementation, concepts such as redefinition of operations play no role in the language. While in C++ there is a need to list the member functions that a class inherits and wishes to redefine, this relisting in IDL is unnecessary and illegal. The code for inherited operations and attributes can be redefined when a derived interface is implemented, for example in C++.

Interface `object`

All IDL interfaces implicitly inherit from interface `Object`. This means, for example, that if type `Object` is used to define the type of an `in` parameter, then a reference to any CORBA object can be passed to this parameter.

3.6 The basic types of IDL

Table 3.1 lists the basic types supported in IDL. Note that there is no type `int` in IDL, and `char` cannot be qualified by `unsigned` (in IDL, a char is neither signed nor unsigned; it is not a 'small integer' as it is in C).

There are no pointer types in IDL: this is one reason why there is a `string` type in IDL; it is not possible to use `char*` as in C++. The fact that IDL does not

Table 3.1 *Basic types.*

IDL identifier	Description
`float`	IEEE single-precision floating point numbers
`double`	IEEE double-precision numbers
`long`	$-2^{31}..2^{31}-1$ (32bit)
`short`	$-2^{15}..2^{15}-1$ (16bit)
`unsigned long`	$0..2^{32}-1$ (32bit)
`unsigned short`	$0..2^{16}-1$ (16bit)
`char`	An 8-bit quantity (the ISO-Latin subset of ASCII)
`boolean`	`TRUE or FALSE`
`octet`	An 8-bit quantity that is guaranteed not to undergo any conversion during transmission. (The other 8-bit data type, `char`, may undergo conversion.)
`any`	The `any` type allows the specification of values that can be of an arbitrary IDL type
`NamedValue`	A pair consisting of a name (a `string`) and a value (of type `any`). See Section 3.15, p.64

include pointers is very helpful when mapping it to a programming language, such as Java, that too does not support pointers. It also means that the rules for passing values across a network (the so-called **marshaling rules**) are significantly easier.

The any type allows an interface to specify that a parameter or result type may contain an arbitrary type of value to be determined at runtime:

```
// IDL
interface I {
    void op(in any a);
};
```

A process that receives an any must determine what type of value it contains and then extract the value. The any type is described in detail in Chapter 14, 'Type any.' Type any should be used sparingly because it makes interfaces more difficult to understand, as it is not clear what types of values should be passed; and also because no compile-time type checking can be performed.

A number of new basic types were added in October 1996:

wchar	represents characters from any wide character set.
wstring	represents unbounded strings of wide characters. (in anticipation of this type, some of the CORBAservices typedef the type Istring to be string, with the aim of replacing this with a typedef that maps Istring to wstring).
wstring<length>	represents bounded strings of wide characters.
long long	represents 64 bit integer values.
unsigned long long	represents 64 bit unsigned integer values.
fixed<x, y>	represents exact numeric values, that have an integer and a fixed length decimal fraction part. For example, 123.45 is of type fixed<5, 2>.
long double	represents IEEE Std 754-1985 double-extended floating point numbers.

These new basic types have not been not covered in this book because they are not yet widely implemented.

3.7 Constructed types

As well as the basic types listed above, IDL provides three constructed types: struct, union, and enum.

3.7.1 Structures

Section 2.12 (p.39) defines two struct data types:

```
// IDL
struct Place {
      char row;
      unsigned long seat;
};

struct CreditCard {
      string id;
      Date expiry;
};
```

`Place` and `CreditCard` are valid type names, therefore there is no need to use a `typedef` when defining a `struct` (see Section 3.11, p.62). (Use of a `typedef` when defining a struct is considered bad style, because it introduces two type names.)

Structures are an important part of many IDL defintions. For example, `struct Place` is a natural choice within the cinema/theater example. The alternatives are not as useful:

- The row and seat numbers could be passed as individual parameters. This increases the number of parameters for each operation, and the resulting clutter can make it more difficult to understand an operation. Also, two separate values cannot be used for a return value to an operation, or as an attribute type. It must be said, of course, that passing two parameters to an operation can often require fewer statements than passing a structure, but the increased clarity of structures compensates for this.
- The row and seat numbers could be combined into a single value, say of type `long` or `string`. The required encoding and decoding can be confusing, error prone and expensive.
- Places could be represented as objects; that is, `struct Place` could be replaced with an object reference. This is a suitable approach, but it appears too heavyweight in this case. Also, some operation would be required to return object references for places to a client, given row and seat numbers, and this operation could require the reintroduction of `struct Place`.

3.7.2 Enumerated types

An enumerated type allows the members of a set of values to be represented by identifiers, for example:

```
// IDL
enum seatQuality {high, medium, low};
```

This is more readable than defining `seatQuality` as a `short`. The order in which the identifiers are named in the specification of an enumerated type defines the relative order of the identifiers. This order may be used by a specific programming language mapping which allows two enumerators to be compared.

3.7.3 Discriminated unions

The IDL `union` type provides a way to pass a value of one of a small number of types. A tag field is used to specify which member of a `union` instance is currently assigned a value:

```
// IDL
union Token switch (long) {
            case 1 : long l;
            case 2 : float f;
            default: string str;
};
```

`Token` is the name of a new type, therefore there is no need to use a `typedef` when defining a `union` (see Section 3.11, p.62).

IDL unions must be discriminated: that is, the `union` header must specify a tag or **discriminant** field that determines which `union` member is assigned a value. In the example, the discriminant is of type `long`. Each expression that follows the `case` keyword must be compatible with the discriminant type. The discriminant type, specified in parentheses after the `switch` keyword, must be one of the integer types, `char`, `boolean` or an `enum` type. A default case can appear at most once in a `union` declaration.

For `Token`, if the discriminant value is `1`, then the member called `l` is valid; if the discriminant value is `2`, then the member called `f` is valid; otherwise the member called `str` is valid.

In C++ and C, unions are used to save space: the space required for a union is the space required for its largest member. However, IDL makes no such statement, because this may not be possible in all programming languages that IDL is mapped to.

Because unions can make it difficult to understand some interfaces, they should not be overused. In fact, a union does not appear in any of the application-level IDL definitions in this book. They do appear in three places in the IDL for the CORBAservices shown in Appendix A, 'IDL interfaces for selected CORBAservices.' In one case, in the Query Service, a union is used to represent the types of values that can be stored in a collection:

```
// Part of the Query Service:
     union Value switch (ValueType) {
          case TypeBoolean: boolean b;
          case TypeChar: char c;
          case TypeOctet: octet o;
          case TypeShort: short s;
          case TypeUShort: unsigned short us;
          case TypeLong: long l;
          case TypeULong: unsigned long ul;
          case TypeFloat: float f;
          case TypeDouble:double d;
          case TypeString: string str;
          case TypeObject: Object obj;
          case TypeAny: any a;
          case TypeSmallInt: short si;
          case TypeInteger: long i;
          case TypeReal: float r;
          case TypeDoublePrecision: double dp;
          case TypeCharacter: string ch;
          case TypeDecimal: Decimal dec; // Decimal is a struct.
          case TypeNumeric: Decimal n;
     };
```

In the two other cases, a union is used to handle null values; that is, to define a type that can be null or any valid value. For example:

```
union FieldValue switch (boolean) {
     case FALSE: Value v;
};
```

For example, an `out` parameter of type `FieldValue` can either contain no value at all (if the discriminant is `TRUE`), or valid `Value` (if the discriminant is `FALSE`).

3.8 Arrays

IDL provides multidimensional fixed-size arrays to hold lists of elements of the same type. The size of each dimension must be specified in the definition. Some example array types are:

```
// IDL
// A one-dimensional array.
typedef Booking Bookings[100];

// A two-dimensional array.
typedef Place BlockOfPlaces[10][20];
```

Types `Bookings` and `BlockOfPlaces` can be used, for example, to define parameters to an operation.

Section 3.9.1 discusses the fact that IDL requires array-type definitions to be made with a `typedef`, as shown above.

3.9 Template types

IDL provides two template types, `sequence` and `string`, which are described in the following subsections. Other user-defined template types are not supported.

3.9.1 Sequences

A sequence is a variable length list of elements, of any IDL type. Sequences are used to pass lists of elements in either direction between a client and a target object, especially where the length of the list cannot be determined statically. If the length could be determined statically, either a sequence or an array could be used.

A sequence may be **bounded** or **unbounded**, depending on whether or not the maximum size is specified when the sequence type is defined. For example, the type declaration:

```
// IDL
typedef sequence <Place, 10> TenPlaces;
```

defines a bounded sequence type. An instance of this type may be of any length up to the bound, 10. The type declaration:

```
// IDL
typedef sequence <Place> Places;
```

defines an unbounded sequence type of `Place` structs. An instance of this type can be of any size.

A bounded sequence therefore has a maximum length, whereas an unbounded sequence does not. Every sequence has a current length, and only that number of elements is transmitted when a sequence is sent as a parameter or return value.

An array differs from a sequence because a fixed number of these elements are always transmitted when an array is transmitted.

A sequence (or array) that is used as a parameter, an attribute or a return value must be named by a `typedef` declaration (see Section 3.11, p.62) before it can be used as the type of an attribute definition or as a parameter to an operation. For example:

```
// IDL

// The following two definitions are not allowed:
attribute sequence<Place> illegalVector;
void illegalOperation (in sequence<Place> p);

// but the following two are legal:
typedef sequence<Place> Places;
attribute Places legalVector;
void legalOperation (in Places p);
```

This restriction is made so that variables of these sequence types can be defined in programming languages that IDL is mapped into. Clearly, when a `typedef` is used, a variable of type `Places` can be defined (for example, in C++ when the IDL types are translated into C++). If a `typedef` is not used, the sequence type will be anonymous in IDL, and some ad hoc rule would have to be used to allow variables of this type to be defined in C++ or another programming language.

A sequence (or array) that appears within a struct or union definition does not have to be named by a `typedef`. Therefore, the following is legal:

```
// IDL
struct Place {
      char row
      unsigned long seat;
      sequence<Place> placesCloseBy;
};
```

However, it is better style always to name sequence (and array) types using a `typedef`.

As examples of the use of exceptions, structs, and sequences, the cinema application includes the following IDL definitions:

```
interface FrontOffice {

      exception NoSuchPlace { Place where; };
      exception PlaceAlreadyBooked
                              { Place where; Date when; };
      exception InvalidCreditCard { CreditCard invalidCard; };
      exception InvalidDate { Date when; };
      exception GroupTooSmall { unsigned long chosenSize;
                                unsigned long minimumSize;
                              };

      readonly attribute string name;
```

```
     readonly attribute char lastRow;
     readonly attribute unsigned long seatsPerRow;

          boolean checkIfOpen (in Date when,
                                    out Date nextAvailableDate)
                    raises (InvalidDate);

     Places listAvailablePlaces(in Date when)
               raises (InvalidDate);

     Price getPrice (in Place chosenPlace,
                    in Date when)
               raises (NoSuchPlace, invalidDate);

     Booking makeBooking (in Places chosenPlaces,
                         in Date when,
                         in CreditCard payment)
               raises (NoSuchPlace, PlaceAlreadyBooked,
                       InvalidCreditCard, InvalidDate);

     GroupBooking makeGroupBooking (in Places chosenPlaces,
                                   in Date when,
                                   in CreditCard payment,
                                   in string organizer,
                                   in string groupName)
               raises (NoSuchPlace, PlaceAlreadyBooked,
                       InvalidCreditCard, InvalidDate,
                       GroupTooSmall);
};
```

3.9.2 Strings

We have already used type `string`, which is list of `char`. A string can contain any ASCII ISO-Latin character, except ASCII NUL. A `string` may be bounded or unbounded depending on whether or not its maximum length is specified in its declaration. A maximum length may be specified for a `string` as shown in the example below:

```
// IDL
interface FrontOffice {
     // Other details as before.

     typedef string<10> ShortString;
     attribute ShortString shortName; // Max length is 10 chars.

};
```

The simple type `string` represents unbounded strings, that is, strings with no maximum length.

For a bounded string, the stated bound is the number of valid characters that can appear in the string, and this does not count the terminating NUL character required in programming languages such as C++. Therefore, in C++, the space required to store a bounded string will be one byte longer than the bound.

An array of `char` and a `string` differ in the following ways:

- The full array is transmitted when an array is passed as a parameter or return value, whereas only the current number of characters in a string is transmitted. The transmission of an array of `char` causes difficulties if all of its elements are not initialized, if some of the elements are not valid ASCII ISO-Latin characters.
- There is no array equivalent of an unbounded string.

3.10 Constants

A constant can be defined as follows:

```
// IDL
interface FrontOffice {

    const unsigned long lengthOfShortString = 10;
    const unsigned long lengthOfLongString =
                                  lengthOfShortString * 4;

    typedef string<lengthOfShortString> ShortString;
    typedef string<lengthOfLongString> LongString;

    attribute ShortString shortName;
    attribute LongString longName;
    // Rest of interface not shown.
};
```

The value of an IDL constant cannot change. Constants may be defined in an interface or module, or at the global scope (that is, at the file level, outside of any interface or module).

Constants of type `long`, `unsigned long`, `short`, `unsigned short`, `char`, `boolean`, `float`, `double`, and `string` can be declared. Note that constants of type `octet` cannot be declared. Integer literals can be specified in decimal, octal, or hexadecimal. Character literals support all of the C++ escape sequences, such as `'\n'`, `'\t'`, `'\031'`, and so on.

3.11 `Typedef` declarations

A `typedef` declaration can be used to define a meaningful or a more simple name for a basic or a user-defined type. For example:

```
// IDL
typedef string Date;
```

defines `Date` as a synonym for `string`. Consequently, the parameter declaration in

```
// IDL
void op1( in Date when );
```

is equivalent to:

```
// IDL
void op1( in string when );
```

The definition

```
// IDL
typedef Booking Bookings[100];
```

allows a subsequent definition (for example, as a member of a structure):

```
// IDL
Bookings arrayOfBookings;
```

Type definitions can be made in terms of other type definitions, such as:

```
typedef Date DateOfBirth;
```

3.12 Type definitions in interfaces

Types can also be defined in interfaces. For example, we might decide to define struct `Place` inside the scope of interface `FrontOffice`:

```
interface FrontOffice {

     struct Place {
          char row
          unsigned long seat;
     };
```

```
        // Other definitions not shown here.
};
```

Definitions inside of interface `FrontOffice` can then refer to the struct type as `Place`, but definitions outside of the interface must refer to it using its fully scoped name `FrontOffice::Place`. Of cource there is no concept of the struct being private to interface `FrontOffice`: the concept of private definitions has no place in IDL, since it is not concerned with implementation details.

Module and interface definitions cannot appear within an interface.

3.13 Forward references; self-referential types

If one interface uses another, then there is a natural order for these definitions in the IDL file. However, if both use each other, we need to forward reference one in order to prevent the IDL compiler from reporting an error. Hence, the following is valid IDL:

```
// IDL
interface FrontOffice; // A forward reference.

interface Booking {
        // Other definitions not shown here.
        readonly attribute FrontOffice officeMadeAt;
};

interface FrontOffice {
        // Other definitions not shown here.
        Booking makeBooking ( /* . . . . */ );
};
```

Some types are **self-referential** – meaning that they use themselves. Hence, we might have a definition of struct `Person` that uses itself:

```
// IDL
struct Person {
        readonly attribute float height;
        // Other definitions not shown here.
        readonly attribute Person spouse;
};
```

3.14 The preprocessor

IDL provides preprocessing directives that allow macro substitution, conditional compilation, and source file inclusion. The IDL preprocessor is identical to the C++ preprocessor, as defined in *The Annotated C++ Reference Manual* (Ellis and Stroustrup, 1990). For example, the `#include` directive allows an IDL file to be included in other files.

As in a C++ include file, we should remember that an IDL file can potentially be included in many other IDL files. Hence, one IDL file might include two IDL files, one of which includes the other. The second time that the IDL compiler processes the IDL file that is included twice, it will issue a set of error messages complaining of attempted redefinition of IDL types.

To handle this, all IDL files should be protected with the same use of directives that are common in C++ header files. For example, in file `Front.idl`, we would typically write:

```
#ifndef Front_IDL
#define Front_IDL

/* Body of the IDL file, not shown here. */

#endif
```

The first time that this file is included by the IDL compiler, the macro `Front_IDL` will not be defined, and therefore the file will be properly included. `Front_IDL` will be defined the second time the file is included, and the body of the IDL file will be skipped.

✚ Other preprocessing directives available in IDL are: `#define`, `#undef`, `#include`, `#if`, `#ifdef`, `#ifndef`, `#elif`, `#else`, `#endif`, `#defined`, `#error`, and `#pragma`. These directives should not be overused, as they tend to make IDL files difficult to read. In contrast to C++, where directives such as `#ifdef` are used to protect alternative code for different platforms, these porting issues do not arise in IDL, and the need for such directives is very rare. ✚

✚ 3.15 NamedValue

The built-in type, `NamedValue`, represents a pair: a name of type `string` and a value of type any. It is a valid parameter, return, attribute, and member type, but it is not frequently used in the definition of application IDL interfaces. It is used in standard interfaces, such as in some of the CORBAservices (see Part 5), and in the dynamic invocation interface (see Section 15.3, p.247).

3.16 Context clause

An IDL operation may also have a `context` clause associated with it. A client can maintain one or more CORBA context objects, which provide a mapping from identifiers (string names) to string values. An IDL operation can specify that it is to be provided with the client's mapping for particular identifiers – it does this by listing these identifiers following the operation declaration. For example, the definition of `makeGroupBooking()` could be changed as follows:

```
// Old
     GroupBooking makeGroupBooking (in Places     chosenPlaces,
                                    in Date       when,
                                    in CreditCard payment,
                                    in string     organizer,
                                    in string     groupName)
                raises ( /* . . . . */ );

// New
     GroupBooking makeGroupBooking (in Places     chosenPlaces,
                                    in Date       when,
                                    in CreditCard payment)
                raises ( /* . . . . */ )
                context ("organizer", "groupName");
```

The caller of the new version of `makeGroupBooking()` must pass a context object as a parameter; and this context can contain entries for the organizer's name and the group's name. In this case, there is no particular benefit in doing this, but there would be an advantage if many of the operations called by a client took the same context entries. The client could then set these values up once in a context, and pass this to the operation calls, rather than passing two parameters, as required in the old version of the operation.

In general, the advantage of a context is that a set of *identifier:string* mappings can be specified in one location of a large program, and a subset of these mappings can be passed to IDL operation calls spread throughout the program. The mappings can then be maintained easily in one location.

Nevertheless, context clauses are one of the least important features of IDL, and extensive use should be avoided. One of the dangers associated with contexts is that it is not clear from the normal parameters to a call what values are being passed to it; another is that there is no type-checking for the values passed. If the documentation for an operation states that one of the context strings is to be a string of digits, or one of a fixed set of strings, then this cannot be checked at compile time. Further, there is some possibility that contexts will be removed in some future version of CORBA.

Each identifier name in a context clause must begin with an alphanumeric character and can only contain alphanumerics, digits, '`_`' and '`.`'. An identifier specified in a `context` clause can also contain the character '`*`', but this character must appear at the end; it indicates that the operation is to receive the mapping for all identifiers in the client context with matching leading names. (A '`*`' can only appear in a `context` clause; it cannot appear in an identifier in a `Context` object.) For example, an identifier '`sys_*`' in a `context` clause would match entries such as 'sys_printer' and 'sys_quality' in the client's context.

3.17 The orb.idl include file

The interface names for the CORBA pseudo types NamedValue, Principal, and TypeCode are available in an IDL file only if it includes the directive:

```
#include <orb.idl>
```

Interface name Object (the implicit base interface of all interfaces) is available in all files. ✚

3.18 Identifier rules and conventions

An identifier in IDL can contain letters and digits, and the underscore ('_') character, but it cannot begin with an underscore. The language is case-sensitive (hence if type Place is defined, it cannot be used as if it were defined with the name place). Furthermore, two identifiers in the same scope cannot differ just in the case of any of the letters. Hence, if type Place is defined, another type called place cannot be defined in the same scope. This rule makes it easier to map IDL to programming languages that are case-insensitive (if Place and place were allowed in the same scope, this would cause difficulties when mapped to a language that would view these two identifiers as the same).

The following are useful conventions for identifiers in IDL:

- Type names should begin with an upper case letter, and use a capital letter to begin any concatenated words; for example, FrontOffice. This applies to names for interfaces, types, and exceptions.
- Other names should begin with a lower case letter, and use a capital letter to begin any concatenated words; for example, checkIfOpen(). This applies to names for operations, attributes, structure members, exception members, and union members.
- Underscore ('_') characters should not be used, as these can cause problems when translating IDL to some programming languages. Many of the identifiers in the CORBAservices (see Part 5) do contain underscores, so ad hoc workarounds must be used for programming languages that have difficulties with underscores.

- Programming language keywords should be avoided; for example, `while`, `class`, `namespace`, and so on.

3.19 Example IDL

Section 2.12 (p.39) shows the IDL definitions that are used in a number of the subsequent chapters.

4 IDL to C++ mapping of simple types

This chapter and the next describe how IDL definitions are translated into C++, and the rules that C++ clients and servers must obey when, respectively, using and implementing IDL interfaces. Instead of just aiming at completeness, these chapters attempt to make these rules easier to understand. Nevertheless, some readers will need to know more than the basics, so advanced and detailed material has been included. This is marked so that it can be skipped on first reading. Indeed, many readers will not need to be concerned with this level at all.

The IDL to C++ mapping rules are defined by the CORBA standard but certain detailed decisions have been left to the implementer of each ORB. Decisions made when implementing Orbix will be pointed out to allow you to understand which details are covered by the standard and which are ORB-specific. A **conforming** client or server program is one that makes no assumptions about details that CORBA has left to individual ORB vendors.

The rules are explained for each data type, starting with IDL basic types and then dealing with each complex type in turn. For each IDL data type, the static mapping rules to C++ are presented, then how this type is mapped when it appears as a parameter to an operation, and finally the memory management rules that must be obeyed by the client and the server to avoid the leakage of memory.

On first reading, it is sufficient to understand the rules for basic types, interfaces, strings, and object references (Sections 4.1–4.4, respectively). The other data types (structs, sequences, arrays, and unions) are covered in Chapter 5. The handling of IDL type `any` is covered in Chapter 14. CORBA exceptions are discussed in Chapter 9.

4.1 Basic types and enums

The mappings for basic types are shown in Table 4.1.

Table 4.1 *Mapping for basic types.*

IDL	C++ typedefs
`short`	`CORBA::Short`
`long`	`CORBA::Long`
`unsigned short`	`CORBA::UShort`
`unsigned long`	`CORBA::ULong`
`float`	`CORBA::Float`
`double`	`CORBA::Double`
`char`	`CORBA::Char`
`boolean`	`CORBA::Boolean`
`octet`	`CORBA::Octet`

In Orbix, on a 32-bit architecture, these C++ typedefs map to basic C++ types as shown in Table 4.2.

Table 4.2 *Example C++ types.*

Typedef name	Orbix mapping to C++ on a 32-bit architecture
`CORBA::Short`	`short`, if this is a 16-bit integer value
`CORBA::Long`	`long`, if this is a 32-bit integer value
`CORBA::UShort`	`unsigned short`, if this is a 16-bit unsigned integer value
`CORBA::ULong`	`unsigned long`, if this is a 32-bit unsigned integer value
`CORBA::Float`	`float`
`CORBA::Double`	`double`
`CORBA::Char`	`char` (provided this is 8 bits)
`CORBA::Boolean`	`unsigned char`
`CORBA::Octet`	`unsigned char`, if this is an 8-bit value

Why are types such as `CORBA::Short` used as a level of indirection between the IDL and C++ types? This indirection is used because the detailed storage requirements of many of the C++ types are not defined by the C++ language; for example, nowhere does it state that a C++ `short` occupies 16 bits. IDL, on the other hand, requires this rigor, so that applications can interoperate between different machine architectures. The mapping from IDL basic types to C++ is therefore defined in terms of typedefs such as `CORBA::Short`, and each ORB on each platform must ensure that these are mapped to appropriate types on that platform. `CORBA::Short`, for example, must always be mapped to an integer type that occupies 16 bits. Programmers are encouraged to use typedefs such as `CORBA::Short` to isolate themselves from platform differences.

`CORBA::Boolean` could have been a typedef for the ANSI C++ data type `bool`, but insistence on ANSI C++ is not a requirement of CORBA at this time, hence `CORBA::Boolean` can be a typedef for the C++ type `unsigned char`. IDL's `octet` data type must also occupy 8 bits; it maps to `CORBA::Octet`, which might be typedef-ed to C++'s `unsigned char`.

✚ The CORBA IDL to C++ mapping rules do not insist that types `boolean`, `octet`, and `char` map to the different C++ types (the first two map to the same type in Orbix). There are a few small features of the overall IDL to C++ mapping that must allow for the fact that these three IDL data types can map to the same underlying C++ type. ✚

The C++ namespace `CORBA` contains some built-in application-independent definitions used by C++ clients and servers. (If the chosen C++ compiler does not support namespaces, a C++ class, `CORBA`, will be used instead.) Putting these definitions in a C++ namespace (or class) means that their names do not clash with names used in any other library or application.

Enum types

An `enum` in IDL is mapped to the equivalent C++ `enum`. Hence the IDL definition

```
enum x {a,b,c};
```

maps to

```
enum x {a,b,c};
```

✚ An instance of the C++ enum must occupy 32 bits, and some C++ compilers must be forced to use this much space through the addition of a constant added at the end; for example:

```
enum x {a,b,c};
```

can map to

```
enum x {a,b,c, IT__ENUM_I_x=CORBA_ULONG_MAX);
```

Here, `IT__ENUM_I_X` is the extra constant, and `CORBA_ULONG_MAX` is a constant that ensures that instances of the enum type occupy 32 bits. The addition of this constant and its name are ORB implementation dependent. ✚

4.1.1 Parameter passing table for basic types

When a basic type is passed as a parameter to an operation or appears as the return type, then the corresponding C++ formal parameter types are as shown in Table 4.3. The rules are very simple: `out` and `inout` parameters are passed by reference so that the called function can change them, and `in` parameters and return values are passed by value.

Table 4.3 *Parameter passing modes for basic types.*

IDL type	in	out	inout	return
short	CORBA::Short	CORBA::Short&	CORBA::Short&	CORBA::Short
long	CORBA::Long	CORBA::Long&	CORBA::Long&	CORBA::Long
unsigned short	CORBA::UShort	CORBA::UShort&	CORBA::UShort&	CORBA::UShort
unsigned long	CORBA::ULong	CORBA::ULong&	CORBA::ULong&	CORBA::ULong
float	CORBA::Float	CORBA::Float&	CORBA::Float&	CORBA::Float
double	CORBA::Double	CORBA::Double&	CORBA::Double&	CORBA::Double
char	CORBA::Char	CORBA::Char&	CORBA::Char&	CORBA::Char
boolean	CORBA::Boolean	CORBA::Boolean&	CORBA::Boolean&	CORBA::Boolean
octet	CORBA::Octet	CORBA::Octet&	CORBA::Octet&	CORBA::Octet

The parameter passing for enum types are shown in Table 4.4.

Table 4.4 *Parameter passing modes for `enum` data types.*

IDL type	in	out	inout	return
enum E	E	E&	E&	E

4.1.2 Memory management for basic types

Since basic types in IDL do not map to pointer types in C++, there are no memory management issues to be discussed when basic types are passed as `in`, `out`, or `inout` parameters or as return values. Nevertheless, for completeness and to introduce the format used to discuss more complex data types, the following subsections discuss the rules for passing basic values to and from operations.

`in` parameters

Consider the interface:

```
interface T {
      void op1 (in long l);
};
```

A C++ client of this interface simply passes a `CORBA::Long` value, for example:

```
T_var p = . . . . ;
CORBA::Long l = 278989;
p->op1(l);
```

The implementation of operation `T::op1()` may be coded as follows:

```
void T_i::op1(CORBA::Long l)
          throw (CORBA::SystemException) {
      cout << l;
}
```

`out` parameters and return values

Consider the interface:

```
interface T {
      float op1 (out char c);
};
```

A C++ client of this interface can use it as follows:

```
T_var p = . . . . ;
CORBA::Char c;
CORBA::Float f;
f = p->op1(c);
// c and f should have sensible values now
```

The implementation of operation `T::op1()` may be coded as follows:

```
CORBA::Float T_i::op1(CORBA::Char& c)
          throw (CORBA::SystemException) {
      c = 'y';
      return 3.14;
}
```

inout parameters

Consider the interface:

```
interface T {
      void op1 (inout Boolean b);
};
```

A C++ client of this interface passes a value that may be updated by the target object:

```
T_var p = . . . . ;
CORBA::Boolean b = 1; // Pass 'true' to op1()
p->op1(b);
// b may be different now
```

The implementation of operation `T::op1()` may be coded as follows:

```
void T_i::op1(CORBA::Boolean& b)
           throw (CORBA::SystemException) {
      if (b) cout << "b is true" << endl;
      b = 0;
}
```

4.2 Interfaces, scopes, modules, and constants

An IDL interface maps to a C++ class. For example:

```
interface T {
      attribute long l;
      readonly attribute char c;
      void op1();
};
```

maps to

```
class T : public virtual CORBA::Object {

      CORBA::Long l()    // Get the value
            throw (CORBA::SystemException);
      void l(CORBA::Long)    // Modify the value.
            throw (CORBA::SystemException);
```

```
      CORBA::Char c()    // Get the value.
            throw (CORBA::SystemException);

      virtual void op1()
            throw (CORBA::SystemException);
};
```

Each operation maps to a member function; each normal attribute maps to two member functions (to read and modify the attribute value); and each `readonly` attribute maps to one member function (to read the attribute value).

The IDL compiler also adds a number of member and static functions, which are described in Section 4.4.4.

Class T inherits from the system-provided class `CORBA::Object`, which acts as the uppermost root class for all CORBA objects. A reference of type `CORBA::Object_ptr` or `CORBA::Object_var` can reference any CORBA object.

✚ The same mapping is used for both normal and `oneway` operations. However, the IDL compiler ensures that each `oneway` operation has no return value, no `out` or `inout` parameters, and no `raises` clause. On the client side, the generated C++ stub code (in Orbix, the member function of the proxy code) does not wait for a reply from the target object. ✚

Scopes

When an IDL type definition is made within an interface definition, the corresponding C++ type appears within the generated C++ class and its name is therefore scoped by the name of that class. Consider the IDL definition:

```
interface T {
      enum e {a,b,c};
      struct nested1 {
            . . . . // Details not shown.
      };
};
```

This is translated into the following C++:

```
class T : public virtual CORBA::Object {
      enum e {a,b,c};
      struct nested1 {
            . . . .
      };
};
```

This gives the scoped names `T::e` and `T::nested1`, and these must be used instead of the simple names `e` and `nested`.

✚ Some C++ compilers do not allow structs or classes to appear in a class definition. The IDL compiler caters for this restriction by making the definition of the C++ struct `nested1` outside of any class and renaming it to `T_nested1`. Further, because the struct `nested1` may use the enum type `e`, the latter is also defined outside of any C++ class and renamed to `T_e`. ✚

Modules

IDL modules are mapped to C++ namespaces. Consider:

```
module M {
      typedef float money;
      interface I {
            // . . . . Details not shown.
      };
};
```

This is translated into:

```
namespace M {
      typedef CORBA::Float money;
      class I : public virtual CORBA::Object {
            . . . .
      };
};
```

Therefore, the scoped name of the interface is `M::I`.

✚ Some C++ compilers do not support namespaces, in which case namespace `M` is replaced with class `M`. If a C++ compiler that does not support namespaces also does not support nested classes, then module `M` is not translated into any feature in the C++ code, but interface `I` is translated into a class called `M_I` and the typedef is called `M_money`. ✚

Constants

Constants that are defined globally in an IDL file are translated directly into their C++ equivalents. Therefore:

```
const long MaxLen = 4;
```

maps to the following C++ definition

```
const CORBA::Long MaxLen = 4;
```

Constants defined in IDL interfaces must map to both a declaration (within the generated C++ class) and a definition (at the C++ file level). Hence:

```
interface I {
      const long MaxLen = 4;
      // Other details not shown.
};
```

maps to:

```
class I : public virtual CORBA::Object {
      static const CORBA::Long MaxLen; // Declaration
      // Other details not shown.
};
```

and the following definition at the C++ file level:

```
      const CORBA::Long I::MaxLen = 4;
```

✚ The fact that the constant value is assigned in a definition statement in the code file means that it is illegal in C++ to define an array that uses this constant as a bound:

```
      long myArray [i::MaxLen]; // Illegal C++
```

The workaround is to write:

```
      long* myArray = new long [I::MaxLen];
```

If an ISO C++ compiler is being used, then simple constants can be defined and initialised within a class. IDL constants defined in a module are mapped like those defined globally, provided that an IDL module maps to a C++ namespace. If an IDL module maps to a C++ class, then constants defined in modules are handled like constants defined in interfaces. ✚

4.3 Strings

IDL type `string` maps to `char*` in C++. Such C++ pointers must point to null-terminated character strings. In addition, as we will see later in this section, a **helper class**, `CORBA::String_var`, is also defined to make the memory management of strings easier. This is the first such helper class that we have introduced, but, as we will see, many such classes are predefined or generated by the IDL compiler.

Allocation and de-allocation of space

All strings passed as `out` or `inout` parameters or return values to IDL operations, or returned as attribute values, must be allocated using one of the following two C++ functions that are defined in the `CORBA` scope:

```
// In namespace (or class) CORBA
char *string_dup (const char*);
char *string_alloc(CORBA::ULong len);
```

(Note that, unlike many C/C++ functions, the length *excludes* the space for the terminating '\0' character. `CORBA::string_alloc()` returns zero if it cannot allocate the required storage.)

`CORBA::string_alloc()` allocates space for a string, and any function (such as `strcpy()`) can be used to initialize this space. `CORBA::string_dup()` allocates space, and copies the specified string parameter into this space. For example, strings can be allocated as follows:

```
char* p1 = CORBA::string_dup("hello1");

char *p2 = CORBA::string_alloc(6);
strcpy(p2,"hello2");
```

Strings allocated with `CORBA::string_alloc()` or `CORBA::string_dup()` must be de-allocated using:

```
void string_free(char*);
```

For example:

```
CORBA::string_free(p1);
CORBA::string_free(p2);
```

It is not legal to use the normal `new` and `delete` operators. At first this appears to be an unfortunate restriction, but the motivation for it is strong. Remember that CORBA aims to give a system integration platform that is the same across many different operating systems, and the vagaries of `new` and `delete` across these operating systems must be avoided. In particular, on Windows, it is not safe to allocate storage for a string (or any data type) in one DLL and de-allocate it in another. Therefore, it is not safe for one DLL (for example, the CORBA runtime) to use `new` to allocate some memory and for another DLL (for example, an application) to use `delete` to de-allocate it.

Instead, because all three functions, `string_alloc()`, `string_dup()`, and `string_free()`, appear in the one DLL, any DLL can call `CORBA::string_alloc()` or `CORBA::string_dup()`, and the same or any other DLL can safely call `CORBA::string_free()`.

✚ An alternative mechanism would have been to redefine the global `new` and `delete` operators, but this would have caused incompatibilities with other libraries that already redefine these.

Another reason for `string_alloc()`, `string_dup()`, and `string_free()` is that they allow an ORB to have complete control of memory allocation. For example, it can allocate all of the `out` parameters for an operation in a contiguous storage block, and only de-allocate this block when the client is finished using all of the parameters. ✚

CORBA::String_var

The class `CORBA::String_var` is defined as a helper class to aid the memory management of strings for clients and servers. (Note the capital letter in the type name `CORBA::String_var` and the small letter in function names such as `CORBA::string_dup()`). It is similar to `char*` in that an instance of `CORBA::String_var` references a null-terminated character string; but it differs in that the destructor of `CORBA::String_var` de-allocates the referenced character string. Hence, the following code does not leak memory:

```
{
      CORBA::String_var s1 = CORBA::string_dup("hello");

}     // s1 goes out of scope, and its destructor
      // de-allocates the string
```

We say that a `CORBA::String_var` variable **owns** the memory that it points to; that is, it de-allocates it in its destructor.

Typical usages of `CORBA::String_var` are shown in the following subsections. Of course, programmers are not required to use `CORBA::String_var`: it is provided only for convenience. Frequently, use of `CORBA::String_var` simplifies code, but programmers must be careful never to assign a string pointer to a `CORBA::String_var` variable when it is not safe for that variable to own the string.

Class `CORBA::String_var` defines the usual copy constructor and `operator=()`, both of which make a deep copy; that is, they copy the string value. Class `CORBA::String_var` also provides `operator[]()`, which can be used to index into a string (it returns the `char` value at a given index).

`CORBA::String_var` has a conversion to and from `char*`, as shown in the following code:

```
char* p1 = . . . .;
char* p2 = . . . .;
CORBA::String_var v1 = . . . .;
CORBA::String_var v2 = . . . .;

// The following statements should be read
// separately, and not as a statement sequence:
p1 = p2;    // No copy; no de-allocation.       Note 1
p1 = v1;    // No copy; no de-allocation.       Note 2
v1 = p1;    // No copy; de-allocation.          Note 3
v1 = v2;    // de-allocation. Copy;             Note 4
```

The final statement is the only one that makes a copy of the string. An assignment that involves a `char*` does not make a copy; only an assignment that involves two

`CORBA::String_var` variables makes a copy of the string, because each `CORBA::String_var` must own its own string.

An assignment into a `CORBA::String_var` de-allocates the string that the `CORBA::String_var` previously pointed to.

✚ The details are described in the following notes.

- *Note 1*: after the call, `p1` and `p2` will point to the same string, and of course no string copying will occur. There will be a memory leak if `p1` is the only pointer to the string it previously pointed to.
- *Note 2*: after the call, `p1` and `v1` will point to the same string, no string copying will occur. `v1` retains ownership of the string; that is, it de-allocates the string in its destructor (therefore, `CORBA::string_free(p1)` should not be called). There will be a memory leak if `p1` is the only pointer to the string it previously pointed to.

  Note that it is not always safe to modify the string value that `p1` points to after the assignment, because the string managed by `v1` (and now pointed to by `p1`) may have been allocated in read-only memory. Therefore, it is safer to define `p1` to be a `const char*`, rather than simply a `char*`.
- *Note 3*: after the call, `v1` and `p1` will point to the same string; no string copying will occur. `v1` assumes ownership of the string. If `v1` previously referenced a string, it will be de-allocated automatically before the assignment is made. Because `v1` assumes ownership of the string, `CORBA::string_free(p1)` should not be called. Note also that the string pointed to by `p1` must have been allocated using `CORBA::string_alloc()` or `CORBA::string_dup()`, because `v1` will eventually de-allocate it using `CORBA::string_free()`.
- *Note 4*: after the call, `v1` and `v2` will point to separate copies of the string (a copy of the string will be made). If `v1` previously referenced a string, it will be de-allocated automatically before the assignment is made. `v1` and `v2` will own the (separate) strings that they point to. ✚

The following statement is likely to cause a runtime error because a literal string cannot be owned by the `CORBA::String_var` (because it cannot be freed), and yet it is not copied:

```
CORBA::String_var v3 = "literal"; // Dangerous!
```

Instead, the following should be written:

```
CORBA::String_var v3 = CORBA::string_dup("literal");
```

Ensure ownership

CORBA::String_var can be used to make the management of strings easier. But always remember that a CORBA::String_var variable expects to own the string it references. Be careful, therefore, not to assign a string to such a variable when it is clear that it cannot own the string. As well as showing typical uses of CORBA::String_var variables, the following subsections, which describe the general memory management rules, show some inappropriate uses where this ownership rule is broken.

4.3.1 Parameter passing table for strings

The formal parameter and return types for IDL string are shown in Table 4.5. Note that CORBA::String_var is not used by the IDL compiler; it is for application use only.

Table 4.5 *Parameter passing modes for string.*

IDL type	in	out	inout	return
string	const char*	char*&	char*&	char*

For in parameters, the target object is given a pointer that it cannot change. For out parameters, the target object is given a pointer that it can change to point to a new string (that the caller assumes ownership of). The same applies to inout parameters. A return value is passed as a pointer to a string (that the caller assumes ownership of).

All strings passed as out or inout parameters or return values to IDL operations, or returned as attribute values, must be allocated using CORBA::string_dup() or CORBA::string_alloc() (and freed using CORBA::string_free()). This does not apply to in parameters: because the client retains ownership of the strings passed, it can decide how to allocate and de-allocate strings (in parameters are discussed in more detail in Section 4.3.2).

Be careful not to pass or return a zero pointer – instead, pass an empty string. The C++ notion of a zero pointer has no correspondence in other languages, so such values cannot be safely passed across an IDL interface.

4.3.2 Memory management for strings

Since IDL string maps to a pointer type (char*), memory management rules must be defined to prevent memory being leaked in the client or server. The need for memory management rules is not particular to CORBA, of course. Consider a C++ function that returns a char* value: there is a clear need to define whether or not the caller of this function must de-allocate the space pointed to by the char* after it is finished with it. It is a serious error if the caller de-allocates the storage in cases where the function's code does not expect the caller to do this, or for the caller to fail to de-allocate the storage in cases where the function's code expects it to.

The difference in CORBA is that the memory management rules for each data type are defined by the standard, rather than being left to the implementer of an interface. The latter would mean that the client would have to depend on documentation to know how to act.

Memory management rules are a contract between the caller of a function and the actions of the function itself. In CORBA there may be a number of contracts: between the client code and the ORB on the client side; and between the ORB on the server side and the target object. In cases where the client and target object are in the same address space, the contract is directly between the client and the target object. When the client and target object are in different address spaces, the ORB on the client and server cooperate to ensure that the rules are the same as in the local case. This is an important aim of CORBA, and one that has had a significant effect on the memory management rules.

In fact, this aim also explains why the memory management rules must be defined by the standard rather than being ad hoc. The rules between the client and the client-side ORB must be determined by the IDL definitions, and certainly not by ad hoc documentation (which cannot be understood by the ORB). Similarly for the rules between the server-side ORB and the target object. And, of course, these ORB-enforced rules must then be the same for clients and target objects in the same address space.

The rules form a consistent pattern for each data type, and the rules for strings (and object references; see Section 4.4.2) will be explained in detail so that the rules for the other data types need not be presented in such detail. The memory management rules for strings are straightforward, and they can be summarized as follows:

(1) `in` parameters: the caller *retains* ownership of the string passed in. The target object is given *temporary* access to the string, but not ownership of it. The string can be allocated and de-allocated in any way that the client wishes (on the stack, using `new` and `delete`, or using the CORBA functions `string_dup()`, `string_alloc()`, and `string_free()`. The top half of Figure 4.1 shows a local call, and the bottom half shows a remote call. The rules are the same for both caller and target object in both cases. Of course the target object is not allowed to change the string (actually, this applies to all non-object parameter types).

(2) `out` parameters; return values; attribute values: the target object *gives up* ownership of the returned string, and the caller is *given* ownership of it (and hence it should de-allocate it). Because the string returned by the target object will be de-allocated, typically it will copy a string (using `string_dup()`, or `string_alloc()`

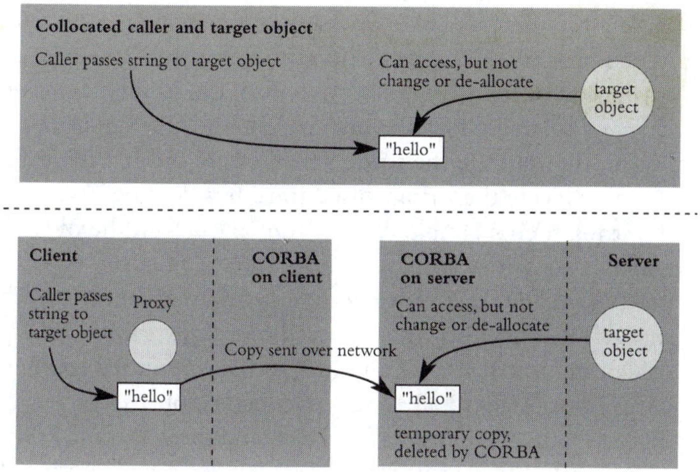

Figure 4.1 `in` *string.*

and `strcpy()`) and return this copy to the caller, or it will construct a string specifically to return to the caller. It should never return the only copy of a string that it wishes to keep. The caller must assume that the string has been allocated in *read-only* memory, and cannot change it in place. (Actually, this rule applies to all `out` parameters of any non-object type.) The top half of Figure 4.2 shows a local call, and the bottom half shows a remote call. The rules are the same for both caller and target object in both cases.

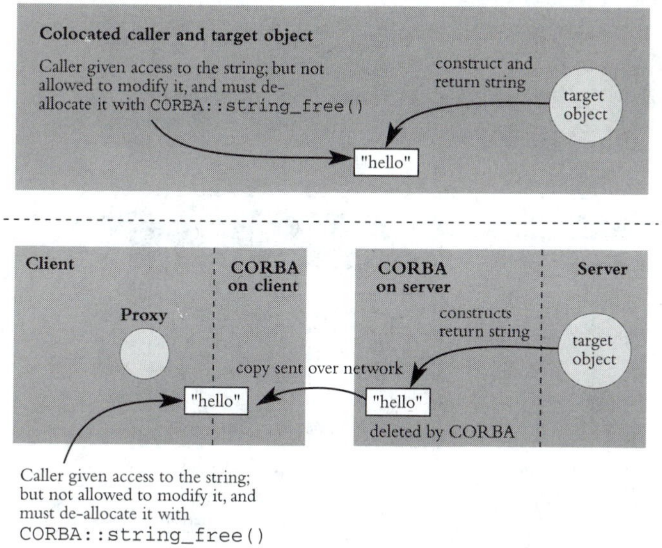

Figure 4.2 `out` *and return string.*

(3) `inout` parameters: The ownership of the string is *temporarily* passed to the target object. After the call, the caller *retains* ownership of the string (but, of course, the string may have changed to a new location and/or value). If the target object does not need to change the string's memory location, then it should not de-allocate the string passed to it. If it does need to change the string then it should call `string_free()` on the old string, and allocate a new string using `string_dup()` or `string_alloc()`. After the call, it gives up ownership of the new string. The target object is allowed to modify the `inout` string or deallocate it and allocate a new one that is returned to the caller. (This rule applies to all `inout` parameters, of any type). The top half of Figure 4.3 shows a local call, and the bottom half shows a remote call. Once again, the rules are the same for both caller and target object in both cases.

The client-side rules can be summarized by the simple statement that *if a client receives a pointer from a call, then it must de-allocate the space.* Most of the server-side rules can be summarized by the statement that *it loses ownership of strings it passes to the caller.*

✚ Further details

The remainder of this subsection restates these memory management rules for strings in more detail and gives examples to show their implications.

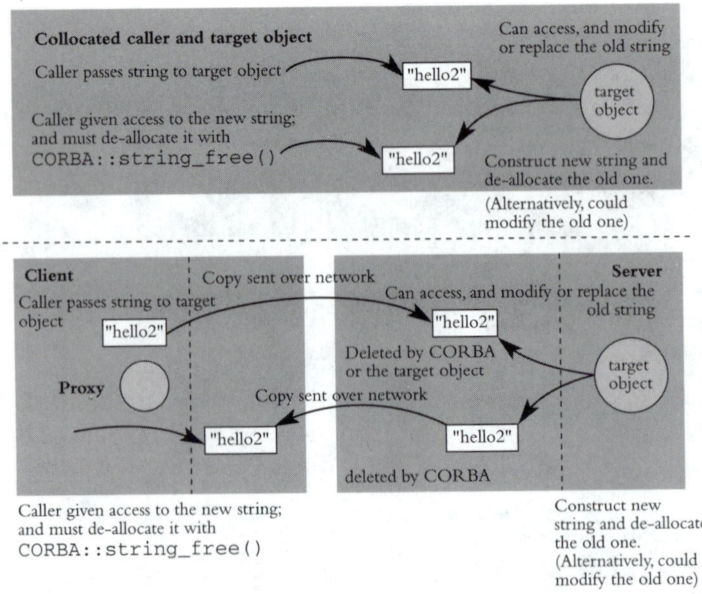

Figure 4.3 `inout` *string.*

`in` *parameters*

If a target object receives a string as an `in` parameter, then it must not de-allocate it, and it must assume that it is in read-only memory. The caller retains ownership of the parameter; the target object is given temporary access to it for the duration of the call. If the client and target object are in the same address space, then the client will pass a string that it retains ownership of, and it will de-allocate the string sometime after the call. If the client and target object are in different address spaces, then the ORB on the client side will pass a copy of the string to the ORB on the server side. This copy on the server side will be made available to the target object for the duration of the call, but it is the responsibility of the ORB on the server side to de-allocate the string, not that of the target object.

Consider the interface:

```
interface T {
      void op1 (in string s);
};
```

A C++ client can use this interface as follows:

```
T_var p = . . . . ;
p->op1("hello");
```

Alternatively, the string that is passed can be allocated using `new` (and then de-allocated using `delete`); or the string can be allocated using the `CORBA::string_dup()` or `CORBA::string_alloc()` functions. For example:

```
T_var p = . . . . ;
char *s1 = CORBA::string_dup("hello");
p->op1(s1);
//Sometime later, de-allocate the string: CORBA::string_free(s1).
```

If `s1` were defined to be of type `CORBA::String_var` then the allocated string would be automatically de-allocated when `s1` goes out of scope, and the risk of a memory leak due to programmer error would be reduced:

```
T_var p = . . . . ;
CORBA::Sting_var s1 = CORBA::string_dup("hello");
p->op1(s1);
// The string will be de-allocated automatically
// when s1 goes out of scope.
```

The implementation of operation `T::op1()` may be coded as follows:

```
void T_i::op1(const char* s)
          throw (CORBA::SystemException) {
      cout << s;
}
```

Note that the function must not de-allocate the string, because the caller retains ownership. This is a natural rule if the client and target object are in the same address space and the same rule has been adopted if the target object is remote (the server-side ORB will allocate and then de-allocate the string's storage).

There would be an error if the implementation of `op1()` assigned the parameter, `s`, to a `CORBA::String_var` variable (without copying the string). Because `s` is of type `const char*`, the string it points to would be copied if it were assigned to a `CORBA::String_var` variable. The `CORBA::String_var` variable would then own the copy; and the caller of `op1()` would own the original string.

`out` *parameters; return values; attribute values*

If a client receives a string as an `out` parameter, return value, or attribute value, then it is the client's responsibility to de-allocate that storage when it no longer needs it (the client 'owns' the storage for `out` parameters and return values). The client must assume that the string is in read-only memory. If the client and target object are in the same address space, then clearly the target object must return a string that it expects the client to de-allocate (the target object gives up ownership of the returned string), and the same rules must hold if the client and target object are in different address spaces.

Consider the interface:

```
interface T {
      string op1 (out string s);
};
```

A C++ client of this interface can use it as follows:

```
T_var p = . . . . .;
char *s1, *s2;
s2 = p->op1(s1);
// De-allocate s1 and s2 when finished with them,
// using CORBA::string_free().
```

If the variables `s1` or `s2` pointed to storage before the call to `op1()`, then this storage would be leaked at the time of the call to the operation.

If `s1` and `s2` were defined to be of type `CORBA::String_var` then the returned strings would be de-allocated automatically when `s1` and `s2` are deleted. Further, if `s1` or `s2` previously pointed to a string, then `CORBA::string_free()` would be called automatically when that variable is changed because of the call to `op1()`.

The implementation of operation `T::op1()` may be coded as follows:

```
char* T_i::op1(char*& s)
          throw (CORBA::SystemException) {
      s = CORBA::string_dup("hello");
      // Now construct the return value:
      return CORBA::string_dup("hello2");
      // or
      // char* tmp = CORBA::string_dup("hello2");
```

```
        // return tmp;
}
// The two strings will be de-allocated by the caller.
```

Note that `CORBA::string_alloc()` could be used as follows:

```
        s = CORBA::string_alloc(5);
        strcpy(s,"hello");
```

Since the two strings are de-allocated by the caller, the implementer of the function needs to be careful not to return (as an `out` parameter or a return value) a string that it wishes to keep; it should make a copy and return the copy. Note that neither the `out` parameter nor the return value can legally be allocated using the C++ `new` operator.

While it is true to say that the two strings will be de-allocated by the caller, more detail can be added to this statement. If the client and target object are separated, the ORB on the server side will send the two strings to the client side, and then de-allocate the two strings created by the `op1()` function. The client will be given pointers to two strings allocated by the client-side ORB, and the client can de-allocate these when it wishes to. If the client and target object are in the same address space, pointers to the two strings allocated by `op1()` will be passed directly to the client, and it can de-allocate these when it wishes, as before.

There would be an error if `tmp` were defined to be of type `CORBA::String_var`: the string it referenced would be deleted by the destructor of `tmp` at the end of the call, and would not be available to return to the client. `tmp` cannot own the string because ownership must be given to the caller of the `op1()` function. This and similar breakage of the ownership rules show that programmers must be careful how they use type `CORBA::String_var`.

inout *parameters*

If a target object receives an `inout` parameter, then it can read it, and/or modify it. If it wishes to change the string then it can either change it in-place, or it can de-allocate the incoming string and allocate space for another string that is passed back to the caller. If the target object returns a different string, it must claim ownership of the old string (that is, it must de-allocate its storage) and give the caller ownership of the new string.

On the client side, if the string pointer is unchanged then the client retains ownership of the string; if it is changed then the old string will have been de-allocated and the client will assume ownership of the new string.

Consider the interface:

```
interface T {
        void op1 (inout string s);
};
```

A C++ client of this interface passes a value that may be updated by the target object:

```
T_var p = . . . . ;
char* s1 = CORBA::string_dup("hello");
```

```
p->op1(s1);
// the string or s1 itself may have changed
// use CORBA::string_free(s1) later to de-allocate the string.
```

There are no difficulties if the variable `s1` is defined as a `CORBA::String_var` variable (rather than `char*`); it too can be updated by the call:

```
T_var p = . . . . ;
CORBA::String_var s1 = CORBA::string_dup("hello");
p->op1(s1);
```

Finally, on the client side, another example of violating the rules for string ownership can be seen from the following:

```
T_var p = . . . . ;
char* s1 = CORBA::string_dup("hello");
CORBA::String_var s2 = s1;
p->op1(s1);
```

`s2` cannot be given ownership of the string pointed to by `s1` because ownership is also temporarily given to (the `inout` parameter of) `op1()`. There would be difficulties when `s2` goes out of scope: it would attempt to de-allocate the storage that `s1` referred to before the call, and this storage may not exist at that time (because it may be deallocated by `op1()`).

The implementation of operation `T::op1()` may be coded as follows:

```
void T_i::op1(char*& s)
        throw (CORBA::SystemException) {
    cout << s;
    // Now change s. First de-allocate the old string:
    CORBA::string_free(s);
    // then create the new value:
    s = CORBA::string_dup("hello2");
}
```

Instead of explicitly de-allocating the old storage, the implementation of `op1()` can assign it to a `CORBA::String_var` variable. For example:

```
void T_i::op1(char*& s)
        throw (CORBA::SystemException) {
    cout << s;
    CORBA::String_var killer = s;
    // then create the new value:
    s = CORBA::string_dup("hello2");
};
```

However, it is not safe to make this assignment to `killer` if the `inout` parameter is not changed by a particular call to `op1()`. Note also that `op1()` could instead change the string value in-place.

4.4 Object references

Each IDL interface maps to a C++ class with the same name; for example, interface `FrontOffice` maps to class `FrontOffice`. Since CORBA can pass references to objects as parameters and return values of operations, it is important to understand the mapping of object references. In C++, object references of type `FrontOffice` are mapped to variables of type `FrontOffice_ptr` and `FrontOffice_var`.

`FrontOffice_ptr` is the fundamental object reference type. (For backward compatibility, type `FrontOfficeRef` is also defined, as a typedef for `FrontOffice_ptr`.) A variable of this type must behave like a pointer, and in particular, the object it references can be invoked using the -> operator. In fact, `FrontOffice_ptr` is a normal C++ pointer type in Orbix:

```
typedef FrontOffice* FrontOffice_ptr; // Orbix-specific.
```

However, programs that may run on other implementations of CORBA must not assume this typedef, and should perform only assignments and function invocations using object references.

✚ They should not, for example, perform pointer arithmetic because `FrontOffice_ptr` may map to some more complex type in another CORBA implementation. Nor should a program convert `FrontOffice_ptr` to `void*` or invoke any relational operators (for example, `operator==()`) on this type. ✚

The use of the helper class `FrontOffice_var` will be explained while object reference counts are being introduced.

A variable of type `CORBA::Object_ptr` or `CORBA::Object_var` can reference any CORBA object (recall from Section 4.2 that the C++ classes that are generated from IDL interfaces inherit from class `CORBA::Object`).

Object reference counts

Each CORBA object has a reference count that indicates the number of local references that refer to it. This reference count should be incremented when a new local reference to the object is created, and decremented when a local reference to the object is deleted. Once an object's reference count falls to zero, it will be de-allocated automatically.

When assigning between two object references of type `FrontOffice_ptr`, the programmer must explicitly increment the reference count:

```
FrontOffice_ptr p1 = . . . .;
FrontOffice_ptr p2;
p2 = FrontOffice::_duplicate(p1);
```

The IDL compiler automatically adds the function `FrontOffice::_duplicate()`.

✚ Because IDL identifiers cannot begin with character '_', there cannot be a name clash between `_duplicate()` and an IDL operation, attribute, constant, or type name. ✚

If the programmer simply makes the assignment:

```
p2 = p1;
```

then the two object references will refer to the same object, but the object's reference count will not be incremented. The number of pointers to the object will then not be reflected in its reference count. Such assignments can be made and their lightweight nature is sometimes useful, but programmers must be careful, for example, not to decrement the reference count using one pointer and then access the target object using the other.

Reference counts are decremented through calls to `CORBA::release()`. For example:

```
FrontOffice_ptr p1 = . . . .;
{
        FrontOffice_ptr p2;
        p2 = FrontOffice::_duplicate(p1);
        // Use p2, then sometime later:
        CORBA::release(p2);
}
// Continue to use p1, then:
CORBA::release(p1);
```

If the initialization of `p1` created the target object, then that object will be released in this case when `CORBA::release(p1)` is called (provided the reference count did not become corrupted by unbalanced increments and decrements).

If `CORBA::release(p2)` were not called, the reference count on the referenced object would be incorrect after the execution of the inner statement sequence. Similarly, `CORBA::release(p1)` must be called to return the object's reference count to its original value after the full code fragment has been executed.

Note that programmers are not allowed to delete an object by executing:

```
delete p1; // Error.
```

In Orbix, this will in fact be safe if the object that `p1` references has a reference count of 1; otherwise a global function is called, whose *default action* is to halt the program.

✚ The reference count of an object can be determined as follows (this function is Orbix specific):

```
p1->_refCount();
```

✚

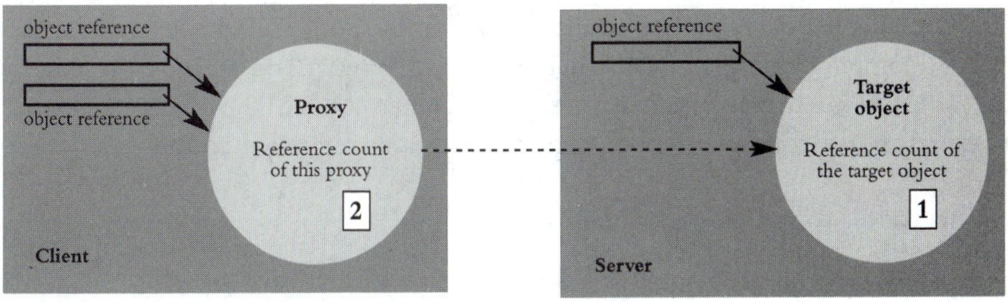

Figure 4.4 *Separate reference counts on objects and proxies.*

Local, not distributed, memory management

It is important to note that reference counts on CORBA objects support local memory management: management of space for objects in servers, and management of space for proxies in clients. For example, if a client receives two separate references to the same object, then Orbix will ensure that there is only one proxy (with a reference count of 2) in its address space. Provided that the memory management rules are obeyed, the reference count management will ensure that the proxy will exist as long as the client retains any reference to it.

Because the aim is to support local memory management, reference counts are maintained separately on a real object and on the (possibly many) proxies for it in different client address spaces. A call to `_duplicate()` in a server (more accurately, in the *holder* of the object, because clients also can hold objects) will only affect the real object's reference count. Similarly, if a client calls `_duplicate()` then the only change will be to the reference count of the proxy in its address space. Figure 4.4 shows how the reference counts on objects and their proxies are separate.

There are two reasons why reference counts are maintained locally in this way, rather than having a global reference count on a real object that counts the number of references to it in the local address space and in all clients. Firstly, a server does not wish to have a rogue client affect the reference counts of its objects, setting them to artificially high values that would prevent or delay subsequent deletion of these objects. A variation on this is that a server would not wish a rogue client to call `CORBA::release()` often enough to cause the deletion of some of the server's objects; servers typically wish to retain full control of when an object is deleted. Secondly, maintaining global reference counts is expensive, typically requiring a remote call for each duplication and release in any client.

✚ In Orbix, global reference counts can be implemented where required using smart proxies. Smart proxies are discussed in Chapter 19. ✚

Reference counts and `_var` variables

Maintenance of reference counts using `_duplicate()` and `CORBA::release()` is, of course, an extra burden on programmers. Therefore, the IDL compiler generates _var types that handle reference counts automatically. So, for interface FrontOffice, the IDL compiler also produces a helper class, FrontOffice_var. An instance of FrontOffice_var automatically handles the reference count of the object it references, and therefore the following code correctly maintains reference counts:

```
FrontOffice_var p1 = . . . .;
{
      FrontOffice_var p2;
      p2 = p1; // Automatic reference count increment.
      // Now use p2.
      . . . . .
} // Automatic decrement of reference count.
// Continue to use p1. For example,
p1->name();
// The reference count of the target object will be
// decremented automatically when p1 goes out of scope.
```

We say that each _var variable *owns* the object that it points to (to be more exact, it shares ownership with the other local references to the same object). This means that the destructor of an _var variable decrements the reference count of the object it points to.

Note that FrontOffice_var defines operator->() to allow the operations and attributes of the target object to be used. Therefore, instances of FrontOffice_var are **smart pointers**. Naturally, programmers should not treat these as real pointers (and perform address arithmetic and other low level functions using them). Use of _var types is optional for programmers, as is the case for CORBA::String_var.

FrontOffice_var has a conversion to and from FrontOffice_ptr, as shown in the following code:

```
FrontOffice_ptr p1 = . . . .;
FrontOffice_ptr p2 = . . . .;
FrontOffice_var v1 = . . . .;
FrontOffice_var v2 = . . . .;

// The following statements should be read
// separately, and not as a statement sequence:
p1 = p2;    // No duplication;† no releasing.     Note 1
p1 = v1;    // No duplication;‡ no releasing.     Note 2
v1 = p1;    // No duplication; releasing.         Note 3
v1 = v2;    // Duplication; releasing.            Note 4
```

An object's reference count is incremented when one _var variable is assigned to another, but not in other cases. The reference count must be incremented because each _var variable expects to own (or, more accurately, to share ownership of) the

† Should normally write: p1 = FrontOffice::_duplicate(p2);

‡ Should normally write: p1 = FrontOffice::_duplicate(v1);

object it references. Also, an _var variable always calls CORBA::release() on the object or proxy it previously pointed to when it is assigned to point to another object or proxy (because it no longer owns the object it previously pointed to).

✚ The details are discussed in the following notes.

- *Note 1*: this may lead to reference count errors. After the call, p1 and p2 will point to the same object, but no reference count maintenance will be done. Also, there will be a memory leak if p1 is the only pointer to the object or proxy it previously pointed to.
- *Note 2*: this may lead to reference count errors. After the call, p1 and v1 will point to the same object, but no reference count maintenance will be carried out. v1 retains ownership of the target object. Also, there will be a memory leak if p1 is the only pointer to the object or proxy it previously pointed to.
- *Note 3*: after the call, v1 and p1 will point to the same object; no reference count maintenance will be carried out for the object pointed to by p1. v1 assumes ownership of the target object. If v1 previously referenced an object or proxy, its reference count will be decremented automatically before the assignment is made.
- *Note 4*: after the call, v1 and v2 will point to the same object, and that object's reference count will be incremented automatically. v1 and v2 will both own the target object (or, if you prefer, they share this ownership). If v1 previously referenced an object or proxy, its reference count will be decremented automatically before the assignment is made. ✚

Ensuring ownership

Always remember that an _var variable expects to own its target object: its destructor expects to decrement the reference count of the object. Be careful, therefore, not to assign a pointer to an _var variable if it is not safe for that variable to own that target object. As well as showing typical uses of _var variables, the following subsections, which describe the general memory management rules, show some inappropriate uses where this ownership rule is broken.

4.4.1 Parameter passing table for object references

When an object reference is passed as a parameter to an operation or appears as the return type, the corresponding C++ formal parameter types are as shown in Table 4.6.

Table 4.6 *Parameter passing modes for object references.*

IDL type	in	out	inout	return
interface T	T_ptr	T_Ptr&	T_Ptr&	T_Ptr

Programmers must also be careful when passing or returning a null object reference. For example, if operation `FrontOffice::makeBooking()` wishes to return a null object reference then it should execute the following code:

```
return Booking::_nil();
```

It is not compliant to pass or return a zero value. Remember that equating of a zero pointer with a null reference is too specific to C++ to be accepted generally in CORBA (which does not even have a notion of pointer).

✚ Use of `_ptr` rather than `_var` for parameters

Since `_var` variables are often easier to use than `_ptr` variables, it may be a surprise that the IDL compiler uses `_ptr` parameters and not `_var` parameters. For example, the IDL definition:

```
interface T {
      void op1 (in FrontOffice f);
};
```

translates to the following C++:

```
class T : public virtual CORBA::Object {
      void op1 (FrontOffice_ptr a);
};
```

In fact, a parameter of type `FrontOffice_var` instead of `FrontOffice_ptr` would not be any more useful. If an `_var` formal parameter type was used *and if an `_var` variable was passed to it*, then the reference count of the object pointed to by the actual parameter might be incremented (depending on the implementation details of the C++ compiler) as the function is called, and then decremented at the end of the call (by the parameter's destructor). This does not cause any particular difficulty, but it shows that `_var` parameter types have little to recommend them. Moreover, it is likely to be an error to pass an `_ptr` variable to such a function: the reference count of the target object would not be incremented at the start of the call, and yet it would be decremented at the end when the `_var` parameter is destroyed.

In addition, many applications must use other libraries in addition to CORBA. Since parameters are `_ptr` types, and a CORBA implementation may map `FrontOffice_ptr` to `FrontOffice*`, there is no difficulty ensuring compatibility between pointer types in CORBA and other libraries. For example, the Orbix and ObjectStore integration benefits from the fact that both systems treat object references as pointers. The Orbix and Versant integration benefits from the fact that Orbix treats object references as pointers, and whereas Versant has a special type for references, it allows simple interworking with pointers. This simple interworking may not have held if CORBA had used `_var` types for parameters. ✚

4.4.2 Memory management for object references

Since an object reference maps to a pointer type (either to an `_ptr` or an `_var` type, both of which behave like pointers), memory management rules must be defined to prevent memory being corrupted on the client or server side. By memory corruption, in this case, we mean that an object or proxy has the wrong reference count, which will cause it to stay in existence when there are no references for it; or it will be deleted prematurely and a subsequent use of an object reference will fail. As is the case for strings (Section 4.3), CORBA defines the memory management rules for object references, rather than leaving these to the implementer of an interface.

When discussing the memory management rules for strings, it was pointed out that there are two ways in which a C++ function that implements an IDL operation can be called: either directly if the client and target object are in the same address space, or via the ORB on the client side sending the request to the server-side ORB, which actually calls the function. As for strings, the object reference memory management rules for the client and target object must be the same in both cases. In the case of object references, the aim is to keep the reference count of each object consistent at all times.

The following brief statements summarize the memory management rules for object references, and the full rules and examples are given in the rest of this section:

(1) `in` parameters: the caller *retains* ownership of the object reference passed in. The target object is given *temporary* access to the object pointed to by the object reference, but it is not given ownership.

(2) `out` parameters; return values; attribute values: the target object *gives up* ownership of the returned object reference; and the caller is *given* ownership (hence it should call `CORBA::release()` on that object reference). Because the target object gives up ownership, typically it will call the relevant `_duplicate()` static function on the object reference that it returns. That is, it makes a 'copy' of the object references and passes back the copy. (Less frequently, the target object will wish that one of the results of the call is that the reference count of the returned object is decremented by one, even if this means that the object will be de-allocated. The most common example of this is where the target object locates an object remote to it, and returns a reference to this object to the caller. If the target object does not wish to retain the proxy for the remote object, then it will return the object reference without calling the relevant `_duplicate()` static function on it.)

(3) `inout` parameters: the ownership of the object reference is temporarily passed to the target object. After the call, the caller retains ownership of the object reference (but, of course, it could point to a different object or proxy). If the target object does not need to change the object reference, then it should not call `CORBA::release()` on it. If it does need to change the object reference, then it should call `CORBA::release()` on the old value, and normally it should call the relevant `_duplicate()` static function on the new value.

The client-side rules can be summarized by the simple statement that if a client receives an object reference from a call, then it must release that object reference when it no longer needs it. Most of the server-side rules can be summarized by the simple statement that it gives up ownership of a reference it passes to a client (that is, the reference count is decremented by 1; and hence it normally calls the relevant `_duplicate()` function before returning the reference).

✚ Further details

The remainder of this subsection restates these memory management rules for object references in more detail and gives examples to show their implications.

`in` *parameters*

If a target object receives an object reference as an `in` parameter, then it must not call `CORBA::release()` on it. Instead, the caller retains ownership, and will release the object reference when it wishes. If the client and target object are in the same address space, then the client will pass an object reference that it retains ownership of, and it will call `CORBA::release()` on it when it wishes. If the client and target object are in different address spaces, then the ORB on the client side will pass a copy of the object reference to the ORB on the server side. The object's reference count will be incremented automatically when the object reference reaches the server (if the object was not previously known to the server then a proxy for the object will be created, and its reference count will be set to 1), and the copy of the object reference will be made available to the target object for the duration of the call. At the end of the call, it is the responsibility of the ORB on the server side to call `CORBA::release()` on this reference, not that of the target object.

Consider the interface:

```
interface T {
      void op1 (in FrontOffice a);
};
```

A C++ client can use this interface as follows:

```
T_var p = . . . . . .;
FrontOffice_ptr a1 = . . . . . .;
p->op1(a1);
// Call CORBA::release(a1) now or later.
```

If `a1` were defined to be of type `FrontOffice_var` then `CORBA::release()` would be called automatically when `a1` goes out of scope, and the risk of a memory leak due to programmer error would be reduced.

The implementation of operation `T::op1()` may be coded as follows:

```
void T_i::op1(FrontOffice_ptr a)
          throw (CORBA::SystemException) {
      // Can use reference a:
      cout <<  a->name();
      // Do not call CORBA::release(); this is
      // done by the caller.
}
```

Note that the function does not call `CORBA::release()` on the parameter; this will be done by the caller. This is a natural rule if the client and target object are in the same address space, and the same rule has been adopted if the target object is remote (the server-side ORB will increment the reference count at the start of the call and then decrement it at the end).

If the implementation of the function wishes to retain the object reference passed to it, then it must duplicate it (by using `_duplicate()` and retaining the returned pointer).

Because the called function is not given ownership of the object reference passed as an `in` parameter, there would be an error if the implementation of `op1()` assigned the parameter, `a`, to a `FrontOffice_var` automatic variable (without calling `_duplicate()` on it). At the end of the call, the automatic variable would be deleted, thereby calling `CORBA::release()` on the object or on the proxy it references. However, there would be a second attempt to call `CORBA::release()` after the call completes (either in the server-side ORB if the client and target object are separated, or in the client if it is in the same address space as the target object). Of course, there is no error if the assignment to the `FrontOffice_var` automatic variable is done using `_duplicate()`.

`out` *parameters; return values; attribute values*

If a client receives an object reference as an `out` parameter or return value, then it is the client's responsibility to call `CORBA::release()` when it no longer needs that object reference. The client is given ownership of the object reference. If the client and target object are in the same address space, then clearly the target object must return an object reference that it expects the client to call `CORBA::release()` on; this normally means that the target object should call `_duplicate()` on the object reference before returning it to the caller. The same rule holds if the client and target object are in different address spaces.

Consider the interface:

```
interface T {
      FrontOffice op1 (out FrontOffice a);
};
```

A C++ client of this interface can use it as follows:

```
T_var p = . . . . ;
FrontOffice_ptr a1, a2;
a2 = p->op1(a1);
// Call CORBA::release() when finished with each
// of the object references.
```

If the variables a1 or a2 pointed to an object, then memory would be leaked at the time of the call to operation op1().

If a1 and a2 were defined to be of type FrontOffice_var then CORBA::release() would be called automatically on the returned object references when a1 and a2 are destroyed, and this would reduce the risk of memory leaks due to programmer error. Further, if a1 or a2 previously referenced an object or proxy, then CORBA::release() would be called automatically when these variables are changed because of the call to op1() (shared ownership of the previous target objects or proxies would be given up).

The implementation of operation T::op1() may be coded as follows:

```
FrontOffice_ptr T_i::op1(FrontOffice_ptr& a)
            throw (CORBA::SystemException) {
      // Assuming that m_someFrontOffice1 and
      // m_someFrontOffice2 are members or
      // global variables of type FrontOffice_ptr
      // or FrontOffice_var.
      a = FrontOffice_ptr::_duplicate(m_someFrontOffice1);
      return FrontOffice_ptr::_duplicate(m_someFrontOffice2);
}
// The caller will call CORBA::release() on the
// out and return references.
```

Since CORBA::release() will be called on the two object references by the caller of the function, the implementer of the function needs to be careful not to return (as an out parameter or a return value) an object reference that it wishes to keep without calling _duplicate() as shown above. It is very important to note the need for these calls to _duplicate().

While it is true to say that CORBA::release() will be called on the two object references, more detail can be added to this statement. If the client and target object are in different address spaces, the ORB on the server side will send the two object references to the client side, and then call CORBA::release() on the two object references returned by the op1() function. The calling code on the client will be given references to local objects or proxies, and it can call CORBA::release() on the two object references when it wishes to. (If a returned reference is to an object or existing proxy in the client, its reference count will be incremented automatically by the client-side ORB. If a returned reference is to an object previously unknown to the client, a proxy will be created with a reference count of 1.) If the client and target object are in the same address space, object references will be passed directly to the client, and it can call CORBA::release() on these when it wishes, as before.

`inout` *parameters*

If a target object receives an `inout` object reference parameter, then it can change that parameter to refer to another object. If it makes such a change, it claims (shared) ownership of the object or proxy that the parameter previously pointed to, and the caller is given (shared) ownership of the object or proxy that the parameter is changed to point to. In other words, the target object is responsible for calling `CORBA::release()` on the object that was previously pointed to; and the target object must ensure that it is safe for the caller to call `CORBA::release()` on the object that the `inout` parameter is changed to point to. As explained before, this normally means that the target object will call `_duplicate()` on the object reference before returning it. On the client side, if the object reference is unchanged then the client retains ownership without any change in reference count of the object or proxy pointed to; if the object reference is changed then the reference count of the object or proxy previously pointed to will be decremented, and that of the object newly pointed to will be incremented.

Consider the interface:

```
interface T {
      void op1 (inout FrontOffice a);
};
```

A C++ client of this interface passes an object reference that may be updated by the target object:

```
T_var p = . . . . ;
FrontOffice_ptr a1 = . . . .;
p->op1(a1);
// a1 may be different now.
// Call CORBA::release(a1) later.
```

If the object reference is changed, then the reference count of the previously referenced object or proxy will be decremented as the object reference is changed. The reference count of the new object pointed to will be incremented. If the value of the actual parameter, `a1`, is unchanged by the call to `op1()` then the value of the reference count of the object it points to will also be unchanged.

If the variable `a1` were defined as a `FrontOffice_var` variable (rather than `FrontOffice_ptr`) then it can be updated by the call, in the same way as shown in the above code fragment. If it is updated, the reference count of the object previously pointed to will be decremented, and that of the new object pointed to will be incremented.

The implementation of operation `T::op1()` may be coded as follows:

```
void T_i::op1(FrontOffice_ptr& a)
          throw (CORBA::SystemException) {
      // Can use parameter a:
      cout << a->name();
      // Now change a. First decrement the reference
      // count of the current object:
      CORBA::release(a);
```

```
        // then assign a new object reference:
        a = FrontOffice_ptr::_duplicate(m_someFrontOffice1);
}
```

Instead of explicitly calling `CORBA::release()` on the parameter, the implementation of `op1()` can assign it to a `FrontOffice_var` variable. For example:

```
void T_i::op1(FrontOffice_ptr& a)
             throw (CORBA::SystemException) {
        // Can use a:
        cout << a->name;
        FrontOffice_var killer = a;
        // then assign it to reference a new object:
        a = FrontOffice_ptr::_duplicate(m_someFrontOffice1);
}
```

However, it is not correct to make this assignment to the automatic variable, `killer`, if the `inout` parameter is not changed by a particular call to `op1()`. ✚

4.4.3 Widening and narrowing object references

Consider the following outline of IDL interface definitions:

```
interface Booking {
        /* . . . . */
};
interface GroupBooking: Booking
{
        /* . . . . */
};
```

These result in the definition of C++ data types `Booking`, `GroupBooking`, `Booking_ptr`, `Booking_var`, `GroupBooking_ptr`, and `GroupBooking_var`. This section discusses the assignment compatibility between the last four of these types.

We will assume the following four definitions:

```
Booking_ptr pb = . . . .;
Booking_var vb = . . . .;
GroupBooking_ptr pgb = . . . .;
GroupBooking_var vgb = . . . .;
```

Widening

As is normal in object-oriented systems, if you have a reference to a `GroupBooking` object, you can assign it to a reference of type `Booking`. Moving from a derived interface to a base interface is termed **widening** in CORBA (C++ uses the term **`up-cast`**).

The following assignments automatically **widen** a reference from a `GroupBooking` reference to a `Booking` reference (these assignment statements should be read independently, not as a statement sequence):

```
pb = pgb;   // Allowed but no reference count increment.
pb = vgb;   // Allowed but no reference count increment.
vb = pgb;   // Allowed but no reference count increment.
            // The reference count of the object that vb
            // previously pointed to is decremented.
vb = Booking::_duplicate(vgb);
            // It is a (compile time) error to write
            //        vb = vgb;
            // such implicit widening between _var types is
            // illegal in the CORBA specification.
```

To increment the reference counts in the first three assignments, the `_duplicate()` function should be used:

```
pb = Booking::_duplicate(pgb); // Reference count incremented.
pb = Booking::_duplicate(vgb); // Reference count incremented.
vb = Booking::_duplicate(pgb); // Reference count incremented.
            // In the last case, the reference count of the object
            // that vb previously pointed to is decremented.
```

Narrowing

The term **narrowing** is used in CORBA when moving from a base interface to a derived interface (C++ uses the term **`down-cast`**). If you have a base interface reference then you can assign it to a reference to a derived interface, but only if the base reference actually references an instance of the derived interface. There is no way to statically determine whether this condition holds, so there must be a runtime test to determine the safety of the assignment. Non-ISO C++ compilers do not support dynamic casts with runtime type checking; also, down-casts are disallowed if `virtual` inheritance is used. The `_narrow()` function shown here overcomes these restrictions.

The following statements **narrow** a reference from a `Booking` reference to a `GroupBooking` reference (these `if` statements should be read independently, not as a statement sequence):

```
pgb = GroupBooking::_narrow(pb);
if (!CORBA::_is_nil(pgb))
     { /* all ok, pb did reference a GroupBooking */ }
else { */ the narrow failed */ }

pgb = GroupBooking::_narrow(vb);
if (!CORBA::_is_nil(pgb))
     { /* all ok, vb did reference a GroupBooking */ }
else { */ the narrow failed */ }
```

```
vgb = GroupBooking::_narrow(pb);
if (!CORBA::_is_nil(vgb))
      { /* all ok, vb did reference a GroupBooking */ }
else { */ the narrow failed */ }
```

Note that the static function `_narrow()` returns a nil object reference if the parameter passed to it is not a reference to an object of the correct interface, or a derived interface. A successful call to `_narrow()` increments the reference count of the target object; a failed call does not.

4.4.4 Extra member and static functions

In addition to the member functions that correspond to operations and attributes, each interface class has the member functions listed in Table 4.7.

Table 4.7 *Extra member functions.*

Function name	Description
`_deref()`	When invoked on a TIE object, this returns a pointer to the real object. When invoked on a BOAImpl object, this returns a pointer to the BOAImpl aspect of the object. This function is Orbix specific
`_marker()`	Returns a pointer to the object's marker. This function is Orbix specific
`_refCount()`	Returns the reference count of the object or proxy. This function is Orbix specific
`_get_interface()`	Returns a pointer to the `CORBA::InterfaceDef` object in the IFR that describes the target object's interface (see Chapter 16)
`_loader()`	Returns a pointer to the target object's loader (see Chapter 20). This function is Orbix specific
`_create_request()`	Creates a `CORBA::Request` object for use with the DII (see Chapter 15)
`_request()`	Similar to `_create_request()`
`_is_equivalent()`	Returns True if the parameter and the object invoked on are the same object; returns False otherwise
`_non_existent()`	Returns True if the target object does not exist; returns False otherwise. Normally this is invoked on a proxy, which will determine if the real object still exists

`_is_a()`	Takes a type and returns true if the target object is of that type or a derived type; returns false otherwise
`_hash()`	Returns a hash value of type `CORBA::ULong` for this object
`_save()`	Calls `save()` on the target object's loader (see Chapter 20). This function is Orbix specific

The static functions listed in Table 4.8 are also provided.

Table 4.8 *Static Functions.*

Function name	Description
`_bind()`	(This is redefined within each class in a class hierarchy so that the return type can be different.) Returns a reference to an object (see Chapter 7). `_bind()` is Orbix specific
`_duplicate()`	(This is redefined within each class in a class hierarchy) Increments the reference count of the parameter passed
`_release()`	`CORBA::_release()` decrements the reference count of the parameter passed
`_narrow()`	(This is redefined within each class in a class hierarchy.) Narrows an object reference to a derived interface (`A::_narrow(p)` narrows `p` to interface `A`.). Returns a valid object reference if the object reference does in fact reference an instance of the derived interface (or an interface derived from this in turn), returns a nil object reference otherwise
`_nil()`	(This is redefined within each class in a class hierarchy.) `_nil()` returns a nil object reference for the class. Simple zero values cannot be assumed to represent nil object references (because some ORBs might not map `_ptr` types to normal pointers)
`_is_nil()`	Returns true if the reference passed is a nil reference; returns false otherwise

4.5 Allocation and de-allocation of strings and object references

To dynamically allocate and de-allocate a string or object reference, the allocation and de-allocation functions shown in Table 4.9 should be used.

Table 4.9 *Allocation and de-allocation rules for strings and object references.*

	Allocation	De-allocation
`string`	`CORBA::string_dup()` or `CORBA::string_alloc()`. One extra byte is allocated (for the terminating '`\0`' character)	`CORBA::string_free()`
Object reference	Member function: `_duplicate()`. (Objects themselves can be created using `new`, or they can be automatic or static. `_duplicate()` increases the reference count of an existing object or proxy.)	`CORBA::release()`

5 IDL to C++ mapping of compound types

This chapter describes how IDL definitions for structs, sequences, arrays, and unions are translated into C++. Much of this material is for reference. Section 5.5 (p.122) gives a summary table for how these types can be allocated and de-allocated.

5.1 Structs

IDL struct data types are mapped to C++ structs, and each member of an IDL struct is mapped to a public member of the C++ struct. For example:

```
struct FixedSizedStruct {
      long i;
      char c;
      float f;
};
```

maps to the following C++:

```
struct FixedSizedStruct {
      CORBA::Long i;
      CORBA::Char c;
      CORBA::Float f;
};
```

(Some other member functions are also added by Orbix, but these need not concern us here.)

Because the C++ version of FixedSizedStruct does not contain any explicitly defined contructors or operator=(), it is therefore legal to initialize an instance of it as follows:

```
fixedSizedStruct s1 = {125466545,'x',3.14};
```

The IDL compiler also generates a C++ type called `FixedSizedStruct_var` that can be used to manage dynamically allocated structures. Therefore, structures can be dynamically allocated using either of the following two statements:

```
FixedSizedStruct* p1 = new FixedSizedStruct;
FixedSizedStruct_var p2 = new FixedSizedStruct;
```

The difference is that the structure pointed to by `p2` will be de-allocated automatically when `p2` goes out of scope, whereas the structure pointed to by `p1` must be de-allocated explicitly using `delete p1`.

Structs with string members

Structs with all fixed sized members are called fixed sized structs in CORBA, because their storage requirements can be determined at compile time. (Fixed sized data types are the basic types, and arrays/unions/structures of fixed sized elements/members. Variable sized data types are `string`, object references, sequences, `any`, and arrays/unions/structures that include any variable sized elements/members.) Other structs (for example, those with string or object reference members) are called variable sized, because they contain pointers that can reference varying sizes of storage.

If a struct contains a string member, such as:

```
struct VariableSizedStruct1 {
      string member1;
};
```

the string is de-allocated when the struct is deleted.

✚ This means that it is important that the string is copied if one `VariableSizedStruct1` variable is assigned to another. Rather than adding an `operator=()` and copy constructor to the struct itself, the IDL compiler uses a special type for the string member of the C++ struct:

```
struct VariableSizedStruct1 {
      CORBA::String_mgr member1;  // Type CORBA::String_mgr is an
                                  // implementation detail, and is
                                  // not for application-level use.
};
```

Type `CORBA::String_mgr` acts like `CORBA::String_var`, but it is reserved for use in structures (and some other complex data types). A minor complexity of the CORBA specification prevents `CORBA::String_mgr` being replaced with `CORBA::String_var`. Also note that CORBA specifies the behavior of the `CORBA::String_mgr` type but *not* its name. The string is copied if any of the following occur:

(1) one `CORBA::String_mgr` variable is assigned to another;
(2) a `CORBA::String_var` variable is assigned to `member1`;
(3) `member1` is assigned to a `CORBA::String_var` variable;
(4) a `const char*` value is assigned to a `CORBA::String_mgr` variable;

but not if the assignment is to or from a normal `char*`. The old string that a `CORBA::String_mgr` variable points to is de-allocated if a new string is assigned.

Therefore, if two `VariableSizedStruct1` variables are assigned to each other, the string will be copied. This copying and the other properties of `CORBA::String_mgr` are shown in the following code sequence:

```
char* s1 = CORBA::string_dup("first");
char* s2 = CORBA::string_dup("second");

VariableSizedStruct1 vs1, vs2;

vs1.member1 = s1; // Now vs1.member1 points to the
                  // same string as s1.

vs2 = vs1; // The string is copied. If vs2 previously
           // contained a string, this would be de-allocated.

vs1.member1 = s2;      // No memory leak: "first" is de-allocated.
                       // No string copy is made.
```

After this code sequence, it is not safe to use the memory pointed to by s1, and the lifetime of the string pointed to by s2 is determined by vs1. That is, the string is owned by the struct.

Use of the default constuctor for any struct initializes any string members to null. Assigning or copying any struct does deep copying (including copying any string members).

Structs with object reference members

An object reference member of an IDL struct is mapped to an _mgr type in the equivalent C++ struct. For example:

```
struct VariableSizedStruct2 {
     FrontOffice member2;
};
```

is mapped to the following C++:

```
struct VariableSizedStruct2 {
      FrontOffice_mgr member2;
                 // Type CORBA::FrontOffice_mgr is an
                 // implementation detail, and is
                 // not for application-level use.
};
```

✚ Type FrontOffice_mgr is generated by the IDL compiler. It acts the same as FrontOffice_var, but is reserved for use in structs (and some other complex data types). (A minor complexity of the CORBA specification prevents FrontOffice_mgr being replaced with FrontOffice_var. Also note that CORBA specifies the behavior of the FrontOffice_mgr type but *not* its name. The reference count is incremented if one FrontOffice_mgr variable is assigned to another, or if a FrontOffice_var variable is assigned to member2, or if member2 is assigned to a FrontOffice_var variable, but not if the assignment is to or from a normal FrontOffice_ptr. The reference count of the old object that a FrontOffice_mgr variable points to is decremented if a new value is assigned. Types such as FrontOffice_mgr should never be used in user code.) Therefore, if two VariableSizedStruct2 variables are assigned to each other, the reference count of the target object will be incremented. This and other properties of FrontOffice_mgr are shown in the following code sequence:

```
VariableSizedStruct2 vs1, vs2;
FrontOffice_ptr a1 = . . . .;
FrontOffice_ptr a2 = . . . .;

vs1.member2 = a1; // Now vs1.member2 points to the
                  // same object as a1 - no reference count
                  // increment occurs.

vs2 = vs1; // Reference count of target object is incremented.
           // If vs2 previously contained an object reference,
           // then the reference count of the object
           // pointed to would be decremented.

vs1.member2 = a2; // The reference count of the object or proxy
                  // pointed to by the old value of vs1.member2 is
                  // decremented; no change occurs to the reference
                  // count of the object or proxy pointed to by a2.
```

After this code sequence, it is not safe to use a1; and the lifetime of the object or proxy pointed to by a2 is determined (in part) by vs2, but not by a2 (since it is of type FrontOffice_ptr rather than FrontOffice_var). ✚

Use of the default constuctor for any struct initializes any object reference members to nil. Assigning or copying any struct does deep copying (including duplication of any object reference members).

5.1.1 Parameter passing table for structs

When a struct is passed as a parameter to an operation or appears as the return type, the corresponding C++ formal parameter types are as shown in Table 5.1.

Table 5.1 *Parameter passing modes for structs.*

IDL type	`in`	`out`	`inout`	`return`
`struct S` of only fixed sized members	`const S&`	`S&`	`S&`	`S`
`struct S` with one or more variable sized members	`const S&`	`S*&`	`S&`	`S*`

Remember that pointers are not a valid IDL type, so a zero pointer cannot be returned when a valid pointer to a struct is expected.

✚ Note the differences between fixed and variable sized structs for `out` parameters and return values. Before explaining this, we will first confirm that the parameter passing rules for `in` and `inout` parameters are reasonable. For an `in` parameter, the target object is given access to a struct that it cannot change; and it is passed by reference for efficiency. An `out` parameter is passed by reference so that the target object can change it. For an `inout` parameter, the natural choice is to pass a struct by reference: the target object is passed a struct that it can change.

Variable sized structs: `out` parameters and return values

A variable sized struct can be very large because it can contain strings and other large members, which must be copied when it is copied. Therefore, the standard must allow a target object to pass a variable sized struct to a client with the minimum of copying.

Consider a collocated client and target object. The target object may construct a struct to pass as an `out` parameter to the client, and the most efficient way to achieve this is to allow the target object to pass a pointer to the client. Hence the parameter type is a pointer reference: the client passes a pointer by reference, and the target object changes this to point to the struct it wishes to pass to the client. The client is responsible for de-allocating this struct.

If the client and target object are in different address spaces, the ORB on the client and server cooperate to enforce the same rules. The server-side ORB de-allocates the returned struct after it has copied it to the client-side ORB. Once the returned struct has been allocated by the client-side ORB, it passes a pointer to it to the caller. The caller must de-allocate this struct.

Similar reasons explain why a variable sized struct return value is passed to the caller as a pointer.

The same scheme could have been used for fixed sized structs, but these are normally much smaller and it was felt better to avoid requiring the client and target object to deal with dynamically allocated memory. Indeed, it is more efficient to copy a small struct than to dynamically allocate and free memory.

For a fixed sized struct, `out` parameters are therefore passed by reference so that they can be changed by the target object. The caller can allocate the space for the struct on the stack (or on the heap if it wishes), and avoid any memory management overheads.

Fixed sized return values are passed by value so that they can be assigned to a struct in the caller. For example: if `op1()` returns a `struct` of type `Struct1`, then a client can allocate the space for the returned struct on the stack:

```
{
        Struct1 s1;
        s1 = p->op1();
}
```

✚

Use of `_var` hides any complexity

The parameter passing rules are easy to remember once they are understood. In any case, they will be checked by any C++ compiler. In addition, an `_var` variable can be passed as an `out` parameter without concern for the different rules for fixed and variable sized structs: the `_var` variable need only be passed, and conversion operators will handle the differences.

5.2 Sequences

An IDL sequence type is mapped to a C++ class that behaves similarly to an array type, but with a current length and a maximum length. The maximum length is fixed for a bounded sequence, but it can be changed in the case of an unbounded sequence (the maximum is simply an initial value set in an unbounded sequence's constructor). The details of the generated C++ class differ slightly for bounded and unbounded sequences, and these will be discussed in turn in the following subsections.

An `_var` type is also produced for each IDL sequence type; this can optionally be used to manage the storage of dynamically allocated sequences.

5.2.1 Bounded sequences

Given the following IDL typedef:

```
typedef sequence<long,10> seq10;
```

an instance of this type can be defined as follows in C++:

```
seq10 x1;
```

Elements can be added using `operator[]`, for example:

```
CORBA::ULong i;
x1.length(5);
for (i=0; i < 5; i++) { // Enter five elements.
      x1[i] = i;
}
```

Note that the length must be set explicitly using the `length()` member function; `operator[]` does not change the length. Note that `operator[]` should not be used to access or change an element outside of the current length. The maximum number of elements in this sequence is fixed at 10, the bound of the sequence type. Setting the length to a value larger than the sequence's bound produces undefined behavior. Figure 5.1 shows the resulting sequence.

A sequence can be dynamically allocated using either of the following two statements:

```
seq10* p1 = new seq10;
seq10_var p2 = new seq10;
```

The difference is that the sequence pointed to by `p1` must be de-allocated explicitly with `delete p1`, whereas the sequence pointed to by `p2` will be de-allocated automatically when `p2` goes out of scope.

✚ Although it is less often used, it is also possible to allocate the buffer space for a sequence externally to the definition of the sequence itself, as follows:

```
// Create the data buffer:
CORBA::Long *buf = seq10::allocbuf(7);
// Initialize that buffer:
CORBA::ULong i;
for (i=0; i<7; i++)
      buf[i] = i; // Normal operator[] for C++ arrays.

// Now create the sequence:
seq10 x2(7,buf,1); // Length is 7.
```

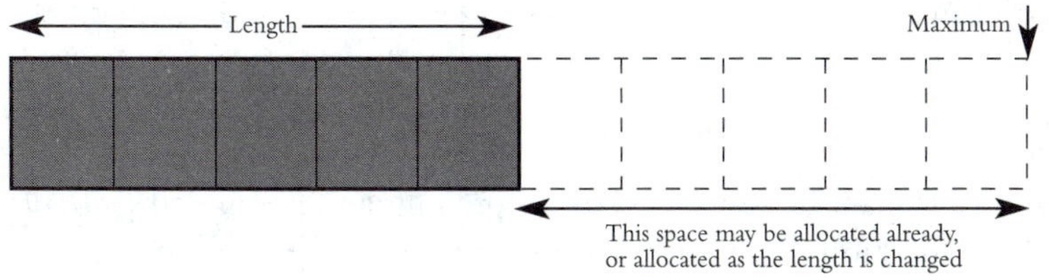

Figure 5.1 *Bounded sequence.*

Because the last parameter to x2's constructor is 1, the data buffer will be de-allocated automatically when x2 goes out of scope. If the last parameter were 0, the data buffer would have to be de-allocated at some later time (when x2 no longer needs it) by calling `seq10::freebuf(buf)`. (Programmers need only be concerned with `freebuf()` if the data buffer is allocated explicitly and the last parameter to the constructor is 0.)

General mapping for bounded sequences

The generated C++ class `seq10` is declared as follows:

```
public:class seq10 {
      seq10();     // Allocates space for 10 elements,
                   // but sets the length to zero.
      seq10(const seq10&); // Deep copy.
      seq10(CORBA::ULong initial_length,
            CORBA::Long *data_buffer,
            CORBA::Boolean release = 0);

      ~seq10();

      seq10& operator=(const seq10&); // Deep copy.

      static CORBA::Long* allocbuf(CORBA::ULong number_elements);
      static void freebuf(CORBA::Long* data);

      // Get the maximum number of elements:
      CORBA::ULong maximum() const;

      // Get and set the length:
      CORBA::ULong length() const;
      void length(CORBA::ULong new_length);

      CORBA::Long& operator[] (CORBA::ULong index);
      const CORBA::Long& operator[] (CORBA::Ulong index) const;
};
```

5.2.2 Unbounded sequences

The difference between a bounded and an unbounded sequence is that the former has a fixed maximum length while the latter has no theoretical maximum. A sequence of any length can be passed (for example, as a parameter to an IDL operation) where an unbounded sequence is expected. Therefore, unbounded sequences are normally used in preference to bounded ones, unless the maximum length can be determined confidently.

Nevertheless, in the C++ class that represents an unbounded sequence, there is a `maximum()` function that returns the sequence's current maximum. This is only an indication of the amount of space that is currently allocated to the sequence (this

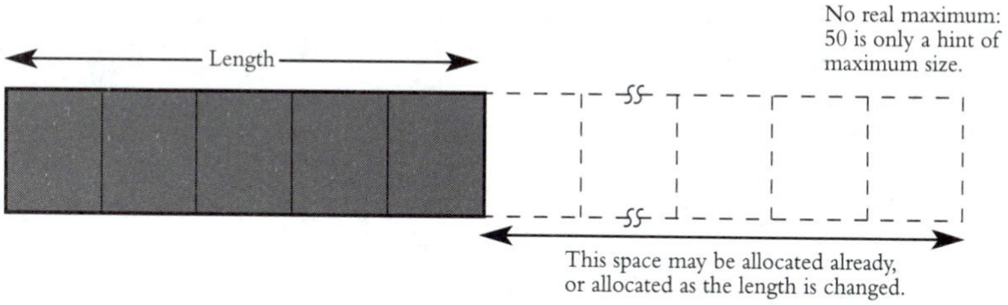

Figure 5.2 *Unbounded sequence.*

may, of course, be larger than the amount of space currently being used), and it is normally not very important. The maximum is automatically increased if the length is increased to require more space than is currently allocated.

Given the following typedef:

```
typedef sequence<float> seq;
```

an instance of this type can be defined as follows:

```
seq x2(50); // Initial maximum of 50.
```

A sequence can be dynamically allocated by either of the following two statements:

```
seq p1 = new seq(50);
seq_var p1 = new seq(50);
```

The length must be set using `length()` as before (otherwise the length will be zero). Elements can then be added using `operator[]`. `operator[]` should not be used to access or change an element outside of the current length. Figure 5.2 shows an unbounded sequence.

An unbounded sequence's maximum length will be automatically increased if the length is set to a value greater that the current maximum. This may cause the data buffer inside the sequence to be de-allocated and a new one allocated. Remember that this may happen whether the buffer was allocated in the sequence's constructor or explicitly using the static function `allocbuf()` and then passed to the sequence's constructor. However, the automatic de-allocation step will not be carried out if the release parameter (the fourth parameter; see p.112) is set to 0 when the constructor is called; and the application is then responsible for freeing the memory. Re-allocation of a sequence's buffer will only happen when the length is changed to exceed the current maximum.

An unbounded sequence defined using the default constructor as follows

```
seq x3;
```

allocates some implementation-dependent amount of initial space for the sequence.

✚ As for bounded sequences, it is also possible to allocate the buffer space for an unbounded sequence externally to the definition of the sequence itself. For unbounded sequences the maximum number of elements must also be set, as follows:

```
// Create the data buffer:
CORBA::Long *buf = seq::allocbuf(50);
// Initialize that buffer:
CORBA::ULong i;
for (i=0; i<27; i++)
      buf[i] = i; // Normal operator[].

// Now create the sequence:
seq10 x2(50, 27, buf, 1); // Length is 27.
```

The initial maximum has been set here to 50 (when the buffer is allocated and in the first parameter to the sequence's constructor). The length is 27 after this code sequence.

General mapping for unbounded sequences

The generated C++ class `seq` is declared as follows (the two small differences to bounded buffers are shown in italics):

```
class seq {
      seq(); // Sets the length to zero.
      seq(const seq&); // Deep copy.
      seq(CORBA::ULong maximum);
      seq(CORBA::ULong maximum,
                   CORBA::ULong initial_length,
                   CORBA::Long *data,
                   CORBA::Boolean release = 0);

      ~seq();

      seq& operator=(const seq&); // Deep copy.

      static CORBA::Long* allocbuf(CORBA::ULong number_elements);
      static void freebuf(CORBA::Long* data);

      CORBA::ULong maximum() const;

      // Get and set length:
      CORBA::ULong length() const;
      void length(CORBA::ULength new_length);

      CORBA::Long& operator[] (CORBA::ULong index);
      const CORBA::Long& operator[] (CORBA::Ulong index) const;
};
```

✚

5.2.3 Parameter passing table for sequences

When a sequence is passed as a parameter to an operation or appears as the return type, the corresponding C++ formal parameter types are as shown in Table 5.2.

Table 5.2 *Parameter passing modes for sequences.*

IDL type	in	out	inout	return
sequence S	const S&	S*&	S&	S*

Remember that pointers are not valid IDL types, so a programmer should not pass or return a zero pointer. It is of course valid to return (or pass as an `out` parameter) a pointer to an empty sequence.

✚ For an `in` parameter, the target object is given access to a sequence that it cannot change. For an `inout` parameter, it is given access to a sequence that it can change.

For a return value, the target object allocates the sequence and for efficiency it returns a pointer to this to the caller. The same applies to `out` parameters (the caller passes a pointer that the target object changes to point to the sequence that it wishes the caller to receive). `out` parameters and return values are not passed by reference because the target object is expected to create a sequence that the caller is to receive; and given the fact that the sequence may be large, the most efficient way to pass this to the caller is to pass a pointer to it. The client assumes responsibility for freeing any returned sequence. ✚

Memory management for sequences

The memory management rules for sequences can be summarized as follows. For an `in` parameter, the client is responsible for memory management. For an `out` paraemter or return value, the target object must allocate the sequence, and return a pointer to this to the client. The client must de-allocate the returned sequence when it no longer needs it. For an `inout` sequence, the client must allocate an initial sequence, which is passed by reference to the target object, and can be changed by it. The client remains responsible for de-allocating the memory.

✚ When the four-parameter constructor is used to create a sequence, its release flag can be set to determine whether or not the sequence's buffer space is to be de-allocated when the sequence is deleted. A release flag of `1` can be considered the default because it is chosen if the (`CORBA::ULong maximum`) constructor is used. Further, the release flag can be explicitly set to `1`, however, if the (`CORBA::ULong maximum`, `CORBA::ULong initial_length`, `CORBA::Long *data`, `CORBA::Boolean release = 0`) constructor is used.

If the client and target object are in different address spaces, the receiver's copy of the sequence will have a release flag of `1` (so de-allocating the sequence will release the buffer space). If the client and server are in the same address space, then the creator of the sequence will have determined whether or not the buffer space is to be released. If the release flag is 0, the creator must have arranged for some other part of the code to release the space.

`in` *parameters*

When a sequence is passed as an `in` parameter to an operation, the sequence itself is passed as (a reference to) a C++ object (an instance of the class that the sequence maps to). There are no memory management implications because the sequence is not passed by pointer. The target object is given access to the sequence for the duration of the operation call, and assumes no ownership of the data buffer.

`out` *parameters*

When a sequence with a release flag of `1` is passed as an `out` parameter, the caller receives a pointer to a C++ object (an instance of the class that the sequence maps to), and it must delete this object when it no longer needs it. Deleting that object will de-allocate the sequence's storage buffer. Therefore, the called operation gives up ownership of the sequence. By assigning the returned pointer to an `_var` variable, the caller can avoid mistakes that lead to memory leaks.

When a sequence with a release flag of 0 is passed as an `out` parameter (the release flag can be set to 0 by allocating the sequence's data buffer explicitly and setting the `release` parameter to the sequence's constructor to 0), the called operation gives up ownership of the sequence, as before. However, the creator of the sequence retains responsibility for de-allocating the storage buffer. In this case, it is useful to discuss separately the details when the client and target object are remote and when they are in the same address space. When they are remote, the creator of the sequence in the server remains responsible for de-allocating the buffer. The copy of the sequence constructed on the client side will have a release flag of `1`. Having a release flag of `1` allows the client simply to delete the returned sequence.

If the client and server are in the same address space, then as the client eventually deletes the sequence the storage buffer will not be de-allocated. This is the required behavior because the creator of the sequence will be in the same address space and it retains responsibility for de-allocating the storage buffer.

Return values

A return value is passed by pointer. It is the caller's responsibility to delete the sequence when it no longer needs it.

`inout` *parameters*

Passing a sequence as an `inout` parameter causes no particular memory management difficulties if the release flag is `1`. The target object is given access to the sequence, which it can change. If it increases the length of the sequence, then the old buffer space may be de-allocated and a new buffer allocated (both of these will be done automatically by the sequence's internal code).

There is a special rule that must be understood if the release flag of an `inout` sequence is 0. If the target object is in the same address space as the client, and the target object increases the length of the sequence, then the old buffer space will not be de-allocated. In this case, the client needs to ensure that some other part of the code de-allocates the old buffer space. In addition, the client must not de-allocate the old buffer space until the sequence has been deleted.

The latter rule arises because the client cannot know whether or not the call has resulted in the sequence having a new buffer space. Therefore, it cannot de-allocate the old space until the sequence has been deleted (because the sequence may still be using the buffer).

If the client and target object are in different address spaces, the client-side and server-side ORBs cooperate to ensure the same rules for the client and target object. (If the buffer space changes, the release flag of the sequence will be `1` at the end of the call. Deleting the sequence will de-allocate the new buffer space, and the client is responsible for deleting the old buffer space, because the release flag was originally zero.)

Note that the target object does not need to assume any responsibility for memory management of a sequence (or its storage buffer) passed to it as an `inout` parameter. ✚

5.3 Arrays

An IDL array type is mapped directly to a C++ array type, and two other C++ types. The first of these types is an `_var` type that can optionally be used to manage the storage of dynamically allocated arrays; the second is a `slice` type that is used for return values and for some `out` parameters, as we will see.

Given the following IDL typedef:

```
typedef long vector[10];
```

an instance of the array type can be defined in C++ as follows:

```
vector x1; // A normal C++ array (size 10).
```

An array can be dynamically allocated using either of the following two statements:

```
long* p1 = vector_alloc(); // Size is 10, of course.
vec10_var p2 = vector_alloc(); // Size is 10, of course.
```

(A C++ type, `vector_slice`, is generated as an alias for `long`; so the first of these statements can also be written as:

```
vector_slice* p1 = vector_alloc(); // Size is 10, of course.
```

The difference is that the sequence pointed to by `p1` must be de-allocated explicitly with `vector_free(p1)`, whereas the sequence pointed to by `p2` will be de-allocated automatically when `p2` goes out of scope. The functions `vector_alloc()` and `vector_free()` are generated by the IDL compiler, and they must be used to allocate and deallocate arrays, respectively (see Section 5.5).

The type `vec10_var` defines `operator[]()` to allow easy access to the underlying array. Hence, statements such as the following are valid:

```
p2[4] = p1[7];
```

✚ For most element types, the type of the C++ elements is the same as that of the original definition in IDL. However, this is not the case for `string` and object reference types. Instead, implementation- specific types (`_mgr` types in Orbix) are used to ensure that an array manages its own storage. Therefore, if an array of strings is deleted, so too are the strings it refers to; if an array of object references is deleted, the reference counts of the objects it refers to are decremented. ✚

5.3.1 Parameter passing table for arrays

When an array is passed as a parameter to an operation or appears as the return type, then the corresponding C++ formal parameter types are as shown in Table 5.3. Array slice types are explained in the next subsection. (As for the other data types that are passed or returned by pointer, programmers should not return or pass the zero pointer, because it has no correspondence in IDL.)

Table 5.3 *Parameter passing modes for arrays.*

IDL type	`in`	`out`	`inout`	`return`
Array `A` of fixed sized elements	`const A`	`A`	`A`	`A_slice*`
Array `A` of variable sized elements	`const A`	`A_slice*&`	`A`	`A_slice*`

✚ Hence, if an IDL operation has an `in` parameter of type `A` (which might be defined by `typedef long A[10]`), then the corresponding C++ parameter will be of type `const A`. Of course, in C++, a pointer is actually passed to the function.

For `in` and `inout` parameters, the target object receives a pointer to the first element in the array. For a return value, the caller receives a pointer to space allocated by the target object, and the caller assumes ownership of this space.

The rules differ for `out` parameters between arrays of fixed and variable sized elements. (Fixed sized element types are basic types, and arrays/unions/structures of fixed sized elements. Variable sized element types are `string`, object references, sequences, `any`, and arrays/unions/structures that include variable sized elements.)

For arrays of fixed sized elements, the target object can write into the array space allocated (possibly on the stack) by the caller. For arrays of variable sized elements, the target object can construct an array and pass a pointer to this space back to the caller. The caller assumes ownership of the storage space. The motivation for this has been explained when discussing the parameter passing rules for structs (see Section 5.1.1, p.109).

The parameter passing rules are easy to remember once they are understood. In any case, they will be checked by any C++ compiler. In addition, an `_var` variable can be passed as an `out` parameter without concern for the different rules for fixed and variable sized arrays: the variable need only be passed and conversion operators will handle the differences.

For example, if there is an operation `op1()` defined within interface `T` and this takes an array of type `A1` as an `inout` parameter, then the programmer can use a variable of type `A1_var` to hide any complexity in the parameter passing rules. For example:

```
T_var p1 = . . . . ;
A1_var va1; // Setting of initial value not shown.
// No need to worry about whether A1 is a fixed or
// variable sized array type:
p1->op1( va1 );
```

Array slice types

Conventionally in C++, a function that returns an array of elements is written to return a pointer to the first element or row:

```
long* func();
```

This convention is followed by the IDL to C++ mapping. For example:

```
typedef long vector[10];

interface T {
      vector op1 (in vector a);
};
```

maps to (ignoring the `vector_var` type):

```
typedef CORBA::Long vector[10];
typedef CORBA::Long vector_slice;

public:class T : public virtual CORBA::Object {
      vector_slice *op1 (const vector a);
};
```

Type `vector_slice` differs from type `vector` by dropping the first array dimension (the only one in this case). Of course, there is no real need to have the `vector_slice` type defined, since type `CORBA::Long` would have sufficed in this case. Array type slices become a little more useful when multidimensional array types are considered. For example:

```
typedef float matrix[10][20];
```

maps to:

```
typedef float matrix[10][20];
typedef float matrix_slice[20];
```

Hence, the following IDL operation:

```
matrix op2 (in matrix m);
```

maps to:

```
matrix_slice* op1 (const matrix m);
```

That is, a pointer to the first row of the array is returned, as is normal in C++. The array slice type can also be explicitly used by programmers; for example:

```
// Allocate a 10 by 20 matrix:
matrix_slice* p1 = matrix_alloc();
cin >> p1[1][5];
// De-allocate using matrix_free(p1), now or later.
```

In this case, however, the `matrix_var` type is more commonly used because it automatically de-allocates the array:

```
matrix_var p2 = matrix_alloc();
```

Memory management for arrays

The memory management rules for arrays are based on those of strings (pointers to an array of characters); see Section 4.3.2, p.81. The following differences should be noted:

- The size of an `inout` string can be changed, but that of an array obviously cannot.
- The client allocates the storage for a fixed-length `out` parameter array; however, the target object allocates the storage for an `out` parameter string and passes a pointer to the client.

5.4 Unions

An IDL `union` is mapped to a C++ class that allows the value of the union to be set and read, and the current type to be determined. For example, the following IDL:

```
union U switch (long) {
      cass 1: long x;
      case 2: float y;
      default: string z;
};
```

maps to a C++ class that allows an instance of `U` to be created and one of the members `x`, `y`, or `z` to be set and read:

```
U i1;
i1.y(2.45); // Set the y member.
cout << i1.y() << endl; // Output the value.
```

Given an instance of `U`, a programmer can determine which of its members is currently set using the `_d()` member function:

```
switch (i1._d()) {
      case 1: cout << i1->x(); break;
      case 2: cout << i1->y(); break;
      default: cout << i1->z();
}
```

The call to `_d()` returns the **discriminant** value, which is of the IDL union's discriminant type (IDL `long` in this case). The result of calling one of the selector functions is undefined if the discriminant value is set inappropriately (for example, it is an error to call any selector function except `x()` if the union's discriminant is 1).

As is the case with the other IDL data types, the IDL compiler also produces an `_var` type that can (optionally) be used to manage dynamically allocated storage. A union can therefore be allocated dynamically using either of the following statements:

```
U* p1 = new U;
U_var p2 = new U;
```

The difference is that the instance pointed to by `p1` must be de-allocated explicitly using `delete p1`, whereas the instance pointed to by `p2` will be de-allocated automatically when `p2` goes out of scope. When a union itself is de-allocated, any space that the current member of the union points to will be de-allocated (or, in the case of an object reference, the target object's reference count will be decremented).

When a member of a union is assigned a new value, the old value is de-allocated. Therefore, there is no memory leak in the following code:

```
i1.z = (const char*) "hello"; // Copied in this case.
i1.x(4);    // The string is de-allocated.
// i1._d() would now return 1.
```

Generated class for union

The IDL definition:

```
typedef char Arr[10];
union U2 (switch unsigned long) {
      case 1: short a;
      case 2: string b;
      case 3: FrontOffice c;
      case 4: Arr d;
};
```

results in the generation of the following C++ class, with one selector function and one or more modifier functions per IDL union member:

```
class U2 {
public:
      U2();
      U2(const U2&);
      ~U2();
      U2& operator=(const U2&);

      void _d(CORBA::ULong);
      CORBA::ULong _d();

      void a(CORBA::Short);
      CORBA::Short a() const;

      void b(char*);   // Free old; no copy of new.
      void b(const char*); // Free old; copy new.
      void b(const CORBA::String_var&); // Free old; copy new.
      const char* b() const; // No copying.

      void c(FrontOffice_ptr); // Release old; duplicate new.
      FrontOffice_ptr c() const; // No duplication.

      void d(Arr);
      Arr_slice* d() const;
};
```

The member function `b(char*)` adopts ownership of the string passed to it, whereas the member function `b(const char*)` copies the parameter passed to it and adopts ownership of the copy. The accessor function `b()` does not copy the string before returning a `(const)` pointer to it.

The member function `c(FrontOffice_ptr)` de-allocates/releases any old storage and calls duplicate on the object reference passed to it. The `c()` function does not duplicate the object reference that the union holds before returning it.

All member functions that modify the union call the appropriate de-allocation function on the old value; for example, they call `CORBA::release()` if the union previously contains an object reference (see Section 5.5 for a full list of the de-allocation functions). The fact that IDL unions map to C++ classes with modifier and selector functions, rather than to C++ unions, makes it significantly easier to do this de-allocation. Each modifier function can determine the nature of the currently held member and de-allocate its storage if appropriate.

Note that the discriminant of a union can be changed using the `_d()` member function. This is not frequently required, and it is only valid in the cases listed below. Consider the following union:

```
union U switch (short) {
      case 1:
      case 2: long x; // This is active if the value is 1 or 2.
      case 5: string y;
      default: char z;
};
```

If the `long x` member is active, then the `_d()` function can be used to change the discriminant value from `1` to `2`, or vice versa. If the `char z` member is active, `_d()` can be used to change the discriminant to any value other than `1`, `2`, or `5`. If the string `y` member is active, `_d()` can only be used to set the value to `5`, but this is not of any use since this is the value it will have already. `_d()` cannot be used to make a different member active (thus, in this example, `_d()` cannot be used to change the discriminant from `5` to `7`).

When an IDL union does not have a `default` case and there are unused discriminant values, the corresponding C++ class has a (parameterless) function, `_default()`, that can be used to set the union to hold no member. ✚

5.4.1 Parameter passing table for unions

When a union is passed as a parameter to an operation or appears as the return type, then the corresponding C++ formal parameter types are as shown in Table 5.4.

Table 5.4 *Parameter passing modes for unions.*

IDL type	in	out	inout	return
Union `U` of all fixed sized members	`const U&`	`U&`	`U&`	`U`
Union `U` with one or more variable sized members	`const U&`	`U*&`	`U&`	`U*`

As for the other data types that are passed or returned by pointer, programmers should not return or pass the zero pointer, because it has no correspondence in IDL.

✚ For an `in` parameter, the target object is given a reference to a union that it cannot change. For an `inout` parameter, it is give a reference to a union that it can change.

The `out` parameter and return value rules differ for unions that are constructed from all fixed sized members, and ones with one or more variable sized members. (Fixed sized member types are basic types, and arrays/unions/structures of fixed sized elements. Variable sized member types are `string`, object references, sequences, `any`, and arrays/unions/structures that include at least one variable sized element.)

The motivation for the rule differences are the same as for structs (see Section 5.1.1, p.109). Space for a fixed sized `out` parameter union is allocated by the caller, and this space can be modified by the target object. A fixed sized union return value is passed by value because this is normally more efficient that using memory allocation and de-allocation.

Variable sized unions can potentially be very large. Space for a variable sized `out` parameter union is allocated by the target object, and, for efficiency, a pointer to this space is passed back to the caller. The caller passes a pointer which will be changed by the target object to point to the space. For a return value, the caller receives a pointer to space allocated by the target object, with no further copying required. The caller assumes ownership of returned `out` parameters and return values.

As explained in Section 5.3.1 (p.118), `_var` types can be used to hide these differences in parameter passing modes for fixed and variable sized `out` parameters and return values.

5.5 Allocation and de-allocation

To dynamically allocate and de-allocate a type, the allocation and de-allocation functions shown in Table 5.5 should be used.

Table 5.5 *Allocation and de-allocation rules for all data types.*

	Allocation	**De-allocation**
`string`	`CORBA::string_dup()` or `CORBA::string_alloc()`. One extra byte is allocated (for the terminating '`\0`' character)	`CORBA::string_free()`
Object reference	Member function: `_duplicate()`. (Objects themselves can be created using `new`, or they can be automatic or static. `_duplicate()` increases the reference count of an existing object or proxy)	`CORBA::release()`

Sequence	Sequences themselves can be allocated using `new()`. A sequence's data buffer can be allocated automatically using a constructor that allocates the buffer, or the buffer can be allocated using the static function `allocbuf()` and then the sequence can be given to this buffer as a parameter to its constructor	Sequences themselves can be deallocated using `delete()`. A sequence's data buffer is normally de-allocated automatically when the sequence is deleted, unless the buffer was pre-allocated using `allocbuf()` and the release parameter was set to `0` (in which case the static `freebuf()` function should be used to de-allocate the buffer)
Array	For array type `vector`, use function `vector_alloc()`. (If the array type is defined in an interface, then the C++ function will be static in the class)	For array type `vector`, use static function `vector_free()`, or assign the array to a `vector_var` variable
Other data types	Use normal `new()` operator	Use normal `delete()` operator

5.6 C++ keywords

C++ keywords can be used in IDL definitions, but when such definitions are translated into C++ an '_' character is prepended to give the C++ identifier. For example, IDL identifier `while` is translated to identifier `_while` in C++.

6 The cinema example

This chapter further develops the cinema application introduced in Chapter 2. It presents many details of CORBA not covered in previous chapters, and in particular it covers some of the details ignored in Chapter 2.

The IDL for the cinema application was presented in Section 2.12 (p.39). Normally, the definitions below would be made within an IDL module, as follows:

```
module Cinema {
      // As above.
};
```

This has not been done here to avoid having to scope each of the definitions in the C++ code with `Cinema::`.

```
// In, for example, "front.idl."

typedef float Price;

struct Place {
      char row;
      unsigned long seat;
};
typedef sequence<Place> Places;

typedef string Date; // In format DD.MM.YYYY.

struct CreditCard {
      string id;
      Date   expiry;
};
```

```
interface Booking {
      readonly attribute Date when;
      readonly attribute Places seats;
      void cancel();
};

interface GroupBooking : Booking {
      readonly attribute string organizer;
      readonly attribute string groupName;
};

interface FrontOffice {

      exception NoSuchPlace { Place where; };
      exception PlaceAlreadyBooked {
                  Place where; Date when; };
      exception InvalidCreditCard  {
                  CreditCard invalidCard; };
      exception InvalidDate { Date when; };
      exception GroupTooSmall {
                  unsigned long chosenSize;
                  unsigned long minimumSize;
      };

      // Name of the cinema:
      readonly attribute string name;
      // Highest lettered row:
      readonly attribute char lastRow;
      // Number of seats in each row:

      readonly attribute unsigned long seatsPerRow;

      boolean checkIfOpen (in Date when,
                           out Date nextAvailableDate)
                  raises (InvalidDate);

      Places listAvailablePlaces (in Date when)
                  raises (InvalidDate);

      Price getPrice (in Place chosenPlace,
                      in Date when)
                  raises (NoSuchPlace, invalidDate);

      Booking makeBooking (in Places chosenPlaces,
                           in Date when,
                           in CreditCard payment)
                  raises (NoSuchPlace,
                          PlaceAlreadyBooked,
                          InvalidCreditCard,
                          InvalidDate);
```

```
      GroupBooking makeGroupBooking (
                         in Places     chosenPlaces,
                         in Date       when,
                         in CreditCard payment,
                         in string     organizer,
                         in string     groupName)
            raises (NoSuchPlace,
                    PlaceAlreadyBooked,
                    InvalidCreditCard,
                    InvalidDate,
                    GroupTooSmall);
};
```

On the server side, the overall aim will be to create a server, called `FrontOfficeSrv`, which contains both `FrontOffice` and `Booking` objects. In this case, the server contains a single `FrontOffice` object that will accept operation calls such as `makeBooking()` from clients. In this example, all of the objects (both `FrontOffice` and `Booking` objects) will be in a single server, although in a real system several servers may be used and objects may also exist in clients. Note that a server can, without difficulty, manage objects of many different interfaces.

The remainder of this chapter will cover the following programming steps:

- Compiling the IDL definitions.
- Writing a simple client.
- Implementing the two interfaces, `Booking` and `FrontOffice`.
- Writing a server main function which creates a `FrontOffice` object.
- Registering the server.

Chapter 9, 'Exception handling,' shows how operations can raise user-defined exceptions and how clients can handle user- and system-defined exceptions. Chapter 10, 'Inheritance,' discusses inheritance, and in particular interface `GroupBooking`, which inherits from `Booking`.

6.1 Files generated by the IDL compiler

Once the IDL source file, `front.idl`, is passed through the IDL compiler, a number of C++ source files are generated:

- `front.hh`: A shared header file used by both clients and servers for the cinema.
- `frontC.C`: An implementation file containing the proxy support for the interfaces defined in `front.idl`. This should be compiled and linked with the client.
- `frontS.C`: An implementation file containing server-side support for the interfaces defined in `front.idl`. This should be compiled and linked with the server. In Orbix, this file contains `front.C`.

The name of the file containing these IDL definitions is not important; it simply determines the names of the files generated by the Orbix IDL compiler.

It is essential that the programmer understands the IDL to C++ mapping, and thus understands the interface to the C++ classes generated by the IDL compiler. These correspond directly to the interfaces defined in the IDL source. The details of the IDL to C++ mapping were presented in Chapters 4 and 5, but most programmers need to understand only a subset of these rules.

In the case of our cinema example, there are two C++ classes generated, as follows (interface `GroupBooking` is discussed in Chapter 10):

```
// C++
// The file "front.hh".
#include <CORBA.h>

class Booking : public virtual CORBA::Object {
public:
      // Various details for Orbix.

      // IDL attributes:
      virtual Date when ()
          throw (CORBA::SystemException);
      virtual Places* seats ()
          throw (CORBA::SystemException);

      // IDL operations:
      virtual void cancel ()
          throw (CORBA::SystemException);
};


class FrontOffice : public virtual CORBA::Object {
public:
      // Various details for Orbix.

      // IDL attributes:
      virtual char * name ()
          throw (CORBA::SystemException);
      virtual CORBA::Char lastRow ()
```

```
        throw (CORBA::SystemException);
    virtual CORBA::ULong seatsPerRow ()
        throw (CORBA::SystemException);

    // IDL operations:

    virtual CORBA::Boolean checkIfOpen
            (const char* when,
             Date& nextAvailableDate)
         throw (CORBA::SystemException,
                FrontOffice::InvalidDate);

    virtual Places* listAvailablePlaces
            (const char* when)
         throw (CORBA::SystemException,
                FrontOffice::InvalidDate);

    virtual Price getPrice
            (const Place& chosenPlace,
             const char* when)
         throw (CORBA::SystemException,
                FrontOffice::NoSuchPlace,
                FrontOffice::InvalidDate);

    virtual Booking_ptr makeBooking
            (const Places& chosenPlaces,
             const char* when,
             const CreditCard& payment)
         throw (CORBA::SystemException,
                FrontOffice::NoSuchPlace,
                FrontOffice::PlaceAlreadyBooked,
                FrontOffice::InvalidCreditCard,
                FrontOffice::InvalidDate);

    virtual GroupBooking_ptr makeGroupBooking
            (const Places& chosenPlaces,
             const char* when,
             const CreditCard& payment,
             const char * organizer,
             const char * groupName)
         throw (CORBA::SystemException,
                FrontOffice::NoSuchPlace,
                FrontOffice::PlaceAlreadyBooked,
                FrontOffice::InvalidCreditCard,
                FrontOffice::InvalidDate,
                FrontOffice::GroupTooSmall);
};
```

Both `Booking` and `FrontOffice` inherit from class `CORBA::Object`. This is a CORBA library class, which provides functionality common to all C++ classes generated from IDL interfaces. It is defined in `CORBA.h`.

6.2 A client program

From the point of view of the client, the functionality provided by the cinema application is defined by the IDL interface definitions. A typical client program obtains references to one or more remote objects, and then invokes operations on those objects.

In the first client code shown, the Orbix `_bind()` call is used to find a `FrontOffice` object. Alternatives to using `_bind()` are discussed later. (`_bind()` is shown first because it is very simple to use. Nevertheless, use of the Naming Service is the preferred way to obtain object references to an initial set of remote objects; and the passing of object references as parameters and return values is the preferred way to obtain further object references.)

```
// C++
#include "front.hh"
#include <iostream.h>

mainint() {
      FrontOffice_var foVar;

      try {

            // Bind to any FrontOffice object in the
            // FrontOfficeSrv server:
            foVar = FrontOffice::_bind(":FrontOfficeSrv");

            // Check if the cinema is open on a given date:
            CORBA::String_var nextDate;
            CORBA::Boolean b =
                        foVar->checkIfOpen("1.1.1998", nextDate);
            if (b)
                  cout << "The Cinema is Open on that date." << endl;
            else {
                  cout << "The Cinema is Closed on that date." << endl;
                  cout << " The next available date is "
                              << nextDate << endl;
            }

      }
      catch(CORBA::SystemException& se) {
            cerr << "Unexpected exception" << endl
                  << se; *†
            exit(-1);
      }
}
```

† This `operator<<()` is Orbix-specific.

The static member function `FrontOffice::_bind()` requests Orbix to search for an object offering the `FrontOffice` interface. The parameter '`:FrontOfficeSrv`' instructs Orbix to search for the required object in the `FrontOfficeSrv` server. Orbix will first search for that server, activating a process to run the server if necessary, and then it will search for a `FrontOffice` object within that server. The client could also specify which `FrontOffice` object to locate in the `FrontOfficeSrv` server – this would be useful if it contained more than one `FrontOffice` object (these more selective requests will be shown in Chapter 7).

In this case, the bind is being made to an object outside of the caller's address space, therefore Orbix will construct a proxy for that object in the client's address space (unless one exists already).

The `_bind()` function returns a reference to the proxy object; in the example, the client assigns this to a `FrontOffice_var` variable which manages the memory of the proxy. The proxy will initially have a reference count of 1, and the destructor of the `FrontOffice_var` variable will decrement this to zero, and so cause the proxy to be de-allocated.

Recall that the IDL compiler generates an `_var` class from each IDL interface definition (Section 4.4, p.89).

Calling `_bind()` is not always required before communicating with a particular object, and, as discussed in Chapter 2, there are two other ways in which a client can obtain an object reference to an object that it needs to communicate with:

- The server can register the object with the Naming Service – giving it a name – and a client that knows that name can resolve it in the Naming Service to obtain a reference to the object.
- A client may receive an object reference as a return or attribute value, or as an `out` parameter to an IDL operation call. This will result in the creation of a proxy in the client's address space. Operation `makeBooking()`, for example, returns a reference to a `Booking` object, and a client that calls this operation can then make operation calls on the new object. A `FrontOffice` object may also provide an operation to return an object reference for a `Booking`, given a customer name or a Booking number.

The Naming Service is just one special case of using an IDL interface that returns object references to the caller. However, because it is a standard interface, it is worth considering it separately.

Normally, a process must call `_bind()` or use the Naming Service at least once in order to communicate with objects outside of its address space. However, it should not overuse either `_bind()` or the Naming Service, since, for many applications, it is better for a server to make its objects known to its clients through the various IDL interfaces provided by its objects. Further information on `_bind()` and the Naming Service is given in Chapter 7.

Finally, note that a program should always test for exceptions. All system exceptions can be caught by catching the `CORBA::SystemException` type, as shown in the first `catch` clause in the first code segment of this chapter. The class `CORBA::SystemException` declares an output operator, `operator<<()`, which outputs a description of the exception. We will defer further discussion of exception handling until Chapter 9.

Further examples of client code

The client can call the operation `getPrice()` as follows. This shows how to pass a struct to an operation (it assumes that variable `foVar` has been assigned to, as shown in the previous client code):

```
try {
      Place aPlace;
      cout << "Enter row:  ";
      cin >> aPlace.row;
      cout << "Enter seat: ";
      cin >> aPlace.seat;

      CORBA::String_var date = CORBA::string_alloc(10);
      cout << "Enter Date [DD.MM.YYYY]: ";
      cin >> date;

      Price thePrice = foVar->getPrice (aPlace, date);
      cout << "Price: " << thePrice << endl;
}
catch (CORBA::SystemException& se) {
      cerr << endl << "System Exception: " << endl
           << se << endl;
      exit(-1);
}
```

A call to `listAvailablePlaces()` can be coded as follows. This shows how to handle a sequence returned by an operation:

```
try {
      CORBA::String_var date = CORBA::string_alloc(10);
      cout << "Enter Date [DD.MM.YYYY]: ";
      cin >> date;

      Places_var avail = foVar->listAvailablePlaces(date);

      cout << "Available places:" << endl;
      for (CORBA::ULong i = 0; i < avail.length(); i++ ) {
            cout << '\t' << avail[i].row << avail[i].seat << endl;
      }
}
catch (CORBA::SystemException& se) {
```

```
        cerr << endl << "System Exception: " << endl
             << se endl;
        exit(-1);
}
```

A call to `makeBooking()` can be coded as follows. This shows how to pass a sequence of structs to an operation:

```
Booking_var theBooking;
try {
        // Date of the booking:
        CORBA::String_var date = CORBA::string_alloc(10);
        cout << "Enter Date [DD.MM.YYYY]: ";
        cin >> date;

        // Places to be booked:
        cout << "Number of places required: ";
        unsigned long numPlaces;
        cin >> numPlaces;

        Places thePlaces(numPlaces);
        thePlaces.length(numPlaces);
        for (CORBA::ULong i = 0; i < numPlaces; i++) {
              Place where;
              cout << "Enter row: ";
              cin >> where.row;
              cout << "Enter seat: ";
              cin >> where.seat;
              thePlaces[i] = where;
        }

        // Credit card information:
        CreditCard card;
        cout << "Credit card number: ";
        char* ccn = CORBA::string_alloc(30);
        cin >> ccn;
        card.id = ccn;
        cout << "Credit card expiry date [DD.MM.YYYY]: " ;
        char *cced = CORBA::string_alloc(10);
        cin >> cced;
        card.expiry = cced;

        // Make the call to makeBooking():
        theBooking = foVar->makeBooking(thePlaces, date, card);

        cout << "Confirmation of date booked: " ;
        CORBA::String_var when = theBooking->when();
        cout << when << endl;
}
catch (CORBA::SystemException& se) {
        cerr << endl << "System Exception: " << endl
```

```
        << se endl;
    exit(-1);
}
```

6.3 The server: implementing interfaces

To implement an interface, a C++ programmer must provide a C++ class (in Orbix terminology, a C++ **implementation class**) which has a member function definition for each of the operations and attributes of the interface. A C++ implementation class must provide (at least) the operations and attributes defined in the IDL interface that it is declared to implement. Orbix supports two mechanisms for relating such an implementation class to its IDL interface: the BOAImpl approach and the TIE approach. These will be discussed in turn in Sections 6.3.1 and 6.3.2. Most server programmers use one of these approaches exclusively, but there is no difficulty mixing them in the same server.

Client programmers need not be concerned with which of the two mechanisms a server programmer chooses to use.

6.3.1 The BOAImpl approach

Recall that for each IDL interface, Orbix generates a C++ class with the same name, and with member functions that correspond to the IDL operations and attributes. Orbix also generates a second C++ class for each IDL interface, using the name of the interface appended with the letters `BOAImpl`. For example, it generates the class `BookingBOAImpl` for the IDL interface `Booking` (the name of this class differs between ORBs for example, it may be `_sk_Booking` in some other ORBs). To indicate that a C++ class implements a given IDL interface, that class should inherit from the corresponding BOAImpl class.

Each BOAImpl class inherits from the proxy C++ class (for example, `BookingBOAImpl` inherits from `Booking`).

The BOAImpl approach is shown in Figure 6.1 for the `Booking` IDL interface. The Orbix IDL compiler produces the C++ classes `Booking` and `BookingBOAImpl`. The programmer defines a new class, `Booking_i`, to implement the functions defined in the IDL interface. In addition to having functions that correspond to IDL operations and attributes, class `Booking_i` can have user-defined constructors, a destructor, and private and protected member variables and functions.

We use the convention that interface `A` is implemented by class `A_i`. This naming scheme does not have to be adhered to – and in any case some applications may need to implement interface `A` a number of times.

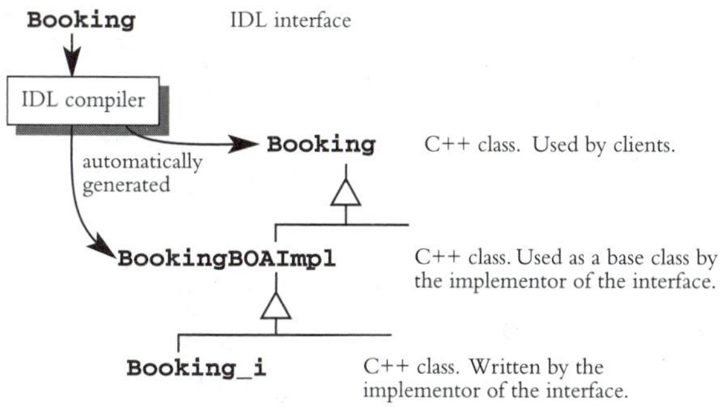

Figure 6.1 *The BOAImpl approach to defining a C++ implementation class.*

6.3.2 The TIE approach

In the second approach, the programmer implements the IDL operations and attributes within a class that does *not* inherit from the BOAImpl class. In this case, the programmer must indicate to Orbix that the class implements a particular IDL interface, by using a C++ macro to *tie together* the programmer's class to the IDL interface. This second approach is termed the **TIE approach**. (Section 6.9 on p.156 gives a comparison of the BOAImpl and TIE approaches.)

The corresponding diagram for the TIE approach is shown in Figure 6.2. The implementer defines a class `Booking_i`, and `TIEs` it to the IDL interface.

To use the `TIE` mechanism, the server programmer indicates that a particular class implements a given interface by calling a `DEF_TIE` macro, which has the general form:

```
// C++  macro
DEF_TIE_<InterfaceName>( <C++ implementation class name> )
```

(In the future, this may be replaced with a C++ template class.)

Each call to this macro declares a `TIE` class – a class that records that a particular interface is implemented by a particular implementation class.

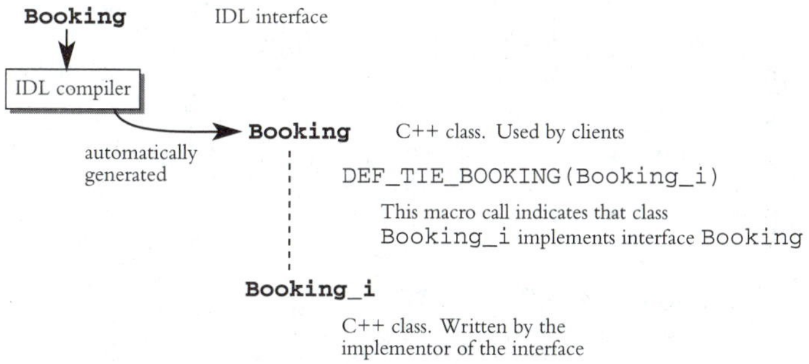

Figure 6.2 *Use of TIE to define a C++ implementation class.*

The macro call:

```
DEF_TIE_Booking(Booking_i)
```

generates a class named `TIE_Booking(Booking_i)`. An instance of a TIE class is known as a `TIE`.

Naturally, the new class has a proper legal C++ name, and the macro call `TIE_Booking(Booking_i)` expands to this name. However, the server programmer need not be concerned with this name; instead, the programmer just uses the name `TIE_Booking(Booking_i)`. The TIE approach is illustrated in Section 6.4.3 (p.145).

6.4 The server: coding the implementation classes

In this section, we show a very simple implementation of the cinema application illustrating both the BOAImpl and TIE approaches. We have ignored any error checking, which would be necessary in a full cinema application – for example, checking that places and dates are valid. The data structures used to record what places have been booked on each date have also been removed here because they are non-trivial and they add nothing to the understanding of CORBA programming. In a non-persistent prototype, a linked list of structures holding dates and places may be used; in a real implementation, a relational table or object search structure with various indices would be required.

We will code two implementation classes:

- `FrontOffice_i`: implements the `FrontOffice` interface.
- `Booking_i`: implements the `Booking` interface.

✚ Note that to assist the sever programmer, a skeleton version of the class and function definitions for `FrontOffice_i` and `Booking_i` can be generated automatically automatically by specifying the `-S` switch to the Orbix IDL compiler. ✚

Either the BOAImpl or the TIE approach may be used to relate the implementation classes to their interfaces. These will be discussed in turn. Client programmers need not be concerned with which of these approaches is chosen by an interface implementer.

6.4.1 The BOAImpl approach

We can indicate that a class implements a specific IDL interface by inheriting from the corresponding BOAImpl class generated by the IDL compiler:

```
// C++. In the file "FrontOffice_i.h".
#include "FrontOffice.hh"

class Booking_i : public BookingBOAImpl {
protected:
      CORBA::String_var m_when;†
      Places_var m_seats;
      FrontOffice_i* m_office;
public:
      Booking_i(FrontOffice_i* office,
                Places& chosenPlaces,
                Date when);

      virtual ~Booking_i();

      // IDL attributes:
      virtual Date when ()
          throw (CORBA::SystemException);
      virtual Places* seats ()
          throw (CORBA::SystemException);

      // IDL operations:
      virtual void cancel ()
          throw (CORBA::SystemException);

      // Could add other public or private non-IDL functions.
};

class FrontOffice_i : public FrontOfficeBOAImpl {
protected:
      const CORBA::String_var m_name;
      const CORBA::Char m_lastRow;
      const CORBA::ULong m_seatsPerRow;
      const CORBA::Char m_firstExpensiveSeat;
      Price m_priceForCheapSeat;
      Price m_priceForExpensiveSeat;
      Price m_addForNewYear; // Price increase for New Year's day.
      CORBA::ULong m_minGroupSize;
      // Also, data structure to hold bookings; not shown here.
public:
      FrontOffice_i (const char* name,
                     const CORBA::Char lastRow,
```

† This could have been declared as a simple `char*`, but use of `CORBA::String_var` ensures that we do not forget to de-allocate it. Only strings that are passed as `out` or `inout` parameters, returned as attribute values or return values need to be allocated using `CORBA::string_dup()` or `CORBA::string_alloc()`; but in some cases it is convenient to use `CORBA::string_var` elsewhere so that automatic de-allocation and `CORBA::string_dup()` can both be used.

```
                const CORBA::ULong seatsPerRow,
                const CORBA::ULong minGroupSize,
                const CORBA::Char firstExpensiveSeat,
                const Price priceForCheapSeat,
                const Price priceForExpensiveSeat,
                const Price addForNewYear);

virtual ~FrontOffice_i ();

// IDL attributes:
virtual char* name ()
    throw (CORBA::SystemException);
virtual CORBA::Char lastRow ()
    throw (CORBA::SystemException);
virtual CORBA::ULong seatsPerRow ()
    throw (CORBA::SystemException);

// IDL operations:

virtual CORBA::Boolean checkIfOpen
                                  (const char* when,
                                   Date& nextAvailableDate)
      throw (CORBA::SystemException,
             FrontOffice::InvalidDate);

virtual Places* listAvailablePlaces
                                  (const char* when)
      throw (CORBA::SystemException,
             FrontOffice::InvalidDate);

virtual Price getPrice
                                  (const Place& chosenPlace,
                                   const char* when)
      throw (CORBA::SystemException,
             FrontOffice::NoSuchPlace,
             FrontOffice::InvalidDate);

virtual Booking_ptr makeBooking
                                  (const Places& chosenPlace,
                                   const char* when,
                                   const CreditCard& payment)
      throw (CORBA::SystemException,
             FrontOffice::NoSuchPlace,
             FrontOffice::PlaceAlreadyBooked,
             FrontOffice::InvalidCreditCard,
             FrontOffice::InvalidDate);

virtual GroupBooking_ptr makeGroupBooking
                                  (const Places& chosenPlaces,
                                   const char* when,
                                   const CreditCard& payment,
```

```
                                    const char* organizer,
                                    const char* groupName)
        throw (CORBA::SystemException,
              FrontOffice::NoSuchPlace,
              FrontOffice::PlaceAlreadyBooked,
              FrontOffice::InvalidCreditCard,
              FrontOffice::InvalidDate,
              FrontOffice::GroupTooSmall);

    // Could add other public or private non-IDL functions.
};
```

Classes `FrontOffice_i` and `Booking_i` redefine each of the functions inherited from their respective BOAImpl classes; they may add constructors, destructors, and member variables. Other public member functions can be added, and these will be available to the server (but of course not to the client, since they were not defined in IDL).

6.4.2 Outline of the cinema implementation (BOAImpl approach)

This subsection shows an outline of the implementation of each of the member functions of classes `FrontOffice_i` and `Booking_i`. Throughout this code, C++ comments of the form `/* some comment */` are used whenever a real expression has been removed to keep the code simple.

`FrontOffice_i::FrontOffice_i()`

```
FrontOffice_i:: FrontOffice_i
                    (const char* aName,
                     const CORBA::Char lastRow,
                     const CORBA::ULong seatsPerRow,
                     const CORBA::ULong minGroupSize,
                     const CORBA::Char firstExpensiveSeat,
                     const Price priceForCheapSeat,
                     const Price priceForExpensiveSeat,
                     const Price addForNewYear)
    :   FrontOfficeBOAImpl (aName), // Marker (see later).
        m_lastRow (toupper(lastRow)),
        m_seatsPerRow (seatsPerRow),
        m_minGroupSize (minGroupSize),
        m_firstExpensiveSeat (toupper(firstExpensiveSeat)),
        m_priceForCheapSeat (priceForCheapSeat),
        m_priceForExpensiveSeat (priceForExpensiveSeat),
        m_addForNewYear (addForNewYear)
{
    m_name = CORBA::string_dup (aName);
}
```

FrontOffice_i::~FrontOffice_i()

```
FrontOffice_i::  ~FrontOffice_i ()
{}
```

FrontOffice_i::name()

```
char* FrontOffice_i::  name ()
  throw (CORBA::SystemException)
{
     return CORBA::string_dup (m_name);
}
```

FrontOffice_i::lastRow()

```
char FrontOffice_i::  lastRow ()
  throw (CORBA::SystemException)
{
  return  m_lastRow;
}
```

FrontOffice_i::seatsPerRow()

```
long FrontOffice_i::  seatsPerRow ()
  throw (CORBA::SystemException)
{
  return m_seatsPerRow;
}
```

FrontOffice_i::checkIfOpen()

```
CORBA::Boolean FrontOffice_i :: checkIfOpen
                                           (const char* when,
                                            Date& nextAvailableDate)
     throw (CORBA::SystemException, FrontOffice::InvalidDate)
{
     // Check if the date is valid. Code not shown here.

     if ( /* the cinema is open on that day */ ) {
           nextAvailableDate = CORBA::string_dup("");
           return 1;
     }
     else {
           nextAvailableDate = CORBA::string_dup( /* some date */);
           return 0;
     }
}
```

FrontOffice_i::listAvailablePlaces()

```
Places* FrontOffice_i:: listAvailablePlaces (const char* when)
           throw (CORBA::SystemException,
                  FrontOffice::InvalidDate)
{
```

```
    // Check if the Cinema is open on Date. Not shown here.

    int rows  = lastRow ()-'A'+1;
    int seats = seatsPerRow ();
    Places* available = new Places (rows*seats);
    available->length(rows*seats);
    // Find the places that are still available on the
    // specified date. Code not shown here.
    // (Enter each one into available using operator[].)
    available->length( /* actual number of places */ );

  return available;
}
```

In `FrontOffice_i::listAvailablePlaces()`, the length of the sequence `available` is initially set to be the theoretical maximum required, that is, the product of the number of rows by the number of seats. Once the correct number of places has been found, the length of the sequence can be changed. This approach means that we need not be concerned with the possible inefficiency of repeatedly increasing the buffer size of the sequence within the loop.

FrontOffice_i::getPrice()

```
Price FrontOffice_i:: getPrice (const Place& chosenPlace,
                                const Date   when)
        throw (CORBA::SystemException,
               FrontOffice::NoSuchPlace,
               FrontOffice::InvalidDate)
{
    // Code to check if the date and place are both
    // valid. Not shown here.

    // Nobody wants to sit in the first few rows...
    Price p;
    p = ((toupper(chosenPlace.row) < m_firstExpensiveSeat)
                    ? m_priceForCheapSeat :
                      m_priceForExpensiveSeat);

    if ( /* the date is 1st January */ )
        // New Year's Day movies are more expensive...
        p += m_addForNewYear;

    return p;
}
```

FrontOffice_i::makeBooking()

```
Booking* FrontOffice_i:: makeBooking
                                        (const Places& chosenPlaces,
                                         const char* when,
                                         const CreditCard& payment)
```

```
        throw (CORBA::SystemException,
               FrontOffice::InvalidDate,
               FrontOffice::InvalidCreditCard,
               FrontOffice::PlaceAlreadyBooked,
               FrontOffice::NoSuchPlace)
{
    // Code to check that the date and all of the places are
    // valid. Not shown here.

    // Check that none of the places in chosenPlaces has already
    // been booked for the date when. Code not shown here.

    // Update the record of what places have been booked.
    // Code not shown here.

    // Finally, make the booking:
    Booking_ptr newBooking = new Booking_i (
                                     this, chosenPlaces, when);

    Booking::_duplicate(newBooking);
    return newBooking;
}
```

The new `Booking` object has a reference count of one when it is created. The call to `Booking::_duplicate()` increases this to two; and it is decremented to one because a reference to it is returned from the operation.

Booking_i::Booking_i()

```
Booking_i::  Booking_i
                 (FrontOffice_i* office,
                  const Places& where,
                  const char* when)
    : m_office (office)
{
    m_seats = new Places(where);
    m_when = CORBA::string_dup(when);
}
```

Booking_i::~Booking_i()

```
Booking_i::  ~Booking_i ()
{}
```

Booking_i::when()

```
Date Booking_i::  when ()
     throw (CORBA::SystemException)
{
     return CORBA::string_dup(m_when);
}
```

Booking_i::seats()

```
Places* Booking_i::  seats ()
     throw (CORBA::SystemException)
{
     return new Places(*m_seats); // Make a copy and return it.
}
```

Booking_i::cancel()

```
void Booking_i:: cancel()
     throw (CORBA::SystemException)
{
     // Communicate with the FrontOffice (using m_office)
     // and request it to remove the booking from its
     // data structures.
}
```

6.4.3 The TIE approach

Using the TIE approach, an implementation class does not have to inherit from any particular base class. Instead, we indicate that a class implements a specific IDL interface by using the `DEF_TIE` macro. A version of this macro is available for each interface. This has the general form:

```
DEF_TIE_<InterfaceName>( <C++ implementation class name> )
```

The macro takes one parameter – the name of a C++ class which implements this interface:

```
// C++
class Booking_i {
     . . .  // As in Section 6.4.2.
};
// Indicate that class Booking_i implements interface Booking:
DEF_TIE_Booking(Booking_i)
// We now have a class TIE_Booking(Booking_i).


class FrontOffice_i {
     . . .  // As Section 6.4.2.
};
// Indicate that class FrontOffice_i implements
// interface FrontOffice:
DEF_TIE_FrontOffice(FrontOffice_i)
// We now have a class TIE_FrontOffice(FrontOffice_i).
```

The `TIE_Booking(Booking_i)` construct is a preprocessor macro call that expands to the name of a C++ class which represents the relationship between the `Booking`

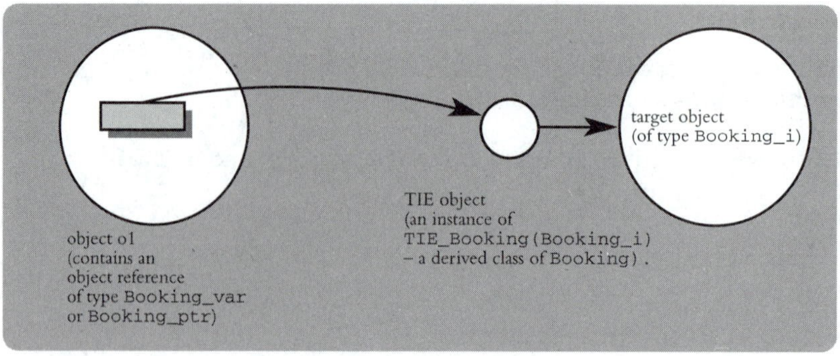

Figure 6.3 *A TIE object is used as a local intermediary.*

and `Booking_i` classes. This class is defined by the `DEF_TIE_Booking(Booking_i)` macro call, and it has a constructor which takes a pointer to a `Booking_i` object as a parameter.

Figure 6.3 shows a TIE object – an instance of `TIE_Booking(Booking_i)`. Object `o1` has an object reference of type `Booking_ptr`, which is a reference to a `TIE` object. The `TIE` object contains a pointer of type `Booking_i*` to the target object. Any invocation on the TIE object will be passed (*delegated*) by it to the real target object.

Figure 6.4 shows the class hierarchy for interface `Booking`, which has been implemented by a C++ class `Booking_i`. It shows that the `TIE` class, `TIE_Booking(Booking_i)`, is a derived class of the C++ class `Booking`.

Note that the TIE approach gives a *complete* separation of the class hierarchies for the C++ classes generated from the IDL interfaces and the class hierarchies of the C++ classes that are used to implement the IDL interfaces.

Consider an IDL operation that returns a reference to a `Booking` object; for example, `FrontOffice::makeBooking()`. In the generated C++ class, this is translated into a function returning a `Booking_ptr` (in Orbix, a `typedef` for `Booking*`). However, using the TIE approach, the actual object to which a reference is to be returned would be of type `Booking_i` – which is not a derived class of `Booking` (see Figure 6.4). Therefore, the server should create an object of type `TIE_Booking(Booking_i)`. This `TIE` object would reference the `Booking_i` object, and a reference to the `TIE` object should be returned by the function. This is legal because, as explained earlier, the class `TIE_Booking(Booking_i)` is a derived class of class `Booking`. All invocations on the TIE object are automatically forwarded by it to the associated `Booking_i` object.

6.4.4 An example of using the TIE approach

`FrontOffice_i::makeBooking()` creates a `Booking` object and must therefore be coded differently to the way shown in Section 6.4.2:

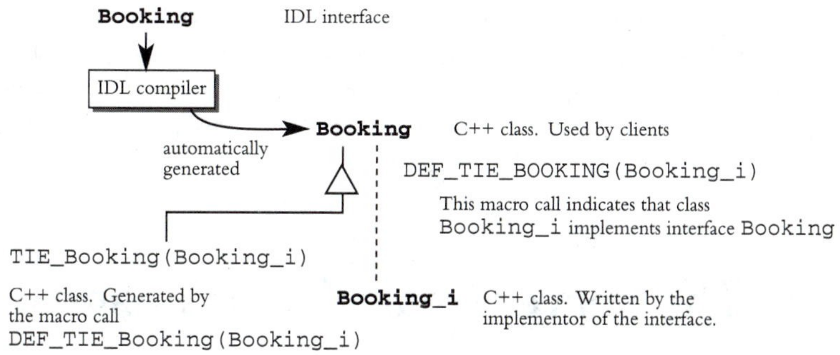

Figure 6.4 *Relationships between interface, implementation class and TIE class.*

```
Booking* FrontOffice_i:: makeBooking
                              (const Places& chosenPlaces,
                               const char* when,
                               const CreditCard& payment)
        throw (CORBA::SystemException,
              FrontOffice::InvalidDate,
              FrontOffice::InvalidCreditCard,
              FrontOffice::PlaceAlreadyBooked,
              FrontOffice::NoSuchPlace)
{
    // Code to check that the date and all of the places are
    // valid. Not shown here.

    // Check that none of the places in chosenPlaces has already
    // been booked for the date when. Code not shown here.

    // Update the record of what places have been booked.
    // Code not shown here.

    // Finally, make the booking:
    Booking_i* p = new Booking_i ( this, chosenPlaces, when );
    Booking_ptr newBooking = new TIE_Booking(Booking_i)(p);
    Booking::_duplicate(newBooking);

    return newBooking;
}
```

The variable `newBooking` is initialized to reference a `TIE` object, which points in turn to the new `Booking_i` object. The code:

```
Booking_ptr newBooking = new TIE_Booking(Booking_i) (p);
```

has the form:

```
Booking_ptr newBooking = new CLASSNAME (POINTER);
```

Note that, by default, the object that a TIE object points to *must* be dynamically allocated (using the C++ operator `new`). This is because by default, when a TIE object is destroyed, it deletes the object that it points to (normally this is the desired behavior; however, a programmer may control this behavior where necessary), and it would be an error if that object were not dynamically allocated.

6.5 The server: main function and object creation

This section shows the main function of the `FrontOfficeSrv` server, using both the BOAImpl and the TIE approaches. Both examples start by creating a single `FrontOffice` object (and other objects are created later; in particular, `Booking` objects are created in `FrontOffice::makeBooking()`).

6.5.1 The BOAImpl approach

The main function for the server shows the creation of a `FrontOffice` object. It takes the following form:

```
// C++
#include "front.hh"
#include <iostream.h>

main() {
      int try {
            // Create a new FrontOffice_i object.
            FrontOffice_var foVar =
                        new FrontOffice_i ( "Savoy", 'H', 12, 5,
                                            'E', 3, 5, 10);
            // Wait for incoming requests.
            CORBA::Orbix.impl_is_ready();†
      }
      catch (CORBA::SystemException& se) {
            cerr << "Unexpected exception:" << endl
                 << &se;
            exit(-1);
      }
      // Resume here when Orbix shuts us down.
      cout << "FrontOfficeSrv shutting down...." << endl;
}
```

† See Section 6.5.3.

The code initializes a `FrontOffice_var` object reference to refer to a new `FrontOffice_i` object.

Having created a `FrontOffice` object, the server calls `impl_is_ready()` on the `CORBA::Orbix` object to indicate that it has completed initialization and is ready to receive operation requests on its objects.

6.5.2 The TIE approach

The implementation of the server main function is similar in the TIE approach. The difference is that the server creates a `TIE` object as well as a `FrontOffice_i` object:

```
// C++
#include "front.hh"
#include <iostream.h>

main() {
      int try {
            // Create a new FrontOffice_i object.
            FrontOffice_i* p =
                        new FrontOffice_i ( "Savoy", 'H', 12, 5,
                                            'E', 3, 5, 10);
            FrontOffice_var foVar =
                        new TIE_FrontOffice(FrontOffice_i) (p);

            // Wait for incoming requests.
            CORBA::Orbix.impl_is_ready();†
      }
      catch (CORBA::SystemException& se) {
            cerr <<"Unexpected exeception:" << endl
                 << se;
            exit(-1);
      }

      // Resume here when Orbix shuts us down.
      cout << "FrontOffice shutting down...." << endl;
}
```

The code initializes a `FrontOffice_var` object reference with a pointer to a new `TIE` object.

6.5.3 Initialization of the ORB

As well as issuing and receiving operation calls, CORBA clients and servers need to communicate with the ORB itself – to control the ORB and to request it to carry

† See Section 6.5.3.

out actions. For example, the code in the previous two subsections (Sections 6.5.1 and 6.5.2) shows how the `impl_is_ready()` function can be called using the `CORBA::Orbix` variable.

The CORBA standard defines how a client or server can obtain a reference to the ORB so that they can communicate with it. In Orbix, this call will normally be as follows:

```
CORBA::ORB_ptr orb = CORBA::ORB_init(argc,argv,"Orbix");
```

Functions such as `object_to_string()` can then be called using the `orb` pointer defined above.

Servers should carry out a further step, to obtain a reference to the Object Adapter, and in particular to the Basic Object Adapter (BOA):

```
CORBA::BOA_ptr boa = orb->BOA_init(argc,argv,"Orbix_BOA");
```

Functions such as `impl_is_ready()` are then called using the `boa` pointer defined above.

For simplicity, we will continue to write code such as

```
CORBA::Orbix.impl_is_ready( /* . . . . */ );
```

Nevertheless use of `ORB_init()` and `BOA_init()` is recommended for portability.

6.5.4 impl_is_ready()

A server is normally coded so that it initializes itself and creates an initial set of objects. It then calls `CORBA::Orbix.impl_is_ready()` to indicate that it has completed its initialization and is ready to receive operation requests on its objects. `CORBA::Orbix` is a static object (of class `CORBA::BOA` in the server, and `CORBA::ORB` in the client), which is used to communicate directly with Orbix, to determine or change its settings.

The `impl_is_ready()` function normally does not return immediately: it blocks the server until an event occurs, handles the event, and re-blocks the server to await another event. A server must call `impl_is_ready()`; a client must not call it.

The function `impl_is_ready()` is declared as follows:

```
// C++
// In class CORBA::BOA.
void impl_is_ready(
      const char* server_name = "",
      CORBA::ULong timeOut = CORBA::ORB::DEFAULT_TIMEOUT,
      CORBA::Environment& = CORBA::default_environment);
```

The `CORBA::Environment` parameter is used for error handling when the C++ compiler does not support exception handling. The `server_name` parameter is the name of the server calling `impl_is_ready()`, as given to the `putit` command (see Section 6.6).

✚ When a server is launched by Orbix, the server name will already be known to Orbix and therefore does not need to be passed to `impl_is_ready()` (but, if it is passed, it must be correct). However, when a server is launched manually or externally to Orbix, the server name must be communicated to Orbix, and one way to do this is as the first parameter to `impl_is_ready()`. To allow a server to be launched either automatically or manually, it is recommended, therefore, that the `server_name` parameter be specified. ✚

The `impl_is_ready()` function returns only when a timeout occurs or an exception occurs while waiting for or processing an event. The `timeout` parameter indicates the number of milliseconds to wait between events: a timeout will occur if Orbix has to wait longer than the specified timeout for the next event. A timeout of zero indicates that `impl_is_ready()` should timeout and return immediately *without* checking if there is any pending event. A timeout does not cause `impl_is_ready()` to raise an exception.

Note that a server can timeout either because it has no clients for the timeout duration, or because none of its clients uses it for that period. The system can also be instructed to make the timeout active only when the server has no current clients – that is, the server should remain running as long as there are current clients.

The default timeout can be passed explicitly as `CORBA::ORB.DEFAULT_TIMEOUT`. An infinite timeout can be specified by passing `CORBA::ORB.INFINITE_TIMEOUT`.

6.5.5 Construction and markers

If we wanted clients to be able to find an individual `FrontOffice` object given a name for it, we could do one, or both, of the following:

- Register the `FrontOffice` with the Naming Service, and allow the client to know the chosen name. The client can then resolve that name to obtain a reference to the required `FrontOffice`. Section 7.3 (p.162) shows how to do this.
- The name of an Orbix object contains its server's name, its interface, and a unique name (called the **marker**; the CORBA standard refers to this part of an object's name as the **reference data**) within that server and interface. A meaningful marker name can be assigned to each `FrontOffice` object, and then clients can specify one of these marker names when calling the `FrontOffice::_bind()` function. Section 7.1 (p.159) shows how to do this. Note that the details of assigning markers are Orbix specific. The issues need not concern us here because we have only one `FrontOffice` object.

6.6 Registration, activation, and the daemon

The last step in developing and installing our cinema application is to register the `FrontOfficeSrv` server. The CORBA Implementation Repository records each server's name and executable code file name. Registration has the advantage that it allows the Orbix daemon (`orbixd`) to launch a server that is not running when one of its objects is used.

The Implementation Repository maintains its data in Implementation Repository entries. Every node in a network which is to run servers must have access to an Implementation Repository, but repositories can be shared using a network file system.

Registration

Registration of a server can be achieved by the `putit` shell command, which takes the following simplified form:

```
$ putit serverName fullPathName [command-line-args-for-server]
```

For example, our `FrontOfficeSrv` server might be registered as follows:

```
$ putit FrontOfficeSrv /usr/users/joe/FrontOfficeExec
```

The executable file `/usr/users/joe/FrontOfficeExec` will then be registered as the implementation code of the server called `FrontOfficeSrv` at the current host. The `putit` command does not execute the indicated file: this can be executed explicitly from the shell (or otherwise), or it will be launched automatically by Orbix in response to an incoming operation invocation. A given executable file can be used by any number of servers.

Further information on the `putit` command is given in Chapter 8.

Activation

The activation modes defined by CORBA are explained in Section 8.2 (p.178).

Server environment

When a server is launched by the daemon, its working directory, environment variables, and standard file descriptors become those of the daemon. On UNIX, the user-id and group-id of an automatically launched server will be those of the daemon (unless this is `root`).

6.7 Debugging

The client and server code can be debugged using the normal C++ debugger. For example, breakpoints can be set at the start of some member functions that implement operations and attributes.

During program development it is normally better to start servers manually (in CORBA terms, in the **persistent activation mode**). This allows you to see the output of each server in a separate window. If a server is activated by the daemon, then the server will output its diagnostics to the daemon's windows, which may be cluttered with other diagnostics. Automatic activation can be used for servers that have been debugged.

6.8 Execution trace

Let us now consider the events that occur as our `FrontOfficeSrv` server and our client are run. The TIE approach will be used to show the initial trace, and then the BOAImpl approach will be discussed.

First a server with name '`FrontOfficeSrv`' is registered using the `putit` command as follows:

```
$ putit FrontOfficeSrv /usr/users/joe/FrontOfficeExec
```

When an invocation arrives from a client, Orbix will launch the server using the specified executable file (`/usr/users/joe/FrontOfficeExec`). This process creates a new `TIE` object (of class `TIE_FrontOffice(FrontOffice_i)`) for an object of class `FrontOffice_i`, and waits on `CORBA::Orbix.impl_is_ready()`:

```
// C++
main() {
      int try {
            FrontOffice_i* p =
                        new FrontOffice_i ( "Savoy", 'H', 12, 5,
                                            'E', 3, 5, 10);
            FrontOffice_var foVar =
                              new TIE_FrontOffice(FrontOffice_i) (p);

            // Wait for incoming requests.
            CORBA::Orbix.impl_is_ready();
      }
      // Catch clauses not shown here.
}
```

The state of the server, at the time of the `impl_is_ready()` call, is shown in

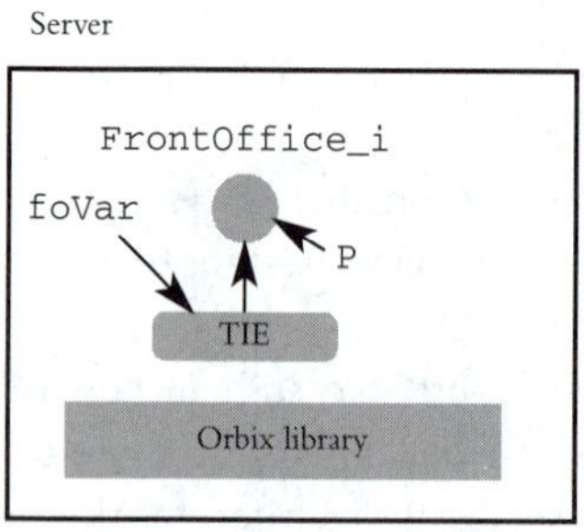

Figure 6.5 *Server launched.*

Figure 6.5. The server is now quiescent, waiting for incoming requests. If `impl_is_ready()` timesout, the server will terminate.

Now let us consider the client: it first finds a `FrontOffice` object, using `_bind()` or the Naming Service; for example:

```
// C++
main() {
      int try {
            // Bind to any FrontOffice object in FrontOfficeSrv
            // server. (Alternatively, the Naming Service could
            // be used.)
            FrontOffice_var cinema =
                              FrontOffice::_bind(":FrontOfficeSrv");
      }
      . . . . .
}
```

No object name (marker) is specified, so Orbix will choose any `FrontOffice` object within the chosen server (`FrontOfficeSrv`). When the `FrontOffice::_bind()` call is made, Orbix will launch an appropriate process (if it is not already running).

We will assume that the `FrontOffice::_bind()` call will bind to our newly created `TIE_FrontOffice(FrontOffice_i)` object. The result of the binding is an automatically generated proxy object in the client, which acts as a 'stand-in' for the remote `FrontOffice` object in the server. The object reference `cinema` within the client is now a **remote object reference**, as shown in Figure 6.6.

The client programmer will not be aware of the TIE object (nevertheless, all remote operation invocations on our `FrontOffice_i` object will go via the TIE).

The client program now proceeds by asking the `FrontOffice` to creating a new `Booking`:

```
// C++
// Obtain a new FrontOffice Booking.
Booking_var myBooking;
try {
```

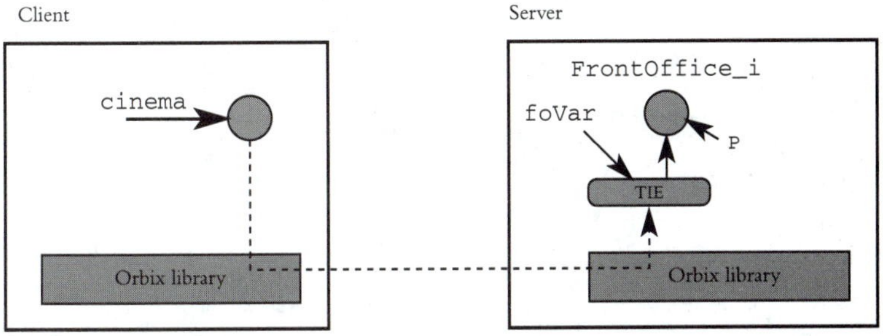

Figure 6.6 *Client binds to server, TIE approach.*

```
    myBooking = cinema->makeBooking( /* . . . . */ );
}
```

When the `cinema->makeBooking()` call is made, the function `FrontOffice_i::makeBooking()` is called (via the `TIE`) within the server. This generates a new `Booking_i` object and associated `TIE` object. Finally, `makeBooking()` returns the `Booking` reference (in C++, a pointer to the `TIE`) back to the client (`makeBooking()` calls `Booking::_duplicate()` because returning the object reference will decrement the reference count of the `Booking`).

At the client side, a new proxy will be created for the `Booking` object, and this will be referenced by the `myBooking` variable; see Figure 6.7. The CORBA specification uses the term **stub** to refer to the client-side code that accepts local requests and transmits them to the server; in Orbix, the proxy executes this code. CORBA also uses the term **skeleton** to refer to the code in the server that accepts incoming requests, extracts the parameters, and passes the call to the target object.

Using the BOAImpl approach, the final diagram would be as shown in Figure 6.8.

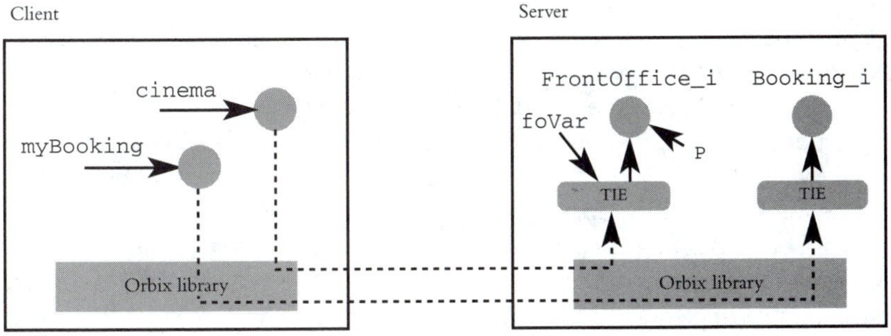

Figure 6.7 *Client creates object, TIE approach.*

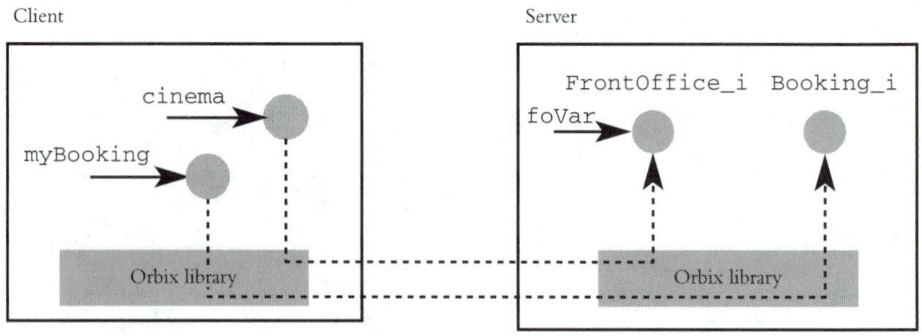

Figure 6.8 *Client creates object, BOAImpl approach.*

6.9 Comparison of the TIE and BOAImpl approaches

This section highlights further ways in which the TIE and BOAImpl approaches can be used to provide implementation classes. It then compares the two approaches.

✚ 6.9.1 Wrapping existing code

CORBA facilitates application integration for both new and existing applications. An application can allow other code to use its services by providing a number of IDL interfaces and making these available to the overall system. This allows new applications to be written by combining the facilities of existing applications. Since the components of the system are objects whose internals are hidden from their clients, these objects can provide the basis for integration with legacy systems. Over time, these legacy systems can be replaced with newer systems which nevertheless provide the same CORBA interfaces.

In some systems, one aspect of this wrapping of existing code is the ability to implement an IDL interface using some existing C++ class. This is discussed in this subsection.

The TIE approach is clear cut in whether or not it supports this. If you are lucky enough that the existing C++ class has *exactly* the correct member functions (each function has exactly the correct name and correct parameter types), then a call to the appropriate `DEF_TIE` macro is all that is required. (The existing code may have other functions that do not correspond to IDL attributes or operations in the IDL interface in question.) It is more likely that the existing C++ code will not have exactly the correct member functions, in which case the TIE approach does not offer any special advantage.

To use the BOAImpl approach for existing code, the programmer may use C++ multiple inheritance to specify the relationship between the generated C++ class and the previously written implementation class. Instances of the derived class are then valid implementations of the IDL interface. Figure 6.9 shows how the BOAImpl approach can be used to allow a pre-existing class, `OldBooking`, to implement an IDL interface. The

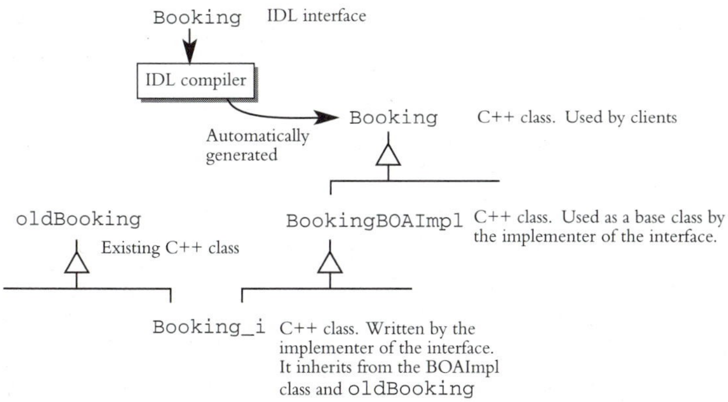

Figure 6.9 *BOAImpl approach to allow an existing class to implement an IDL interface.*

programmer has already implemented the class `oldBooking`, which provides an implementation of some or all of the functions of the IDL interface. To indicate that this class implements the IDL interface, a class `Booking_i` has been defined which inherits from both the BOAImpl class and the class, `oldBooking`, which provides the function implementations. Class `Booking_i` is the class that is said to implement the IDL interface.

This is more difficult to code than the corresponding code for the TIE approach (where a call to the appropriate `DEF_TIE` macro may be all that is required). However, the BOAImpl approach is significantly more flexible in its use of existing code. In particular, the code for class `Booking_i` can manipulate any call that it receives before passing it on to the code for class `oldBooking`. This manipulation can compensate for differences in function names and parameters, and differences in function semantics.

Instead of using multiple inheritance to code `Booking_i` (that is, inheriting from `oldBooking` and `BookingBOAImpl`), `Booking_i` could inherit from just `BookingBOAImpl`, and use delegation to pass the call to an instance of `oldBooking`. That is, each `Booking_i` object could have a private instance of `oldBooking`, to which it passes requests (possibly after doing some manipulation of the parameters, and so on). This form of delegation can also be coded using the TIE approach (the TIE class would remain unchanged, but class `Booking_i` would delegate to `oldBooking`).

6.9.2 Interfaces and implementations

It is straightforward to implement an IDL interface a number of times in the same or different servers, possibly to give different space/time tradeoffs, or simply to cater for different operating systems. It is also possible to provide more than one IDL interface to the same object. This is more straightforward in the TIE approach than in the BOAImpl approach; in the BOAImpl approach it is recommended to combine the multiple IDL interfaces together using IDL multiple inheritance and then to implement the combined interface.

6.9.3 Summary of comparison of the BOAImpl and TIE approaches

This section briefly compares the BOAImpl and TIE approaches to implementing IDL interfaces in C++. Actually, these do not differ greatly in their power, and it is frequently a matter of personal taste which one is preferred. Note also that the TIE and BOAImpl approaches can be mixed without difficulty within the same server. Personally, I prefer the BOAImpl approach.

The TIE approach has a small advantage in that it allows an advanced feature known as 'per-object' filtering to be used (see Section 18.2, p.301). This allows a programmer to specify additional code that is to be executed when an invocation (from the same or a different address space) is made on a particular object. Both the BOAImpl and the TIE approaches allow a programmer to specify additional code that is to be executed when an attribute or operation invocation is made across an address space boundary (using *per-process* filters): from a client–server to a client–server on the same or a different host.

Section 6.9.1 discussed the differences between the BOAImpl and TIE approaches when an existing class must be used. The BOAImpl approach is more flexible, but the TIE approach is easier if the existing class has *exactly* the correct interface.

The TIE approach has a disadvantage if a server deletes the implementation object: the TIE will not be deleted automatically. This can be handled in one of two ways. Firstly, the application could instead delete the TIE, which will in turn, by default, delete the implementation object. Secondly, the implementation object could hold a pointer to its TIE, and its destructor could delete the TIE, but this must be coded by the application programmer. This is one example of the disadvantage of having two objects (the real object and the TIE) instead of just one.

7 Naming and binding

This chapter presents the details of naming and locating objects in a distributed system. These topics were introduced in Chapters 2 and 6. This chapter covers the issues in more detail, and in particular it explains:

- the notion of a **marker**, and how to assign a marker to an object,
- the `_bind()` function,
- the CORBA Naming Service.

The Naming Service is the most important of the ways to name an object.

7.1 Assigning markers to objects

Each object in the system has a unique **object reference**, which includes a name that is unique within its server. We refer to this name as the object's **marker**, and this can be chosen either by the application writer or by Orbix. Naturally, each object's marker must be unique within its server, so that its overall object reference will be unique. For example, if a server creates many `Booking` objects, then it must give each one a unique marker, or rely on Orbix to do this. The details of how markers are assigned and used are Orbix-specific; also note that CORBA uses the term **reference data** for this part of an object reference.

The `_bind()` function takes a marker as a parameter so that a client can specify which particular object in a server it wishes to bind to.

Choosing a marker

Once an object has been created, its marker can be set using the `_marker(const char*)` function; for example:

```
// C++
FrontOffice_i myFrontOffice ( /* . . . . */ ;
myFrontOffice._marker("Savoy");
```

In fact, Orbix assigns a marker to this object when it is created, and then the `_marker(const char*)` function changes this to the one chosen by the application. In many cases, it is more sensible to assign the application-chosen marker to an object when it is being created.

For the BOAImpl approach, this can be done by passing the marker to the constructor of the BOAImpl class, as follows:

```
class FrontOffice_i : public virtual FrontOfficeBOAImpl {
            // State as before.
public:
        // Other details as before, except for the constructor:
        FrontOffice_i (const char* marker, /* . . . . */ );
};

FrontOffice_i::FrontOffice_i(const char *marker, /* . . . . */ )
        : FrontOfficeBOAImpl (marker)
{
        /* code as before */
}
```

Then a `FrontOffice_i` object can be created and named by passing its marker to its constructor:

```
FrontOffice_i myFrontOffice("Savoy", /* . . . . */ );
```

In the TIE approach, the marker can be passed as the second parameter to the TIE macro. Consider the following implementation of interface `FrontOffice`:

```
class FrontOffice_i {
        // Details as before.
};
DEF_TIE_FrontOffice(FrontOffice_i);
```

Then a `FrontOffice` object can be created and assigned an initial marker by passing a string as the second parameter to the TIE macro:

```
FrontOffice_i* p = new FrontOffice_i ( /* . . . . */ );
FrontOffice_var fo = TIE_FrontOffice(FrontOffice_i)(p,"Savoy") ;
```

Determining an object's marker

An object's marker can be determined using the `_marker()` function. For example, if `aPtr` is a reference to any CORBA object, its marker can be output as follows:

```
cout << "The marker of the object is "
          << aPtr->_marker() << endl;
```

✚ Whereas this will work on both the client and server sides, object references are **opaque** to clients: that is, they should not attempt to understand the format of an object reference, or even access the marker it contains. ✚

7.2 Binding to objects

The Orbix `_bind()` function finds a particular object and creates a proxy for it in the client's address space. When an operation is invoked on the proxy, Orbix transmits the request to the target object. The `_bind()` function may be used to specify the exact object required or, by using default parameters, Orbix may be allowed certain degrees of freedom when choosing the object.

The `_bind()` function is presented before the Naming Service so that the benefits of the Naming Service will be clear when they are presented in Section 7.3. Most applications should use the Naming Service in preference, but some will benefit from the simplicity and directness of `_bind()`.

The `_bind()` function is a static member function automatically generated by the IDL compiler for each interface. For interface `FrontOffice`, the full declaration of `_bind()` is:

```
// C++
static FrontOffice_ptr _bind(const char* markerServer,
                             const char* host,
                             const CORBA::Context&)
      throw (CORBA::SystemException);
```

A number of overloaded versions of this function are generated, and, together with default parameters, this allows a great deal of flexibility in what parameters are passed.

A typical use of `_bind()` is:

```
try {
      FrontOffice_var p =
            FrontOffice::_bind("Savoy:FrontOfficeSrv",
                               "host2");
}
// Catch any exceptions here.
```

This call searches for an object with the `FrontOffice` interface, with marker `"Savoy"` in server `FrontOfficeSrv` on host `host2`.

`FrontOfficeSrv` is the name of a server, registered with the `putit` command. It is not necessarily the name of a class or an interface (although a programmer is free to make a server name the same as that of a class or interface, it is, nevertheless, clearer to make the server name something different from the name of any IDL interface).

If the `FrontOffice` on host `host2` does not contain an object with interface `FrontOffice` and marker `"Savoy"`, then Orbix will return an exception to the caller of `_bind()`. (In fact, Orbix will first call any **loaders** in the server's address space; see Chapter 20.)

Specifying a host name to `_bind()` has the strong disadvantage that the locations of objects are not transparent to clients, and therefore the host name is commonly left blank (the next subsection discusses how this is handled). However, some applications, such as management systems, do need to specify host names, and in these cases the low-level nature of `_bind()` is an advantage.

✚ Defaults for some parameters

Some of the parameters to `_bind()` can be defaulted. In particular, the caller can decide to leave the marker and/or host name blank.

The marker can be defaulted as follows:

```
FrontOffice_var p =
        FrontOffice::_bind(":FrontOfficeSrv", "host2");
```

This searches for any object with the `FrontOffice` interface in server `FrontOfficeSrv` on host `host2`.

The `host` parameter to `_bind()` specifies the internet host name or the internet address of a node on which to find the object. An internet address is a string of the form `xxx.xxx.xxx.xxx`, where `x` is a decimal digit.

If, as is common, the host name is defaulted, Orbix will pass the search for the server to the **locator**. The default locator uses configuration files to specify a set of machines that each server can be found at, and it can use these to locate a server at the time that `_bind()` is called. An application can replace the locator with one that uses a different form of configuration file, or uses another mechanism, such as broadcasting, to locate servers.

Although the server name can also be defaulted (it defaults to the IDL interface name), this is not recommended. ✚

7.3 The CORBA naming service

The CORBAservices extend the core CORBA specification with a set of optional utilities that are useful in many applications. The Naming Service is one of the simplest and most useful of these. Its role is to allow a name to be **bound** to (associated with) an object and to allow that object to be found subsequently by **resolving** that name within the Naming Service.

A server that holds an object reference can register it with the Naming Service, giving it a name that can be used by other components of the system subsequently to find the object. The Naming Service has a number of interfaces defined in IDL that allow clients and servers to use its facilities.

As we will see, most applications will find it easier to use the Naming Service rather than the Orbix `_bind()` function call in order to find the objects they need to use. However, as is the case for `_bind()`, programmers are strongly encouraged to pass object references as parameters and return values. In this way, programs can find some initial objects using the Naming Service or `_bind()`, and they can find the others as part of their normal interaction with other objects.

One of the advantages of the Naming Service is that the names it associates with objects are independent of any properties of the objects they refer to: in particular, a name is independent of an object's interface, server, or host name. This is not the case with `_bind()`, in which the server name must be specified (or it defaults to the interface name) and the host name can optionally be specified.

The Orbix `_bind()` function, therefore, provides a more primitive mechanism for obtaining an object reference because the caller must know the marker name – unless any object of the correct interface will suffice – and the server name. The caller must also know the host name if the locator has not been configured. In contrast, finding an object using the Naming Service simply requires the caller to know the name that has been bound to the object. Successfully resolving a name within the Naming Service gives an object reference to the required object, and although it is possible to find the marker, server, and host names of the returned object reference, it is not compliant to do so.

There are two ways in which an application can use the Naming Service. Firstly, the Naming Service can be used to name a significant number of the objects in the system in much the same way that all files in a system are named by a filing system. Alternatively, some important objects in each service can be named, and these objects can act as entry points for the other objects. The Naming Service does not dictate which of these two models is used.

Roadmap

The remainder of this chapter describes the features of the Naming Service specification, including the following:

- Section 7.3.1 introduces some terminology and the IDL module in which all of the Naming Services's IDL definitions are contained.
- Section 7.3.2 describes the format of names within the Naming Service.

- Section 7.3.3 introduces the interfaces `NamingContext` and `BindingIterator`. The `NamingContext` interface is central to the Naming Service because it defines the operations to bind and resolve names.
- Section 7.3.4 shows how to list the contents of a naming context.
- Section 7.3.5 describes the exceptions that can be raised by the operations introduced in Section 7.3.3.
- Section 7.3.6 gives more details about the `BindingIterator` interface described in Section 7.3.3.

Section 7.4 shows some examples of using the Naming Service.

7.3.1 Terminology and the `CosNaming` module

The Naming Service maintains a 'database' of **bindings** between names and object references. A binding is an association between a name and an object reference. The Naming Service provides operations to **resolve** a name, and operations to create new bindings, delete existing bindings, and to list the bound names.

The interfaces that are provided by the Naming Service are defined within the IDL module `CosNaming`:

```
// IDL
module CosNaming {
      /* . . . . */
};
```

7.3.2 Format of names within the Naming Service

A name is always resolved within a given **naming context** (which is similar to a directory or folder in a file system). The naming context objects in the system are organized into a naming graph, which may form a naming hierarchy, much like that of a filing system. This gives rise to the notion of a compound name. The first component of a compound name gives the name of a `NamingContext`, in which the second name in the compound name is looked up. This process continues until the last component of the compound name has been reached.

The notion of a compound name is so common that it has appeared in slightly different forms in different systems. For example, in UNIX, compound names take the form `/aaa/bbb/ccc`; in Windows they take the form `c:\aaa\bbb\ccc`.

A compound name in the Naming Service takes a more abstract form: an IDL sequence of name components. There is, therefore, no concrete form such as `/aaa/bbb/ccc` or `c:\aaa\bbb\ccc`. Instead, the choice of concrete forms has been avoided by making a compound name an IDL sequence of name components. (However, for convenience, we will sometimes use the notation `aaa.bbb.ccc` to represent examples of compound names.)

There is one other difference between Naming Service names and common names such as `/aaa/bbb/ccc` or `c:\aaa\bbb\ccc`. The name components (that make up a sequence to form a name) are not simple strings; instead, a name component is defined as a struct, `NameComponent`, that holds two strings:

```
// IDL
typedef string  Istring; // now wstring

struct NameComponent {
      Istring id;
      Istring kind;
};
```

The most important member is `id`, which is the real name component; the member `kind` is not interpreted in any way by the Naming Service. Instead, the `kind` member can be used by the application layer in any number of ways. For example, it may be used to distinguish whether the `id` member should be interpreted as a disk name or a directory/folder name. Alternatively, it could be used to describe the type of the object being referred to. Remember, however, that the Naming Service does not interpret the `kind` member.

The type `Istring` is a place holder for a future IDL internationalized string which may be defined by the OMG.

A name is defined as a sequence of name components:

```
typedef sequence<NameComponent> Name;
```

Figure 7.1 shows an example name aaa.bbb.ccc, with the `kind` member being empty in all cases.

A `Name` with no components (that is, a name of length zero) is illegal.

7.3.3 The `NamingContext` interface

The IDL interface `NamingContext` defines the core of the Naming Service:

`id`	**aaa**	**bbb**	**ccc**
`kind`	**nil**	**nil**	**nil**

Figure 7.1 *Example name: aaa.bbb.ccc.*

```
// In module CosNaming.
interface NamingContext {
     // Details shown in this section.
};
```

A `NamingContext` object acts much like a directory in a filing system. However, there is no root `NamingContext` object; instead, there is a call on the ORB, which returns a default `NamingContext` object. By passing the string "NameService" to the following C++ function on the ORB (the `CORBA::Orbix` object), an application can obtain a reference to its default naming context:

```
Object_ptr resolve_initial_references (const char* identifier)
```

The result must be narrowed (using `CosNaming::NamingContext::_narrow()`) to obtain a reference to the naming context.

The `NamingContext` interface provides operations to:

- Bind a name to an object reference.
- Resolve a name to find an object reference.
- Unbind a name, to remove a binding.
- List the names within a naming context.

These operations are described in the following subsections. Section 7.3.5 (p.170) describes the exceptions that may be raised by operations defined within interface `NamingContext`.

Resolving names

Name resolution is the process of looking up a name to obtain an object reference.

resolve()

```
Object resolve(in Name n)
          raises ( NotFound, CannotProceed, InvalidName );
```

The `resolve()` operation returns the object reference bound to the specified name, relative to the target naming context (that is, the one that the operation is invoked on). The first component of the specified name is resolved in the target naming context.

Note that the return type is IDL object `Object`, which translates to type `CORBA::Object_ptr` in C++. The result must therefore be narrowed (for example, using `FrontOffice::_narrow()`) before it can be properly used by an application.

Binding

bind()

```
void bind(in Name n,  in Object o)
          raises ( NotFound, CannotProceed,
                   InvalidName, AlreadyBound );
```

The `bind()` operation creates a binding (relative to the target naming context) between a name and an object.

If the name passed to `bind()` is a compound name with more than one component then all except the last name component are used to find the naming context to which to add the binding; these naming contexts must already exist. The last name component names the specified object name in the desired naming context.

The `bind()` operation raises an exception if the specified name is already bound within the final naming context.

bind_context()

```
void bind_context(in Name n,
                  in NamingContext nc)
          raises ( NotFound, CannotProceed,
                   InvalidName, AlreadyBound );
```

The `bind_context()` operation creates a binding (relative to the target naming context) between a name and a specified naming context (the parameter `nc`). Note that this new binding may be used in any subsequent name resolutions: that is the entries in naming context `nc` can be resolved using compound names.

✚ All but the final naming context specified in parameter `n` must already exist. This operation raises an exception if the name specified by `n` is already in use. ✚

Note that the naming graph built using `bind_context()` is not restricted to being a tree: it can be a general naming graph in which any naming context can appear in any other.

✚ Because interface `NamingContext` is a derived interface of interface `Object`, it is also possible to create a binding between a name and a naming context using `bind()`. That is, an object reference to an object of type `NamingContext` can be passed as the second parameter to `bind()`. Note, however, that the resulting binding cannot be used as part of a compound name: only bindings created with `bind_context()` or `rebind_context()` (see later) can be used as part of a compound name. ✚

rebind()

```
void rebind(in Name n,  in Object o)
           raises ( NotFound, CannotProceed, InvalidName );
```

The `rebind()` operation creates a binding between a name that is already bound in the context and an object. The previous name is unbound and the new binding is made in its place. As is the case with `bind()`, all but the last component of a compound name must name an existing `NamingContext`.

rebind_context()

```
void rebind_context(in Name n,
                    in NamingContext nc)
           raises ( NotFound, CannotProceed, InvalidName );
```

The `rebind_context()` operation creates a binding between a name that is already bound in the context and a naming context, `nc`. The previous name is unbound and the new binding is made in its place. As is the case for `bind_context()`, all but the last component of a compound name must name an existing `NamingContext`.

Deleting a binding

unbind()

```
void unbind(in Name n)
           raises ( NotFound, CannotProceed, InvalidName );
```

The operation `unbind()` removes the binding between the specified name and the object it resolved to.

Creating naming contexts

Two operations are provided to create naming contexts.

new_context()

```
NamingContext new_context()
```

The operation `new_context()` creates a new naming context, without entering it into the naming graph (that is, without binding it to any name). The returned naming context can subsequently be entered into the naming graph using `bind_context()` or `rebind_context()`.

bind_new_context()

```
NamingContext bind_new_context(in Name n)
      raises ( NotFound, CannotProceed,
               InvalidName, AlreadyBound);
```

The operation `bind_new_context()` creates a new naming context and binds it using the specified name, relative to the target naming context. The operation `bind_new_context()` is equivalent to calling `new_context()` followed by `bind_context()`.

Deleting contexts

`destroy()`

```
void destroy()
     raises (NotEmpty);
```

The operation `destroy()` deletes the naming context on which it is invoked. The target naming context must be empty; that is, it must contain no bindings.

7.3.4 Listing a naming context

Before describing the `list()` operation on a `NamingContext`, the different types of bindings must be explained.

Types of bindings

The operations `bind()`, `rebind()`, `bind_context()`, and `rebind_context()` create bindings, but it can be seen from the previous sections that the first two create different forms of binding than the latter two. The functions `bind()` and `rebind()` allow a name to be bound to any object, while `bind_context()` and `rebind_context()` are used to construct the naming network supported by the Naming Service.

The two binding types are captured by the following IDL types:

```
// In IDL module CosNaming:

enum BindingType { nobject, ncontext };

struct Binding {
     Name binding_name;
     BindingType binding_type;
};
```

When browsing a network of naming contexts, an application can list a `NamingContext` and determine the type of each binding in it.

The operations `bind_context()`, and `bind_new_contexts` and `rebind_context()` create bindings of type `ncontext`; the operations `bind()` and `rebind()` create bindings of type `nobject`.

The important difference is that a binding of type `nobject` cannot be used in a compound name, except as the last element in that name. To draw from familiarity with a filing system, readers can view bindings of type `ncontext` as naming 'directories,' while those of type `nobject` name 'files.'

Listing names

```
// In IDL module CosNaming:

typedef sequence<Binding> BindingList;

interface BindingIterator;

interface NamingContext {
      /* rest not shown here */
      void list(in unsigned long how_many,†
                out BindingList bl,
                out BindingIterator bi);
};
```

`list()`

The operation `list()` obtains a list of the name bindings in the target naming context.

The parameter `how_many` specifies the maximum number of bindings that should be returned in the `BindingList` parameter `bl`. The `BindingList` parameter is a sequence of `Binding` structs, where each `Binding` indicates the name and type of the binding – the type indicates whether the name is that of an object or whether it is a name of a node in the naming graph which participates in name resolution.

If the naming context contains more than the requested number (`how_many`) of bindings, the `list()` operation returns a `BindingIterator` (see Section 7.3.6) in parameter `bi`, which contains the remaining bindings (the first `how_many` bindings will be in parameter `bl`). If the naming context does not contain any additional bindings, the parameter `bi` will be a nil object reference.

7.3.5 Exceptions raised by operations in `NamingContext`

The exceptions in NamingContext are defined as follows:

```
// In IDL module CosNaming:
```

† The three parameters used here are an example of a pattern used often in the CORBAservices. They allow a sequence of manageable size to be returned to a client, and the entries that would not fit into that sequence to be obtained using an *iterator*.

```
interface NamingContext {
      enum NotFoundReason { missing_node,
                            not_context, not_object};

      exception NotFound {
            NotFoundReason  why;
            Name  rest_of_name;
      };

      exception CannotProceed {
            NamingContext  cxt;
            Name  rest_of_name;
      };

      exception InvalidName {};
      exception AlreadyBound {};
      exception NotEmpty {};
      /* . . . . */
};
```

These exceptions are raised under the following conditions:

- `NotFound`: indicates that some component of the specified name is not bound. To aid debugging, the remainder of the name is returned in the exception. The first component in the returned name is the component that failed.
- `CannotProceed`: indicates that the Naming Service cannot continue with the operation request for some reason.
- `InvalidName`: indicates that the specified name is invalid. A `Name` of length zero (that is, without any name components) is invalid. A `Name` which contains a `NameComponent` whose `id` member is zero or is an empty string is also invalid.
- `AlreadyBound`: indicates that an object is already bound to the specified name. At any time, only one object can be bound to a given name in a naming context.
- `NotEmpty`: indicates that the target naming context contains at least one binding. A naming context cannot be destroyed if it contains any bindings.

7.3.6 The `BindingIterator` interface

Recall that interface `NamingContext` provides an operation `list()` to obtain the list of name bindings within a context:

```
// In IDL interface NamingContext:
void list(in unsigned long how_many,
          out BindingList bl,
          out BindingIterator bi);
```

This operation returns a maximum of `how_many` structs of type `Binding` in the parameter `bl`. If the target context contains more than `how_many` bindings then the `BindingIterator` parameter can be used to access the remaining entries. The relevant IDL definitions are:

```
// In IDL module CosNaming:
enum BindingType { nobject, ncontext };

struct Binding {
      Name binding_name;
      BindingType binding_type;
};

typedef sequence<Binding> BindingList;

interface BindingIterator {

      boolean next_one(out Binding b);

      boolean next_n(in unsigned long how_many,
                     out BindingList bl);

      void destroy();
};
```

The operations `next_one()` and `next_n()` can be used to access the additional entries (that is, the entries other than those returned by the `out BindingList bl` parameter of the `list()` operation). Each entry will be returned at most once; hence consecutive calls to `next_one()` and/or `next_n()` can be used to retrieve all of the additional entries in a naming context. The operation `next_n()` returns at most `n` entries; it may return fewer.

The operation `next_one()` returns true if an entry can be returned; otherwise it returns false. The operation `next_n()` returns true if `n` (or fewer) entries can be returned; if no entries can be returned, `next_n()` returns false.

A `BindingIterator` object can be deleted by calling its `destroy()` operation. ✚

7.4 Examples of using the Naming Service

Consider a portion of the Naming Service maintained as part of a tourism application. Cinemas, theaters, restaurants, and hotels would be just some of categories of objects that would be named by this. Figure 7.2 shows part of a naming context graph designed for this purpose. The nodes `tourism`, `cinemas`, `hotels`, and `hostels` represent naming contexts. A name such as `tourism.hotels.Central` names an object (the notation `aaa.bbb.ccc` is used here to show examples of compound names). In addition, it is convenient to use 'abstract' names so that, for example, the best hotel can be found by looking up the name `tourism.hotels.best`.

The remainder of this section shows some sample code based on the naming context graph in Figure 7.2. (The nodes shown in solid black are of type `ncontext`; the others are of type `nobject`.)

7.4.1 Creating a naming context graph and binding names

The following code segment shows how to build the `tourism` and `tourism.cinemas` naming contexts shown in Figure 7.2, and then to bind the name `tourism.cinemas.Savoy` to the object referenced by the variable `SavoyVar`:

```
// C++. A client of a Naming Service.
#include <Naming.hh>

/* . . . . . */
{
      FrontOffice_var SavoyVar =
                        new FrontOffice_i("Savoy", /* . . . . */);
      . . . . .
      CosNaming::NamingContext_var initContext,
                                    tourismContext,
                                    cinemasContext;
      CosNaming::Name_var name;
      CORBA::Object_var objVar;
```

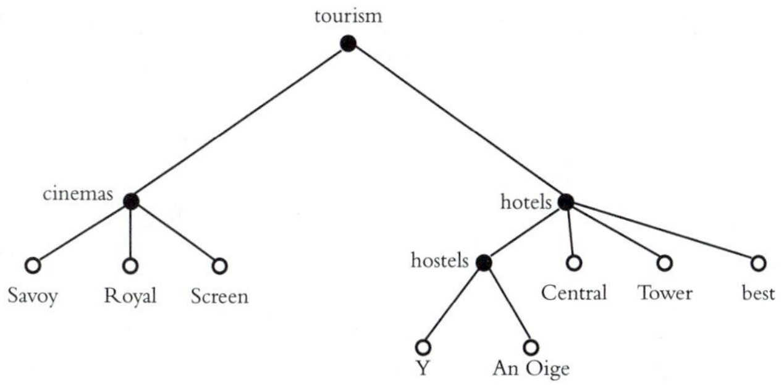

Figure 7.2 *A naming context graph.*

```
    try {
          // Find the initial naming context:
             objVar = CORBA::Orbix.
                     resolve_initial_references("NameService");
             initContext =
                     CosNaming::NamingContext::_narrow(objVar);

          // A CosNaming::Name is simply a sequence of structs.
          name = new CosNaming::Name(1);

          name->length(1);
          name[0].id = CORBA::string_dup("tourism");
          name[0].kind = CORBA::string_dup("");

          // (In one step) create a new context, and bind it
          // relative to the initial context:
          tourismContext = initContext->bind_new_context(name);

          name[0].id = CORBA::string_dup("cinemas");
          name[0].kind = CORBA::string_dup("");
          // (In one step) create a new context, and bind it
          // relative to the tourism context:
          cinemasContext = tourismContext->bind_new_context(name);

          name[0].id = CORBA::string_dup("Savoy");
          name[0].kind = CORBA::string_dup("");
          // Bind name to object SavoyVar in context
          // tourism.cinemas:
          cinemasContext->bind(name,SavoyVar);
    }
    // Catch clauses not shown here.
}
```

7.4.2 Resolving names

For a client, a typical use of the Naming Service is to find the initial naming context and then to resolve a name to obtain an object reference. The following code segment illustrates this. It finds the object named `tourism.hotels.best` and then prints that hotel's name.

The following IDL definition is assumed:

```
// IDL
interface Hotel {
     readonly attribute string name;
     . . . . .
};
```

The client is written as:

```
// C++. An Orbix client.
#include <Naming.hh>

main (int argc, char** argv) {
      /* . . . . . */
      CosNaming::NamingContext_var initContext;
      CosNaming::Name_var name;
      Hotel_var hotelVar;
      CORBA::Object_var objVar;

      try {
            // Find the initial naming context:
            objVar = CORBA::Orbix.
                        resolve_initial_references("NameService");
            initContext =
                        CosNaming::NamingContext::_narrow(objVar);

            name = new CosNaming::Name(3);
            name->length(3);
            name[0].id = CORBA::string_dup("tourism");
            name[0].kind = CORBA::string_dup("");
            name[1].id = CORBA::string_dup("hotels");
            name[1].kind = CORBA::string_dup("");
            name[2].id = CORBA::string_dup("best");
            name[2].kind = CORBA::string_dup("");

            objVar = initContext->resolve(name);
            if(!CORBA::is_nil(hotelVar)) { (hotelVar =
                                    Hotel::_narrow(objVar) ;
                  CORBA::String_var hotelName = hotelVar->name();
                  cout << hotelName
                        << " is the best hotel!" << endl;
            } else { /* Deal with failure to _narrow() */ }
      } // Catch clauses not shown here.
}
```

Iterating through a context's bindings

The following code segment shows a simple example of using the `BindingIterator` interface (see Section 7.3.6, p.171) to list the bindings in a context. Here, we list the bindings in the context `tourism.cinemas`.

```
// C++
CosNaming::NamingContext_var initContext, cinemasContext;
CosNaming::BindingList_var bList;
CosNaming::BindingIterator_var bIter;
CosNaming::Name_var name;
CORBA::Object_var objVar;
try {
```

```
            // Find the initial naming context:
            objVar = CORBA::Orbix.
                         resolve_initial_references("NameService");
            initContext =
                         CosNaming::NamingContext::_narrow(objVar);

        name = new CosNaming::Name(2);
        name->length(2);
        name[0].id = CORBA::string_dup("tourism");
        name[0].kind = CORBA::string_dup("");
        name[1].id = CORBA::string_dup("cinemas");
        name[1].kind = CORBA::string_dup("");

        objVar = initContext->resolve(name);
        cinemasContext =
                 CosNaming::NamingContext::_narrow(objVar)
                     if (!CORBA::_is_nil(cinemasContext)) {

            // Maximum number of bindings to be returned in bList:
            const CORBA::ULong batchSize = 10;

            cinemasContext->list(batchSize, bList, bIter);
            CORBA::ULong i;
            for (i = 0; i < bList.length(); i++)
                  cout << bList[i].binding_name[0].id << endl;

            // If more than batchSize bindings in context,
            // obtain them using next_n():
            if ( ! CORBA::is_nil(bIter) ) {
                 while( bIter->next_n(batchSize, bList) ) {
                    for (i = 0; i < bList.length(); i++)
                         cout << bList[i].binding_name[0].id << endl;
                 }
            }
        } else { ..... } // Deal with failure to _narrow().
} // Catch clauses not shown.
```

7.5 Other features

The Names Library is an optional mechanism within the CORBA Naming Service for creating names required by the Naming Service; that is, for creating sequences of `NameComponent` records. In C++, as we have seen in Section 7.4 (p.172), it is not difficult to create such sequences and populate them using `operator[]()`. Therefore, this aspect of the Naming Service is not covered here.

8 Registration and activation of servers

This chapter describes the Implementation Repository, the component of Orbix that maintains registration information about servers and controls their activation. This facility is implemented by the Orbix daemon, which is responsible for launching servers and connecting clients and servers (but, of course, it is not involved in normal communication between clients and servers).

8.1 Registering servers

The Implementation Repository maintains a mapping from a server s name to the file name of the executable code which implements that server. A server must be registered, using the `putit` command or a GUI tool, so that it can be included in this mapping table. This has the advantage that the server will be launched automatically by Orbix (if this has not been done already) when an operation invocation is made on one of its objects, or when a client binds to one of its objects.

The `putit` command has the following general format:

```
putit <Server_name> <Executable_command_and_arguments>
```

✚ Although there is very little burden in registering a server in this way, some applications may benefit from not having to register servers at all. This may arise in some unusual applications because servers may have to be created dynamically at runtime: that is, the names and number of servers of a particular type may not have been known at compile time. Even though servers can be registered dynamically at runtime (using the daemon's IDL interface), such applications may be simpler if they do not need to register servers at all.

Another example is that a software vendor may package a number of servers in his system and may not wish to include an install script that will use `putit` to register these servers.

In these cases, the ordixd daemon can be run with a switch (`-u`). Any server process can then be started manually: when it calls the `impl_is_ready()` function it can pass any string as its server name, and the daemon will not check that this is a server name known to it. The disadvantage of this approach is that an unregistered server will not be known to the daemon, so the daemon will not be able to launch it automatically when a client binds to or invokes an operation on one of its objects.

Another useful switch is `-p`, which runs the daemon in protected mode – in which only the user that started the daemon can register servers with it. This prevents rogue users from registering dangerous commands for servers to run. It is especially important for daemons that must be run as the root user on UNIX, which by default will start servers with root privileges. Only the owner of the daemon is allowed to register servers, and in addition this must be done from the machine that the daemon is running and not remotely (for example, from a machine that a rogue user could use to masquerade as the owner of the daemon).

The `putit` command is in fact implemented using Orbix IDL calls: the daemon itself contains an Orbix object that exports an IDL interface that is used by `putit` and other utility commands. This means that the `putit` command finds the daemon that it must communicate with, and invokes one or more operations on it. The other utilty commands are implemented in a similar manner:

- `lsit`: lists the registered servers
- `catit`: outputs details about a particular server
- `rmit`: removes the entry for a particular server, but this does not kill any process or processes associated with that server
- `killit`: kills the process or processes associated with a particular server, but this does not remove the entry from the Implementation Repository
- `psit`: lists the current processes associated with Orbix servers.

The functionality these commands provide is also available via a GUI tool.

In addition, server names can be hierarchic, so there are utility commands for creating and managing (possibly nested) directories within the Implementation Repository.

Since the Implementation Repository has an IDL interface, it is straightforward to write a graphical user interface to display the registered servers, and allow these to be managed. This facility is being provided on a growing number of operating systems.

8.2 Activation modes

CORBA provides a number of different mechanisms, or **modes**, for launching servers, giving the programmer control over how servers are implemented as processes by the underlying operating system. In the default **shared activation mode**, each server has a single process if it is active, and of course a server has no associated process if it has not yet been activiated or if it has been activated and has timed out. However, a small number of applications need to use a different process structure.

This section explains the available modes, for the most part using diagrams to illustrate the processes created. Switches to the `putit` command are used to choose between the modes, but these details are not covered here.

The following primary activation modes are supported:

- **Shared activation mode**: in this mode, all of the objects with the same server name on a given host are managed by the *same* process on that host . This is the most commonly used activation mode, and it is the default. If the process is already launched when a function invocation arrives for one of its objects, then Orbix will route the invocation to that process; otherwise Orbix will launch the process (using the Implementation Repository's mapping from server name to file name to determine which executable file to use).

+

- **Unshared activation mode**: in this mode, individual objects of a server are registered with the Implementation Repository. All invocations for an individual object are handled by a single process. This server process is activated by the first invocation of that object, and one process is created per active registered object. Each object managed by a server can be registered with a different executable file, or any number of them can share the same executable file. The motivation for this mode is that some servers may have objects that cannot or should not be run in the same process. Some objects may use such large amounts of system resources that it would be better to run them separately, or it may be impossible to run them together in the same process. In some cases, there could be risks in running objects together: if one object corrupts its memory then it should be possible to ensure the validity of the memory of the others. In addition, this mode can increase parallelism because each object has its own process that can be scheduled. (Chapter 21 discusses the use of lightweight threads for increasing concurrency.)
- **Per-method-call activation mode**: in this mode, individual operation (or attribute) names are registered with the Implementation Repository. Interprocess calls can be made to these operations – and each invocation will result in the creation of an individual process. A process is created

to handle each individual operation call, and that process is destroyed once the operation has completed. A different executable file can be specified for each operation, or any number of them can share the same executable file. This mode is primarily supported to allow operations to be executed by running command scripts. These should run as separate processes that terminate after the call completes.

For the **shared** and **unshared** modes, there are three variations that an application can choose between:

- **Per-client**: in this sub-mode, activations of the same server by different end users (that is, different principals) will cause a different process to be created for each such end user. Two processes owned by the same end user will share a server process; two processes owned by different end users will each communicate with their own server process. By default, Orbix uses the clients' user names to determine if two clients belong to the same or different end users.
- **Per-client-process**: in this sub-mode, activations of the same server by different client processes will cause a different process to be created for each such client process. Thus, two processes owned by the same end user (or different end users) will each communicate with its own server process.
- **Multiple-client**: in this sub-mode, activations of the same server by different end users will share the same process, in accordance with whichever fundamental activation mode (shared or unshared) is selected. This is the default.

In addition, if a server is registered in the shared mode, then it can be launched manually (or by some mechanism external to Orbix, for example by a debugger), prior to any invocations on its objects. Launching servers in this way is useful for a number of reasons. Some servers take considerable time to initialize themselves (for example, because they open a database and read from it), therefore it is sensible to launch such servers before any client wishes to use them. Also, during development it may be clearer to launch a server in its own window, allowing its diagnostic messages to be seen more easily.

Manually launched servers, once they have called `impl_is_ready()`, behave in a similar way to shared activation mode servers. If a server is registered as unshared or per-method, then, in line with the CORBA specification, `impl_is_ready()` will fail if the server is launched manually.

Usually, clients are not concerned with the activation details of a server or aware of what server processes are launched. To a client, a server is viewed as a single unit; an object in a server can be bound to and communicated with without considering activation mode details.

✚ A server process can determine the mode in which its server is registered. In the unshared mode, it can also obtain a reference to the object that was invoked to cause it to be launched, and in the per-method-call mode, it can determine the name of the operation or attribute that it was created to handle a call to. These facilities are supported so that processes can share the same executable file, where this is appropriate, and yet each can determine the object or method that it was created to handle. ✚

Illustration of the activation modes

The remainder of this section illustrates each activation mode. The main object or objects in each server process are of type `FrontOffice`, but each process also contains objects of type `Booking`. Clients belonging to different users are also shown.

Shared activation mode (with the default multiple-client option)

Each of the clients uses one or more `FrontOffice` and `Booking` objects in the server. All of these objects run in the same server process (Figure 8.1).

✚ *Shared activation mode (with the per-client option)*

Each set of processes owned by a single user is connected to its own server process, which holds all of the objects that are created by that server process. This set of objects may be the same for each client, or it can be different, depending on the application. If there is an overlap between the set of objects that each client uses, then it is the responsibility of the application to coordinate any updates, where this is required. In the example shown in Figure 8.2, the application must coordinate the two copies of `Savoy` and the two copies of `Screen`.

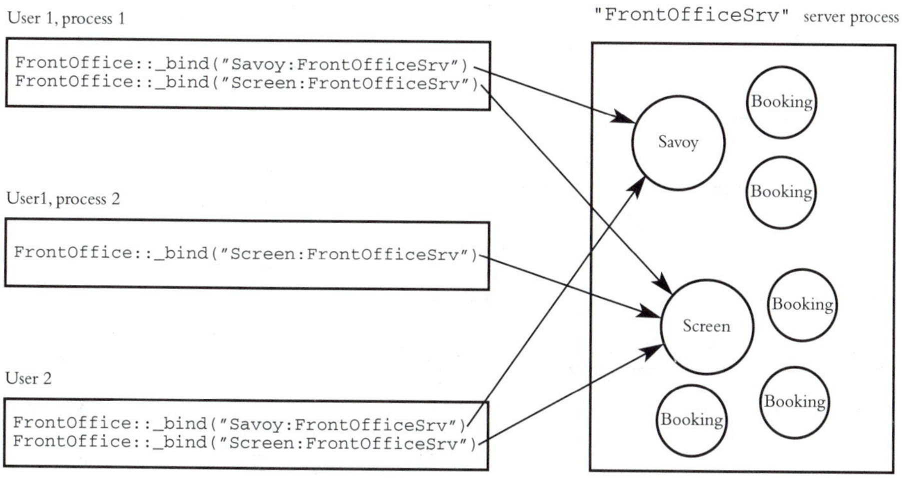

Figure 8.1 *Shared activation.*

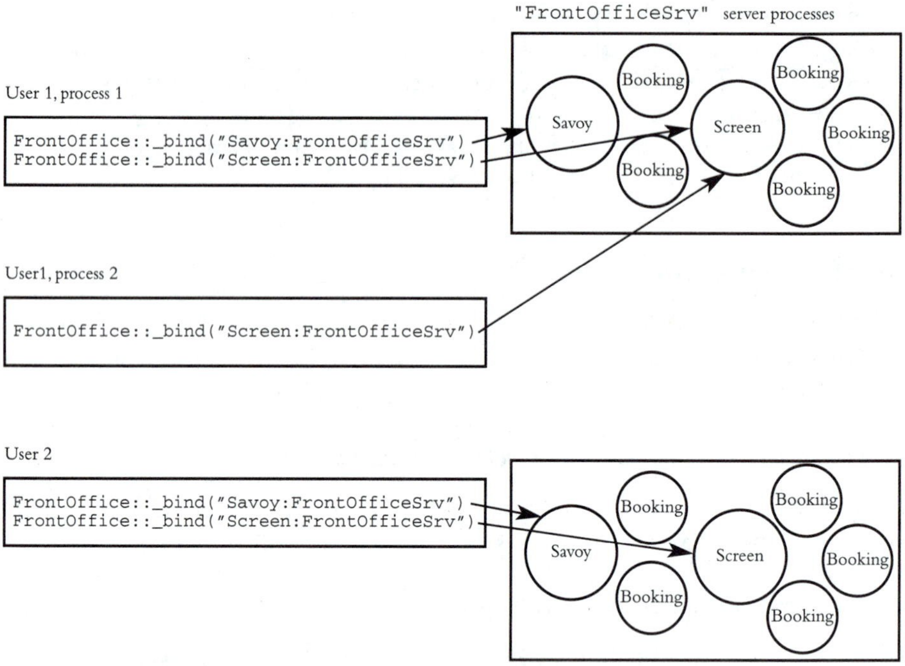

Figure 8.2 *Shared activation, with the per-client option.*

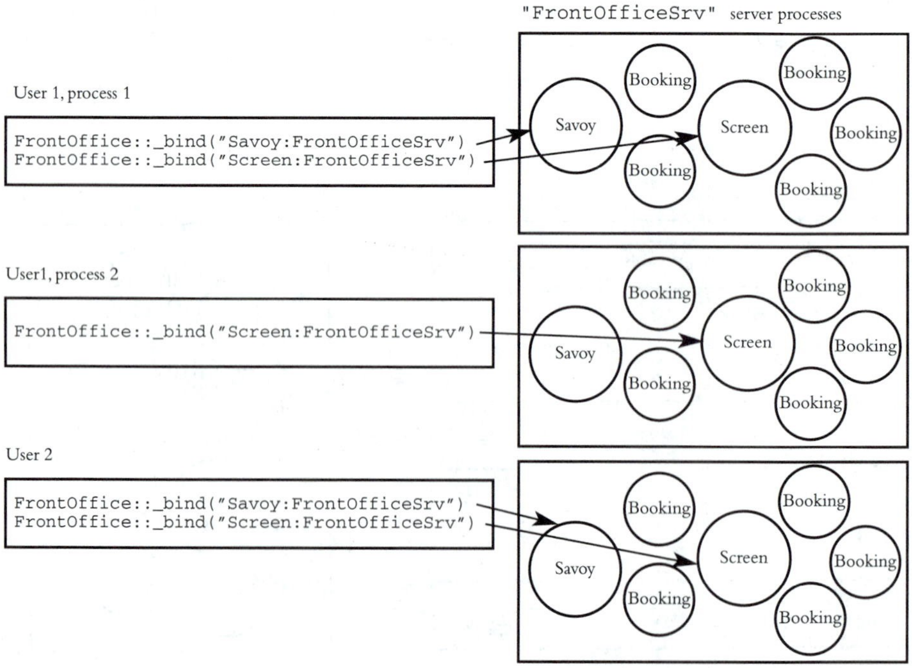

Figure 8.3 *Shared activation, with the per-client-process option.*

Shared activation mode (with the per-client-process option)

This is different from the previous case because each client process, irrespective of its owner, is connected to its own server process, which holds all of the objects that are created by that server process (Figure 8.3).

Unshared activation mode (with the default multiple-client option)

In all of the illustrations of the unshared activation mode, we have assumed that each of the `FrontOffice` objects (`Savoy` and `Sceen`) has been individually registered using `putit` (but that none of the `Booking` objects has been registered in this way). Therefore, each `FrontOffice` object runs in its own server process. In Figure 8.4, `Savoy` and `Screen` run in their own processes.

An invocation on an unregistered object will not launch a server process, and a call on an unregistered object will fail unless the reference to that object was passed by the process holding the object to the client making the call.

Unshared activation mode (with the per-client option)

This is different to the mode shown in Figure 8.4 because each set of processes owned by a given client will have a set of processes in the server to handle its calls. There will be one server process (per set of processes owned by a given client) for each registered object (Figure 8.5).

Unshared activation mode (with the per-client-process option)

This is different to the mode shown in Figure 8.5 because each client process, irrespective of its owner, will have a set of processes in the server to handle its call. There will be one server process (per client process) for each registered object (Figure 8.6).

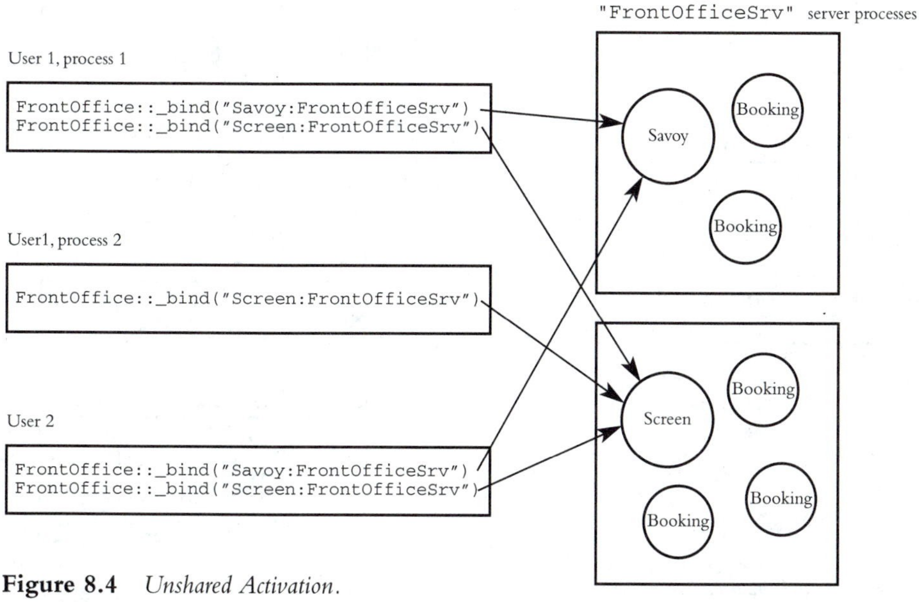

Figure 8.4 *Unshared Activation.*

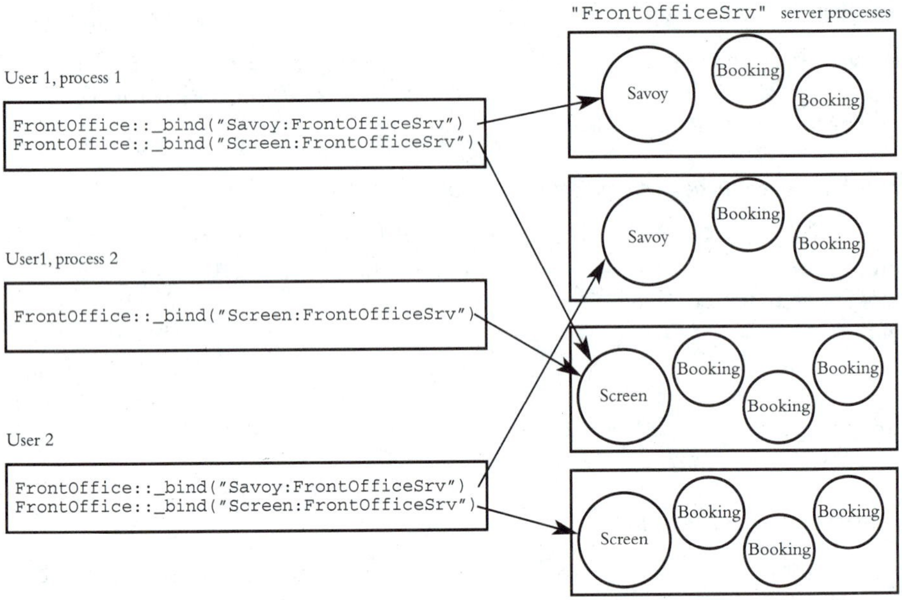

Figure 8.5 *Unshared activation, with the per-client option.*

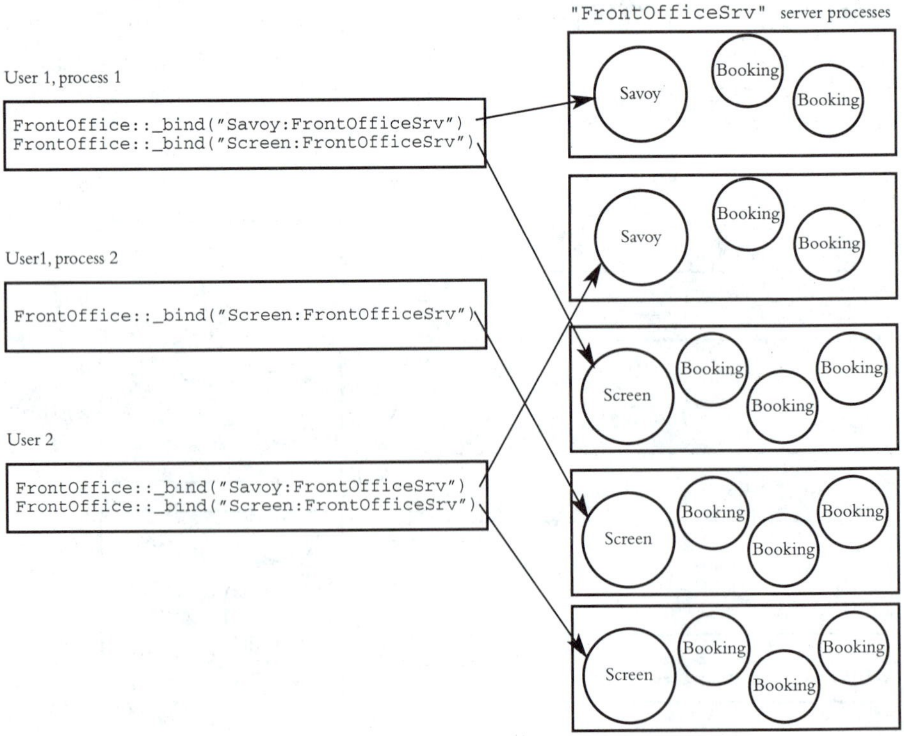

Figure 8.6 *Shared activation, with the per-client-process option.*

Per-method-call activation mode

In this mode, a server process is created for each registered operation or attribute call, and this process terminates when this call completes. Here we have assumed that the two operations `getPrice()` and `makeBooking()` have been registered (Figure 8.7). An invocation on an unregistered operation or attribute will fail.

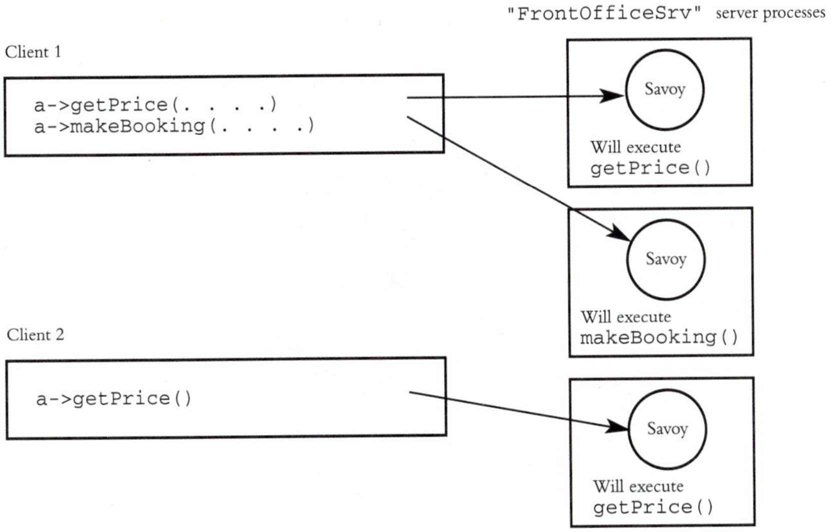

Figure 8.7 *Per-method-call activation mode.*

9 Exception handling

In this chapter, we extend the cinema example of Chapter 6, to include user-defined IDL exceptions, and to show how to raise such exceptions in the server code and handle them in the client. System-defined exceptions are also explained.

In the examples in this chapter, and throughout this book, we assume that the host C++ compiler supports C++ exception handling. Lower level facilities are used to handle IDL exceptions when using other compilers, but these facilities are not explained here.

9.1 The IDL definitions

We begin by recognizing the fact that `getPrice()` may raise an exception if an invalid place or date is passed to it. Exceptions `FrontOffice::NoSuchPlace` and `FrontOffice::InvalidDate` are defined and used as follows:

```
// IDL
interface FrontOffice {

      exception NoSuchPlace { Place where; };
      exception InvalidDate { Date when; };

      Price getPrice (in Place chosenPlace,
                      in Date when)
                 raises (NoSuchPlace, InvalidDate);

      // Rest not shown here.
};
```

Operation `FrontOffice::getPrice()` can raise either `FrontOffice::NoSuchPlace` or `FrontOffice::InvalidDate`, or any system-defined exception (see Section 9.2.1). Read or write access to any IDL attribute can also raise any system-defined exception.

9.1.1 The generated code

IDL exception `FrontOffice::InvalidDate` is translated into a C++ class with the same name:

```
class FrontOffice: public virtual CORBA::Object {
public:
      // Rest not shown here.

      class InvalidDate: public CORBA::UserException {
      public:
            CORBA::String_mgr when;

            InvalidDate(const char* _when);
            InvalidDate();

            static FrontOffice::InvalidDate* _narrow()
                        throw (CORBA::SystemException);

            // Various other details for Orbix.
      };

      // Rest not shown here.
};
```

(Note that `String_mgr` behaves like `String_var`, see Section 4.3 (p.77). Type `String_mgr` is not for use by application programmers. It converts to `char*` and `CORBA::String_var` so that its value can be used.)

Here, the `InvalidDate` class is defined as a nested class within class `FrontOffice`. Each C++ class that corresponds to an IDL exception has a constructor that takes a parameter for each member of the exception. Since the `InvalidDate` exception has one member (`when`, of type `Date`, which is an alias for `string`), class `FrontOffice::InvalidDate` has a constructor that allows that single member to be initialized. It also has a default constructor that initializes none of the members.

9.2 The client: handling exceptions

A client (or server) that calls an operation or attribute should use an appropriate C++ `catch` clause to handle the user- and system-defined exceptions that can be raised. Our client can be programmed as follows:

```
// C++
#include "front.hh"
#include <iostream.h>
#include <stdlib.h>

int main() {
      FrontOffice_var foVar;
      Price thePrice;

      try {
            // Bind to the FrontOffice with marker Savoy
            // in the FrontOfficeSrv server:
            foVar = FrontOffice::_bind("Savoy:FrontOfficeSrv");
            // We used _bind(), but better to use the Naming Service

            Place aPlace;
            cout << "Enter row:  ";
            cin >> aPlace.row;
            aPlace.row = toupper(aPlace.row);
            cout << "Enter seat: ";
            cin >> aPlace.seat;

            CORBA::String_var date = CORBA::string_alloc(10);
            cout << "Enter Date [DD.MM.YYYY]: ";
            cin >> date;

            thePrice = foVar->getPrice (aPlace, date);
            cout << "Price is " << thePrice << endl;
      }
      catch (FrontOffice::InvalidDate &ivd) {
            cerr << "Invalid Date: " << ivd.when << endl;
            exit(1);
      }
      catch (FrontOffice::NoSuchPlace &nsp) {
            cerr << "No Such Place ["
                  << nsp.row << "," <<
                  << nsp.seat << "]." << endl;
            exit(1);
      }
      catch (CORBA::SystemException& se) {
            cerr << "Unexpected system exception" << endl
                  << se << endl; // Output description text.†
            exit(-1);
      }
      // Continue here if no exception.
      /* . . . . . */
}
```

† The printing of a system exception using `operator<<()` is Orbix-specific.

The handlers for the `FrontOffice::InvalidDate` and `FrontOffice::NoSuchPlace` exceptions output an error message and exit the program. Note that the parameter to the `catch` clause (for any CORBA exception) is passed by reference.

The `operator<<()` defined on class `SystemException` outputs a text description of the individual system exception that was raised. (This text is read from a standard file, and so can be modified for individual installations.)

A programmer who wishes to catch all user-defined exceptions in one clause can use the following:

```
catch (CORBA::UserException& ue) {
      /* . . . . */
}
```

All CORBA exeptions can be caught as follows:

```
catch (CORBA:Exception& ue) {
      /* . . . . */
}
```

Continuing after catching an exception

If the handlers for the `FrontOffice::InvalidDate` and `FrontOffice::NoSuchPlace` exception do not exit the program, then the programmer must be careful with the value of the variable `thePrice`. In particular, if an exception occurs in `getPrice()`, then (as specified by the C++ exception model) the return value of this operation call would be undefined, and hence `thePrice` would be undefined. (Similarly, the C++ exception model specifies that the values of `out` and `inout` parameters will be undefined if an operation raises an exception.) A simple way to address this is shown in the following code fragment, in which a flag is used to record whether or not `thePrice` has a valid value:

```
unsigned char haveThePrice = 0;
try {
      /* . . . . . */

      // Make a booking:
      thePrice = foVar->getPrice( /* . . . . */ );
      haveThePrice = 1;
}
catch (FrontOffice::InvalidDate &ivd) {
      cerr << "Invalid Date: "
            << ivd.when << endl;
}
catch (FrontOffice::NoSuchPlace &nsp) {
      cerr << "No Such Place ["
             << nsp.row << "," <<
             << nsp.seat << "]" << endl;
```

```
    }
    catch (CORBA::SystemException& se) {
          cerr << "Unexpected system exception"
               << endl << se << endl;
          exit(-1);
    }

    if (haveThePrice) {
          // No exception occurred before or during the call
          // to getPrice():
          /* . . . . */
    }
```

9.2.1 Handling specific system exceptions

A client may also provide a handler for a specific system exception. For example, to explicitly handle a `CORBA::COMM_FAILURE` exception that might be raised from a call to `_bind()`, the client could write code as follows:

```
// C++
#define EXCEPTIONS    // Orbix
#include "front.hh"
#include <iostream.h>

int main() {
      FrontOffice_var foVar;

      try {
            // Bind to the FrontOffice with marker Savoy
            // in the FrontOfficeSrv server:
            foVar = FrontOffice::_bind("Savoy:FrontOfficeSrv");
      }
      catch (CORBA::COMM_FAILURE& se) {
            cerr << "Communications failure exception" << endl
                 << se << endl;
            /* . . some actions specific to this exception . . */
      }
      catch (CORBA::SystemException& se) {
            // Handle the other system exceptions.
            cerr << "Unexpected system exception" << endl
                 << se << endl;
            exit(-1);
      }
      /* . . . . */
}
```

Although `_bind()` is used as an example here, the same points apply when calling operations and attributes.

Note that the handler for a specific system exception must appear before the handler for `CORBA::SystemException`. In C++, `catch` clauses are attempted in the order specified, and the *first* matching handler is called. Because of implicit casting, a handler for `CORBA::SystemException` matches all system exceptions (because all system exception classes are derived from class `CORBA::SystemException`), and therefore it should normally appear after all handlers for specific system exceptions.

Note that if the programmer simply wishes to know the type of system exception that occurred, then the message output by `operator<<()` on class `CORBA::SystemException` is sufficient. A handler for an individual system exception is only required when specific action is to be taken if that exception occurs. It is also possible to catch `CORBA::SystemException` and narrow it to a specific system exception.

9.3 The server: throwing an exception

This section shows how to extend the definition of the function `FrontOffice_i::getPrice()` to raise an exception, using the normal C++ `throw` statement. The function `getPrice()` can be coded as follows:

```
// C++
Bookingt_ptr FrontOffice_i::getPrice( const Place& where,
                                       const char* when)
        throw (CORBA::SystemException,
               FrontOffice::NoSuchPlace,
               FrontOffice::InvalidDate ) {
    // If ( /* the date is invalid */ ) {
        // Throw a FrontOffice::InvalidDate exception:
        throw FrontOffice::InvalidDate(when);
    }
    else if ( /* the place does not exist */ ) {
        throw FrontOffice::NoSuchPlace(where);
    }
    else {
        // Create the new booking, and return its reference:
        // (assuming the BOAImpl approach):
        Booking_ptr p = new Booking_i (this, where, when);
        Booking::_duplicate(p);
        return p;
    }
}
```

The code uses the automatically generated constructors of class `FrontOffice::InvalidDate` and `FrontOffice::NoSuchPlace` to initialize the exception thrown.

Propagating an exception

If the implementation of `getPrice()` must call another operation, then it is easy for it to propagate an exception back to the original caller. There are actually two cases here. Firstly, the operation that `getPrice()` calls may have a raises clause that is a subset of that of `getPrice()`. In this case, `getPrice()` can safely propagate the original exception to its caller. For example, if all that `getPrice()` has to do is to call an operation named `findPrice()` on some object reference `m_p`, then this can be coded simply as follows:

```
// C++
Bookingt_ptr FrontOffice_i::getPrice( const Place& where,
                                      const char* when)
        throw (CORBA::SystemException,
               FrontOffice::NoSuchPlace,
               FrontOffice::InvalidDate ) {
    // On the assumption that findPrice() can only throw a system
    // exception, NoSuchPrice or InvalidDate, then it is safe
    // to automatically propagate any exception:
    return m_p->findPrice(where, when);
}
```

If, on the other hand, `findPrice()` can raise a different exception, say `PriceFinder::InvalidPlace`, then the code must be written as follows:

```
// C++
Bookingt_ptr FrontOffice_i::getPrice( const Place& where,
                                      const char* when)
        throw (CORBA::SystemException,
               FrontOffice::NoSuchPlace,
               FrontOffice::InvalidDate ) {
    try {
        return m_p->findPrice(where, when);
    }
    catch (PriceFinder::InvalidPlace& ex) {
        throw FrontOffice::NoSuchPlace(where);
    }
    // Other exceptions are propagated automatically.
}
```

9.3.1 Other aspects of system exceptions

System exceptions have two member functions that are of use in some applications. The first, `completed()`, returns an enumerated type that indicates how far the operation or attribute call progressed before the exception was raised. The values are:

- `COMPLETED_NO`: the system exception was raised before the operation or attribute call began to execute.
- `COMPLETED_YES`: the system exception was raised after the operation or attribute call completed its execution.
- `COMPLETED_MAYBE`: it is uncertain whether or not the operation or attribute call started execution, and, if it did, whether or not it completed. For example, the status will be COMPLETED_MAYBE if a client's host receives no indication of success or failure after transmitting a request to a target object.

The second function, `minor()`, returns a value (IDL `unsigned long`) to give more details of the particular system exception raised. For example, if the `COMM_FAILURE` system exception is caught by a client, it can access the minor field of the system exception to determine why this occurred. Each system exception has a set of minor values associated with it; for example, those for `COMM_FAILURE` include `TCP_TIMEOUT` and `TCP_UNKNOWN_HOST`. The minor codes are not specified by CORBA, but must be chosen by each ORB.

Finally, because some C++ compilers do not support native exceptions, the CORBA standard defines how programs written for these compilers can throw and catch exceptions. The key to this support is that each C++ member function that corresponds to an IDL operation or attribute takes a parameter of type `CORBA::Environment`. This can be assigned to by a function's implementation and tested by a function's caller. Orbix provides a set of macros (`TRY`, `CATCH`, and so on) to make this testing easier.

Exceptions can be raised in this way in a server, and caught using native C++ exceptions in a remote client. On the other hand, native exceptions raised by a server can be caught by testing the `CORBA::Environment` parameter in a remote client compiled with a C++ compiler that does not support native exceptions. ✚

10 Inheritance

IDL allows a new interface to be defined by extending the functionality provided by an existing one. The new interface is said to inherit or **derive** from the **base** interface. IDL also supports multiple inheritance, allowing an interface to have several immediate base interfaces.

10.1 Example using inheritance

As an example of single inheritance, consider extending the cinema example of Chapter 6 with group bookings:

```
// IDL

interface Booking {
      /* as before */
};

interface GroupBooking : Booking {
      readonly attribute string organizer;
      readonly attribute string groupName;
};
```

The new interface `GroupBooking` derives from interface `Booking`. It has added two new attributes: to return the name of the organizer and the name of the group.

Interface `FrontOffice` includes an operation, `makeGroupBooking()`, that uses this new type:

```
interface FrontOffice {

      // Rest not shown here.

      exception GroupTooSmall {
                unsigned long chosenSize;
                unsigned long minimumSize;
      };

      GroupBooking makeGroupBooking (
                        in Places     chosenPlaces,
                        in Date       when,
                        in CreditCard payment,
                        in string     organizer,
                        in string     groupName)
                raises (NoSuchPlace,
                        PlaceAlreadyBooked,
                        InvalidCreditCard,
                        InvalidDate,
                        GroupTooSmall);
};
```

The IDL compiler produces the following C++ classes from these interfaces. Note, in particular, that class `GroupBooking` inherits from `Booking`:

```
// C++
#include <CORBA.h>

class Booking : public virtual CORBA::Object {
      // As before.
};


class GroupBooking : public virtual Booking {
      // Various details for Orbix.
public:
      // Various details for Orbix.

      virtual char* organizer ()
                throw (CORBA::SystemException);

      virtual char* groupName ()
                throw (CORBA::SystemException);
};


class FrontOffice : public virtual CORBA::Object {
      // Various details for Orbix.
public:
      // Rest not shown here.
```

```
      virtual GroupBooking_ptr makeGroupBooking
                                        (const Places& chosenPlaces,
                                         const char* when,
                                         const CreditCard& payment,
                                         const char* organizer,
                                         const char* groupName)
          throw (CORBA::SystemException,
                 FrontOffice::NoSuchPlace,
                 FrontOffice::PlaceAlreadyBooked,
                 FrontOffice::InvalidCreditCard,
                 FrontOffice::InvalidDate,
                 FrontOffice::GroupTooSmall);
};
```

10.1.1 Usage from a client

A client can proceed to manipulate a `GroupBooking` object in a similar way to the `Booking` objects of Chapter 6:

```
// C++
#include "front.hh"
#include <iostream.h>
#include <stdlib.h>

int main() {
      try {
         // Bind to any FrontOffice object in the
         // FrontOfficeSrv server.
         FrontOffice_var foVar =
                  FrontOffice::_bind(":FrontOfficeSrv");
         // We used _bind(), but better to use the
         // Naming Service.

         // Obtain a reference to a new GroupBooking object:
         GroupBooking_var ourClubsBooking =
               foVar->newGroupBooking( /* . . . . */ );

         String_var org = ourClubsBooking->organizer();
         cout << "Organizer is " << org << endl;

         ourClubsBooking->cancel(); // Calls correct implementation
      }
      catch(FrontOffice::GroupTooSmall& e) {
         cerr << "Error: Group too small!"
              << " Minimum Size is " << e.minimumSize
              << "    (specified size was "
              << e.chosenSize << ")."<< endl;
         exit(1);
      }
```

```
      catch (CORBA::SystemException& se) {
         cerr << "Unexpected exception:" << endl
              << se;
         exit(-1);
      }
      // And so on.
}
```

Polymorphic assignments and dynamic binding

Certain assignments are legal between base and derived interface reference variables. The following code shows how an object reference of type `GroupBooking` can be assigned to one of type `Booking` (the full rules for `_ptr` and `_var` types are explained in Section 4.4.3, p.100):

```
Booking_var myBooking = /* . . . . */;
GroupBooking_var ourClubsBooking = /* . . . . */;

myBooking = Booking::_duplicate(ourClubsBooking);

// Note that the following is illegal:
myBooking = ourClubsBooking; // Illegal: cannot implicitly widen.
```

Once `myBooking` has been assigned in this way, a call of the form:

```
myBooking->cancel();
```

will call the correct implementation of the `cancel()` operation, that is, the one defined for the implementation of the target object, which has an interface of type `GroupBooking`. The type of object reference used to access an object does not determine the code executed for its operations and attributes. Instead, this is determined by the implementation class that the object is an instance of.

An object reference of type `Booking` can be assigned to one of type `GroupBooking`, but only if the object that is referenced actually has an interface of type `GroupBooking`:

```
ourClubsBooking = GroupBooking::_narrow(myBooking);
if (!CORBA::_is_nil(ourClubsBooking)) {
          /* All ok, myBooking did reference a GroupBooking. */

// Note that the following is illegal:
ourClubsBooking = myBooking; // Illegal.
```

Polymorphic parameter passing

Consider an IDL operation defined as follows:

```
interface I {
     void op1 (in Booking p);
};
```

The variable `ourClubsBooking`, or any variable of type `Booking_ptr`, `Booking_var`, `GroupBooking_ptr`, or `GroupBooking_var`, can be passed to `I::op1()`.

10.1.2 The implementation classes

This following two subsections show how to implement the `GroupBooking` interface using the BOAImpl and TIE approaches.

The BOAImpl approach

The class definitions:

```
class GroupBooking_i: public virtual Booking_i,
                      public virtual GroupBookingBOAImpl
{
public:

     GroupBooking_i (FrontOffice_i* office,
                     const Places& where,
                     const char* when,
                     const char* organizer,
                     const char* groupName);

     // IDL attribute access methods:

     virtual char* organizer ()
                throw (CORBA::SystemException);

     virtual char* groupName ()
                throw (CORBA::SystemException);

     // Functions to redefine:
     virtual void cancel ()
                throw (CORBA::SystemException);

private:
     CORBA::String_var m_organizer;
     CORBA::String_var m_groupName;
};
```

The constructor and members functions can be coded as follows:

```
GroupBooking_i::  GroupBooking_i
                      (FrontOffice_i* office,
                       const Places& where,
```

```
                              const char* when,
                              const char* organizer,
                              const char* groupName)
                             : Booking_i (office, where, when)
{
  m_organizer = CORBA::string_dup(organizer);
  m_groupName = CORBA::string_dup(groupName);
}


char* GroupBooking_i:: organize ()
           throw (CORBA::SystemException)
{
  return CORBA::string_dup (m_organizer);
}


char* GroupBooking_i::  groupName ()
           throw (CORBA::SystemException)
{
  return CORBA::string_dup (m_groupName);
}


void GroupBooking_i::cancel()
           throw (CORBA::SystemException) {
     // Record the group and organizer as being unreliable.
     // Then call
     Booking_i::cancel();
}
```

The `makeGroupBooking()` operation can be coded as follows:

```
GroupBooking_ptr FrontOffice_i:: makeGroupBooking
           (const Places& where,
            const char* when,
            const CreditCard& payment,
            const char* organizer,
            const char* groupName)
     throw (CORBA::SystemException,
            FrontOffice::NoSuchPlace,
            FrontOffice::PlaceAlreadyBooked,
            FrontOffice::InvalidCreditCard,
            FrontOffice::InvalidDate,
            FrontOffice::GroupTooSmall)
{
     // Code to check that the date and all of the places are
     // valid. Throw NoSuchPlace or InvalidDate if
     // they are invalid. Not shown here.

     if (where.length() < m_minGroupSize)
```

```
            throw FrontOffice::GroupTooSmall (where.length(),
                                              m_minGroupSize

      // Check that none of the places in where has already
      // been booked for the date when. Code not shown here.
      // Throw PlaceAlreadyBooked if any place is not available.

      // Update the record of what places have been booked.
      // Code not shown here.

      // Finally, make the group booking:
      GroupBooking_ptr newGroupBooking = new GroupBooking_i (
                                             this, where, when,
                                             organizer, groupName);

      return GroupBooking::_duplicate(newGroupBooking);
}
```

The TIE approach

The TIE approach is similar, except for the following

```
// Assuming that Booking_i has also been implemented using
// the TIE approach:

class GroupBooking_i: public virtual Booking_i {
      // as before.
};

DEF_TIE_GroupBooking(GroupBooking_i);
// We now have a class TIE_GroupBooking(GroupBooking_i)
```

The creation of a new group booking object can be coded as follows (within, for example, `newGroupBooking()`):

```
      GroupBooking_i* p = new GroupBooking_i ( this, where, when,
                                               organizer, groupName);
      GroupBooking_ptr newGroupBooking =
                      new TIE_GroupBooking(GroupBooking_i)(p);
```

Redefinition

An IDL interface cannot redefine an operation that it inherits from its base interface. This may appear as a restriction to some C++ programmers, who are familiar with the declaration of a derived class having to list the member functions that it wishes to redefine. However, it must be remembered that IDL is not an implementation language, and therefore redefinition has no place in the language. A derived interface should simply list the operations and attributes that it wishes to add, and it inherits without modification the *declarations* of all operations and attributes in its base interface(s).

When a derived interface is implemented, different code can be provided for its operations compared to that provided by a class that implements its base interface. That is, redefinition is a concern of the implementation, not of the IDL definitions.

For example, the implementation of `cancel()` can be different in an implementation of `GroupBooking` compared to that of an implementation of `Booking`:

```
void Booking_i::cancel()
      throw (CORBA::SystemException) {
      // Remove the booking from the FrontOffice's data structures.
}


void GroupBooking_i::cancel()
      throw (CORBA::SystemException) {
      // Record the group and organizer as being unreliable.
      // Then call
      Booking_i::cancel();
}
```

10.2 Multiple inheritance of IDL interfaces

IDL supports multiple inheritance. A (slightly contrived) example of this follows:

```
// IDL

interface Booking {
      // As before.
};

interface GroupBooking : Booking {
      readonly attribute string organizer;
      readonly attribute string groupName;
};

interface PriorityBooking: Booking {
      /* . . . . */
};

// Use of multiple inheritance:
interface PriorityGroupBooking : GroupBooking, PriorityBooking{
      /* . . . . */
};
```

The C++ class `PriorityGroupBooking` (generated by the IDL compiler) is defined using multiple inheritance, as follows:

```
class Booking : public virtual CORBA::Object {
     /* . . . . */
};

class GroupBooking : public virtual Booking {
     /* . . . . */
};

class PriorityBooking : public virtual Booking {
     /* . . . . */
};

class PriorityGroupBooking
                    : public virtual GroupBooking,
                      public virtual PriorityBooking {
     /* . . . . */
};
```

Part two

Other Object Systems and Languages

This part addresses other object systems and languages of the book.

Chapter 11, **CORBA and OLE integration**, introduces the interworking of CORBA and OLE, showing how OLE languages such as Visual Basic can be used to write both clients and servers in a distributed heterogeneous environment.

Chapter 12, **Java and CORBA**, shows how CORBA can be programmed using Java.

11 CORBA and OLE integration

Applications on Windows are frequently integrated using Microsoft s Object Linking and Embedding (OLE). An application can export one or more OLE interfaces, which can be called by other applications on the same machine. For example, the interface to our cinema application could be defined in OLE, and then implemented and used from a range of languages. The interaction between Microsoft s Word and PowerPoint, for example, is defined as OLE interfaces. One of the interesting features of OLE is that a client can be written in a scripting language, such as Visual Basic (VB) or Delphi, which provides rapid development of user interfaces. Packages such as Excel can also make OLE calls to other applications; in the case of Excel this is possible because it incorporates a VB interpreter. This can be used to extract financial or other data from an application, and analyse and present it using Excel.

OLE consists of many subsystems. Those such as the cut-and-paste, drag-and-drop, and compound document subsystems need not concern us here. It is the ability to define and call application-level OLE interfaces that is of interest. OLE is underpinned by the Component Object Model (COM) subsystem, which provides the infrastructure for communicating between applications and hence it plays a similar role to the core of an ORB.

CORBA—OLE integration provides transparent two-way interworking between CORBA and OLE applications. A CORBA client can call a CORBA or an OLE object, treating both as CORBA objects — that is, treating both as objects with CORBA IDL interfaces that it can understand. An OLE client can call an OLE or a CORBA object, treating both as OLE objects — that is, treating both as objects with OLE interfaces that it can understand. Figure 11.1 shows the forms of interworking that are allowed, and these are described in the following list:

(1) A simple usage of this integration is for a programmer to provide an OLE graphical interface for a new or existing CORBA server,

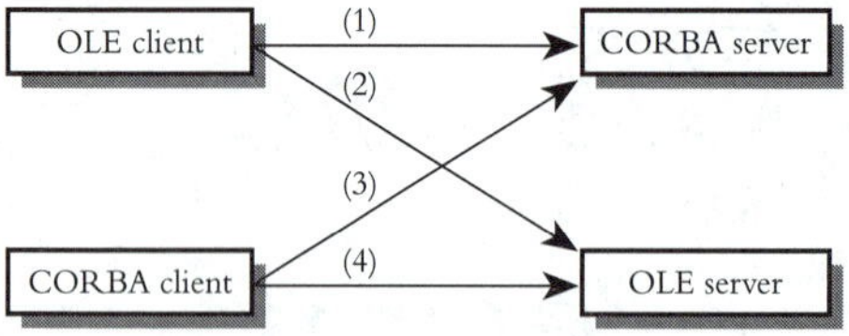

Figure 11.1 *CORBA-OLE interworking.*

implemented, say, in C++ on UNIX. The programmer (automatically) translates some or all of the server's IDL interfaces into OLE interfaces, so that they can be called from, say, VB.

✚ The client calls may also be made by C++ code, which means that there are two ways to program a C++ client. The first has been the topic of Part I of this book: the objects in the target application can be viewed by a C++ client as C++ CORBA objects (no matter what language they are actually implemented in). Alternatively, they can be viewed as OLE objects and called using OLE rules. ✚

(2) An IDL interface can be implemented as an OLE interface, and, in particular, it can be implemented in an OLE language such as VB. In this case, the IDL definitions are (automatically) translated into OLE interfaces for both the client and the server. When called from a different process or machine, CORBA is used as the underlying integration layer, giving the advantages of distribution, operating system independence, and standards compliance.

(3) CORBA client–server interaction requires no OLE involvement.

(4) A CORBA IDL interface can be implemented as an OLE server, and invoked by CORBA clients using normal CORBA programming conventions. In this case, the IDL definitions are translated into OLE for use by the server side only.

In addition, an *existing* OLE server can be used from a CORBA client or an OLE client across machine, programming language, and operating system boundaries. To achieve this, the OLE interfaces within that server can automatically be identified and translated into IDL. This IDL can then be translated into C++ to facilitate C++ clients; into Java for Java clients, and so on.

Some details on OLE

Before explaining how the CORBA–OLE integration is achieved, some aspects of OLE must be better understood.

Each OLE object has one or more OLE interfaces, each defining a number of functions that a client can call. Physically, these interfaces appear as arrays of function pointers. Interfaces can be **static**, meaning that a client must know which offset to use into the correct interface array of pointers in order to call the correct function, or **dynamic**, allowing a client to determine which functions are provided by each of an object s interfaces. Using an interface known as `IDispatch`, a client can determine which functions and properties (akin to CORBA attributes) an object supports. Given a name of a function, `IDispatch::GetIDsOfNames()` can be called to find the **dispatch identifier** for a function of a given name; and this identifier can be used in a subsequent call to `IDispatch::Invoke()`. The latter function takes a dispatch identifier of a function that the caller wishes to call on the target object, as well as the parameters to the call.

Interfaces can also be marked as **dual**; that is, they can be called both statically and dynamically. Interfaces are, in fact, defined in two separate languages. Microsoft IDL (MIDL) is used to define the details of how to call an interface. ODL (Object Definition Language) is used to populate the Type Library, the OLE equivalent of the CORBA Interface Repository (see Section 11.4, p.213).

Any OLE object with an `IDispatch` interface is known as an Automation Server (object). The mechanism for using an Automation Server is primitive, but this is hidden by languages such as VB. When a VB statement to call a function on an Automation Server is interpreted, VB determines the dispatch identifier of the function, and then uses `IDispatch::Invoke()` to call the function. Code that can call an Automation Server is termed an Automation Controller.

An Automation Server can be in-process or local. In-process means collocated with the client; local means in a separate process.

11.1 CORBA–OLE interworking: OLE to CORBA calls

The basis of the CORBA—OLE interworking is that an IDL interface is translated into an OLE Automation interface, which can be called dynamically. In fact, a dual interface is used to allow it to be called dynamically or statically, depending on the client programming language. In addition, the IDL to OLE translator generates the implementation of this OLE interface — this code is known as th**OLE Broker**, and it converts OLE calls into IDL calls. The caller is therefore only aware of OLE, and the target object is only aware of IDL and the CORBA rules.

Figure 11.2 shows an OLE client and OLE Broker, and a set of remote objects.

An OLE Broker can support many interfaces. It is given a name so that client programmers can refer to it as the gateway through which CORBA objects can be used. Similarly to when the Orbix `_bind()` call and the Naming Service are used, the name of an OLE Broker need only be used when locating a few initial object references (one of which could be a reference to the Naming Service, of course).

Figure 11.3 shows the result of the client acquiring an object reference to a CORBA object. Invocations on the proxy are made using OLE rules, and these are

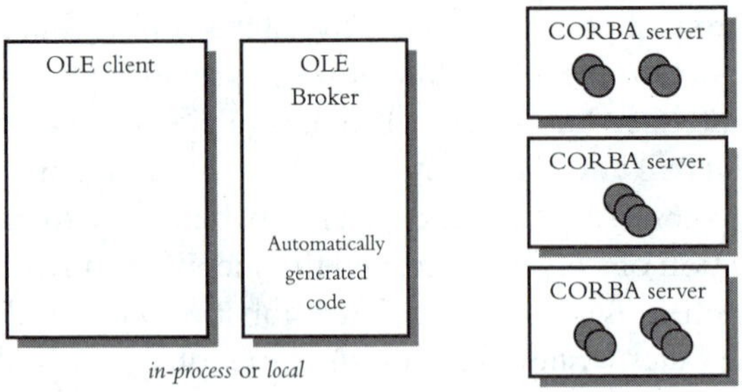

Figure 11.2 *OLE Broker.*

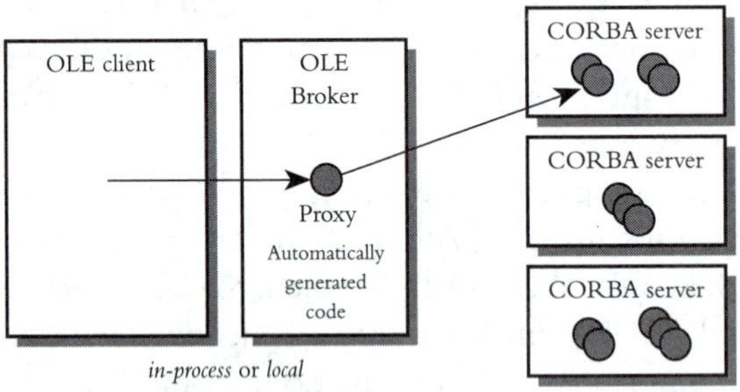

Figure 11.3 *OLE Broker and proxy.*

forwarded to the target object in the server. The target object is not aware that the call originated from OLE.

11.2 CORBA–OLE interworking: CORBA to OLE calls

OLE Automation can handle OLE to CORBA interworking, but not CORBA to OLE calls. For this, an IDL interface must be translated into an OLE Custom Control (OCX). An OCX provides an `IDispatch` interface, in the same way as an OLE Automation server, but it can also make calls to its environment (to its container in OLE terms). It defines a set of calls that it makes on its environment when some application-specific events occur. An OCX does not implement these functions – it calls them, and code interested in these events must act upon these calls.

To use an example with a GUI theme, an OCX may represent a scroll bar on the screen, and the user can use the mouse to move the scroll bar up and down. The OCX can define four functions that it calls when the scroll bar is moved up, moved down, reaches the low limit, and reaches the high limit. An application that includes this OCX (that is, that provides its environment) can define what these function calls actually do. OLE refers to these function calls (from the OCX to its container) as events.

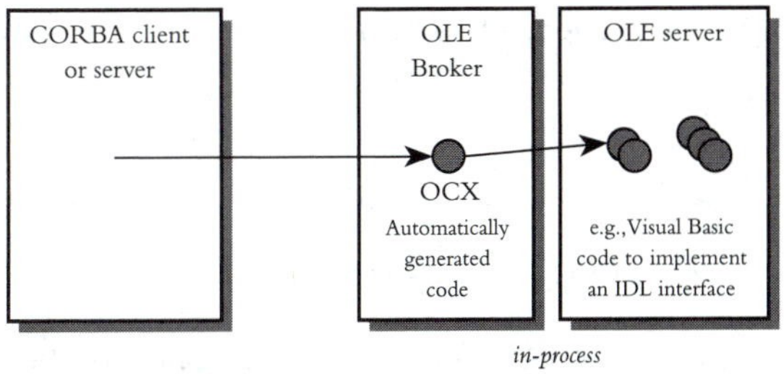

Figure 11.4 *A CORBA to OLE call.*

Physically, this call-back interface from an OCX to its environment is an OLE Automation `IDispatch` interface. There is, therefore, an `IDispatch` interface into the OCX (it is therefore an OLE Automation server), and an `IDispatch` interface in the opposite direction; that is, within the container that defines the OCX s environment.

To achieve CORBA to OLE calls, an IDL interface is translated into an OCX that defines an event for each IDL operation and attribute. This OCX code is installed in the OLE Broker as before, but now it can receive CORBA calls and call code defined in the application containing it. This code actually implements the calls made from the CORBA world, but it does so using an OLE language and using OLE rules. Therefore, a scripting language such as VB can be used to implement a CORBA interface (either one that was defined prior to the writing of the VB code, or one that was generated from an OLE interface definition).

One use of this is to allow a VB program that implements a GUI front-end to a CORBA server to receive **call-backs** from the server to inform it of important events. In our cinema application, such calls may include notifications of cancellations, or of price changes. The cinema server would act as if it were calling CORBA objects in the client; but these would actually be OLE objects.

Of course, in other cases, the use of CORBA to OLE calls can go beyond that of simple call-backs, and OLE can actually be used to implement a CORBA server.

Figure 11.4 shows a CORBA client calling an operation on a CORBA interface; this call is delivered to an OCX in an OLE Broker. The OCX translates the call into an OLE call on an OLE object that implements the interface. Once again, transparency is achieved because the caller and callee live within their own paradigms (CORBA and OLE, respectively).

11.3 Example usage

The code examples which follow assume that the variable `FO` has been initialized to reference a `FrontOffice` object. `cinemaBroker` is the chosen name for the OLE Broker.

A simple call to `FrontOffice::checkIfOpen()` can be coded as follows:

```
On Error GoTo ErrorTrap

Dim isOpen As Boolean
Dim nextAvailableDate As String
isOpen = FO.checkIfOpen ("12.6.1997",nextAvailableDate)
if Not isOpen then
      MsgBox ("Sorry the cinema is closed on the specified day, _
              but we're open again on the " & nextAvailableDate)
End If
      ExitSub

ErrorTrap:
' Handle or report the error here. Code not shown.
```

`FrontOffice::getPrice()` can be called as follows (for place `A7`):

```
On Error GoTo ErrorTrap

Dim thePrice As Single
Dim aPlace As cinemaBroker.DIPlace

'aPlace is a struct, so we have to create an object:
Set aPlace = ORBFactory.CreateType(Nothing,"cinemaBroker.Place")
aPlace.row = Asc("A")
aPlace.seat = 7

thePrice = FO.getPrice(aPlace,"12.6.1997")
      ExitSub

ErrorTrap:
' Handle or report the error here. Code not shown.
```

`FrontOffice::makeBooking()` can be called to obtain a reference to a `Booking` object. In the following code, an exception parameter is passed to `makeBooking()` and then a number of `If` statements are used to determine which exception has been raised. This structure is necessary if a different error message is to be printed for each exception:

```
Dim chosenPlaces As cinemaBroker.DIPlaces
Dim payment As cinemaBroker.DICreditCard
Dim aPlace As cinemaBroker.DIPlace
Dim aBooking As cinemaBroker.DIBooking

'payment is a struct, so we have to create it as follows:
Set payment = ORBFactory.CreateType(Nothing, _
                                    "cinemaBroker.CreditCard")
payment.id = "1234 2345 3456 4567"
payment.expiry = "30.09.1999"
```

```
'chosenPlaces is a sequence, so we have to create it as follows:
Set chosenPlaces = ORBFactory.CreateType(Nothing, _
                                    "cinemaBroker.Places")

' Now enter two places into the sequence (chosenPlaces):
Set aPlace = ORBFactory.CreateType(Nothing,"cinemaBroker.Place")
aPlace.row = Asc("A")
aPlace.seat = 7
chosenPlaces(0) = aPlace
aPlace.row = Asc("A")
aPlace.seat = 8
chosenPlaces(1) = aPlace

' Now make the call to makeBooking:
Set ABooking = FO.makeBooking( _
                         chosenPlaces,"12.6.1997",payment,Excp)

'Excp may contain an exception. Test for each possible exception
' and print a relevant message in each case.
if Not Excp is Nothing then
If Excp.EX_majorCode() = SYSTEM_EXCEPTION Then
     MsgBox (Excp.EX_repositoryID)
ElseIf Excp.EX_majorCode() = USER_EXCEPTION Then
     If TypeOf Excp Is cinemaBroker.DINoSuchPlace Then
          MsgBox ("Invalid Place: " & Excp.Where)
     ElseIf TypeOf Excp Is cinemaBroker.DIPlaceAlreadyBooked Then
          MsgBox ("Place already booked: " & Excp.Where & Excp.when)
     ElseIf TypeOf Excp Is cinemaBroker.DIInvalidCreditCard Then
          MsgBox ("Credit Card Rejected: " & Excp.invalidCard)
     ElseIf TypeOf Excp Is cinemaBroker.DIInvalidDate Then
          MsgBox ("Invalid Date: " & Excp.When)
     Else
          MsgBox (Excp.EX_repositoryID)
     End If
```

The call `Excp.EX_repositoryID` returns a string that describes the exception that has been raised.

11.4 Brief comparison of CORBA and OLE

This section describes some of the major differences between CORBA and OLE:

- OLE is a 'binary interworking' standard, by which we mean that the set of arrays of function pointers (that is, the layout details of its interfaces) that an object supports ultimately determines how to communicate with it. A C program can interact with an OLE object by indexing into an array of function pointers and calling a chosen function. IDL plays a much stronger role in CORBA because IDL is translated into different programming language definitions (C++, Ada, Visual Basic (actually, IDL is translated to OLE), Smalltalk, Java, Eiffel, Objective C, COBOL, and so on). For each language, the translation defines what a client can call, and no low-level implementation details are defined, or are even visible across a network.

- CORBA has a strong notion of object identity; an object has an identifier (an object reference in CORBA) and can be referred to uniquely. Object references can be transmitted as parameters and return values. OLE has no strong notion of object identity. Instead, interfaces have strong identity; a client can obtain a pointer to an interface (an array of function pointers), and can index into the interface to call a function.

- OLE supports inheritance, but **aggregation** is more frequently used. Hence, an object will support many independent interfaces, with no inheritance relationships between these. Sparse use is made of inheritance from base interfaces. Notwithstanding the simple introduction to OCXs given in this chapter, an OCX actually has 13 interfaces: three are related to Automation (one of these is the `IDispatch` interface), and the others are for facilities such as cut-and-paste and persistence. Inheritance plays a strong role in CORBA, and multiple inheritance is supported. Each object supports one interface, which may derive from others. The set of operations and attributes supported is the union of those defined in the various base and defined interfaces. Clients can call all of these operations and attributes, or they can narrow an object reference to a chosen base interface and then use just the operations and attributes available at that level. Support of multiple interfaces is being considered for CORBA objects.

- IDL plays a very strong role in CORBA, not just for defining the type system – that is, what is available to clients – but also how data is transmitted across a network. OLE supports ODL to define the type system (that is, to populate the OLE Type Library), and it supports MIDL to define how parameters and operation identifiers are communicated in a call from a caller to an OLE object. In fact, the NT 4.0 MIDL compiler extends IDL to support ODL constructs, effectively merging the two languages.

- CORBA defines translations to and from OLE.

12 Java and CORBA

This chapter shows simple examples of using CORBA from the Java programming language.

12.1 Java

Besides being easier to program than C++, Java has the strong advantage that code can be loaded over a network into a running application. Hence, a client can locate a service that it is interested in using, and then load a user interface for this and present an interactive screen to the user. Java has therefore been viewed as an internet or Web programming language, which allows clients to locate interesting services anywhere in the world, and then to interact with them. For example, a Java client may locate our cinema application and allow its user to book seats.

Java-based ORBs, for example OrbixWeb, have been written to make these interactions easier. Portions of OrbixWeb can be loaded across the network into Java clients, followed by, say, a user interface to our cinema application. That user interface can then make direct Java calls to CORBA objects on the server. The programming model for the client programmer is familiar to any Java programmer because the IDL operations and attributes are mapped to normal Java function calls. These calls provide a direct and high-level communication facility between the client and server, without any indirection through other servers (such as http servers) and without the creation or involvement of other processes. (CGI scripts are a lower-level communication facility, and also require the creation of a process on the server for each call. Beside being inefficient, this approach also has the disadvantage that servers have difficulties retaining state during a series of calls from one or more clients. This also makes it too difficult to provide transactional rollback facilities across a number of calls. Another disadvantage is that client and server programmers have to deal with the CGI language: in contrast, all CORBA interactions can be programmed directly in the chosen programming language, normally Java on a Web-based client.)

Of course, the CORBA server can be programmed in any programming language supported by CORBA, including Java.

The remainder of this section shows some sample Java code. The OMG are currently defining the standard IDL to Java mapping, but this was not available while this chapter was being finalised. Therefore some of the details shown here are likely to change. The code examples assume that the variable `theFrontOffice` has been initialized to reference a `FrontOffice` object.

A simple call to `FrontOffice::checkIfOpen()` can be coded as follows:

```
boolean isOpen = false;
String nextAvail = "";
try {
      isOpen = theFrontOffice.checkIfOpen("12.6.1997",nextAvail);
}
catch (FrontOffice.InvalidDate ex) {
      System.out.println("Invalid Date");
      System.out.println(ex.toString());
      System.exit(1);
}
catch (IE.Iona.Orbix2.CORBA.SystemException ex) {
      System.out.println("Exception: cannot get available seats");
      System.out.println(ex.toString(1));
      System.exit(1);
}
if (not isOpen) {
      System.out.println ("Sorry the cinema is closed on " +
            "the specified day, but we're open again on " +
            nextAvail);
}
```

`FrontOffice::getPrice()` can be called as follows to find the price of place `A7`:

```
float price = 0;
try {
      Place where = new Place ('A',7);
      price = theFrontOffice.getPrice(where,"12.6.1997");
}
catch (FrontOffice.NoSuchPlace ex) {
      System.out.println("Exception: Invalid place " + row + seat);
      System.out.println(ex.toString());
      System.exit(1);
}
catch (IE.Iona.Orbix2.CORBA.SystemException ex) {
      System.out.println("Exception: can't get available seats");
      System.out.println(ex.toString(1));
```

```
        System.exit(1);
}
```

`FrontOffice::makeBooking()` can be called to obtain a reference to a `Booking` object, which can then be used to interrogate the booking (here we simply read the `Booking::when` attribute):

```
Places seatList = new Places (2);
seatList.buffer[0] = new Place ('A',7);
seatList.buffer[1] = new Place ('A',8);

CreditCard myCard = new CreditCard ("1234 2345 3456 4567",
                                    "30.09.1999");

Booking.ref bookingRef = null;
try {
      bookingRef =
           theFrontOffice.makeBooking(seatList,"12.6.1997",myCard);
      System.out.println("Confirmed date is " +
                                              bookingRef.when());
}
catch (FrontOffice.NoSuchPlace ex) {
      System.out.println("Invalid Seat");
      System.exit(1);
}
catch (FrontOffice.PlaceAlreadyBooked ex) {
      System.out.println("At least one place already booked");
      System.exit(1);
}
catch (FrontOffice.InvalidCreditCard ex) {
      System.out.println("Credit card refused!");
      System.exit(1);
}
catch (FrontOffice.InvalidDate ex) {
      System.out.println("Invalid Date");
      System.exit(1);
}
catch (IE.Iona.Orbix2.COR BA.SystemException ex) {
      System.out.println("Exception: cannot make the booking");
      System.out.println(ex.toString(1));
      System.exit(1);
}
```

The current list of available places can be obtained as follows:

```
Places availableSeats = null;
try {
      availableSeats = theFrontOffice.listAvailablePlaces(
                                                    "12.6.1997");
}
```

```
// Catch clauses not shown here.
for (int idx=0; idx < availableSeats.length; idx++) {
      System.out.println (availableSeats.buffer[idx].row +
                          availableSeats.buffer[idx].seat );
}
```

OrbixWeb is a full implementation of CORBA in Java. It allows clients, interfaces, and servers to be implemented in Java. It also supports all of the Orbix-specific features, such as smart proxies, filters, and loaders.

Part three

Dynamic Aspects of CORBA

This part introduces the dynamic aspects of the CORBA specification. These aspects include the ability to interpret types at runtime, to define parameters to which any type of value can be passed, the ability to construct an invocation to an IDL operation that was not known to the programmer of the calling application, the facilities required to write a server that can accept any operation call rather than a fixed set known at compile time, and the ability to navigate the set of IDL definitions at runtime, for example to determine the parameters taken by a given operation.

Much of this material can be skipped at the first reading of this book, but a basic knowledge of the dynamic invocation interface (Chapter 15) and the Interface Repository (Chapter 16) is useful for most readers.

Chapter 13, **`TypeCode`**, introduces CORBA type codes, which are used to represent data types at runtime. Type codes are used in type `any`, the Dynamic Invocation Interface (DII), the Interface Repository (IFR) and the Dynamic Skeleton Interface (DSI), which are covered, respectively, in the following four chapters.

Chapter 14, **Type `any`**, explains the need for the IDL type `any`, and shows how it is defined and used. Where the type of a (input or output) parameter cannot be fixed at compile time, it can be defined as type `any`, leaving the type of the actual parameter to be specified at runtime.

Chapter 15, **Dynamic Invocation Interface**, shows how to use the DII. The programming of distributed applications is greatly simplified by the generation of proxy classes that allow clients to use normal C++ function invocation syntax. This approach naturally means that the set of interfaces that a client can use is fixed at its compilation time. Although this causes no difficulties for most applications, some applications (such as browsers) need to interact with interfaces that might not even have been defined when they were compiled. To cater for such applications, Orbix supports the DII, which allows an application to issue requests for any interface that exists when it is running. This interface can be used to construct a request for any operation of any interface at runtime and to invoke that request on any object implementing that interface. The basic DII is specified by CORBA, and Orbix extends this with a C++ stream-like interface which makes it significantly easier to use.

Chapter 16, **Interface Repository**, explains how a client, at runtime, can determine the definition of the interface of an arbitrary object; for example, what operations it supports and what types of parameters these take. Such facilities can be important for tools, such as browsers, as well as for parts of applications that need to perform dynamic type checking. The Interface Repository is frequently used in conjunction with the DII: the Interface Repository is used to determine what operations are supported by an object, and the DII is used to call some of these operations.

Chapter 17, **Introduction to Dynamic Skeleton Interface**, explains how a server can be programmed to accept any operation or attribute request, and not just those chosen at compile time. In particular, such servers do not need to be linked with the skeleton code for an IDL interface in order to accept invocations on its operations and attributes. The DSI is specifically designed to make it possible to implement flexible gateways.

13 TypeCode

This chapter describes the IDL type TypeCode, which is used to describe, at runtime, arbitrarily complex IDL types. Given a TypeCode value, an application can determine the full details of the associated type specification.

TypeCode is used for many purposes in a system, including the following:

- As a component of an IDL any value (any is discussed in Chapter 14). An any should be used as a parameter to an operation when the type of the parameter cannot be restricted at compile time. At runtime, an any can be constructed from a value of any type, and then passed to the operation. The target object that receives the any can extract the any's TypeCode and from it determine the type of the value passed to it. The class CORBA::Any has a public member function, type(), which has a return type of CORBA::TypeCode_ptr. This return value can be queried at runtime to determine the type of a CORBA::Any.
- By the Interface Repository (see Chapter 16). This stores IDL definitions and allows them to be listed and browsed at runtime.
- In an IDL specification, a TypeCode can be used as a normal type, for example as an attribute type, or as the type of a parameter or return value to an operation.
  The TypeCode interface is available in an IDL file only if it includes the directive:

```
#include <orb.idl>
```

TypeCode maps to C++ class CORBA::TypeCode, and to types CORBA::TypeCode_ptr and CORBA::TypeCode_var.

13.1 The IDL type TypeCode

This section describes the IDL interface to TypeCode. Each TypeCode value has a **kind**, which determines the overall category of the type that the TypeCode represents. TypeCode::kind() returns an enum value: for example, tk_string, tk_short, or tk_sequence. If the kind indicates that the TypeCode represents an IDL basic type, such as short, then this is all that needs to be understood about the TypeCode.

However, if the kind indicates that the TypeCode represents a constucted type, such as a sequence, then the TypeCode operations must be called to determine the other features of the type: in the case of a sequence, the element type and the bound (if any).

Interface TypeCode defines some operations that can be called on any TypeCode value. However, most of its operations can only be called for certain TypeCode values. For example, operation discriminator_type() can only be called if the TypeCode represents a union. Table 13.1 lists the operations that are valid on each TypeCode value; an attempt to call an operation on an inappropriate TypeCode will raise the TypeCode::BadKind exception. For example, if name() is called on a TypeCode of kind tk_string, then the BadKind exception will be raised.

Table 13.1 *Table of legal operations on different TypeCode values.*

Kind of the TypeCode	Set of operations that can be called
Object type (tk_objref)	equal() kind() id() name()
Struct (tk_struct)	equal() kind() id() name() member_count() member_name() member_type()
Union (tk_union)	equal() kind() id() name() member_count() member_name() member_type() member_label() discriminator_type() default_index()
Enum (tk_enum)	equal() kind() id() name() member_count() member_name()
Alias (tk_alias)	equal() kind() id() name() content_type()
Exception (tk_except)	equal() kind() id() name() member_count() member_name() member_type()
String (tk_string)	equal() kind() length()
Sequence (tk_sequence)	equal() kind() content_type() length()
Array (tk_array)	equal() kind() content_type() length()

✚ TypeCode is defined as follows:

```
// IDL, in module CORBA.
      enum TCKind {
                 tk_null, tk_void,
                 tk_short, tk_long, tk_ushort, tk_ulong,
                 tk_float, tk_double, tk_boolean, tk_char,
                 tk_octet, tk_any, tk_TypeCode,
                 tk_Principal, tk_objref,
                 tk_struct, tk_union, tk_enum, tk_string,
                 tk_sequence, tk_array, tk_alias, tk_except
      };

      interface TypeCode {
            exception Bounds {};
            exception BadKind {};

            boolean equal (in TypeCode tc);
            TCKind kind();

            // Type RepositoryId is defined
            // in Chapter 16.
            RepositoryId id() raises (BadKind);

            // Type Identifier is defined as string
            // in Chapter 16.
            Identifier name() raises (BadKind);

            unsigned long member_count() raises (BadKind);
            Identifier member_name (in unsigned long index)
                                  raises (BadKind, Bounds);

            TypeCode member_type (in unsigned long index)
                                  raises (BadKind, Bounds);

            any member_label (in unsigned long index)
                                  raises (BadKind, Bounds);
            TypeCode discriminator () raises (BadKind);
            long default_index() raises (BadKind);

            unsigned long length() raises (BadKind);

            TypeCode content_type() raises (BadKind);

            // The remaining two operations are for backward
            // compatibility with CORBA 1.x; their use is
            // not recommended:
            long param_count();
            any parameter (in long index) raises (Bounds);
      };
```

✚

Type `TCKind` lists the kinds of type code that can exist. `tk_void` is the kind of type code returned by an operation with a `void` return type. `tk_alias` is the kind of type code created by an IDL `typedef` statement: that is, a statement that creates an alias for another type.

The operations of `TypeCode` have the following meanings:

- `equal()`: returns true if and only if the `TypeCode` passed as a parameter is equal to the target `TypeCode`.
- `kind()`: returns the kind of the `TypeCode`.
- `id()`: returns the repository ID of the target `TypeCode`; see Chapter 16. This is valid only for object types (for example, `Booking`), structs, unions, enums, aliases, and exceptions.

  ✚ The returned string should not be freed by the caller. ✚
- `name()`: returns the name of the target `TypeCode`. This is valid only for object types (for example, `Booking`), structs, unions, enums, aliases, and exceptions.

  ✚ The returned string should not be freed by the caller. ✚
- `member_count()`: returns the number of members in the target `TypeCode`: for example, the number of members in a struct, or the number of enumeration constants in an enum. This is valid only for structs, unions, enums, and exceptions.
- `member_name()`: returns the name of a chosen member of the target `TypeCode`. The chosen member is specified by index, starting at zero. For a struct, union, or exception, this returns the name of a member; for an enum it returns the name of an enumeration constant. This operation is valid only for structs, unions, enums and exceptions. The `Bounds` exception is raised if the index is out of range.

  ✚ The returned string should not be freed by the caller. ✚
- `member_type()`: returns the `TypeCode` of a chosen member of the target `TypeCode`. The chosen member is specified by index, starting at zero. This operation is valid only for structs, unions, and exceptions. The `Bounds` exception is raised if the index is out of range.
- `member_label()`: this is valid only on unions; it returns the label of a chosen member (the label is the value that indicates when the chosen member of the union is valid). The chosen member is specified by index, starting at zero. The label is returned as an `any` because it can be a constant of any valid type. (For the default

member, the label will be `octet` zero; `octet` is not a valid label type so this special value cannot clash with the label of a normal member.)

- `discriminator_type()`: this is valid only on unions; it returns the `TypeCode` of the discriminant of the union.
- `default_index()`: this is valid only on unions; it returns the index of the default member of the union. This index can be used in operations `member_name()`, `member_type()`, and `member_label()`. The value `-1` is returned if the union has no default member.
- `length()`: returns the bound of a string or sequence, or the size of an array. Multidimensional arrays are modeled as arrays of arrays.
- `content_type()`: this is valid for sequences, arrays, and aliases. It returns the element type for a sequence, or array, and the type that an alias maps to.

13.2 Implementation of `TypeCode`

The IDL type `TypeCode` is implemented by the C++ class `CORBA::TypeCode`. An IDL operation with a parameter of type `TypeCode` is translated into a C++ member function with a parameter of type `CORBA::TypeCode_ptr`.

`TypeCode` constants

For each user-defined type which appears in an IDL file, a `CORBA::TypeCode_ptr` constant value can be generated by the IDL compiler. These constant values can be used to compare type codes or to pass contant values to services such as the Interface Repository.

In C++, these constants have names of the form `_tc_<type>` where `<type>` is the name of the user-defined type. For example, consider the following IDL specification:

```
typedef long LongType;
struct Useful {
      LongType l;
};

interface Interesting {
      /* . . . . */
};
```

From these definitions, the following `CORBA::TypeCode_ptr` constants can be generated:

```
_tc_Interesting
_tc_LongType
_tc_Useful
```

✚ In Orbix, type code constants will only be generated if the `-A` switch is specified to the IDL compiler. In this way, the IDL compiler can be instructed to generate `TypeCode` constants for IDL constructs such as interface, `typedef`, struct, union, and enum.

In addition, if struct `Useful` is extended to be the following

```
struct Useful {
      LongType l;
      string<4> st;
};
```

then the `TypeCode_ptr` constant `_tc_string_4` is also generated. ✚

Finally, a number of predefined `CORBA::TypeCode_ptr` constants are always available to allow the user to access `TypeCodes` for standard types. For example:

- `CORBA::_tc_float`: is an object reference for the `TypeCode` for `float`.
- `CORBA::_tc_string`: is an object reference for the `TypeCode` for unbounded `string`.
- `CORBA::_tc_TypeCode`: is an object reference for the `TypeCode` for `TypeCode` (which is a valid parameter type).

C++ `CORBA::TypeCode` class details

The C++ class, `CORBA::TypeCode`, defines 'standard' features such as `operator=()` and `operator==()`, as well as functions that correspond to IDL operations such as `equal()`, `kind()`, `id()`, `name()`, and so on.

13.3 Use of `TypeCode`

Some examples of using `TypeCode` are discussed in the following subsections.

13.3.1 Use of CORBA::TypeCode in type CORBA::Any

Consider an example IDL definition:

```
// IDL
struct Example{
     long l;
};
```

Use of the -A switch to the IDL compiler will cause the CORBA::TypeCode_ptr constant _tc_Example to be generated. Now, assume that a client program invokes the IDL operation op():

```
// IDL
interface Bar {
     void op(in any a);
};
```

with the following code:

```
// C++ - Client code
CORBA::Any a1;
Bar_var bVar = /* . . a reference to a Bar object . . */ ;
// We shall see how to initialize 'a1' in Chapter 14.
bVar->op(a1);
```

At the server side, we may wish to query the actual type of the parameter to op(). For example (assuming that interface Bar is implemented by C++ class Bar_i):

```
// C++
// Server code.
void Bar_i::op(const CORBA::Any& a)
          throw (CORBA::SystemException) {
     CORBA::TypeCode_var t = a.type();
     if(t->equal(_tc_Example)) {
          cout << "The parameter contains a struct, with "
               << t->member_count() << " members." << endl;
          /* . . handle this value .. */
     }
     else /* . . handle other data types . . */
}
```

Function type() on a COBRA::Any returns its TypeCode.

This is a common use of TypeCodes — namely, the runtime querying of type information from a CORBA::Any. The example shown simply compares the TypeCode of the parameter with a TypeCode constant. The other TypeCode operations (for example, `kind()`, `name()`, and `member_count()`) could be used to extract the kind of the `TypeCode` (of the `any`) and then its detailed definition.

IDL type `any` (C++ type `CORBA::Any`) is explained fully in Chapter 14. As we will see, C++ class `CORBA::Any` defines some operations that make the manipulation of `any`s very straightforward.

13.3.2 Use of `CORBA::TypeCode` when interrogating the Interface Repository

Class `CORBA::TypeCode` is frequently useful when using the Interface Repository functions. For example, when finding information about an operation defined in an interface, the number of its arguments can be determined, and then the `TypeCode` of each argument can be obtained. The function `kind()` can be used on each `TypeCode` to determine the kind of the type of each argument; and then functions such as `name()` and `member_count()` can be used to understand the type definition. We will take a detailed look at the Interface Repository in Chapter 16.

14 Type any

This chapter gives the details of the IDL type any, and the corresponding C++ class CORBA::Any. Type any is used to indicate that a value of an arbitrary type can be passed as a parameter or a return value.

Consider the following interface:

```
// IDL
interface Test {
      void op(in any a);
};
```

A client can construct an any to contain any type of value that can be specified in IDL, and then it can pass this in a call to operation op(). An application receiving an any must determine what type of value it stores and then extract the value.

There are a number of ways of constructing and interpreting an any, and these will be introduced in turn. The first of these mechanisms is the use of operator <<= (left-shift assign operator) and operator >>= (right-shift assign operator). This approach is both the simplest to use and the most type-safe. As we will see, however, there are situations where these operators cannot be used.

The IDL type any maps to the C++ class CORBA::Any. This class contains some private member data (accessible via public accessor functions), which store both the type of the any and its value. The type is stored as a CORBA::TypeCode, and the value is stored (presumably) as a void*.

14.1 Using operator <<= ( ) to insert into an any

The C++ class `CORBA::Any` contains a number of left-shift assign operators (<<=), which can be used to assign a value to an IDL `any`. An overloaded version `operator<<=()` is provided for each of the basic IDL types such as `long`, `unsigned long`, `float`, `double`, `string`, and so on. (An operator is not provided for `boolean`, `char`, `octet`, or bounded strings.) In addition, the IDL compiler can generate this operator for each user-defined type which appears in an IDL specification.

For example, consider the following IDL definition:

```
// IDL
interface Flexible {
     void doit (in any a);
};
```

Let us assume that a client programmer wishes to pass an `any` containing an IDL `short` (in C++, a `CORBA::Short`) as the parameter to the `doit()` operation. The following operator, which is a standard member of class `CORBA::Any`, may be used:

```
// C++
void operator<<=(CORBA::Short s);
```

Using this operator, the client programmer can write the following code:

```
// C++
Flexible_var flexVar = /* object ref to any Flexible object */ ;

CORBA::Any param;
CORBA::Short toPass;

toPass = 26;
param <<= toPass;
flexVar->doit(param);
```

The left-shift assign operator inserts a value into an `any`: it sets the `any` s value and `TypeCode`.

If the client wishes to pass an object reference, say to a `FrontOffice` object, the following generated operator can be used:

```
// C++
void operator<<=(CORBA::Any& a, const FrontOffice_ptr t);
```

So, for example, the client programmer might write:

```
CORBA::Any param;
FrontOffice_ptr toPass = /* object ref to any FrontOffice */;

// Now initialize the any, and call doit():
param <<= toPass;
flexVar->doit(param);
```

If the client wishes to pass a more complex user-defined type, such as `LongSeq`, defined below, one of the following generated operators can be used:

```
// IDL
typedef sequence<long, 10> LongSeq;

// C++ operators to insert LongSeq:
void operator<<=(CORBA::Any& a, const LongSeq& t); // Copies
void operator<<=(CORBA::Any& a, LongSeq* p);      // Does not copy
```

These two forms of `operator<<=()` are generated for types that cannot be passed efficiently by value (that is, for all types except `short`, `unsigned short`, `long`, `unsigned long`, `float`, `double`, enums, unbounded strings (`char*`), and object references). For example, the following code can be used to insert a sequence into an `any`:

```
LongSeq *toPass = new LongSeq;
toPass->length(1);
(*toPass)[0] = 27;

CORBA::Any param;

param <<= toPass;  // No copy is made.
flexVar->doit(param);
```

The various forms of `operator<<=()` are easy to use, and their use is also key to providing a type-safe mechanism for insertion into an `any`. In particular, the correct operator is called based on the type of the value being inserted. Furthermore, if an attempt is made to insert a value that has no corresponding IDL type, this will result in a compile-time error.

In addition, any previous value held by the `CORBA::Any` will be properly deallocated (for example, using `CORBA::release()` in the case of object references) when an `operator<<=()` is called.

✚ The default constructor for an `any` initializes it to have a type of `tk_null` (see Section 13.1, p.224) and no value. ✚

14.2 Using operator >>= ( ) to interpret an any

The C++ class `CORBA::Any` contains a number of right-shift assign operators (>>=), which can be used to extract the value in an `any`. These operators correspond to the basic IDL types such as `long`, `unsigned long`, `float`, `double`, `string`, and so on. As for `operator<<=()`, the IDL compiler can generate an `operator>>=()` for each user-defined type that appears in an IDL specification (for example, `LongSeq`, specified in Section 14.1).

The following example illustrates the use of these operators. It takes advantage of the fact that each `operator>>=()` returns a `CORBA::Boolean` value to indicate whether or not a value of the required type could be extracted from the `any`. Each `operator>>=()` returns `1` if the `any` contains a value whose `CORBA::TypeCode` matches the type of the right-hand parameter, and returns `0` otherwise.

The following code uses operator:

```
CORBA::Boolean operator>>=(const Any&, CORBA::Long&);
```

to extract a simple type:

```
// C++
void Flexible_i::doit(const CORBA::Any& a)
        throw (CORBA::SystemException) {

    CORBA::Long extractedValue;

    if (a >>= extractedValue) {
        cout << "I got a long with value "
            << extractedValue << endl;
    }
    else {
        // Normally, we would accept a set of different types,
        // but for simplicity here we just complain if
        // the any does not contain a long:
        cerr << "I can only handle longs ! " << endl;
    }
}
```

An `operator>>=()` is provided for the following types: `short`, `unsigned short`, `long`, `unsigned long`, `float`, `double`, enums, unbounded strings (`string` in IDL; `char*` in C++), and object references. (An operator is not provided for `boolean`, `char`, `octet`, and bounded strings.)

✚ The alternative way to extract a value from an `any` is to find the `any`'s type (using the `type()` function) and to compare that with type code constants (such as `CORBA::_tc_long` below):

```
// IDL
interface Flexible {
     void doit(in any a);
};

// C++
void Flexible_i::doit(const CORBA::Any& a)
          throw (CORBA::SystemException) {

     CORBA::Long extractedValue;
          CORBA::TypeCode_var t = a.type();

     if (t->equal(CORBA::_tc_long)) {
          a >>= extractedValue;
          cout << "I got a long with value "
               << extractedValue << endl;
     }
     else {
          cerr << "I only handle longs ! "<< endl;
     }
}
```

There is a type code constant for each built-in type, and the IDL compiler can be instructed to generate type code constants for each user-defined type. This is discussed in more detail in Chapter 13. ✚

Example of extracting a user-defined type

A different form of `operator>>=()` is required for types that cannot be passed efficiently by value (that is, for all types except `short`, `unsigned short`, `long`, `unsigned long`, `float`, `double`, enums, unbounded strings (`char*`), and object references). For some type, `T`, this operator has the form:

```
CORBA::Boolean operator>>=(const Any&, T*&);
```

The caller passes a pointer variable, which is updated to point to the `any` s storage.

Given the following IDL type:

```
// IDL
typedef sequence<long, 10> LongSeq;
```

an application programmer can extract a `LongSeq` from a `CORBA::Any` as follows:

```
// C++
void Flexible_i::doit(const CORBA::Any& a)
          throw (CORBA::SystemException) {

     LongSeq* extractedValue;
```

```
        if (a >>= extractedValue) {
                cout << "I got a sequence of longs"<< endl;
                // Here we could query the length of the sequence,
                // by calling extractedValue->length() and
                // then accessing each member.
        }
        else {
                cerr << "I can only handle a sequence of "
                     << "(maximum) 10 longs ! " << endl;
        }
}
```

✚ The generated right-shift operator for user-defined types takes a pointer to the generated type as the right-hand parameter. If the call to the operator is successful, this pointer will point to the memory that is managed by the `CORBA::Any`. No attempt should be made to de-allocate this storage: the `CORBA::Any` variable retains ownership of the memory. Note that extraction into an `_var` variable will violate this rule, since the `_var` variable will attempt to assume ownership of the memory. ✚

14.3 Other ways to construct and interpret an `any`

This section presents a number of other ways to construct and interpret an `any`. Operators `>>=` and `<<=` should be used wherever possible, but there are occasions when a more complex approach must be used. (See Figure 14.1 (p.232) for a summary of the various insertion and extraction mechanisms discussed in this chapter.)

14.3.1 Inserting and extracting `boolean`, `octet`, and `char`

The standard CORBA IDL to C++ mapping does not require that the IDL types `boolean`, `octet`, and `char` map to distinct C++ types. Therefore, it is not possible to insert and extract each of these using `operator<<=()` and `operator>>=()`. (Remember that the overloaded right-shift and left-shift assignment operators are distinguished based on the type of the right-hand argument.)

✚ In Orbix, the types `boolean` and `octet` do, in fact, map to the same underlying C++ type (`unsigned char`). Type `char` maps to a different type (C++ `char`), so a separate operator could have been provided for it, but this would not have been CORBA compliant. ✚

The distinction is in fact achieved through the use of helper types, which are nested within the C++ class `CORBA::Any`. Left-shift and right-shift assignment operators are provided for each of these helper types, and these can be used as follows:

```
// C++
CORBA::Any a;

// Insert a boolean into a:
CORBA::Boolean b = 1;
a <<= CORBA::Any::from_boolean(b);

// Extract the boolean from a:
CORBA::Boolean extractedValue1;
if (a >>= CORBA::Any::to_boolean(extractedValue1)) {
      cout << "Success !" << endl;
}


// Insert an octet into a:
CORBA::Octet o = 1;
a <<= CORBA::Any::from_octet(o);

// Extract the octet from a:
CORBA::Octet extractedValue2;
if (a >>= CORBA::Any::to_octet(extractedValue2)) {
      cout << "Success !" << endl;
}


// Insert a char into :
CORBA::Char c = 'b';
a <<= CORBA::Any::from_char(c);

// Extract the char from a:
CORBA::Char extractedValue3;
if (a >>= CORBA::Any::to_char(extractedValue3)) {
      cout << "Success !" << endl;
}
```

14.3.2 Insertion and extraction of bounded (and unbounded) strings

Since bounded and unbounded strings map to `char*` in C++, both cannot be inserted or extracted with the same `operator<<=()` or `operator>>=()`. In fact, the following two operators assume that the string is unbounded:

```
void operator<<=(Any&, const char*);
CORBA::Boolean operator>>=(Any&, char*&);
```

To insert and extract a bounded string, a helper type is provided:

```
CORBA::Any a;

// Insert a bounded string<10> into a:
char* p = CORBA::string_dup("test");
a <<= CORBA::Any::from_string(p,10); // 10 is the string bound.

// Extract the bounded string from a:
char *p2;
if (a >>= CORBA::Any::to_string(p2, 10)) {
      cout << "Success !" << endl;
      // p2 points to the string.
}
```

The use of `from_string` shown above makes a copy of the string passed to it. If this is not required, a value of true should be passed as the last parameter to `from_string`:

```
a <<= CORBA::Any::from_string(p,10,1); // Do not copy.
```

14.3.3 Insertion and extraction of object references

Insertion and extraction of object references can be done simply using `operator<<=()` and `operator>>=()`, as shown in Sections 14.1 and 14.2. However, an object reference can also be widened to a `CORBA::Object_ptr` as it is being extracted using the helper type to_`object()`.

14.3.4 Inserting and extracting array types

Recall that IDL arrays are mapped to regular C++ arrays. This presents a problem for the type-safe operator interface to `CORBA::Any` described in Sections 14.1 and 14.2. Because C++ array parameters decompose to a pointer to their first element, it is not possible to use the operators to insert or extract arrays of different lengths.

Nevertheless, arrays can be inserted and extracted using the operators, because a distinct C++ type is generated for each IDL array – specifically to help with insertion and extraction into or out of `CORBA::Any` variables. The name of this type is the name of the array followed by the suffix '`_forany`.'

Thus, the following example shows type-safe manipulation of arrays and a `CORBA::Any`:

```
// IDL
typedef long LongArray[2][2];

// C++
LongArray arrPointer = { {14, 15}, {24, 25} };
```

```
// (arrPointer could be initialized with any pointer to
// a 2x2 array of long values).

// Insertion:
CORBA::Any a;
a <<= LongArray_forany(arrPointer); // Copies the array.

// Extraction:
LongArray_forany extractedValue;
if (a >>= extractedValue) {
      cout << "Success !" << endl;
      cout << "Element [1][2] is "
           << extractedValue[1][2] << endl;
}
```

`LongArray_forany`, like `LongArray_var` (see Section 5.3, p.117), provides an `operator[]()` to access the array members, but the `LongArray_forany` type does not delete any storage associated with the array when it is destroyed. This is a good match for the semantics of `operator>>=()`; the `CORBA::Any` retains ownership of the memory returned by the operator. Therefore, there is no memory leak in the above code.

14.3.5 Inserting values at construction time

Instead of creating a `CORBA::Any` variable using the default constructor, and then inserting a value using `operator<<=()`, an application can specify the value and its type when the `CORBA::Any` is being constructed. This alternative constructor has the following signature:

```
// C++
CORBA::Any(CORBA::TypeCode_ptr tc,
    void* value,
    CORBA::Boolean release = 0);
```

This is normally not used, because it is more difficult to use than `operator<<=()`, and because it is not type-safe. In particular, the type of the value passed to parameter `value` might not match the type passed in parameter `tc`. A mismatch will not be detected (because the `value` parameter is of type `void*`) and this will lead to subsequent errors.

To illustrate the use of this constructor, a `CORBA::Any` variable can be constructed to contain a bounded string, as follows:

```
// IDL
typedef string<30> Address;

// C++
char* toPass = CORBA::string_dup("test");

CORBA::Any a(_tc_Address, &toPass, 1);
```

The first parameter to the constructor is a pseudo-object reference for a CORBA::TypeCode. In this case, the constant _tc_Address is passed (this is generated by the IDL compiler).

The second parameter is a pointer to the value to be inserted into the CORBA::Any. This value should be of the type specified by the CORBA::TypeCode_ptr parameter. The behavior is undefined if the CORBA::TypeCode_ptr and the value parameters do not agree. Note that when constructing CORBA::Anys for string types, the second parameter is of type char**.

The third parameter, release, specifies which code assumes ownership of the memory occupied by the value in the CORBA::Any variable. If it is 1 (True), then the CORBA::Any will assume ownership of the storage pointed to by the value parameter. If the third parameter is 0 (False), then it is the responsibility of the caller to manage the memory associated with the value. Notice that this is the default.

In the example shown, the CORBA::Any assumes ownership of the memory associated with toPass: the application code is not expected to free this memory.

14.3.6 Low-level access to a CORBA::Any

Three low-level functions are provided by class CORBA::Any, namely:

```
// C++
void replace( CORBA::TypeCode_ptr,
              void* value,
              CORBA::Boolean release = 0);
CORBA::TypeCode_ptr type() const;
const void* value() const;
```

The replace() function is similar to the constructor introduced in Section 14.3.5 and is only intended for use with types that cannot use the type-safe operators or helper types. It can be used at any time after construction of a CORBA::Any to replace the existing CORBA::TypeCode and value. Like the various <<= operators, it releases the previous CORBA::TypeCode and it de-allocates the storage previously associated with the value (the de-allocation is not done if the any has a *release* flag of 0 (False)). The release parameter has the same semantics as the release parameter of the CORBA::Any constructor described in Section 14.3.5.

The type() function returns an object reference for a CORBA::TypeCode which describes the type of the CORBA::Any. As for all object references, the caller must release the reference when it is no longer needed, or assign it to a CORBA::TypeCode_var variable for automatic management.

The value() function returns a pointer to the data stored in the CORBA::Any, or, if no value is stored, it returns the null pointer. This value may be cast to the appropriate C++ type depending on the CORBA::Any's CORBA::TypeCode. The rules for the actual C++ type returned for each different IDL type are listed in Table 14.1 (which shows a subset of the valid types).

Table 14.1 *The C++ types returned for each IDL type.*

IDL type	`value()`
`char`	`CORBA::Char*`
`short`	`CORBA::Short*`
`unsigned short`	`CORBA::UShort*`
`long`	`CORBA::Long*`
`unsigned long`	`CORBA::ULong*`
`float`	`CORBA::Float*`
`double`	`CORBA::Double*`
`Object`	`CORBA::Object_ptr*`
Object reference of interface `I`	`I_ptr*`
`string`	`char**`

14.4 Summary of insertion and extraction mechanisms

Figure 14.1 shows a summary of the insertion and extraction mechanisms.

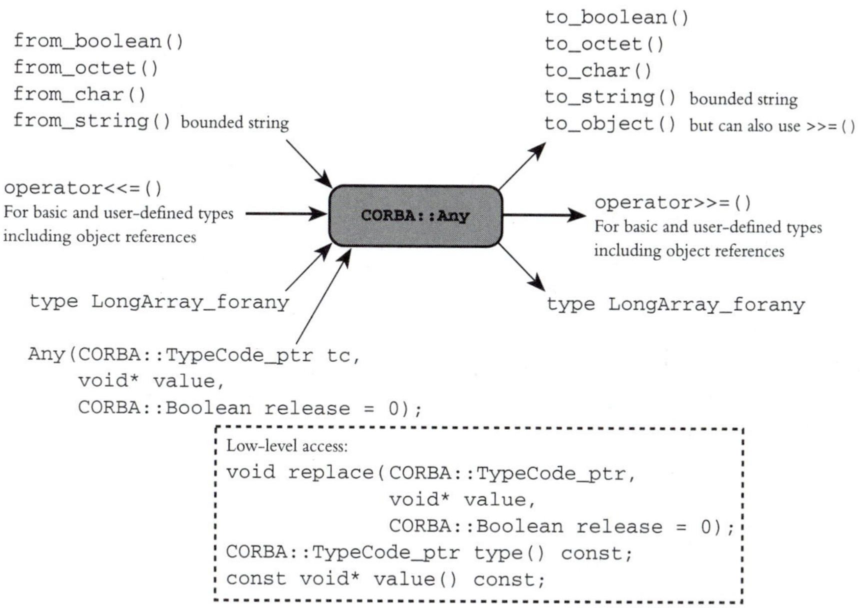

Figure 14.1 *Summary of insertion and extraction mechanisms.*

15 Dynamic Invocation Interface

IDL is used to describe interfaces, and the IDL compiler is used to generate the necessary support to allow clients to invoke remote objects. Specifically, the IDL compiler automatically builds the code for proxies, the code to dispatch incoming requests within a server, and the code to manage the underlying Orbix services.

Using this approach, the IDL interfaces that a client program can use are determined when the client program is compiled. Unfortunately, this is too limiting for a small but important subset of applications. These applications cannot be limited to using those objects that provide the IDL interfaces selected by the client programmer when compiling the code. These application programs and tools require the ability to use an indeterminate range of interfaces: interfaces that perhaps were not even conceived at the time when the applications were developed. Examples include browsers, gateways, management support tools, and distributed debuggers. It certainly is not desirable to limit a browsing tool to a fixed set of predefined interfaces.

CORBA therefore supports a **Dynamic Invocation Interface** (DII), which allows an application to issue requests for any interface, even to an interface that was unknown at the time when the application was compiled.

Note that inheritance of interfaces, as supported in IDL, does provide some help in accessing new interfaces. A tool can be written to use a specific IDL interface, but in fact that tool can successfully use objects that support any interface derived from that base interface. Sometimes, however, use of inheritance in this way is still insufficient; in particular, because the tool would be restricted to using only base interface operations and attributes, and not those added by derived interfaces.

To overcome this general problem, the DII allows invocations to be constructed by specifying, at runtime, the target object reference, the operation/attribute name, and the parameters to be passed. Such calls are termed 'dynamic' because the IDL interfaces used by a program do not have to be 'statically' determined at the time when the program is designed and implemented. In contrast, the use of IDL stubs (for example, in Chapter 6) has become known as the SII (Static Invocation Interface).

It is important to note that an object receiving an incoming invocation request does not know – or care – whether the client that sent the request used the SII or the DII.

15.1 Example

To demonstrate the use of the DII, we will use the familiar cinema example, making use of the following IDL definitions:

```
// IDL
interface FrontOffice {

      boolean checkIfOpen (in Date when,
                           out Date nextAvailableDate)
              raises (InvalidDate);

      // Rest not shown here.
};
```

In the examples that follow, we will show how a programmer can make dynamic invocations by constructing a `Request` object and then causing the specified operation or attribute call to be made. In many of the examples given later, the equivalent of the following call to operation `checkIfOpen()` will be made:

```
// C++
FrontOffice_var foVar = /* obj ref to any FrontOffice */
Date chosenDate = "1.1.1998";
CORBA::String_var nextDate;
foVar->checkIfOpen(chosenDate, nextDate);
```

15.2 Using the DII

To make an invocation using the DII, the following steps are carried out:

(1) An object reference to the target object is obtained.

(2) A `Request` object is constructed.

(3) This `Request` object is populated with the object reference, the name of the operation/attribute, and the parameters to the operation.

(4) The request is invoked.

(5) Finally, the results, if any, are obtained.

The following code illustrates some of these steps (ignoring error handling) using the stream-like interface to the DII that is specific to Orbix:

```
// C++
CORBA::Object_ptr target = /* any object reference */

// Create a Request, specifying the target object
// and the operation name.
CORBA::Request r(target, "checkIfOpen");

// Add parameters to the Request:
Date chosenDate = "1.1.1998";
CORBA::String_var nextDate;
r << CORBA::inMode << chosenDate
  << CORBA::outMode << nextDate;

// Invoke the Request:
r.invoke();
```

It can be seen that the DII is easy to use, especially using the stream-like interface. However, it must be noted that this example is unrealistic since it assumes that we know the name of the operation (`"checkIfOpen"`) and the types of parameters that it takes. In practice, this information will rarely be built into a program that uses the DII, because if that information were known then it would be easier to use the SII. In fact, there are two ways in which the DII is normally used:

(1) A client may find the details of an interface, or some specific operation, by communicating with the Interface Repository (as explained in Chapter 16). It can then construct a correct request using the DII, and issue this to the target object.

(2) A client may simply use the DII to make a call to an object, without determining the interface details. A gateway, for example, may receive a network packet describing a call that it should make. It could interact with the Interface Repository to check that the call is correct, or it could simply make the call, and rely on system level checks to detect errors.

In addition, Section 15.6 shows that the DII can be used to make 'deferred synchronous' operation calls. Since these cannot be made using the SII, some applications may use the DII with built-in knowledge of the operations and their parameters (as shown in the code above), simply so that deferred synchronous calls can be made.

Before continuing the description of the Orbix stream interface to the DII in Section 15.4 (p.250), we will first explain the CORBA compliant approach, showing how to use the DII as specified in the CORBA standard. Section 15.2.1 explains how a DII client will typically obtain an object reference to a target object.

15.2.1 Obtaining an object reference

Assume that there is already some server which contains a number of objects that implement the `FrontOffice` interface. The first step in using the DII is to obtain an object reference of type `CORBA::Object_ptr` which references the target object. Some applications may, of course, use a user-defined object reference type, but it is important to note that the DII can be used with the most general type, `CORBA::Object_ptr`.

Such an object reference may be obtained from an IDL operation or attribute call. A server may receive an object reference as an `in` or `inout` parameter, and a client may receive one as a return value, an `out` or `inout` parameter, or an attribute value. The formal IDL type of these parameters may be `Object`, but in fact any object reference type can be used.

Another way to obtain an object reference is to take an object reference string (the result of a previous call to `CORBA::Object::_object_to_string()`), and call `CORBA::Orbix.string_to_object()` to turn that string into an object reference, of type `CORBA::Object_ptr`. The string could be obtained in any way; for example, from a file or from a mail message. It could even be obtained as a parameter to an IDL operation call, but this would be unusual because it is normally better to use the IDL type `Object` rather than to use a string that holds an object reference.

`CORBA::Object::_object_to_string()` can be called as follows to obtain a 'stringified' object reference:

```
// C++
FrontOffice_var foVar = /* an object ref to any FrontOffice */ ;
char* refStr = foVar->_object_to_string();
```

The string contained in `refStr` can be used later, in any client or server, to obtain an object reference:

```
// C++
CORBA::Object_var target =
        CORBA::Orbix.string_to_object(refStr);
```

15.3 Using the DII: CORBA compliant approach

This section demonstrates how to use the DII using the classes and operations defined in the CORBA specification.

15.3.1 Creating a request

There are two compliant ways to construct a `Request` object:

(1) Using the function `_request()` defined in class `CORBA::Object`. This is declared as:

```
// C++. In class CORBA::Object.
Request_ptr _request(Identifier operation)
        throw (CORBA::SystemException);
```

The `Identifier` parameter is simply the name of the operation.

(2) Using the function `_create_request()`, also defined in class `CORBA::Object`. It is declared as:

```
// C++
// In class CORBA::Object.
Status _create_request(
        Context_ptr ctx,
        const char* operation,
        NVList_ptr arg_list,
        NamedValue_ptr& result,
        Request_ptr& request,
        Flags req_flags)
    throw (CORBA::SystemException);
```

The use of `_create_request()` is described in Section 15.3.2. Section 15.3.3 explains how to actually issue a request once it has been set up.

15.3.2 Setting up a request using `_create_request()`

The following steps can be used to set up a DII request:

(1) Obtain an object reference to the target object, as described in Section 15.2.1. One way to achieve this is to call `string_to_object()` on a stringified object reference; for example:

```
// C++
CORBA::Object_var target =
              CORBA::Orbix::string_to_object(refStr);
```

(2) Initialize the parameters for `_create_request()`:

```
CORBA::Request_var r_var;
CORBA::NVList_ptr arg_list = 0;
CORBA::NamedValue_var result;
CORBA::Flags f(0); // Null flag
```

(3) Construct a `Request` object by calling `_create_request()` on the target object:

```
target->_create_request( CORBA::Conctext::_nil(),
                         "checkIfOpen",
                         arg_list,
                         result,
                         r_var,
                         f);
```

✚ Alternatively, the `CORBA::ORB::create_operation_list()` function could be used to create a partially initialized named value list (`NVList`) . The first parameter to this is of type `OperationDef_ptr`, which can be obtained from the Interface Repository for the required operation. The returned `NVList_ptr` points to a named value list that is of the correct length, with one entry per parameter to the operation; and each of the entries will have the correct parameter passing mode, the name of the parameter, and an initial value of type `CORBA::Any`. The type of this `CORBA::Any` will be correct, but its value will not have been initialized. ✚

(4) The parameters to `checkIfOpen()` must then be added, in the correct order:

```
// Insert the first parameter, in Date when:
char *when_value = "1.1.1998"
r_var->add_arg("when", CORBA::_tc_string,
              &when_value, strlen(when_value),
              CORBA::ARG_IN);

// Insert the second parameter, out Date
nextAvailableDate:
char *nextAvailableDate_value;
r_var->add_arg("nextAvailableDate", CORBA::_tc_string,
              &nextAvailableDate_value, 0,
              CORBA::ARG_OUT);
/* use nextAvailableDate_value, then de-allocate
it using */
```

```
CORBA::string_free(nextAvailableDate_value);

/* invoke the operation here; see Section 15.3.3 */

// After the call, the return value can be obtained
as follows:
CORBA::Any *a = result->value();
CORBA::Boolean b;
if ((*a) >>= CORBA::Any::to_boolean(b))
   // b now tells us if the cinema is open or closed
else /* handle the error */
```

The function `add_arg()` adds a single parameter to the request. The parameter name, type, and value must be specified, as well as the parameter passing mode, which can be one of the following:

- `CORBA::ARG_IN`: input parameters (IDL's `in`).
- `CORBA::ARG_OUT`: output parameters (IDL's `out`).
- `CORBA::ARG_INOUT`: input/output parameters (IDL's `inout`).

The mode must be correctly specified to match the corresponding formal argument of the IDL operation, otherwise the call will fail its dynamic type checking.

15.3.3 Making a request

Once the parameters are inserted, the request can be made as follows:

```
// C++
// Send and get the outcome.
try {
      r_var->invoke();
}
catch (CORBA::SystemException& se) {
      cout << "Unexpected System Exception"
            << se << endl;
      exit(-1);
}
```

Exceptions are handled in the same manner as for static function invocations. Section 15.6 (p.253) shows alternative functions that make a request without blocking the caller.

15.3.4 Setting up a request to read or write an IDL attribute

The DII can also be used to read and write attributes. To read an attribute `size`, for example, the name should be '`_get_size`'; and to write it, the name should be '`_set_size`.'

15.3.5 Interrogating a request

Given a `Request`, the operation name and the target object's object reference can be determined using the functions `operation()` and `target()`, respectively. We will use these functions in Chapter 18, 'Filters.'

15.4 An alternative way of using the DII: the Orbix stream-like interface

This section describes the Orbix stream-like interface to the DII.

As usual, the first step is to obtain an object reference, as described in Section 15.2.1. Assume we have an object reference:

```
// C++
CORBA::Object_ptr target = /* any object reference */;
```

The request may be created as follows:

```
// C++. Create a Request.
CORBA::Request r(target);
```

Next, the operation name for the request should be set using `setOperation()`:

```
// C++
r.setOperation("checkIfOpen");
```

Alternatively, both the target and the operation name can be specified to the constructor:

```
// C++
CORBA::Request r(target, "checkIfOpen");
```

All of the parameters (`in`, `out`, and `inout`) to the request should then be added. Insertion of the parameters is done almost as if `Request` were an I/O stream. In particular, `Request` supports `operator<<()` for all of the basic types except `octet` (see Section 15.4.2):

```
// C++. Insert the two arguments:

r << "1.1.1998"; // operator<<() defaults to in mode.

Date nextDate;
r << CORBA::outMode << nextDate;
```

The parameters must be inserted in the correct order.

The default parameter attribute mode is `in`. Other parameter attribute modes can be set by using one of the (parameterless) manipulators: `CORBA::inMode`, `CORBA::outMode`, or `CORBA::inoutMode`. The use of a manipulator changes the parameter attribute mode for all subsequent parameters for this `Request` object or until another manipulator is used.

Once the parameters are inserted, the request can be made as follows:

```
// C++. Make the call and get the outcome:
try {
      r.invoke();
}
catch (CORBA::SystemException& se) {
      cout << "Unexpected System Exception"
           << se << endl;
      exit(-1);
}
```

Exceptions are handled in the same manner as for static function invocations.

15.4.1 Operation results

Once the invocation has been made, the return value and output parameters can be examined. If there are any `out` and `inout` parameters, then these will be modified by the call, and no special action is required to access their values. For example, after calling `invoke()` on a request to operation `checkIfOpen()`, the actual parameter `nextDate` will be updated automatically.

The operation's return value (if any) can be accessed using the extraction operator, `operator>>()`:

```
// C++
CORBA::Boolean isItOpen;
try {
      r.invoke();
      r >> isItOpen;
}
catch (CORBA::SystemException& se) {
      cout << "Unexpected System Exception"
           << se << endl;
      exit(-1);
}
catch (...) {
      cout << "Unexpected exception << endl;
      exit(1);
}
```

Note that `operator>>()` is used to extract just the return value from the request and *not* to extract the output parameters (which are updated automatically).

After using a `Request` object, the function `Request::reset()` can be called on it to allow it to be reused for another invocation. `reset()` clears any parameters that have been added, and it clears the target object reference and the operation name.

15.4.2 Inserting and extracting user-defined types

Two manipulators, `CORBA::insert` and `CORBA::extract`, are provided to insert and extract user-defined IDL types into and out of a `CORBA::Request` object. For example:

```
// IDL
struct Example {
        long m1;
        char m2;
};

// C++
CORBA::Request r ( /* . . . */ , /* . . . */ );
Example e;
e.m1 = 27;
e.m2 = 'c';
r << CORBA::insert(_tc_Example, &e, CORBA::inMode);
```

`CORBA::insert` uses the `CORBA::TypeCode` constant generated by the IDL compiler for each user-defined type. In this case, `_tc_Example` is the `TypeCode` for the IDL struct `Example`. See Chapter 13 for a full explanation of `TypeCode`.

A return value can be extracted from a `Request` using the `CORBA::extract` manipulator:

```
// C++
CORBA::Request r;
Example s1;
r >> CORBA::extract(_tc_Example, &s1);
```

The `CORBA::insert` and `CORBA::extract` manipulators will also work for primitive types. Special functions are provided for inserting and extracting arrays.

15.5 One-way calls

The `invoke()` function cannot be used to issue a call to a `oneway` operation. Instead, `send_oneway()` must be used. For example, if `Request r` has been set up to make an invocation on a oneway operation, then this call must be made as follows:

```
// C++
try {
      r.send_oneway();
}
catch (CORBA::SystemException& se) {
      cout << "Unexpected System Exception"
           << &se << endl;
      exit(-1);
}
```

As with other functions, `send_oneway()` should always be called within a C++ `try` block. Although a `oneway` operation cannot raise user-defined exceptions, it can result in the raising of a system-defined exception.

The `send_oneway()` function can also be used to make an invocation on a normal (non-`oneway`) operation. The effect of this is that the operation will be treated as `oneway` for this call only. All return values, and `out`/`inout` values, will be discarded. Exceptions that are not raised immediately by Orbix are also discarded.

15.6 Deferred synchronous requests

In addition to supporting the `invoke()` operation on a `Request`, CORBA supports a deferred synchronous invocation mode for operation requests. This allows clients to invoke on a target object and to continue processing in parallel with the invoked operation. At a later point, the client can check to see if a response is available, and, if so, it can obtain the response. This approach can be used to improve parallelism, particularly in the case of long-running invocations (parallelism is discussed in more detail in Chapter 21).

To use this invocation mode, a request should be invoked using `send_deferred()` on the `Request`. The caller will continue in parallel with the processing of the call by the target object. The caller can use the function `poll_response()` on the `Request` to determine whether the operation has completed, and `get_response()` to determine the result.

✚ In addition, `send_oneway()` can be called on a `Request` even for an operation that is not `oneway`, as explained in Section 15.5. The difference between `send_deferred()` and `send_oneway()` is that the former allows the caller to get the results of the call at some later time, but the latter does not.

Finally, note that two functions are provided to allow a set of requests to be made with a single call to the ORB. These are `CORBA::ORB::send_multiple_requests_oneway()` and `CORBA::ORB::send_multiple_requests_deferred()`. Each takes a sequence of `Request` objects, each `Request` describing one call that is to be made. ✚

16 Interface Repository

This chapter describes the Interface Repository (IFR), the component of CORBA that provides persistent storage of IDL modules, interfaces, and other IDL types. Some readers will need to know more than the basics, so advanced and detailed material has been included. This is marked so that it can be skipped by readers who need to have only a basic understanding of the IFR.

A repository can be iterated through to browse or list its contents. Alternatively, given an object reference, the object's type and all information about that type can be determined at runtime by calling functions defined by the IFR. Such facilities are important for some tools, such as:

- Browsers that allow designers and code writers to determine the types that have been defined in the system, and to list the details of chosen types.
- CASE tools that aid software design, writing, and debugging.
- Application-level code that uses the Dynamic Invocation Interface (DII) to invoke on objects whose types were not known to it at compile time. This code may need to determine the details of the object being invoked in order to construct the request using the DII.
- A gateway that requires runtime type information about the type of an object being invoked.

The IFR provides a set of IDL interfaces to browse and list its contents, and to determine the type information for a given object.

Orbix provides a utility (`putidl`) to enter definitions defined in an IDL file into the IFR; use of this utility provides the simplest and safest way to populate the IFR. In addition, the IFR defines IDL operations to update the definitions that it holds and to enter new definitions. However, these IDL operations are designed for use by a coordinated set of application level tools, and not for ad hoc use. Further, if these operations are used, care must be taken to avoid inconsistencies for any application using that information at that time. It is also possible to use the update operations to define interfaces and types that do not make sense (the IFR checks for such updates, but it cannot prevent all non-sensible updates).

16.1 Structure of the Interface Repository data

The data in the IFR is best viewed as a set of CORBA objects where, for each IDL type definition, one object is stored in the repository. For example, interface `FrontOffice` can have a corresponding object in the IFR, as can each of its attributes and operations. Using the IDL interfaces to these objects, at runtime an application can find the full IDL definition of `FrontOffice` and its attributes and operations.

Many IFR objects have a Repository ID (as well as having a normal object identifier, as for any other CORBA object). Any IFR object whose interface inherits from interface `Contained` has an attribute called `id` of type `RepositoryId`.

The CORBA specification allows the set of definitions that are of interest to an application to be divided among a number of repositories. If a particular definition appears in two or more repositories then it will have the same Repository ID in each repository (even though the associated objects in the different repositories will have different CORBA object identifiers).

Objects in the IFR support one of the following IDL interfaces, reflecting the IDL constructs they describe:

- `Repository`: the type of the repository itself, in which all of its other objects are nested.
- `ModuleDef`: each module has a name and can contain definitions of any type (except `Repository`).
- `InterfaceDef`: each interface has a name and a possible inheritance declaration, and can contain definitions of type attribute, operation, exception, typedef, and constant.
- `AttributeDef`: each attribute has a name and a type, and a mode that determines whether or not it is read-only.

- `OperationDef`: each operation has a name, a return value, a set of parameters, and, optionally, `raises` and `context` clauses.
- `ConstantDef`: each constant has a name, a type, and a value.
- `ExceptionDef`: each exception has a name and a set of member definitions.
- `StructDef`: each struct has a name, and also holds the definition of each of its members.
- `UnionDef`: each union has a name, and also holds a discriminant type and the definition of each of its members.
- `EmumDef`: each enum has a name, and also holds its list of member identifiers.
- `AliasDef`: each alias has a name and a type that it maps to. (Objects of this type correspond to `typedef` statements in IDL.)
- `PrimitiveDef`: objects of this type correspond to a type such as `short` or `long`, and are predefined within the IFR.
- `StringDef`: objects of this type correspond to bounded strings. They do not have a name; if they have been defined using an IDL `typedef` statement, then they will have an associated `AliasDef` object.
- `SequenceDef`: each sequence type records its bound (a value of zero indicates an unbounded sequence type) and its element type. Objects of this type do not have a name; if they have been defined using an IDL `typedef` statement, then they will have an associated `AliasDef` object.
- `ArrayDef`: each array type records its length and its element type. Objects of this type do not have a name; if they have been defined using an IDL `typedef` statement, then they will have an associated `AliasDef` object. Each `ArrayDef` object represents one dimension; multiple `ArrayDef` objects are required to represent a multidimensional array type.

In addition, the following abstract types (that is, those without direct instances) are defined: `IRObject`, `IDLType`, `TypedefDef`, `Contained`, and `Container`.

Understanding these types is the key to understanding how to use the IFR. They are nested in a natural manner, corresponding to the IDL definitions. For example, each `InterfaceDef` object is said to contain objects representing the interface's constant, type, exceptions, attribute, and operation definitions. The outermost object is of type `Repository`. The containment rules are shown in Figure 16.1.

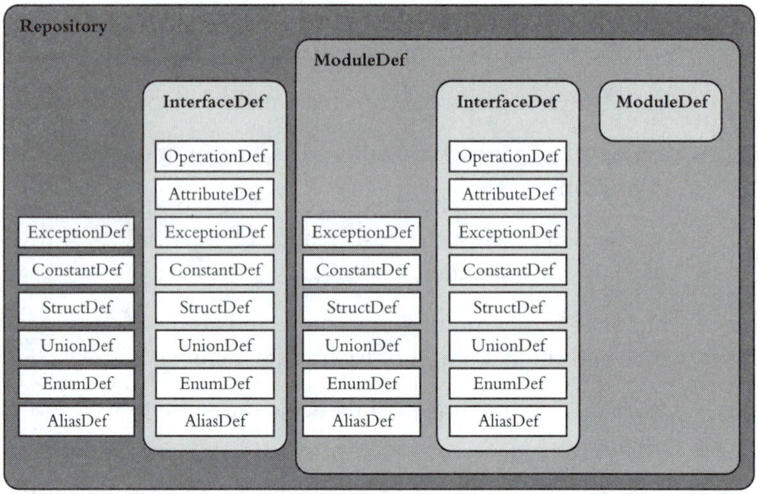

Figure 16.1 *Containment rules for IFR objects.*

Figure 16.2 shows a simple example for the following IDL:

```
module Cinema {
     typedef float Price;

     interface FrontOffice {
          exception InvalidDate { Date when; };
          readonly attribute string name;
          boolean checkIfOpen ( in Date when,
                                out Date nextAvailableDate)
               raises (InvalidDate);
     };
};
```

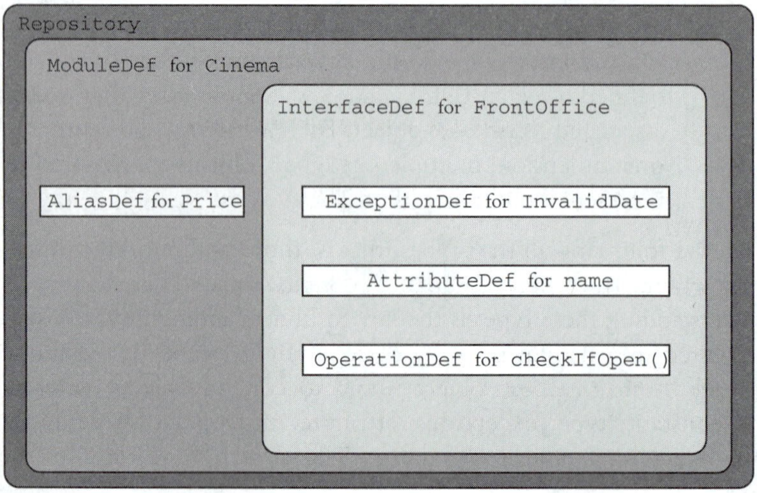

Figure 16.2 *Example IFR objects for part of* `FrontOffice` *example.*

16.1.1 Retrieving information from the Interface Repository

Given an object of any of the IFR types, full information on that definition can be determined. For example, `InterfaceDef` defines operations and attributes to determine an interface's name, its inheritance hierarchy, and the description of each operation and attribute.

In fact, there are three ways to retrieve information from the IFR:

(1) Given an object reference, its corresponding `InterfaceDef` object can be found. From this, all of the details of the object's interface definition can be found.

(2) An object reference to a `Repository` can be obtained, and its full contents can then be navigated.

(3) Given a `RepositoryId`, a reference to the corresponding object in the IFR can be obtained and interrogated.

These are explained in more detail in the following three subsections.

Retrieving information: `CORBA::Object::_get_interface()`

Given an object reference, say `objVar`, to any CORBA object, an object reference to an `InterfaceDef` object can be obtained as follows:

```
CORBA::InterfaceDef_var ifVar = objVar->_get_interface();
```

The member function `_get_interface()` returns a reference to an object within the IFR. Section 16.2 explains how information about that interface can be retrieved, and how references to the IFR objects containing it or contained within it can be obtained.

Retrieving information: browsing or listing a repository

Once a reference to a `Repository` object is obtained, the contents of that repository can be browsed or listed. There are two ways to obtain such an object reference. Firstly, the `resolve_initial_references()` operation can be called on the ORB (of type `CORBA::ORB`), passing the string "InterfaceRepository" as a parameter (see Section 7.3.3, p.165). This returns an object reference of type `CORBA::Object`, which can then be narrowed to a `CORBA::Repository` reference.

Alternatively, the Naming Service or the Orbix `_bind()` function can be used. For example:

```
// C++
Repository_var repVar = Repository::_bind(":IFR","");
```

Section 16.4.1 (p.271) explains how the resulting `Repository` object can be used.

Retrieving information: finding an object using its Repository ID

Given a Repository ID (of type `CORBA::RepositoryId`), this can be passed as a parameter to the `lookup_id()` operation of a `CORBA::Repository`. This returns a reference to an object of type `Contained`, and this can be narrowed to the correct object reference type.

16.1.2 Modifying information in the Interface Repository

Many of the interfaces described here include attributes and operations that can be used to create new IFR definitions or to modify existing ones. Nevertheless, the recommended way to make entries in the IFR is to use the IDL compiler to compile some IDL definitions, and instruct it to register these with the IFR. Similarly, the recommended way to modify the entries in the IFR is to modify the IDL source files and to recompile these using the IDL compiler.

The disadvantages of using the IDL attributes and operations of the IFR objects to directly change them is that these definitions will then be out of step with the IDL source files, and also that it is difficult to make a single IFR update while retaining overall consistency of a set of definitions. Therefore, the IDL interfaces defined in the IFR should be used primarily to retrieve information, not to modify it.

16.2 The interface to the Interface Repository

This section describes the set of IDL interfaces provided by the IFR. The simple types defined by the IFR are described first, followed by four base classes that capture common behavior, and then by the main IFR types (such as `Repository`, `InterfaceDef`, and `OperationDef`).

The description is broken into four distinct parts.

- This section describes the simple types that are used throughout the Interface Repository, and the class hierarchy of the interfaces defined in the IFR.
- Section 16.3 (p.262) discusses the abstract interfaces within the Interface Repository. These interfaces cannot be directly instantiated, but they provide base interfaces for all of the concrete interfaces within the Interface Repository.

- Section16.4 (p.271) discusses the concrete interfaces within the Interface Repository. These interfaces can be instantiated and they allow access to all of the information contained within the Interface Repository.
- Section 16.5 (p.285) shows some simple code that illustrates the use of the Interface Repository.

16.2.1 Simple types

The IFR defines the following simple IDL definitions:

```
// IDL
// In module CORBA.
typedef string Identifier;
typedef string ScopedName;
typedef string RepositoryId;
typedef string VersionSpec;

enum DefinitionKind {
      dk_none, dk_all,
      dk_Attribute, dk_Constant, dk_Exception, dk_Interface,
      dk_Module, dk_Operation, dk_Typedef,
      dk_Alias, dk_Struct, dk_Union, dk_Enum,
      dk_Primitive, dk_String, dk_Sequence, dk_Array,
      dk_Repository
};
```

An `Identifier` is a simple name that identifies modules, interfaces, constants, typedefs, exceptions, attributes, and operations.

✚ A `ScopedName` gives an entity's name relative to a scope. A `ScopedName` that begins with '`::`' is an **absolute scoped name**, one that uniquely identifies an entity within a repository. An example is `::FrontOffice::makeBooking`. A `ScopedName` that does not begin with '`::`' is a relative scoped name, one that identifies an entity relative to some other entity. An example is `makeBooking` within the entity with the absolute scoped name `::FrontOffice`.

A `RepositoryId` is a string that uniquely identifies an object (a constant, exception, attribute, operation, structure, union, enumeration, alias, interface, or module) within a repository, or globally within a set of repositories if more than one is being used.

Type `VersionSpec` is used to indicate the version number of an IFR object; that is, to allow the IFR to distinguish two or more versions of a definition, each with the same name but with details that evolve over time. However, the IFR is not *required* to support such versioning: it is not required to store more than one definition with any given name.

Each IFR object has an attribute (called `def_kind`) of type `DefinitionKind` that records the kind of the IFR object. For example, the `def_kind` attribute of an `interfaceDef` object will be `dk_interface`. The enumerated constants `dk_none` and `dk_all` have special meanings when searching for objects in a repository. ✚

16.2.2 Class hierarchy and abstract base interfaces

The IFR defines five abstract base interfaces (interfaces that cannot have direct instances), which are used to define the other IFR types:

✚

- `IRObject`: this is the base interface of all IFR objects. Its only attribute defines the kind of an IFR object (it is of type `DefinitionKind`).
- `IDLType`: this is the base interface of all IFR interfaces that describe types that can be used as IDL parameters, return values, or attributes. Its only attribute is called `type` and is of type `CORBA::TypeCode` (see Chapter 13).
- `TypedefDef`: this is the base interface for all IFR types (except interfaces) that can have names: structures, unions, enumerations, and aliases (results of IDL `typedef` definitions). `TypedefDef` inherits from `Contained` and `IDLType` but does not define any attributes or operations itself.
- `Contained`: many IFR objects can be contained in others (the exact meaning of contained will be explained later): constants, exceptions, attributes, operations, interfaces, modules, structures, unions, enumerations, and aliases (results of IDL `typedef` statements). This type defines an attribute `name`, and other attributes and operations.
- `Container`: some IFR objects can contain other objects: repositories, modules, and interfaces. This interfaces defines the common properties of containers.

The interface hierarchy for all of the IFR interfaces is shown in Figure 16.3. ✚

16.3 Abstract interfaces in the IFR

This section describes the abstract interfaces introduced in Section 16.2.2: `IRObject`, `IDLType`, `TypedefDef`, `Contained`, and `Container`. Section 16.4 describes the non-abstract (concrete) interfaces that inherit from those described here.

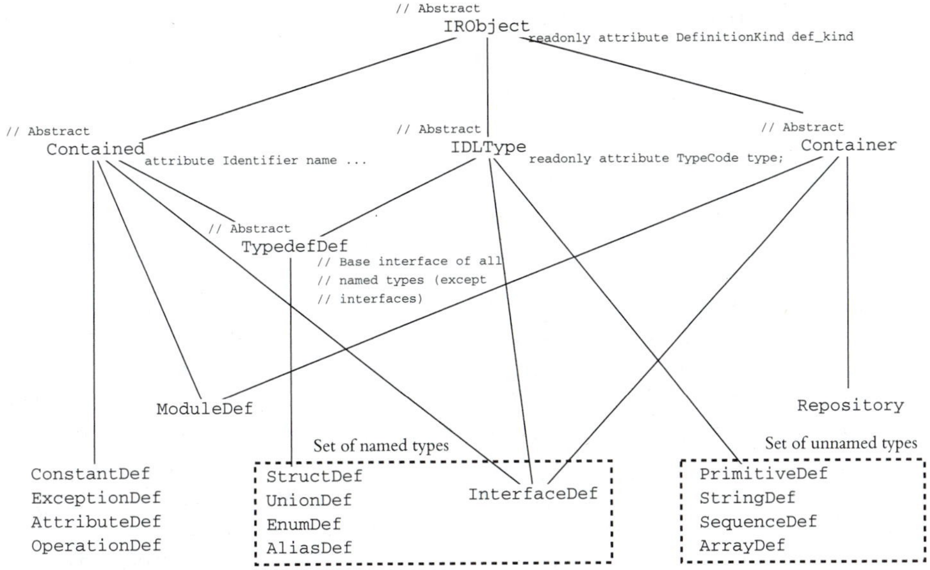

Figure 16.3 *Hierarchy for IFR interfaces.*

16.3.1 Interface `IRObject` (abstract)

Interface `IRObject` is defined as follows:

```
// IDL. In module CORBA:
interface IRObject {
      // read interface
      readonly attribute DefinitionKind def_kind;

      // write interface
      void destroy ();
};
```

This is the base interface of all IFR types. Other than defining an attribute and operation, and acting as the base interface of other interfaces, `IRObject` does not play any other role in the IFR definition.

Modifying objects of type `IRObject`

An IFR object can be deleted by calling its `destroy()` operation. This also deletes any objects contained in the target object. It is an error to call `destroy()` on a `Repository` or a `PrimitiveDef` object.

16.3.2 Interface `IDLType` (abstract)

Interface `IDLType` is defined as follows:

```
// IDL. In module CORBA:
interface IDLType : IRObject {
     readonly attribute TypeCode type;
};
```

Each structure, union, enumeration, alias (that is, IDL `typedef`), interface, primitive, bounded string, sequence, and array type known to the IFR is represented by an object whose interface inherits from `IDLType`. Each such object has an inherited attribute of type `TypeCode`, which encodes its type information (see Chapter 13); but type information can be extracted also using the operations and attributes defined by the IFR, as we will see.

Interface `IDLType` is used extensively within the IFR definitions. It is the base interface of many of the other interfaces, and it contains a `TypeCode` that describes a type in detail. Many IDL interfaces have two attributes that hold the same information, one of type `IDLType` and one of type `TypeCode`, although either one of these would suffice.

16.3.3 Interface `TypedefDef` (abstract)

Interface `TypedefDef` is defined as follows:

```
// IDL. In module CORBA:
interface TypedefDef : Contained, IDLType {
};
```

The `TypedefDef` interface is inherited by all IFR interfaces (except `InterfaceDef`) that define named types – that is, types for which a name must appear in their definition: structures, unions, enumerations, and aliases (the result of an IDL `typedef` statement). Interface `InterfaceDef` (which represents interface types) does not inherit from `TypedefDef`. Anonymous types (`PrimitiveDef`, `StringDef`, `SequenceDef`, and `ArrayDef`) do not inherit from `TypedefDef`. (If these are aliased using an IDL `typedef` statement, then this is captured by an `AliasDef` object in the IFR.)

Interface `TypedefDef` does not play a major role in the IFR definition. It is merely the base interface for `StructDef`, `UnionDef`, `EnumDef`, and `AliasDef`. ✚

16.3.4 Interface `Contained` (abstract)

Interface `Contained` is an abstract interface that is inherited by all IFR interfaces that describe types that can be contained in a module, interface, or repository: `AttributeDef`, `OperationDef`, `TypedefDef`, `ConstantDef`, `ModuleDef`, `InterfaceDef`, `ExceptionDef`, `StructDef`, `UnionDef`, `EnumDef`, and `AliasDef`.

For example, the interface `ModuleDef` inherits from `Contained` because it can be contained in a repository (and in a module).

The IFR defines two notions of contained:

(1) An IFR object is contained by the IFR object in which it is defined. For example, an `InterfaceDef` object is contained by the `ModuleDef` in which it is defined.

(2) An IFR object (of type `AttributeDef` or `OperationDef`) is contained in an object of type `InterfaceDef` if it is inherited into that interface. Therefore, an operation may be contained in an interface because the interface inherits the operation from another interface. An operation may be contained in a module because one of the module's interfaces inherits the operation from an interface defined outside of the module. When the objects contained in an IFR object are listed, there is an option to determine whether or not inherited objects should be included.

Interface `Contained` is central to the IFR. All concrete IFR interfaces inherit from it, except `Repository`, `PrimitiveDef`, `StringDef`, `SequenceDef`, and `ArrayDef`. (A repository cannot be contained in any IFR object, and the other four types define anonymous types that should not have the IDL attributes defined by interface `Contained`.)

`Contained` defines attributes and operations to determine the name (within its scope), Repository ID, and version of an object. It also defines an attribute, `defined_in`, which gives the object reference of the IFR object that the target object was defined in. (The `defined_in` attribute of an object always references the object that it is defined in. For example, `cancel()` is contained in `GroupBooking` because `cancel()` is defined in `Booking`, and `GroupBooking` inherits from `Booking`. Nevertheless, the `defined_in` attribute of the IFR object representing `cancel()` is a reference to `Booking`, not to `GroupBooking`.) The attribute `absolute_name` gives the absolute scoped name of an object. The attribute `containing_repository` references the `Repository` within which the object was defined (alternatively, this could be found by recursively following an object's `defined_in` attribute until the repository level is reached).

The interface is defined as follows:

```
// IDL. In module CORBA:
interface Contained : IRObject {

	// Read/write interface:
	attribute RepositoryId id;
	attribute Identifier name;
	attribute VersionSpec version;
```

```
    // Read interface:
    readonly attribute Container defined_in;
    readonly attribute ScopedName absolute_name;
    readonly attribute Repository containing_repository;

    struct Description {
        DefinitionKind kind;
        any value;
    };

    Description describe ();

    // Write interface:
    void move (
        in Container new_container,
        in Identifier new_name,
        in VersionSpec new_version
    );
};
```

The operation `describe()` returns a `Contained::Description` structure, which contains most (and in most cases, all) of the information for an object in a single call. The `kind` member of the returned structure contains the same value as the `def_kind` attribute that `Contained` inherits from `IRObject`. This can be used to determine how to interpret the `value` member of type `any` (see Chapter 14).

Operation `describe()` can be called on any IFR object of type `ConstantDef`, `ExceptionDef`, `AttributeDef`, `OperationDef`, `StructDef`, `UnionDef`, `EnumDef`, `AliasDef`, `ModuleDef`, or `InterfaceDef`. In each case, the `value` member will be an `any` which will contain a different structure for each type of object. In fact, the structure stored in the `value` member will be one of the following:

```
ConstantDescription
ExceptionDescription
AttributeDescription
OperationDescription
ModuleDescription
InterfaceDescription
TypeDescription
```

The last of these, `TypeDescription`, is used for objects of type `StructDef`, `UnionDef`, `EnumDef`, and `AliasDef` (it is associated with interface `TypedefDef`, from which `StructDef`, `UnionDef`, `EnumDef`, and `AliasDef` inherit).

For example, if an application calls `describe()` on an `ExceptionDef` object, then it will know that the structure contained in the `any` will be of type `ExceptionDescription`. If the application does not know the type of `Contained object` that it calls `describe()` on, then the `kind` member of the returned `Contained::Description` structure should be used to determine the type (alternatively, it can interrogate the `value` member to determine what type of `any` it contains).

Modifying objects of type contained

The id, name, and version attributes can be changed (but not to values that are currently being used). The move() operation moves the target object to another Container object (this must be within the same repository), and specifies the name and version to use in that Container.

16.3.5 Interface Container (abstract)

Interface Container defines attributes and operations common to IFR types that can contain objects: Repository, ModuleDef, and InterfaceDef. It defines four operations that allow its content to be listed or browsed:

- lookup(): finds a single contained object by name. If a relative name is given, the object is looked up relative to the target container. If an absolute name is given the object is looked up relative to the containing Repository.
- contents(): returns a sequence of Contained objects that are *directly* contained in (defined in or inherited into) the target object. The parameters indicate the set of contained objects required:
  - limit_type: limits the objects which will be returned. If it is set to dk_all, all objects will be returned. If set to the DefinitionKind for a particular Interface Repository kind, only objects of that kind will be returned. For example, if operations are of interest, limit_type can be set to dk_operation.
  - exclude_inherited: if set to True, inherited objects are not returned. If set to False, inherited objects are included.
- lookup_name(): locates an object or objects by name within the target container. The named objects can be directly or indirectly defined in or inherited into the target container. A sequence of contained objects is returned because more than one object can exist with the same simple name in a set of nested scopes. The parameters indicate the set of contained objects required:
  - search_name: specifies the simple name of the object to search for.
  - levels_to_search: specifies the number of levels of nesting to be included in the search. For example, if set to 1, the search is restricted to the current object. If set to -1, the search is unrestricted.

  - `limit_type`: limits the objects which are to be returned. If it is set to `dk_all`, all objects will be returned. If set to the `DefinitionKind` for a particular Interface Repository kind, only objects of that kind will be returned. For example, if operations are of interest, `limit_type` can be set to `dk_operation`.
  - `exclude_inherited`: if set to True, inherited objects are not returned. If set to False, inherited objects are included.
- `describe_contents()`: acts like `contents()` except that it returns a sequence of `Container::Description` structures, rather than just a sequence of object references. It achieves the result of calling `contents()`, followed by calling `Contained::describe()` on each returned object reference. The parameters are the same as those for the `contents()` operation with one exception. The `max_returned_objs` parameter places a maximum length on the returned sequence. Setting this parameter to `-1` indicates no restriction.

A typical use of the `Container` interface is to navigate through the hierarchy of definitions – starting, for example, at a `Repository`.

`Container` is defined as follows:

```
// IDL. In module CORBA:

typedef sequence <Contained> ContainedSeq;

interface Container : IRObject {

      // Read interface:
      Contained lookup ( in ScopedName search_name);

      ContainedSeq contents (
            in DefinitionKind limit_type,
            in boolean exclude_inherited
      );

      ContainedSeq lookup_name (
            in Identifier search_name,
            in long levels_to_search,
            in DefinitionKind limit_type,
            in boolean exclude_inherited
      );

      struct Description {
            Contained contained_object;
            DefinitionKind kind;
            any value;
```

```
};

typedef sequence<Description> DescriptionSeq;

DescriptionSeq describe_contents (
      in DefinitionKind limit_type,
      in boolean exclude_inherited,
      in long max_returned_objs
);

// Write interface:

ModuleDef create_module (
      in RepositoryId id,
      in Identifier name,
      in VersionSpec version
);

ConstantDef create_constant (
      in RepositoryId id,
      in Identifier name,
      in VersionSpec version,
      in IDLType type,
      in any value
);

StructDef create_struct (
      in RepositoryId id,
      in Identifier name,
      in VersionSpec version,
      in StructMemberSeq members
);

ExceptionDef create_exception (
      in RepositoryId id,
      in Identifier name,
      in VersionSpec version,
      in StructMemberSeq members
);

UnionDef create_union (
      in RepositoryId id,
      in Identifier name,
      in VersionSpec version,
      in IDLType discriminator_type,
      in UnionMemberSeq members
);

EnumDef create_enum (
      in RepositoryId id,
      in Identifier name,
```

```
        in VersionSpec version,
        in EnumMemberSeq members
    );

    AliasDef create_alias (
        in RepositoryId id,
        in Identifier name,
        in VersionSpec version,
        in IDLType original_type
    );

    InterfaceDef create_interface (
        in RepositoryId id,
        in Identifier name,
        in VersionSpec version,
        in InterfaceDefSeq base_interfaces
    );
};
```

Modifying objects of type `Container`

Compiling IDL definitions is the recommended way to populate a repository. The alternative is to use operations on a `Container` object to create new IFR objects within it:

- `create_module()`
- `create_exception()`
- `create_alias()`
- `create_constant()`
- `create_union()`
- `create_interface()`
- `create_struct()`
- `create_enum()`

Each takes as parameters the information required to construct an IFR object of the corresponding type. The types `StructMemberSeq`, `UnionMemberSeq`, `EnumMemberSeq`, and `InterfaceDefSeq` are defined later in subsections of Section 16.4. The `create_interface()` operation creates an empty interface definition (it records the name of the interface and its base interfaces); this can then be populated with attributes and operations. Type, exception, and constant definitions can be added by treating the new `InterfaceDef` object as a `Container` object. Attribute and operations can be added using, respectively, `InterfaceDef::create_attribute()` and `InterfaceDef::create_operation()`.

16.4 Non-abstract interfaces in the IFR

This section describes the non-abstract interfaces that are defined by the IFR:

- `Repository`
- `ModuleDef`
- `ConstantDef`
- `StructDef`
- `UnionDef`
- `EnumDef`
- `AliasDef`
- `PrimitiveDef`
- `StringDef`
- `SequenceDef`
- `ArrayDef`
- `ExceptionDef`
- `AttributeDef`
- `OperationDef`
- `InterfaceDef`

The remainder of this section describes each of these interfaces in turn.

16.4.1 Repository

The Interface Repository itself is a container for IDL type definitions. Its interface is described by the interface `Repository`, which inherits from `Container` (note, therefore, that it does not have a `name` or `id` attribute):

```
// IDL. In module CORBA:
interface Repository : Container {

      // Read interface:

      Contained lookup_id (in RepositoryId search_id);

      PrimitiveDef get_primitive (in PrimitiveKind kind);
```

```
    // Write interface:

    StringDef create_string (in unsigned long bound);

    SequenceDef create_sequence (
          in unsigned long bound,
          in IDLType element_type
    );

    ArrayDef create_array (
          in unsigned long length,
          in IDLType element_type
    );
};
```

Section 16.1.1 (p.259) explains how to obtain a reference to a `Repository` object.

The operation `lookup_id()` returns a `Contained` object given its `RepositoryId`. Operation `get_primitive()` returns an object reference for the `PrimitiveDef` object whose kind is specified as a parameter. These primitive objects always exist within the IFR, one primitive object per primitive type (for example, `short`, `long`, `unsigned short`, `unsigned long`, `float`, `double`, `boolean`, `char`, `octet`, and (unbounded) `string`). Type `PrimitiveKind` is defined in Section 16.4.8 (p.278).

On a `Repository` object, the inherited `Container::describe_contents()` operation returns a sequence of `Container::Description` structures; one such structure for each top-level item in the repository:

```
// IDL. In module Container:
struct Description {
      Contained  contained_object;
      DefinitionKind kind;
      any value;
};
```

Each structure has a member `contained_object` which references a contained object; the `kind` member indicates its type, and the `value` member gives an `any` that contains a struct. The type of this struct is different for each type of contained object: for a contained interface it will be `InterfaceDescription`; for a module it will be `ModuleDescription`, and so on. These structs are defined later in this chapter, as each IFR type is described. These structs can also be obtained by calling `Contained::describe()`, which returns a struct of type `Contained::description`. This struct in turn holds an `any` that will contain one of these `description` structs.

Modifying objects of type `Repository`

The `Repository` interface defines three operations that create anonymous types: `create_string()`, `create_sequence()`, and `create_array()`. Each anonymous type object must be used in the definition of exactly one other object (actually an object of type `Contained`); the anonymous type object is deleted whenever the `Contained` object it is used in is deleted. It is the application's responsibility to delete an anonymous type object if it cannot subsequently be used successfully in the definition of a `Contained` object.

The operation `create_string()` creates an anonymous bounded string type. `create_sequence()` creates an anonymous bounded or unbounded sequence type of the specified element type (parameter `element_type`). The sequence type will be unbounded if the `bound` parameter is `-1`. The operation `create_array()` creates an anonymous one-dimensional array (multidimensional arrays are created by recursive use of `create_array()`).

The fourth anonymous type, `PrimitiveDef`, cannot be created; instead, an object reference to a desired primitive type is returned by `Repository::get_primitive()`.

16.4.2 Interface ModuleDef

A module can contain constants, typedefs (aliases), exceptions, interfaces, and other modules. A module is also an object of type `Contained`, possessing a name and other attributes (inherited from `Contained`). `Moduledef` is defined as follows:

```
// IDL. In module CORBA:
interface ModuleDef : Container, Contained {
};
```

Result of calling Contained::describe() on a ModuleDef

When the `Contained::describe()` operation is called on a `ModuleDef` object, the returned `Contained::Description` struct will have the following two members (see Section 16.3.4, p.264):

- `kind` will be `dk_Module`.
- `value` will be an any that contains a structure of the following type (defined in module `CORBA`):

```
// IDL
struct ModuleDescription {
    Identifier name;
    RepositoryId id;
    RepositoryId defined_in;
    VersionSpec version;
};
```

16.4.3 Interface ConstantDef

A ConstantDef object represents a named constant:

```
// IDL
interface ConstantDef : Contained {
      readonly attribute TypeCode type;
      attribute IDLType type_def;
      attribute any value;
};
```

The name of the constant is inherited from Contained; its type is given in attributes type and type_def; its value is in attribute value. The two type attributes represent the same data: one as a TypeCode, and the other as an object of type IDLType that contains the same TypeCode value.

✚ Modifying objects of type ConstantDef

The type of a constant can be changed by changing its type_def attribute. This also changes its type attribute. The value of a constant can be changed by changing its value attribute; at that time, the type of the any must be the same as the type attributes of the constant.

Result of calling Contained::describe() on a ConstantDef

When the Contained::describe() operation is called on a ConstantDef object, the returned Contained::Description struct will have the following two members (see Section 16.3.4, p.264):

- kind will be dk_Constant.
- value will be an any that contains a structure of the following type (defined in module CORBA):

```
// IDL
struct ConstantDescription {
    Identifier name;
    RepositoryId id;
    RepositoryId defined_in;
    VersionSpec version;
    TypeCode type;
    any value;
};
```

✚

16.4.4 Interface StructDef

A StructDef object represents an IDL structure:

```
// IDL. In module CORBA:
struct StructMember {
      Identifier name;
      TypeCode type;
      IDLType type_def;
};
typedef sequence <StructMember> StructMemberSeq;

interface StructDef : TypedefDef {
      attribute StructMemberSeq members;
};
```

The name of the structure is in the inherited `Contained::name` attribute. Attribute `members` contains a description of each member of the struct: its `name` and its type (`members type` and `type_def` contain the same information).

✚ Modifying objects of type `StructDef`

Attribute `members` can be modified to give a structure a different set of members. Only the `name` and `type_def` members of each `StructMember` should be set (the `type` member should be set to `_tc_void`, and it will be automatically changed internally to the `TypeCode` of the `type_def` member).

Result of calling `Contained::describe()` on a `StructDef`

When the `Contained::describe()` operation is called on a `StructDef` object, the returned `Contained::Description` structure will have the following two members (see Section 16.3.4, p.264):

- `kind` will be `dk_Struct`.
- `value` will be an `any` that contains a structure of the following type (defined in module `CORBA`):

```
// IDL
struct TypeDescription {
   Identifier name;
   RepositoryId id;
   RepositoryId defined_in;
   VersionSpec version;
   TypeCode type;
};
```

✚

16.4.5 Interface `UnionDef`

A `UnionDef` represents an IDL union definition:

```
// IDL. In module CORBA:
```

```
struct UnionMember {
      Identifier name;
      any label;
      TypeCode type;
      IDLType type_def;
};
typedef sequence <UnionMember> UnionMemberSeq;

interface UnionDef : TypedefDef {
      readonly attribute TypeCode discriminator_type;
      attribute IDLType discriminator_type_def;
      attribute UnionMemberSeq members;
};
```

The name of the union is in the inherited `Contained::name` attribute. Attribute `members` contains a description of each member of the union: its `name`, its `label`, and its type (`type` and `type_def` contain the same information). The union's discriminator type is held in the attributes `discriminator_type` and `discriminator_type_def` (these contain the same `TypeCode`).

Modifying objects of type `UnionDef`

The `members` attribute can be modified to give a union type a different set of members. Only the `name`, `label`, and `type_def` members of each `UnionMember` should be set (the `type` member should be set to `_tc_void`, and it will be automatically changed internally to the `TypeCode` of the `type_def` member).

The type of a union's discriminator can be changed by changing the attribute `discriminator_type_def`; attribute `discriminator_type` will be set automatically to the `TypeCode` of the `discriminator_type_def` attribute.

Result of calling `Contained::describe()` on a `UnionDef`

When the `Contained::describe()` operation is called on a `UnionDef` object, the returned `Contained::Description` structure will have the following two members (see Section 16.3.4, p.264):

- `kind` will be `dk_Union`.
- `value` will be an `any` that contains a structure of the following type (defined in module `CORBA`):

```
// IDL
struct TypeDescription {
    Identifier name;
    RepositoryId id;
    RepositoryId defined_in;
    VersionSpec version;
    TypeCode type;
};
```

16.4.6 Interface EnumDef

An EnumDef represents an IDL enumerated type definition:

```
// IDL. In module CORBA:
typedef sequence <Identifier> EnumMemberSeq;

interface EnumDef : TypedefDef {
      attribute EnumMemberSeq members;
};
```

The attribute members contains the list of enumerated constants. The name of the enumerated type is in the inherited Contained::name attribute.

✚ Modifying objects of type EnumDef

The set of enumerated constants of an enumerated type can be altered by changing its members attribute.

Result of calling Contained::describe() on a EnumDef

When the Contained::describe() operation is called on a EnumDef object, the returned Contained::Description struct will have the following two members (see Section 16.3.4, p.264):

- kind will be dk_Enum.
- value will be an any that contains a structure of the following type (defined in module CORBA):

```
// IDL
struct TypeDescription {
   Identifier name;
   RepositoryId id;
   RepositoryId defined_in;
   VersionSpec version;
   TypeCode type;
};
```

✚

16.4.7 Interface AliasDef

An AliasDef represents an IDL typedef:

```
// IDL. In module CORBA:
interface AliasDef : TypedefDef {
      attribute IDLType original_type_def;
};
```

The name of the alias is in the inherited `Contained::name` attribute. The attribute `original_type_def` gives the type that it maps to.

✚ Modifying objects of type `AliasDef`

The type of an alias can be changed by changing its `original_type_def` attribute. This automatically sets its inherited `IDLType::type` attribute.

Result of calling `Contained::describe()` on an `AliasDef`

When the `Contained::describe()` operation is called on an `AliasDef` object, the returned `Contained::Description` structure will have the following two members (see Section 16.3.4, p.264):

- `kind` will be `dk_Alias`.
- `value` will be an `any` that contains a structure of the following type (defined in module `CORBA`):

```
// IDL
struct TypeDescription {
    Identifier name;
    RepositoryId id;
    RepositoryId defined_in;
    VersionSpec version;
    TypeCode type;
};
```

✚

16.4.8 Interface `PrimitiveDef`

A `PrimitiveDef` object represents a primitive type, such as `short`. `PrimitiveDef` is defined as follows:

```
// IDL. In module CORBA:
enum PrimitiveKind {
      pk_null, pk_void, pk_short, pk_long, pk_ushort,
      pk_ulong,pk_float, pk_double, pk_boolean, pk_char,
      pk_octet,pk_any, pk_TypeCode, pk_Principal,
      pk_string, pk_objref
};

interface PrimitiveDef: IDLType {
      readonly attribute PrimitiveKind kind;
};
```

A `PrimitiveDef` object is anonymous. Its `kind` attribute specifies which primitive type it represents. A `PrimitiveDef` object of kind `pk_string` represents the unbounded string type. A `PrimitiveDef` object of kind `pk_objref` represents IDL type `Object`.

`PrimitiveDef` objects cannot be created or modified; instead, they are owned by the IFR and are obtained using the `Repository::get_primitive()` operation.

16.4.9 Interface `StringDef`

A `StringDef` object represents a bounded string type:

```
// IDL. In module CORBA:
interface StringDef : IDLType {
      attribute unsigned long bound;
};
```

A `StringDef` object is anonymous. Its `bound` attribute specifies the string's bound (this cannot be zero). Unbounded strings are primitive types (see Section 16.4.8).

✚ Modifying objects of type `StringDef`

The bound of a `StringDef` object can be altered by changing its `bound` attribute. ✚

16.4.10 Interface `SequenceDef`

A `SequenceDef` object represents an IDL sequence definition:

```
// IDL. In module CORBA:
interface SequenceDef : IDLType {
      attribute unsigned long bound;
      readonly attribute TypeCode element_type;
      attribute IDLType element_type_def;
};
```

A `SequenceDef` is anonymous. Its bound is given by its `bound` attribute; a bound of zero indicates an unbounded sequence type. The type of its elements is given by attributes `element_type` and `element_type_def` (these contain the same information).

✚ Modifying objects of type `SequenceDef`

The element type of a sequence type can be altered by changing its `element_type_def` attribute (its `element_type` attribute will be changed automatically). The bound of a sequence type can be changed by changing its `bound` attribute. ✚

16.4.11 Interface `ArrayDef`

An `ArrayDef` object represents a one-dimensional IDL array definition:

```
// IDL. In module CORBA:
interface ArrayDef : IDLType {
      attribute unsigned long length;
      readonly attribute TypeCode element_type;
      attribute IDLType element_type_def;
};
```

Attribute `length` gives the length of an array definition; the type of its elements is given by attributes `element_type_def` and `element_type` (these contain the same information).

A multidimensional array is represented by an `ArrayDef` with an element type that is another array definition. The final element type represents the actual element type for the array.

✚ Modifying objects of type `ArrayDef`

The length of an `ArrayDef` object can be changed by changing its `length` attribute. The type of its elements can be changed by changing its `element_type_def` attribute (its `element_type` attribute will be changed automatically). ✚

16.4.12 Interface `ExceptionDef`

An `ExceptionDef` object represents an IDL exception definition:

```
// IDL. In module CORBA:
interface ExceptionDef : Contained {
      readonly attribute TypeCode type;
      attribute StructMemberSeq members;
};
```

`StructMemberSeq` is defined in Section 16.4.4 (p.274).

The definition of an exception can be understood from its `members` attribute, or from its `type` attribute.

✚ Modifying objects of type `ExceptionDef`

The members of an `ExceptionDef` can be changed by changing its `members` attribute (see Section 16.4.4, p.274).

Result of calling `Contained::describe()` on an `ExceptionDef`

When the `Contained::describe()` operation is called on an `ExceptionDef` object, the returned `Contained::Description` structure will have the following two members (see Section 16.3.4, p.264):

- `kind` will be `dk_Exception`.
- `value` will be an `any` that contains a structure of the following type (defined in module `CORBA`):

```
// IDL
struct ExceptionDescription {
    Identifier name;
    RepositoryId id;
    RepositoryId defined_in;
    VersionSpec version;
    TypeCode type;
};
```

16.4.13 Interface `AttributeDef`

An `AttributeDef` object represents an attribute definition (within an interface definition):

```
// IDL. In module CORBA:
enum AttributeMode { ATTR_NORMAL, ATTR_READONLY };

interface AttributeDef : Contained {
      readonly attribute TypeCode type;
      attribute IDLType type_def;
      attribute AttributeMode mode;
};
```

Attribute `mode` specifies whether or not the `AttributeDef` is `readonly`. The attribute's name is in the inherited `Contained::name` attribute. Its type is given by attributes `type_def` and `type` (these contain the same information).

Modifying objects of type `AttributeDef`

The mode of an `AttributeDef` object can be changed by changing its `mode` attribute. Its type can be changed by changing its `type_def` attribute (its `type` attribute will be changed automatically).

Result of calling `Contained::describe()` on a `AttributeDef`

When the `Contained::describe()` operation is called on a `AttributeDef` object, the returned `Contained::Description` structure will have the following two members (see Section 16.3.4, p.264):

- `kind` will be `dk_Attribute`.
- `value` will be an `any` that contains a structure of the following type (defined in module `CORBA`):

```
// IDL
struct AttributeDescription {
    Identifier name;
    RepositoryId id;
    RepositoryId defined_in;
    VersionSpec version;
    TypeCode type;
    AttributeMode mode;
};
```

16.4.14 Interface `OperationDef`

An `OperationDef` object represents an operation (defined in an interface):

```
// IDL. In module CORBA:
enum OperationMode {OP_NORMAL, OP_ONEWAY};

enum ParameterMode {PARAM_IN, PARAM_OUT, PARAM_INOUT};

struct ParameterDescription {
      Identifier name;
      TypeCode type;
      IDLType type_def;
      ParameterMode mode;
};

typedef sequence <ParameterDescription> ParDescriptionSeq;

typedef Identifier ContextIdentifier;
typedef sequence <ContextIdentifier> ContextIdSeq;

typedef sequence <ExceptionDef> ExceptionDefSeq;
typedef sequence <ExceptionDescription> ExcDescriptionSeq;

interface OperationDef : Contained {
      readonly attribute TypeCode result;
      attribute IDLType result_def;
      attribute ParDescriptionSeq params;
      attribute OperationMode mode;
      attribute ContextIdSeq contexts;
      attribute ExceptionDefSeq exceptions;
};
```

Attributes `result` and `result_def` give the return type of an operation (both attributes contain the same information). Its parameters are described by attribute `params`; and its `mode` indicates whether or not it is a `oneway` operation. Its `context` and `raises` clauses are represented by attributes `contexts` and `exceptions`, respectively. The context information is a sequence of identifiers. The exception information is a sequence of `ExceptionDef` object references (see Section 16.4.12).

Modifying objects of type `OperationDef`

The `result_def`, `params`, `mode`, `contexts`, and `exceptions` attributes of an `OperationDef` can be modified. Changing the `result_def` attribute automatically changes the `result` attribute.

Result of calling `Contained::describe()` on an `OperationDef`

When the `Contained::describe()` operation is called on an `OperationDef` object, the returned `Contained::Description` structure will have the following two members (see Section 16.3.4, p.264):

- `kind` will be `dk_Operation`.
- `value` will be an `any` that contains a structure of the following type (defined in module `CORBA`):

```
// IDL
struct OperationDescription {
    Identifier name;
    RepositoryId id;
    RepositoryId defined_in;
    VersionSpec version;
    TypeCode result;
    OperationMode mode;
    ContextIdSeq contexts;
    ParDescriptionSeq parameters;
    ExcDescriptionSeq exceptions;
};
```

16.4.15 Interface `InterfaceDef`

An `InterfaceDef` object represents an IDL interface definition:

```
// IDL. In module CORBA:
typedef sequence <InterfaceDef> InterfaceDefSeq;
typedef sequence <RepositoryId> RepositoryIdSeq;
typedef sequence <OperationDescription> OpDescriptionSeq;
typedef sequence <AttributeDescription> AttrDescriptionSeq;
```

```
interface InterfaceDef : Container, Contained, IDLType {

      // Read/write interface:
      attribute InterfaceDefSeq base_interfaces;

      // Read interface:

      boolean is_a (in RepositoryId interface_id);

      struct FullInterfaceDescription {
            Identifier name;
            RepositoryId id;
            RepositoryId defined_in;
            VersionSpec version;
            OpDescriptionSeq operations;
            AttrDescriptionSeq attributes;
            RepositoryIdSeq base_interfaces;
            TypeCode type;
      };

      FullInterfaceDescription describe_interface();

      // Write interface:

      AttributeDef create_attribute (
            in RepositoryId id,
            in Identifier name,
            in VersionSpec version,
            in IDLType type,
            in AttributeMode mode
      );

      OperationDef create_operation (
            in RepositoryId id,
            in Identifier name,
            in VersionSpec version,
            in IDLType result,
            in OperationMode mode,
            in ParDescriptionSeq params,
            in ExceptionDefSeq exceptions,
            in ContextIdSeq contexts
      );
};
```

The interface's name is obtained from the inherited `Contained::name` attribute. Attribute `base_interfaces` lists all of the direct base interfaces of an `InterfaceDef`. Operation `is_a()` returns true if and only if the target `InterfaceDef` object inherits, directly or indirectly, from the `InterfaceDef` object whose `RepositoryId` is passed as a parameter.

Operation `describe_interface()` returns a `FullInterfaceDescription` structure. It gives the interface's name, repository ID, the repository ID of the IFR object that it is defined in, its version number, a description of its operations (struct `OperationDescription` is defined in Section 16.4.14), a description of its attributes (struct `AttributeDescription` is defined in Section 16.4.13), its base interfaces, and the `TypeCode` of the interface itself. Details of contained types, exceptions, and constants can be obtained using `Container::describe_contents()`.

Calling `CORBA::get_interface()` (in C++, this is the `_get_interface()` member function) on any CORBA object returns a reference to the `InterfaceDef` object that defines the CORBA object's interface.

Modifying objects of type `InterfaceDef`

The inheritance specification of an `InterfaceDef` object can be changed by changing its `base_interfaces` attribute.

An attribute or operation can be defined in an `InterfaceDef` object using `create_attribute()` or `create_operation()`, respectively.

Result of calling `Contained::describe()` on an `InterfaceDef`

When the `Contained::describe()` operation is called on an `InterfaceDef` object, the returned `Contained::Description` structure will have the following two members (see Section 16.3.4, p.264):

- `kind` will be `dk_Interface`.
- `value` will be an `any` that contains a structure of the following type (defined in module `CORBA`):

```
// IDL
struct InterfaceDescription {
    Identifier name;
    RepositoryId id;
    RepositoryId defined_in;
    VersionSpec version;
    RepositoryIdSeq base_interfaces;
};
```

16.5 Example of using the Interface Repository

In this section, we show some simple uses of the IFR.

The following code prints the list of operation names and attribute names defined on the interface of a given object:

```
// C++. List the names of the operations valid on
// the object referenced by objVar.

CORBA::InterfaceDef_var interfaceVar;

try {
      // Get interface definition:
      interfaceVar = objVar->_get_interface();
}
catch (...) { /* Handle any exceptions */ }

CORBA::InterfaceDef::FullInterfaceDescription_var full;
try {
      full = interfaceVar->describe_interface();
}
catch (...) { /* Handle any exceptions */ }

// Now print out the operation names:
cout << "The operation names are: " << endl;
CORBA::ULong i;
for (i=0; i < full.operations.length(); i++) {
      cout << '\t' << full.operations[i].name;

// Now print out the attribute names:
cout << "The attribute names are: " << endl;
for (i=0; i < full->attributes.length(); i++) {
      cout << '\t' << full->attributes[i].name;
```

The example can be extended by finding the `OperationDef` object for an operation called `op1()`. The `Container::lookup_name()` can be used as follows:

```
try {
      CORBA::ContainedSeq_var opSeq;
      cout << "Looking up operation op1()" << endl;
      opSeq = interfaceVar->lookup_name(
                  "op1", 1, CORBA::dk_Operation, 0);
      if (opSeq->length() != 1)
            cout << "Incorrect result for lookup_name()";
            exit(1);
      } else {
            // Narrow the result to be an OperationDef:
            CORBA::OperationDef_var opVar;
            opVar = CORBA::OperationDef::_narrow(opSeq[0]);
            if (!CORBA::_is_nil(opVar))
                  // _narrow succeeded
            else
                  // _narrow failed
```

```
        }
        ...
}
catch (...) { /* Handle any exceptions */ }
```

17 Introduction to Dynamic Skeleton Interface

In Chapter 15, the Dynamic Invocation Interface (DII) was introduced to allow clients to construct a request by hand and then invoke it. The advantage of the DII is that it allows a client to make an invocation on an object even when the object's IDL interface is unknown at compile time. The DII is a fundamental part of the dynamic CORBA support for clients; without it, a client would be able to use an IDL interface only if it was linked with the stub code for that interface.

The Dynamic Skeleton Interface (DSI) is the server-side equivalent of the DII. It allows a server to receive an operation or attribute invocation on any object, even one with an IDL interface unknown at compile time. The server does not need to be linked with the skeleton code for an interface to accept operation invocations on it.

Instead, a server can define a function that will be informed of an incoming operation or attribute invocation: that function can determine the identity of the object being invoked, the name of the operation, and the types and values of each argument. It can then carry out the task that is being requested by the client, and construct and return the result.

The client need not be aware that the server is in fact implemented using the DSI; it simply makes IDL calls as normal. (Recall from the DII, that a server need not consider whether the client uses the DII or the SII.)

Since the introduction of the DSI, the normal way of writing a server (implementing a class that uses the BOAImpl or TIE approach, creating instances of that class, and linking with the skeleton code generated by the IDL compiler) has become known as the Static Skeleton Interface (SSI).

In the same manner that use of the DII is significantly less common than use of the SII (that is, the Static Invocation Interface, where the client is linked with the stubs generated by the IDL compiler), use of the DSI is significantly less common

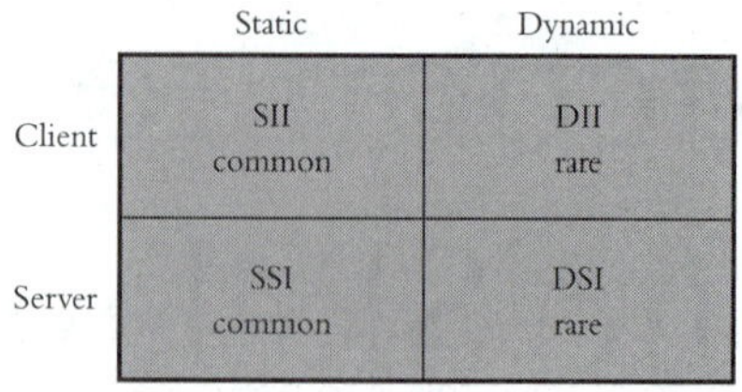
Static
Dynamic
Client
SII
common
DII
rare
Server
SSI
common
DSI
rare

Figure 17.1 *Static/dynamic clients and servers.*

than use of the SSI. Figure 17.1 shows the four possibilities for static/dynamic clients and servers.

To process incoming operation or attribute invocations using the DSI, a server must make a call to the ORB to indicate that it wishes to use the DSI for a specified IDL interface. The same server can use the SSI to handle operation or attribute invocations on other interfaces, but it cannot use the DSI and SSI on the same interface.

This chapter introduces the DSI and its associated interfaces and programming model. The DSI is a recent addition to the CORBA specfication, therefore it is covered only briefly here.

Uses of the DSI

The DSI has been explicitly designed to help programmers to write gateways, specifically gateways to interface between CORBA and some non-CORBA system. A gateway would have to know the protocol used by the non-CORBA system but it would be the only part of the CORBA system that would require this knowledge: the rest of the CORBA system would continue to make and accept IDL calls as usual.

The Internet Inter-ORB Protocol (IIOP protocol) is a very useful interoperability protocol. Because all ORBs must support at least IIOP, it allows an object in one ORB to invoke on an object in another ORB. However, non-CORBA systems do not have to support this protocol, and yet CORBA may have to be interfaced to such systems. One way to achieve this is to recode the ORB to be able to communicate using the non-CORBA protocol, but it is often easier to construct a gateway using the DSI. This gateway would appear as a CORBA server, and clients in the CORBA system would have the impression that it contained many CORBA objects that they could invoke on. In reality, the server would use the DSI to trap the incoming invocations and translate them into calls on the non-CORBA system.

Recall from Chapter 15 that the DII can be used to construct a gateway from a non-CORBA system into CORBA. A process can receive a message from a non-CORBA system and translate it into a CORBA call using the DII. A combination of the DSI and DII therefore gives a process the ability to be a bidirectional gateway. It can receive messages from the non-CORBA system and use the DII to make CORBA calls; and it can use the DSI to receive operation and attribute requests from the CORBA system and translate these into messages in the non-CORBA system.

✚ Other usages of the DSI are also possible, but it is likely that these will be rare. One example is that a server may contain a very large number of non-CORBA objects that it wishes to make available to its clients. One way to achieve this is to provide an individual CORBA object to act as a front-end for each non-CORBA object, but in some cases this multitude of objects may cause too much overhead. Another way is to provide a single front-end object that can be used to invoke on any of the objects, probably by adding a parameter to each call that specifies which non-CORBA object is to be manipulated. This would, of course, change the client's view because the client would not be able to invoke on each object individually, treating it as a proper CORBA object.

The DSI can be used to achieve the same space saving as achieved when using a single front-end object, but clients can be given the view that there is one CORBA object for each underlying object. The server would indicate that it wishes to accept invocations on the IDL interface using the DSI, and, when informed of such an invocation, it would identify the target object, the operation or attribute being called, and the parameters, if any. It would then make the call on the underlying non-CORBA object, receive the result, and return it to the calling client.

In Orbix, the loader mechanism (see Chapter 20) can be used to achieve the same effect: a loader could have a single representative object that it could pass all invocations to, as well as an indication of which object is being invoked. ✚

17.1 Architecture of the DSI support

To use the DSI, a server must create one or more objects that have the `CORBA::DynamicImplementation` interface, and register these with Orbix. This interface is defined as follows:

```
pseudo interface DynamicImplementation {
          void invoke (inout ServerRequest request);
};
```

The single operation, `invoke()`, is informed of incoming operation and attribute requests: it can use the `ServerRequest` parameter to determine what operation or attribute is being invoked and on what object. This parameter is also used to obtain `in` and `inout` parameters, and to return `out` and `inout` parameters and the return value to the caller. It can also be used to return an exception to the caller. An implementation of `invoke()` is known as a Dynamic Invocation Routine (DIR).

Interface `DynamicImplementation` is not visible to clients. In particular, the interfaces that they use do not inherit from it. If they were to, then the fact that the DSI is used at the server side would not be transparent to the clients.

Once an instance of `DynamicImplementation` has been created, it must be registered to handle requests of a specified interface by calling the `setImpl()` operation on the `CORBA::Orbix` object:

```
interface BOA
{
      ...
      void setImpl(in ImplementationDef implDef,
                   in DynamicImplementation impl);
      ...
};
```

The `ServerRequest` object that is passed to `DynamicImplementation::invoke()` will be created by Orbix once it receives an incoming request and recognizes it as one that is to be handled by the DSI: that is, that an instance of `DynamicImplementation` has been registered to handle the target interface. Using the `ServerRequest` passed to it, `DynamicImplementation::invoke()` can determine the name of the operation being called, its actual parameters, and details of the target object; and, using these, it can handle the call.

Part four

Orbix-specific Aspects

Orbix-specific features are explained in this part. It is important to realize that these features are designed to allow system programmers to extend the ORB itself, rather than breaking the CORBA compliance of the system. In many cases these extensions will be to improve performance, provide extra security, or allow integration with other technologies such as databases. The last of the chapters in this part explains some of these technology integrations.

Chapter 18, '**Filters**,' introduces the support necessary to allow a programmer to specify that additional code is to be executed before or after the normal code of an operation. This code might perform security checks, provide debugging traps or information, maintain an audit trail, launch a thread to handle an operation call, and so on. Each process can have a chain of filters, with each element of a chain performing a different task. The following monitoring points are supported: before a request is sent out by a client, when a request arrives at a server, when a reply is sent, and when a reply arrives back at the caller.

Chapter 19, '**Smart proxies**,' shows how to replace normal proxies, used heretofore, with smart proxies. Although Orbix generates the C++ class for proxies of a given interface, it is sometimes beneficial for an application to define a derived class and instruct Orbix to generate proxies using the derived class. Such proxies are called smart proxies. Smart proxies may, for example, cache values locally to reduce the number of remote accesses; or they may access objects or resources local to the client object. Often, apart from an increase in performance, client programmers are not aware of the differences between smart and default proxies.

Chapter 20, '**Loaders: support for persistent objects**,' discusses how loaders can be used to support persistent objects, either in an application-specific manner or using a database management system. In each client and server, Orbix keeps track of what objects and proxies are currently created in its process. If a request is made for an unknown object, then normally an exception is returned to the client. However, a programmer can choose to intervene and be advised of the failure to find the object. The programmer might choose to handle such 'object faults' by reconstructing the required object from a persistent store – such as a flat file, an RDBMS, or an ODBMS. Orbix can then be told to continue the invocation without the client being aware of the object fault.

Chapter 21, '**Multi-threaded servers**,' explains why it is useful to run multiple lightweight threads in a server, and shows how this can be achieved in Orbix. The Solaris threads package is used as an example, but anyone with a basic knowledge of threads should be able to understand the code. Any features of the Solaris threads package that are used are briefly explained. This chapter also explains why it is not sufficient for an Object Request Broker to support asynchronous (non-blocking) communications.

Chapter 22, '**Technology integration**,' shows how a CORBA system can be integrated with other technologies such as multicast communication, OLE, and databases.

✚ Some Orbix-specific extensions have not been explained in this part – including the following:

- Message transformers: these are somewhat similar to filters but they are given access to the full message buffer being transmitted or received (in contrast, filters are given access to a higher level request object). They are specifically designed to provide the 'hooks' necessary to allow messages to be encrypted. For example, a transformer on a client can encrypt a message if it is being sent to one of a set of servers, and a corresponding transformer on the server side can decrypt it.
- Transmission of objects by value: in most cases, when an object reference is passed as a parameter to or from an operation, the correct behavior is that a reference is passed across the network, so that the receiver can use the object in subsequent calls. However, in some cases, it is better to transmit a copy of (some or all of) the object's data, as well as the object reference. The receiver can then use the object with no, or at least fewer, remote calls.

- Locator: a programmer can write a locator to give application-level control over how servers are searched for in a distributed system. The Naming Service provides more powerful support for finding individual objects (the locator finds servers, whereas the Naming Service finds objects), and it is more likely to be used rather than an application-level locator. Nevertheless, a locator can add flexibility when the `_bind()` call is used, and, in particular, it allows the caller of `_bind()` to omit the host name parameter. The default locator uses configuration files to find the correct host for the specified server (when the host name is omitted to a call to `_bind()`); an application-specific locator can use another technique, such as broadcasting for the server to respond. ✚

The common theme in providing the set of extensions described in this part is that there is no single correct or best way of providing features such as authentication, authorization, encryption, persistence, threading, and so on, and therefore these features must not be built into the core ORB. Instead, default implementations should be provided and these should be overridden by system programmers who are customizing the system for a set of applications.

18 Filters

Orbix allows a programmer to specify that additional code is to be executed before or after the normal code of an operation or attribute. This support is provided by allowing applications to create **filters**, which can perform security checks, provide debugging traps or information, maintain an audit trail, and so on.

There are two forms of filters: per-process and per-object filters. Per-process filters see all operation and attribute calls leaving or entering a client's or server's address space, irrespective of the target object. Per-object filters apply to individual objects. Sections 18.1 and 18.2 give a brief introduction to each, and the remainder of the chapter then describes per-process filters in detail.

18.1 Introduction to per-process filters

Per-process filters monitor all incoming and outgoing operation and attribute requests to and from an address space. Each process can have a chain of such filters, with each element of the chain performing its own actions. A new element can be added to the chain simply by:

- Defining a class that inherits from class `CORBA::Filter`.
- Creating a single instance of the new class.

Each filter of the chain can monitor *eight* individual points during the transmission and reception of an operation or attribute request (see Figure 18.1). For a normal operation call: a filter in the client will see four of these points; and a filter in the server will see the other four.

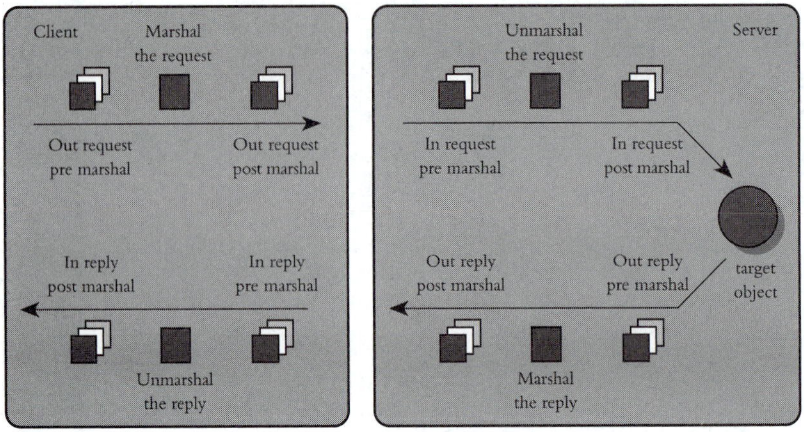

Figure 18.1 *Eight normal filter points.*

The four most commonly used filter points are:

- **Out request pre marshal**: (in the caller's address space) before an operation or attribute request is transmitted from the filter's address space to any object in another address space; in particular, before the operation's parameters have been added to the request packet.
- **In request pre marshal**: (in the target object's address space) once an operation or attribute request has arrived at the filter's address space, but before it has been processed; in particular, before the operation's parameters have been removed from the request packet and the operation has been sent to the target object.
- **Out reply pre marshal**: (in the target object's address space) after the operation or attribute request has been processed by the target object, but before the result has been transmitted to the caller's address space; in particular, before an operation's out parameters and return value have been added to the reply packet.
- **In reply pre marshal**: (in the caller's address space) after the result of an operation or attribute request has arrived at the filter's address space, but before the result has been processed; in particular, before an operation's return parameters and return value have been removed from the reply packet.

The other four monitor points are similar:

- **Out request post marshal**: (in the caller's address space) same as 'out request pre marshal' but after the operation's parameters have been added to the request packet.

- **In request post marshal**: (in the target object's address space) same as 'in request pre marshal' but after the operation's parameters have been removed from the request packet.
- **Out reply post marshal**: (in the target object's address space) same as 'out reply pre marshal' but after the operation's out parameters and return value have been added to the reply packet.
- **In reply post marshal**: (in the caller's address space) same as 'in reply pre marshal' but after the operation's out parameters and return value have been removed from the reply packet.

Since per-process filters are applied only when an invocation leaves or arrives at an address space, they are not informed of invocations between collocated objects.

A particular filter may perform actions for any number of these filter points. For example, a server that wishes to record all incoming requests and their replies might define code for just two monitor points; for example, 'in request pre marshal' and 'out reply pre marshal.' In Figure 18.1, the white filter points in the client belong to a single filter object: they are member functions of the one C++ object of type `CORBA::Filter`.

Each filter point must indicate (using its return value) how the handling of the request should be continued once the filter point itself has completed. In particular, a filter point can indicate whether or not Orbix is to continue to process the request or to return an exception to the caller. This is a very useful feature for many filters: for example, a filter that adds some application-specific security checks can code the 'in request pre marshal' filter point to determine whether each incoming request should be accepted or rejected. (If the C++ compiler supports native exceptions then rejection is chosen by raising an exception, and acceptance is chosen by returning the value `1` from the filter point. If native exceptions are not supported, then rejection is chosen by returning the value `0`.)

As well as monitoring incoming and outgoing requests, a filter on the client side and a filter on the server side can cooperate to pass data between them, in addition to the normal parameters of an operation (or attribute) call. For example, the 'out' filter points of a filter in the client can be used to insert extra data into the request package (for example, in 'out request pre marshal') and the 'in' filter points of a filter in the server can be used to extract this data (for example, in 'in request pre marshal').

Failure points

In addition to the eight monitor points described already, there are two failure points that are informed of exceptions or rejection of a call by one of the eight monitor points. These are:

- **Out reply failure**: (in the target object's address space) this is called if any preceding filter point on the server ('in request' or 'out reply') raises an exception or uses its return value to indicate that the call should not be processed any further; or if Orbix or the target object raises an exception.
- **In reply failure**: (in the caller's address space) this is called if any preceding filter point on the client or server ('out request,' 'in request,' 'out reply,' or 'in reply') raises an exception or uses its return value to indicate that the call should not be processed any further; or if Orbix or the target object raises an exception.

Once an exception is raised, or a filter point indicates that the call should not be processed further, no more of the eight normal monitor points are called. If this occurs in the caller's address space, then 'in reply failure' is called; if it occurs in the target object's address space, then 'out reply failure' and 'in reply failure' are both called (in the target object's and the caller's address spaces, respectively).

Example usages of per-process filter

Filters are a simple mechanism that can be used in many ways by applications. Some examples are:

(1) Since each filter point is passed a reference to an object of type `CORBA::Request`, a filter at the server side can determine the principal making the request, the object reference of the target object, and the name of the operation or attribute call being made. It can then use an access control list, or other authorization mechanism, to determine whether the request should be processed or a system exception (such as `NO_PERMISSION`) raised to the caller.

(2) A filter on the client and a filter on the server can cooperate to allow extra information to be passed with the request. An example is to pass a security ticket (generated by Kerberos, for example) that identifies the caller in a secure way in an open distributed system.

(3) When the server uses a database that contains CORBA objects that the client can invoke on, a filter on the server can start a database transaction if there is none running when a request arrives. It is typically a requirement to access the database only within a transaction, and starting the transaction in an 'in request' filter point ensures that this rule will be obeyed, without intervention by the higher-level application level. Such automatic

starting of transactions is not always required, but it is very useful in some cases.

(4) A filter on the server side, and possibly on the client side, may maintain audit logs of the calls that pass through it. One example of the many applications that may require this is one that manages large foreign exchange orders in a bank. If there is any claim of loss of an order, the bank will need audit logs to determine the validity of the claim; and the software engineers will need a number of audit logs to help find the point of failure in the system.

In addition, there are two special forms of per-process filters, each with its own particular use:

- Authentication filter: a filter that passes authentication information from a client to a server. The ability to verify the identity of the caller is a fundamental requirement for security.
- Thread filter: a filter that creates lightweight threads when an operation invocation arrives at a server. The filter point `inRequestPreMarshal()` actually creates the thread, as explained in Chapter 21.

18.2 Introduction to per-object filters

Per-object filters are associated with a *particular* object, rather than with *all* objects in an address space as in per-process filtering. The following filtering points are supported:

- **Per-object pre**: a filter applied to operation invocations on a particular object – before they are passed to the target object.
- **Per-object post**: a filter applied to operation invocations on a particular object – after they have been processed by the target object.

Unlike per-process filters, per-object filters apply even for intraprocess operation requests.

✚ Note that per-object filters can be used only with the TIE approach; they are not available when the BOAImpl approach is being used. Also, they are designed for use on the server side. ✚

18.3 Per-process filters

The remainder of this chapter gives some of the details of the per-process filtering mechanism. A per-process filter is installed by defining a derived class of class `CORBA::Filter`, and redefining one or more of its member functions:

- `outRequestPreMarshal()`: action to carry out in the caller's filter before outgoing requests (before marshaling).
- `outRequestPostMarshal()`: action to carry out in the caller's filter before outgoing requests (after marshaling).
- `inRequestPreMarshal()`: action to carry out in the receiver's filter before incoming requests (before marshaling).
- `inRequestPostMarshal()`: action to carry out in the receiver's filter before incoming requests (after marshaling).
- `outReplyPreMarshal()`: action to carry out in the receiver's filter before outgoing replies (before marshaling).
- `outReplyPostMarshal()`: action to carry out in the receiver's filter for outgoing replies (after marshaling).
- `inReplyPreMarshal()`: action to carry out in the caller's filter for incoming replies (before marshaling).
- `inReplyPostMarshal()`: action to carry out in the caller's filter for incoming replies (after marshaling).

Each of these member functions takes two parameters, and returns a `CORBA::Boolean` value to indicate whether or not Orbix should continue to make the request (`inRequestPreMarshal()` returns an `int` value; this is discussed in more detail in Chapter 21). For example:

```
CORBA::Boolean
        outRequestPreMarshal(CORBA::Request& r,
                             CORBA::Environment&)
                throw (CORBA::SystemException);
```

The details of the request being made can be obtained by calling member functions on the `CORBA::Request` parameter. Examples of this are shown in Section 18.3.1. The `CORBA::Environment` variable can be used to raise an exception if the C++ compiler does not support native exceptions.

The constructor of class `CORBA::Filter` adds the newly created filter object into the per-process filter chain. Direct instances of `Filter` cannot be created. (the constructor is protected to enforce this.)

Programmers should define derived classes of `Filter` and redefine some subset of the member functions to carry out the required filtering. If any of the eight monitoring functions is not redefined in a derived class of `CORBA::Filter`, then the following implementation is inherited in all cases:

```
// C++
{ return 1; /* Continue the call as normal */ }
```

Failure points

The two failure points are declared as follows:

```
void outReplyFailure (CORBA::Request& r,
                      CORBA::Environment&)
                 throw (CORBA::SystemException);
void inReplyFailure (CORBA::Request& r,
                     CORBA::Environment&)
                 throw (CORBA::SystemException);
```

18.3.1 An example per-process filter

Consider the following simple example of a per-process filter:

```
// C++
#include <CORBA.h>
#include <iostream.h>

class ProcessFilter : public virtual CORBA::Filter {
public:

     CORBA::Boolean
     outRequestPreMarshal(CORBA::Request& r,
                          CORBA::Environment&)
                throw (CORBA::SystemException) {
          CORBA::String_var s;
          s = (r.target())->_object_to_string();
          cout << endl << "Request outgoing to "
               << s << " with operation name "
               << r.operation() << endl;
          return 1; // Continue the call.
     }

     int inRequestPreMarshal(CORBA::Request& r,
                             CORBA::Environment&)
                    throw (CORBA::SystemException) {
          CORBA::String_var s;
          s = (r.target())->_object_to_string();
          cout << endl << "Request incoming to "
```

```
                << s << " with operation name "
                << r.operation() << endl;
            return 1; // Continue the call.
        }

        CORBA::Boolean outReplyPreMarshal(CORBA::Request& r,
                                          CORBA::Environment&)
                    throw (CORBA::SystemException) {
            cout << "Incoming operation "
                << r.operation()
                << " finished." << endl << endl;
            return 1; // Continue the call.
        }

        CORBA::Boolean inReplyPreMarshal(CORBA::Request& r,
                                         CORBA::Environment&)
                    throw (CORBA::SystemException) {
            cout << "Outgoing operation" << r.operation()
                << " finished." << endl << endl;
            return 1; // Continue the call.
        }
};
```

Such classes can have any name; but they must inherit from `CORBA::Filter`.

The function `target()` can be called on a `Request` to find the object reference of the target object; and the function `_object_to_string()` can be applied to an object reference to obtain a stringified form. The function `operation()` can be called on to a `Request` to find the name of the operation being called.

18.3.2 Installation of the per-process filter

To install this per-process filter, the programmer need only create an instance of it:

```
// C++
ProcessFilter myFilter;
```

This object will automatically add itself to the per-process filter chain.

18.3.3 Raising an exception in a filter

Any of the per-process filter points can raise an exception in the normal manner. For example, the `inRequestPostMarshal()` filter point can be changed to raise a `NO_PERMISSION` system exception:

```
// C++
CORBA::Boolean
```

```
ProcessFilter::inRequestPostMarshal(CORBA::Request& r,
                                    CORBA::Environment& env)
                throw (CORBA::SystemException) {
      if ( / . . . . */ ) {
            throw CORBA::NO_PERMISSION(CORBA::INVOKE_DENIED,
                                       CORBA::COMPLETED_NO);
            // The NO_PERMISSION system exception
            // has been  raised here, with a minor
            // code of INVOKE_DENIED, and a
            // completion status of NO.
      }
      /* . . . . */
}
```

Naturally, if native C++ exceptions are used, the return value is of no importance. A value of zero should not be returned if no exception is raised.

18.3.4 Piggybacking extra data to the request buffer

Any of the two `outRequest` filter points in a client can add extra piggybacked data to an outgoing request buffer – and this data will then be made available to the corresponding `inRequest` filter point on the server side. This is illustrated in Figure 18.2. In addition, any of the two `outReply` filter points on a server can add data to an outgoing reply – and this data will then be made available to the corresponding `inReply` filter point on the client side.

At each of the four 'out' monitor points, data can be added by using `operator<<()` on the `Request` parameter; for example:

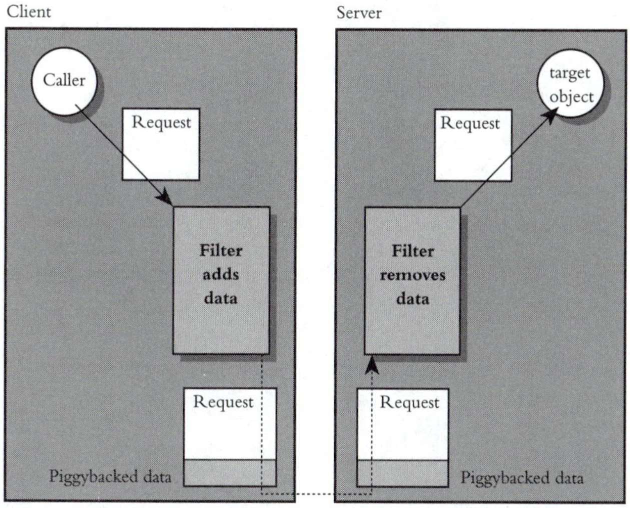

Figure 18.2 *Piggybacking data.*

```
// C++
CORBA::Long l = 27L;
// . . .
r << l;
```

This is the same `operator<<()` that is used in the DII (Chapter 15).

At each of the 'in' monitor points, data can be extracted using `operator>>()`; for example,

```
// C++
CORBA::Long j;
// . . .
r >> j;
```

Care must be taken to match correctly the insertion and extraction points, as follows:

- `outRequestPreMarshal()` matches `inRequestPreMarshal()`
- `outReplyPreMarshal()` matches `inReplyPreMarshal()`
- `outRequestPostMarshal()` matches `inRequestPostMarshal()`
- `outReplyPostMarshal()` matches `inReplyPostMarshal()`

For example, a value inserted by `outRequestPreMarshal()` must be extracted by `inRequestPreMarshal()`.

Piggybacking is a low-level facility and care must be taken when using it. In particular, programmers must be careful not to include piggybacked data in communications with objects in a server that does not expect this extra data in the request packets.

19 Smart proxies

We have seen that proxy classes for IDL interfaces are automatically generated by the IDL compiler, and that these are used to support invocations on remote objects. When a proxy receives an invocation, it packages it for transmission to the target object in another address space on the same or a different host. Normally, therefore, the code for proxy classes is not of concern to programmers.

However, it is sometimes beneficial to be able to implement proxy classes manually. Although we would not expect many client programmers to do this, it is a useful option for the implementers of interfaces. They may provide **smart proxy** code, for example to optimize how clients use the service.

A typical example is where it is desirable to cache some information from a remote object locally at a client site. In our cinema application, we may wish, for example, to cache the price of seats at a client. Requests to obtain the price of a seat could then be satisfied immediately.

We may therefore wish to construct a smart proxy for the `FrontOffice` interface. This is simply achieved by manually programming a class derived from the proxy class `FrontOffice` (which is generated by the IDL compiler). The member functions of class `FrontOffice` package requests for the target object; the member functions of a derived class can provide optimized, application-specific coding.

Client programs can then be linked with this smart proxy code, but they would not have to be changed in other ways. As we will see, when a proxy needs to be created in a client's address space, a smart proxy will be created rather than a default one.

Example usages

As well as the caching example explained previously, smart proxies can be used for a large set of purposes, including the following simple examples:

(1) If it is common to call a set of operations on some set of objects in some repeated complex sequence, then this sequence can be initiated simply by calling an operation on a smart proxy. This means that the client can call a single operation, but in effect make a sequence of calls. In this case, the smart proxy is acting as an abstracter of some underlying complexity, and providing the client with a simple interface that is easier to use. Of course, the target object could be changed to support this operation; but where this is not possible, smart proxies can be used to achieve the same effect for the client code.

(2) If it is common for a client to access more than one of the attributes of an object, then this will require a number of consecutive remote calls. In order to increase efficiency, a smart proxy on the client could call an extra operation on the remote object to retrieve a set of attributes commonly used together. These would then be made available to the application-level client code as the individual attributes are accessed. This would not require a change to the application level of the client code, although the real object's interface would have to be extended (probably using inheritance). The advantage of using smart proxies in this case is that the client code can initially be written without concern for the number of remote attribute accesses it makes, and efficiency can be improved later without changing the client code.

(3) If a client makes a set of changes to a remote object, then it will sometimes be acceptable to batch these change requests in a smart proxy (local to the client, of course). In order to reduce the number of remote calls to the real object, it will have to provide an operation that allows the smart proxy to pass all of the batched updates in one call (possibly as a sequence of structures, one structure for each individual update). This batch-update operation can be visible to the client, but it is more likely that it would be hidden, and only used by the smart proxy code.

(4) If there is more than one object that can satisfy a client's request, then a smart proxy could be used to decide between these objects, choosing, say, one that is running on a lightly loaded machine, or choosing one randomly. This choice could be made on each operation request, or for each set of related requests (ensuring that each request in the consecutive set of operation requests is handled by one object). Alternatively, if an object must be replicated without any system-level support, then a smart proxy can be used to send requests to each of the replicas.

(5) If the system analysis stage identifies an object that is in fact implemented later (or implemented already in a legacy system) by a number of different objects distributed throughout the system, then a smart proxy can be created on the client machine to maintain the correct logical view. Naturally, the same result could be achieved by creating a single real object that provides the correct logical view, but use of a smart proxy is also a valid approach and it has the advantage of performing the required combining of functionality in the client address space rather than in an arbitrary server process. This is not a common requirement, but it is mentioned here as an example of using smart proxies as 'an escape mechanism' from strict object interactions. Such facilities have been called 'get out of jail cards' by some users.

Smart proxies are not part of the CORBA standard, but they can frequently be used even in applications that require CORBA compliance. In particular, in some cases the smart proxy code can be added or removed without affecting the functionality of an application. For example, if a smart proxy is used to improve efficiency, then the application can be ported to any CORBA compliant system simply by removing the smart proxy code. The normal aim in this case is to require no changes to the application level of the client code; and if any additions are made to the real object's interface then these should be acceptable (even if not used) if the smart proxy code is removed. For example, if a smart proxy requires the addition of some operation to the target object, then it should not be an error if the application level of a client were to use this operation.

In fact, such operations are easy to remove if the smart proxy is removed: if they are added by defining a derived interface of the target object's normal interface. The smart proxy should know that the target object is in fact an instance of that derived interface; but the application level of the client's code should only know about the base interface.

In the remainder of this chapter, we first consider the details of how proxy objects are actually generated, and the general steps needed to implement smart proxy support for a given interface. We then proceed to consider how a simple caching smart proxy can be built. In this first example, it is assumed that the cache of seat prices held by a smart proxy (for `FrontOffice`) need never be invalidated. A later example shows how to handle this invalidation where necessary.

19.1 Proxy factories

This section begins by providing the basis for understanding smart proxies by describing how Orbix manages normal proxies. For each IDL interface, the Orbix IDL compiler generates the following classes:

- A **standard proxy class**
- A **proxy factory class** for that class.

The proxy class `FrontOffice`, gives the code for standard proxies for that IDL interface – such a proxy transmits requests to its real object and returns the results it receives to the caller. It is sometimes referred to as the default proxy class. The proxy factory class produced by the IDL compiler is responsible for creating these standard proxies for its class, and there is a single global instance of this factory class linked into the client code. When requested to by Orbix, this instance simply constructs a new standard proxy for its IDL interface.

✚ Therefore, for IDL interface `FrontOffice`, the IDL compiler generates the following:

- `FrontOffice`: the standard proxy class.
- `FrontOfficeProxyFactoryClass`: the standard proxy factory class for interface `FrontOffice`.
- `FrontOfficeProxyFactory`: the single global instance of `FrontOfficeProxyFactoryClass`. ✚

To provide smart proxies for an IDL interface, a programmer must:

- Define the smart proxy class, which must inherit from its standard proxy class.
- Define a smart proxy factory class, which creates instances of the smart proxy class on request. Orbix calls a proxy factory's `New()` member function whenever it wishes to create a proxy for that interface.
- Create a single instance of the proxy factory class.

Examples of these steps are given in the rest of this chapter.

Client programs must be linked with the smart proxy class and the smart proxy factory class, and must create the instance of the smart proxy factory class. The programmer of a smart proxy class will normally provide a header file and a corresponding object file to carry out all of these steps. Very minimal changes are therefore required to clients – and, in particular, their normal operation invocation code remains unchanged.

Once these steps are carried out, Orbix will communicate with the factory whenever it needs to create a proxy of that interface:

- When a reference to an object of that interface is passed back as an `out` or `inout` parameter, a return value, or an attribute value;

or when a reference to a remote object enters an address space via an `in` parameter or when setting an attribute value.

- When the interface's `_bind()` function is called.
- ✚ When `CORBA::Orbix.string_to_object()` is called with a stringified object reference for an object of that interface. ✚

More than one smart proxy class (and associated smart proxy factory class) can be defined for a given IDL interface. Orbix maintains a linked list of all of the proxy factories for a given IDL interface.

✚ A chain of smart proxy factories is allowed for an IDL interface because the same IDL interface might be provided by a number of different servers in the system. It may be useful, therefore, to have different smart proxy code to handle each server, or set of servers. Each factory in turn can examine the marker and server name of the target object for which the proxy is to be created, and decide whether to create a smart proxy for it or to defer the request to the next proxy factory in the chain. ✚

Initially, of course, there is a single entry in this list – the standard proxy factory class described above.

In more detail, the following steps must be carried out in order to create smart proxies:

(1) Implement the smart proxy class. The constructor(s) of this class will be used by the smart proxy factory, in step 2.

(2) Implement a new proxy factory class, derived from the default proxy factory class. It should redefine the `New()` function to create new smart proxy objects of the class defined in step 1; or return zero to indicate that it is not willing to create a smart proxy.

(3) Declare a global object of this new proxy factory class. The constructor of the base class will automatically register this new proxy factory with the factory manager in Orbix.

These steps are illustrated in Figure19.1.

When a new proxy is required, Orbix will call all of the registered proxy factories for the interface until one of them successfully builds a new proxy. The only guarantee on the order of use of smart proxy factories is that the factory manager ensures that an interface's standard proxy factory object is the last factory on the chain. Thus, if no other proxy factory is willing to manufacture a new proxy, then a standard proxy will be constructed.

The factory manager requests each proxy factory to manufacture a new proxy via its `New()` member function, whose first parameter is the full object reference string of the target object:

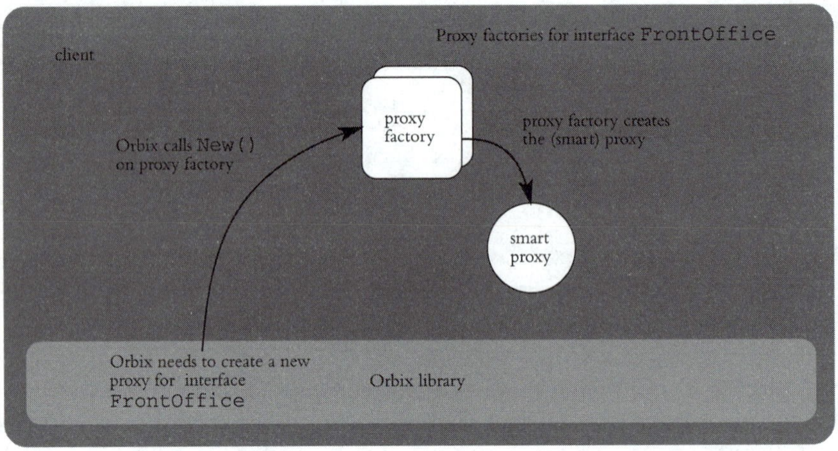

Figure 19.1 *Creation of a proxy.*

```
// C++. The return value is the pointer to the new smart proxy:
void* New(char*, CORBA::Environment&);
```

If the function returns zero, but does not raise an exception, then Orbix will try the next smart proxy factory in the chain.

✚ The code for this function may need to extract the target object's marker and server name. One way to do this is to construct a direct occurrence of `CORBA::Object`, passing the full object reference string as a constructor parameter, and then to call `_marker()` and `_implementation()` on that temporary object. ✚

19.2 Smart proxy example

This section shows how to write a smart proxy for interface `FrontOffice`, to cache the prices of seats. The important subset of interface `FrontOffice` is:

```
// IDL
    interface FrontOffice {

        /* rest not shown here. */

        Price getPrice (  // Get price of a seat.
                in Place chosenPlace,
                in Date when)
            raises (NoSuchPlace, InvalidDate);

};
```

Step A

We will define a smart proxy class, which we will call `SmartFrontOffice`, for class `FrontOffice`. Instances of this class will cache the prices of seats:

```
// C++. In "SmartFrontOffice.h".
#include "front.hh"

class SmartFrontOffice : public virtual FrontOffice {
      // Member variables to hold the cache. Not shown here.
public:
      // The required constructor:
      SmartFrontOffice(char*);

      // Functions for IDL operations and attributes.
      // List only those which require a different
      // implementation in the smart proxy class:
      virtual Price getPrice(
                  const Place& chosenPlace,
                  const char* when)
            throw (CORBA::SystemException
                   FrontOffice::NoSuchPlace,
                   FrontOffice::InvalidDate);
};
```

Note that the constructor must take the stringified object reference as a parameter, but it can take other parameters also.

Class `SmartFrontOffice` inherits from the default proxy code generated by the IDL compiler. It therefore inherits all of the code required to make a remote invocation: each `SmartFrontOffice` function can make an upcall to its base class's function to make a remote call. Virtual inheritance is not strictly necessary in the code shown.

The constructor for the smart proxy class takes a full object reference string as a parameter. As we will see, it must pass this to the constructor of its default proxy class.

The corresponding function definitions might be:

```
// C++. In "SmartFrontOffice.cc".
#include "SmartFrontOffice.h"

SmartFrontOffice::SmartFrontOffice(char* OR) :
      FrontOffice(OR)
{
      // Initialize the cache. Code not shown here.
}


Price SmartFrontOffice::getPrice(
                        const Place& chosenPlace,
```

```
                    const char* when)
               throw (CORBA::SystemException) {
                    FrontOffice::NoSuchPlace,
                    FrontOffice::InvalidDate {
     if ( /* the price is in the cache */ )
          // Return that price.
     else {
          Price pr = FrontOffice::getPrice (chosenPlace, when);
          // Update the cache. Code not shown here.
          return pr;
     }
}
```

The constructor for `SmartFrontOffice` initializes the cache of seat prices. It can initialize this to an empty cache, or alternatively it can call `FrontOffice::getPrice()` to find the prices of popular seats and cache these. The definition of `SmartFrontOffice::getPrice()` uses and maintains this cache. If there is a cache miss, `SmartFrontOffice::getPrice()` calls `FrontOffice::getPrice()`; that is, the function that is generated by the IDL compiler to make a remote call to the target object.

The constructor of `SmartFrontOffice` also makes an upcall to the constructor of `FrontOffice`. This upcall is necessary because the constructor of `FrontOffice` in turn calls the constructor of its base class `CORBA::Object`, which registers the proxy in the object table (this table registers all objects in an address space).

Step B

The next step is to define a new proxy factory to generate our smart proxies at the appropriate time. This step is straightforward, even mechanical. Recall that the standard proxy factory produced by the IDL compiler for interface `FrontOffice` is `FrontOfficeProxyFactoryClass`. We derive from this class:

```
// C++. Possibly also in "SmartFrontOffice.h".

class SmartFrontOfficeFactoryClass :
          public virtual FrontOfficeProxyFactoryClass {
public:
     // Constructor:
     SmartFrontOfficeFactoryClass():
          CORBA::ProxyFactory(FrontOffice_IR) {}

     // The New() member function is called when a
     // proxy is required:
     virtual void* New(char* OR, CORBA::Environment&) {
          // Create and return a new smart proxy:
          return (FrontOffice_ptr) new SmartFrontOffice(OR);
     }
};
```

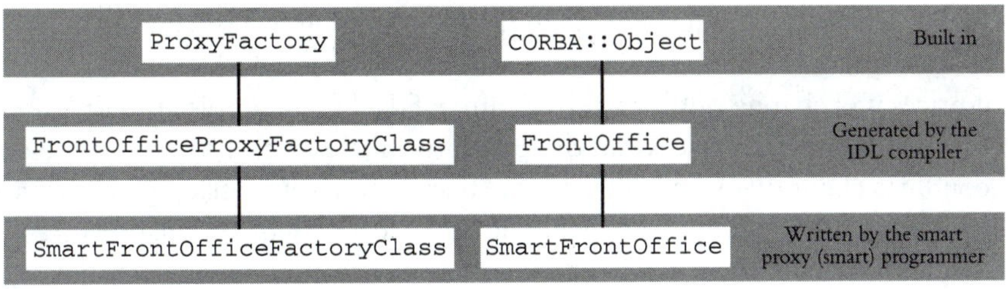

Figure 19.2 *Class hierarchy for smart proxy class.*

The member initialization list of the constructor of class `SmartFrontOfficeFactoryClass` makes a call to the constructor of class `ProxyFactory`, which is the base class of `FrontOfficeProxyFactoryClass`. The parameter passed is `FrontOffice_IR`, an automatically defined macro (it is the string form of the class name; that is, '`FrontOffice`').

✚ Each standard proxy factory class has a default (no parameter) constructor, so the constructor of `SmartFrontOfficeFactoryClass` need not be concerned with calling the constructor of `FrontOfficeProxyFactoryClass`; however, it must call the constructor of `ProxyFactory`. ✚

The various class hierarchies are shown in Figure19.2.

The `SmartFrontOfficeFactoryClass::New()` function is called by Orbix to signal that a smart proxy is to be created. Orbix passes it the (stringified) object reference of the real object for which the proxy is required. If the function decides to create a smart proxy, it must dynamically construct the smart proxy, passing it the stringified object reference (and any other constructor parameters agreed on by the smart proxy and the smart proxy factory).

Step C

Finally, we need to declare a single instance of this new class:

```
// C++. Possibly also in "SmartFrontOffice.cc".
SmartFrontOfficeFactoryClass  SmartFrontOfficeFactory;
```

The constructor of the base class will then register this new factory, entering it into the linked list of factories for interface `FrontOffice`.

19.3 Handling changing seat prices

The example shown so far assumes that the prices of seats do not change during the lifetime of a `SmartFrontOffice` smart proxy. Our implementation of `SmartFrontOffice` was thus able to ignore the issue of invalidating its cache.

There are a number of ways to handle changing seat prices. Firstly, part of the non-functional contract between a `FrontOffice` object and its clients could be that seat prices will change only at a certain time of day, for example at midnight. A smart proxy that caches seat prices can therefore invalidate its cache at that time each day. Secondly, a client that uses a smart proxy that caches seat prices can give a warning to its user that the prices it quotes may not be exact, so a subsequent call to `makeBooking()` can in fact cost the user a different sum of money than quoted by `getPrice()`. This might be acceptable in some cases because seat prices do not change frequently, and when they do change they do so by small percentages.

Thirdly, the `FrontOffice` object and smart proxy can use a technique common in distributed systems, whereby the cache is treated as a **hint** and is therefore checked on each usage. Section 19.3.1 shows the interfaces and code required to implement this.

Section 19.3.2 (p.320) shows that a `FrontOffice` object can make a **call-back** to the client to inform it when seat prices change. This is a useful addition to both the second and third approaches discussed above, because it allows the client's cache to be updated without undue delay. However, race conditions prevent this approach by itself being a full solution to the caching problem. In particular, a client could use cached seat price data at the same time that a `FrontOffice` object is making call-back calls to inform the client of price changes.

The fourth way to fix the caching problem is to provide a cache coherency algorithm that ensures that the cache value held at any client is always valid. In a loosely coupled distributed system, this requires some form of locking, in which an application that wishes to change the price of a seat must wait until there is no client holding a cached value. Instead of waiting for all of the clients with cached values to exit (or release their locks in some other way), the system could break these locks if a management client wishes to change the seat prices. In either case, it is difficult to implement a system that will scale to many concurrent clients; and it is also difficult to handle clients written by different programmers (possibly in different programming languages).

19.3.1 Treating the cache as a hint

Caching is a common requirement for efficiency in a distributed system. Because of the asynchronous and independent natures of various components in a distributed system, such caches are often treated as **hints**: that is, values that are likely to be correct, but which are checked for validity when they are used. An example is a cache that records which file server each of a set of directories is stored in. Since the file system is servers are used so frequently, clients will benefit from this cache because they will not need to use some expensive lookup to know which file server to use to access a given directory. However, over time a directory may be moved to a different file server, so the cache held in client machines may not be correct at all times.

To handle this, the cache can be treated as a hint, and checked on each use. For efficiency, this checking can be combined with the use of the directories themselves. Therefore, a call to a file server to list a directory is really interpreted to mean 'if you hold the target directory then return a listing, otherwise either return the correct file server for this directory or just inform me that my cache was incorrect.'

An everyday example of using hints is our caching of phone numbers. Frequently, we begin a phone conversation by checking that we are communicating with the correct person, and frequently, in fact, this check is very efficient because the person answering a call announces his or her name or the name of the company we have actually called.

Within the cinema application, the `FrontOffice` interface can be extended to allow a smart proxy to treat its cache as a hint. A call to `getPrice()` can return the value in the cache, or it can call the target object when there is a **cache miss**. Prices can be quoted to the end user, who can choose some seats at a suitable price. However, the price of the seats may change before the call to `makeBooking()` is made, and therefore prices are re-checked at that time.

The required extension to the `FrontOffice` interface is best achieved by inheritance:

```
// In "FrontOfficeForHinting.idl"
interface FrontOfficeForHinting : FrontOffice {

           typedef struct PriceInformation {
                Place where;
                Date when;
                Price amount;
           };
           typedef sequence<PriceInformation> Pricing;

           exception IncorrectPricing {
                Pricing actualPricing;
           };

           Booking makeBookingWithHintCheck (
                                in Places chosenPlaces,
                                in Date when,
                                in CreditCard payment,
                                in Price amount)
                     raises (NoSuchPlace,
                             PlaceAlreadyBooked,
                             InvalidCreditCard,
                             InvalidDate,
                             IncorrectPricing);
};
```

The target object would actually be an instance of `FrontOfficeForHinting`, rather than being a direct instance of `FrontOffice`.

`makeBookingWithHintCheck()` extends `FrontOffice::makeBooking()` by the addition of a parameter, `amount`, which specifies the caller's calculation of the cost of the set of seats being booked. If this value is incorrect, the operation raises the `IncorrectPricing` exception, which returns actual pricing information. The information returned in this exception can be used to update the caller's cache, and make a subsequent call with the correct price (or the caller could revert to calling `makeBooking()`).

Operation `FrontOffice::makeGroupBooking()` should also be extended in a similar way to give another operation, say, `FrontOfficeForHinting::makeGroupBookingWithHintCheck()`.

Notice that this extension to the interface is useful even when the caching of seat pricing information is not implemented to make `getPrice()` more efficient. If a call to `getPrice()` is made in order to quote a price to a customer, then there is no guarantee that the price will not be different when a subsequent call to `makeBooking()` is made a few moments later. Prices should therefore be checked when actually making a booking. There is a strong argument, therefore, to replace operation `FrontOffice::makeBooking()` with the variation shown in this section. The alternative is to have a locking mechanism on prices, so that they cannot be changed between a call to `getPrice()` and `makeBooking()`. A variation on this is for a `FrontOffice` object to freeze the price of a seat for some number of minutes after a call to `getPrice()` for that seat.

Returning to the introduction of `makeBookingWithHintCheck()`, there is no need to change the clients of interace `FrontOffice`; instead, they can continue to use `makeBooking()`. A call to `makeBooking()` can be intercepted by a smart proxy in the client, and the cached pricing information can be used to make a call to `makeBookingWithHintCheck()`. In fact, interface `FrontOfficeForHinting` need not be visible to client programmers. Figure19.3 shows the general approach.

The following gives an outline of the smart proxy code for interface `FrontOfficeForHinting`. To reuse code, class `SmartFrontOfficeForHinting` inherits from `SmartFrontOffice`:

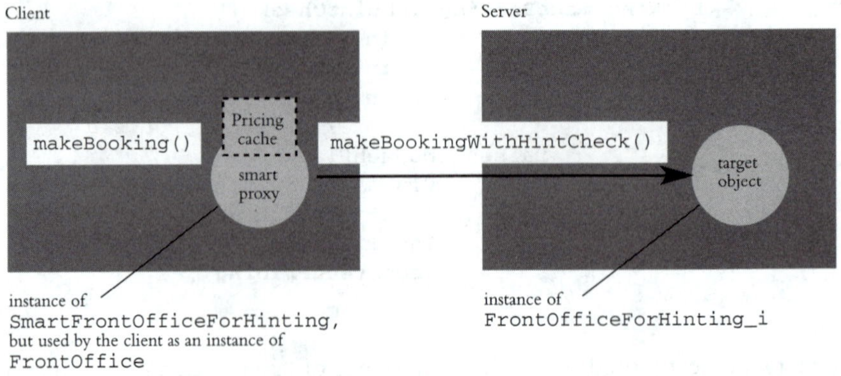

Figure 19.3 *Translating a `makeBooking()` call into a `makeBookingWithHintCache()` call.*

```
// C++
// In "SmartFrontOfficeForHinting.h".
#include "FrontOfficeForHinting.hh"

class SmartFrontOfficeForHinting :
                            public virtual FrontOfficeForHinting,
                            public virtual SmartFrontOffice {
      // The cache is inherited.
public:
      // The required constructor:
      SmartFrontOfficeForHinting(char*);

      virtual Booking_ptr makeBooking(
                                  const Places& where,
                                  const char* when,
                                  const CreditCard& payment)
                        throw (/* .... */);

      // Should also redefine makeGroupBooking(),
      // but this is not shown here.
};
```

Function `SmartFrontOfficeForHinting::makeBooking()` can be coded as follows:

```
// C++
// In "SmartFrontOfficeForHinting.cc".
#include "SmartFrontOfficeForHinting.h"

SmartFrontOfficeForHinting::SmartFrontOfficeForHinting(char* OR) :
      FrontOfficeForHinting(OR), SmartFrontOffice(OR) {}

Booking_ptr SmartFrontOfficeForHinting::makeBooking(
                                        const Places& where,
                                        const char* when,
                                        const CreditCard& payment)
                        throw (/* .... */) {
      if ( /* the prices for all of the places
             in where are in the cache */) {
            // Calculate the price for all places being booked.
            try {
                  FrontOfficeForHinting::makeBookingWithHintCheck
                                                      ( /* .... */);
            }
            catch (FrontOfficeForHinting::IncorrectPricing &e) {
               // Report the change to the user.
               /* . . . . */
            } // Other exceptions can be handled by the caller.
      }
      else
            SmartFrontOffice::makeBooking( where, when, payment );
}
```

This function checks whether or not the prices for all of the places being booked are held in the cache. If they are, it uses this information as a hint; otherwise it calls the normal `makeBooking()` code. Calls on the target object are made by using the base class's implementations of the functions called.

19.3.2 Invalidating the cache

This section shows how a `FrontOffice` object can make a call to each of its smart proxies distributed throughout the system, informing each that the prices of seats have changed. This is a detailed section that need not be studied on the first reading.

The basic strategy is to implement a smart proxy class for `FrontOffice` which can receive call-backs from the real `FrontOffice` object whenever prices are changed. Correspondingly, each real `FrontOffice` object must track which proxies have cached its seat pricing information, and call-back these proxies when this pricing changes.

These changes require modifications to both the implementation of interface `FrontOffice` and the implementation of its smart proxies.

(Section 19.3.3, p.327 describes how OrbixTalk (Section 22.1, p.356) can be used to simplify the mechanisms required to inform clients of price changes, and to make these notifications more efficient.)

The call-back operation must be defined in an IDL interface – so that it can be called across the network. Because it is a separate piece of functionality, it is better to define a new interface specifically to define this call-back operation. We have called this new interface `CacheInvalidate`, since a proxy must invalidate its cache if the call-back operation is used:

```
// IDL
interface CacheInvalidate {
      // The call-back operation.
      oneway void invalidate(in Pricing priceInfo);
};
```

An instance of this interface will exist in each client that has cached prices.

(The sequence type `Pricing` is defined in Section19.3.1. It consists of a sequence of structures, with each structure holding the number of a seat, a date, and the seat's price. A caller of this operation might pass updated pricing information on some popular seat/ dates, or an empty sequence may be passed (which can be interpreted as a request to invalidate all of the cache entries)).

Here, the `invalidate()` operation is specified to be a `oneway` operation because we are assuming that a `FrontOffice` object itself is not interested in receiving any indication from a proxy that the proxy has received and processed the `invalidate()` call. Use of a `oneway` operation here has the advantage that the server will not be blocked while the proxy processes the call-back.

In order to receive incoming operation calls, the client *must* be linked with the server-side code for the `CacheInvalidate` interface. The smart proxies for interface `FrontOffice` will have to implement the `CacheInvalidate` interface, as well as implementing the operations of interface `FrontOffice` itself.

As well as supporting this new interface, a smart proxy will also have to register its presence with its true object. To do so, we can define a further new interface, which will be implemented by our `FrontOffice` objects on the server:

```
// IDL
interface RegisterProxy {
      // Signal that a new proxy has been created for
      // a given FrontOffice:
      void signOn(in CacheInvalidate proxy);

      // Signal that a proxy has been removed:
      void signOff(in CacheInvalidate proxy);
};
```

(Alternatively, we could have added the `signOn()` and `signOff()` operations to interface `FrontOffice`, but we have not done this because it would make these operations visible to clients.)

The parameter to `signOn()` is the object on which the `invalidate()` call is to be made when the `FrontOffice`'s pricing changes; that is, it is an object reference to the `CacheInvalidate` object in the client.

Figure 19.4 shows the objects involved when the TIE approach is used to implement the `FrontOffice` and `CacheInvalidate` interfaces. The interfaces supported by each object are also shown separately for clarity. There are two `TIE` objects: the `TIE` object of type `TIE_RegPxFrontOffice(RegPxFrontOffice_i)` in the server is required to allow the target object to be used remotely; the `TIE` of type `TIE_CacheInvalidate(SmartProxy2)` in the client is required to allow the target object to call `CacheInvalidate::invalidate()`. The arrows in Figure 19.4 indicate that an object uses another. Of course, the BOAImpl approach could also be used.

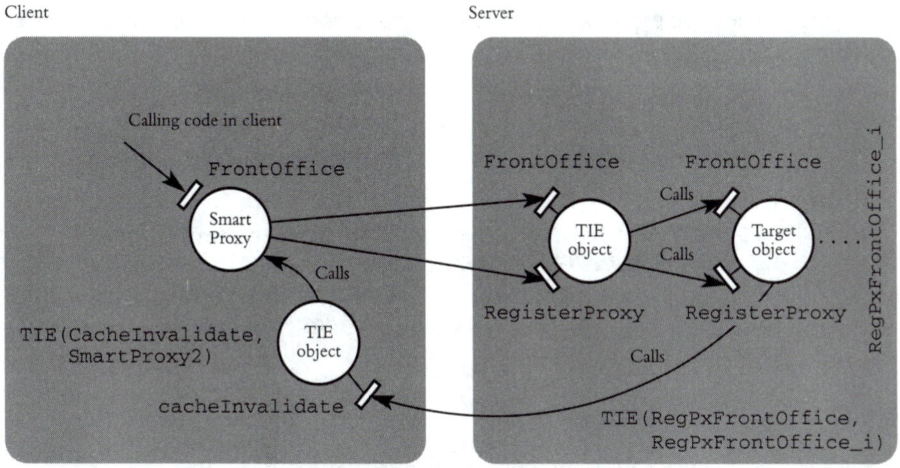

Figure 19.4 *Communication between a client and a* `FrontOffice`.

Implementing RegisterProxy in the server to allow sign on and sign off

The general approach to implement `signOn()` is to add the calling object to a list of proxies maintained for each `FrontOffice`: each proxy in the list is notified when prices change. `signOff()` is implemented by removing the proxy from the list. It is useful to implement this interface separately, say by class `RegisterProxy_i`. (The data structures within the implementation class `RegisterProxy_i` have deliberately been kept simple here.)

```
// C++
// A very simple implementation of the RegisterProxy interface.

class RegisterProxy_i {
      // Call-back list:
      CacheInvalidate_ptr m_proxies[20];
      // Size of call-back list:
      CORBA::ULong m_number;
public:
      // Constructor.
      RegisterProxy() : m_number(0) {}

      // Functions for IDL operations.
      virtual void signOn(CacheInvalidate_ptr)
                        throw (CORBA::SystemException);
      virtual void signOff(CacheInvalidate_ptr)
                        throw (CORBA::SystemException);
protected:
      virtual void notify();
};

DEF_TIE_RegisterProxy(RegisterProxy_i);
```

The `notify()` function calls the `CacheInvalidate::invalidate()` operation on all of the proxies in the call-back list. The implementation of the member functions can be as follows:

```
// C++
void RegisterProxy_i::signOn(CacheInvalidate_ptr c)
                        throw (CORBA::SystemException) {
      if (m_number >= 20)
            return; // To keep it (overly) simple here.
      m_proxies[m_number++] = CacheInvalidate::_duplicate(c);
      // The call to _duplicate() is required to avoid having the
      // proxy (in the server) for the object referenced by c
      // destroyed at the end of the call.
}


void RegisterProxy_i::signOff(CacheInvalidate_ptr c)
                        throw (CORBA::SystemException) {
```

```
        // Orbix will have incremented the ref count of the object
        // pointed to by c. First find c in our list.
        CORBA::ULong i;
        for (i = 0; i < m_number; i++)
                if ( c == m_proxies[i] )
                        break;
        // Now remove it if found.
        if ( c == m_proxies[i] ) {
                CORBA::release(m_proxies[i]);
                m_number—;
                while (i < m_proxy)
                        m_proxies[i] = m_proxies[++i];
                // CORBA::release(c) will be called automatically to
                // decrement the reference count of (and presumably
                // destroy) the proxy (local to the server) for the
                // object referenced by c.
        }
}


void RegisterProxy::notify() {
        CORBA::ULong i;
        for (i = 0; i < m_number; i++)
                try {
                        m_proxies[i]->invalidate();
                }
                catch (CORBA::SystemException& se) {
                        cerr << "notification failed: "
                                << se << endl;
                }
        }
}
```

Summary of steps

Up to this point, we have decided that the `FrontOffice` object should make a call-back to each of its smart proxy objects in its clients whenever seat prices change. We have introduced interface `CacheInvalidate` to provide the operation (`invalidate()`) that is to be called by the `FrontOffice` objects. Instances of `CacheInvalidate` will be created in the clients' address spaces.

Each `CacheInvalidate` object must make itself known to (register itself with) its `FrontOffice` object. To allow this, we have introduced a new interface, `RegisterProxy`, on the server side. This provides two operations, `signOn()` and `signOff()`, which can be called by a `CacheInvalidate` object in the client to register and unregister itself.

Design decisions

Of the various ways in which this design could be implemented, we have chosen to do the following in this case:

- The `FrontOffice` object in the server will implement both the `FrontOffice` and the `RegisterProxy` interfaces. To make this easy to program, we will introduce an IDL interface (`RegPxFrontOffice`) that inherits from both `FrontOffice` and `RegisterProxy`. Nevertheless, the application-level code in the client will still see only interface `FrontOffice`.
- The smart proxy class (called `SmartProxy2` in this section) will provide the normal `FrontOffice` interface to the application-level client code, but it will also implement interface `CacheInvalidate` (that is, operation `CacheInvalidate::invalidate()`). Each smart proxy object will create a TIE object for interface `CacheInvalidate`, and register this (using `RegisterProxy::signOn()`) with the server.
- We will assume that the client is multi-threaded (see Chapter 21). If this is not the case, the client will have to make periodic calls to the Orbix `processEvents()` function, to instruct it to process incoming messages, some of which may be cache invalidate calls.

Implementing the design

Our implementation of interface `FrontOffice` will implement the operations of the `RegisterProxy` interface and of the `FrontOffice` interface itself. To facilitate this, we will define an interface that combines these two interfaces:

```
// IDL
interface RegPxFrontOffice: RegisterProxy, FrontOffice {
      // No new operations or attributes.
};
```

To implement this interface in C++, we will inherit from class `FrontOffice_i` (defined in Chapter 6), as well as from class `RegisterProxy_i`, explained earlier in this section:

```
// C++
class RegPxFrontOffice_i : public virtual FrontOffice_i,
                           public virtual RegisterProxy_i {
public:
      RegPxFrontOffice_i( /* . . . . */ ) :
                  FrontOffice_i( /* . . . . */ )
      {}

      // Public C++ (non-IDL) function (it can be called locally):
      void changeSeatPrice ( const Place& where,
                             const char* when,
                             const Price newPrice);
};
DEF_TIE_RegPxFrontOffice(RegPxFrontOffice_i);
```

To facilitate remote communications, objects of this type require a `TIE` of the class `TIE_RegPxFrontOffice(RegPxFrontOffice_i)`.

Implementating `SmartProxy2`

We can now proceed to define the second version of the smart proxy class for interface `FrontOffice`, naming it `SmartProxy2`. As well as implementing the operations defined in interface `FrontOffice`, this class must implement the `invalidate()` operation from interface `CacheInvalidate`.

Class `SmartProxy2` will be used to construct smart proxies for the `RegPxFrontOffice` interface – so it will inherit from the `RegPxFrontOffice` proxy class. This will allow these smart proxies to call all of the operations defined in `RegPxFrontOffice`.

In addition, to reduce the coding effort, `SmartProxy2` will inherit from the simple proxy, `SmartFrontOffice`, which we defined previously in Section 19.2.

The class hierarchy for `SmartProxy2` and related classes is shown in Figure 19.5. The underlined classes are standard proxy classes. The associations labeled `TIE` indicate that the lower class implements the upper proxy class; they do not indicate inheritance. Interface `CacheInvalidate` is called by the server. Interface `RegPxFrontOffice` is called by the client side: the application level on the client calls the `FrontOffice` portion of this (through the smart proxies of type `SmartProxy2`), and the smart proxy objects (of type `SmartProxy2`) call the `RegisterProxy` part.

The definition of `SmartProxy2` is as follows:

```
// C++. In "SmartProxy2.h".
#include "front.hh"

class TIE_CacheInvalidate(SmartProxy2); // Forward reference.

class SmartProxy2 : public virtual RegPxFrontOffice,
                    public virtual SmartFrontOffice {
```

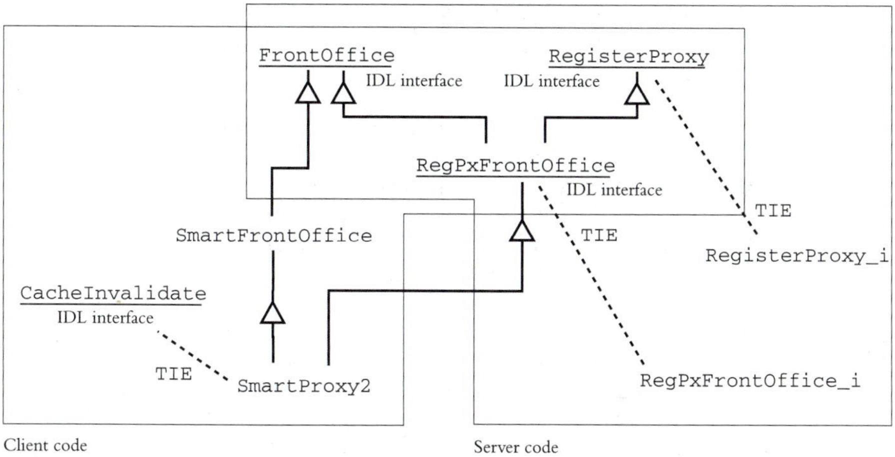

Figure 19.5 *The class hierarchy for the sophisticated proxy example.*

```
	// TIE for call-back:
	TIE_CacheInvalidate(SmartProxy2)* m_self;
public:
	// The required constructor.
	SmartProxy2(char*);

	virtual ~SmartProxy2();

	// IDL operation from interface CacheInvalidate:
	virtual void invalidate ()
			throw (CORBA::SystemException);
};

// Specify that SmartProxy2 implements the
// CacheInvalidate interface:
DEF_TIE_CacheInvalidate(SmartProxy2);
```

The `m_self` member is, in effect, a reference to the smart proxy itself, but it must reference a `TIE` to the smart proxy so that the `FrontOffice` object can remotely call the `invalidate()` function on it (hence the `TIE` is specified to implement the `CacheInvalidate` interface).

The implementation of these functions is as follows:

```
// C++
// In "SmartProxy2.cc".
#include "SmartProxy2.h"

SmartProxy2::SmartProxy2(char* OR)
	// Call the constructor of the proxy class
	// (RegPxFrontOffice) we provide proxies for;
	// also the constructor for any class we inherit
	// code from for ease of implementation; and any required
	// because C++ virtual inheritance is being used:
	: RegPxFrontOffice(OR), SmartFrontOffice(OR),
			FrontOffice(OR), RegisterProxy(OR)
{
	try {
		// Need to talk to the FrontOffice immediately to
		// register with it. First create a TIE for
		// the CacheInvalidate interface of this object:
		m_self = new TIE_CacheInvalidate(SmartProxy2)(this);
		// Register that TIE - which is really self:
		RegPxFrontOffice::signOn(m_self);
	}
	catch (CORBA::SystemException& se) {
		cerr << "Smart Proxy signOn() failed! "
			<< endl << se << endl;
		exit(-1);
	}
}
```

```
SmartProxy2::~SmartProxy2() {
      signOff(m_self);
}


void SmartProxy2::invalidate ()
                      throw (CORBA::SystemException) {
      // Call-back from FrontOffice - so invalidate
      // the cache. Code not shown here.
}
```

Note that `SmartProxy2` provides proxies for the proxy class `RegPxFrontOffice`, and therefore its constructor must call the constructor of `RegPxFrontOffice`. It would not be sufficient for the constructor of `SmartProxy2` to call the constructor of `FrontOffice`.

Figure 19.4 (p.321) shows clearly that the `CacheInvalidate` interface is implemented on the client side, and therefore the client must be linked with the server-side code generated by the IDL compiler for interface `CacheInvalidate` (the client-side stub code is not sufficient to handle incoming calls).

A new proxy factory must be defined to generate the smart proxies at the appropriate time. This code follows the normal pattern:

```
// C++
class SmartProxy2FactoryClass :
            public virtual RegPxFrontOfficeProxyFactoryClass {
public:
      // Constructor.
      SmartProxy2FactoryClass() :
            CORBA::ProxyFactory(RegPxFrontOffice_IR) {}

      virtual void* New(char* OR, CORBA::Environment&) {
            return (RegPxFrontOffice_ptr) new SmartProxy2(OR);
      }
};
```

Finally, the single instance of our proxy factory class can be defined as:

```
// C++
SmartProxy2FactoryClass sfo2;
```

19.3.3 Making the call-backs using OrbixTalk

Section 22.1(p.356) introduces the OrbixTalk multi-cast communication facility. This can be used to make the call-backs from a `FrontOffice` object to the set of clients that are interested in price changes. Using OrbixTalk, use would again be made of interface `CacheInvalidate`, defined in Section 19.3.2:

```
// IDL
interface CacheInvalidate {
      oneway void invalidate(in Pricing priceInfo);
};
```

Each client that caches pricing information would require an object of this type, registered as a listener. When prices change, the `FrontOffice` object would make a single OrbixTalk call to `CacheInvalidate::invalidate()`, and this call would be multi-cast automatically to each listener.

The implementation of `invalidate()` can work closely with the `FrontOffice` smart proxy, and inform it that some or all of its cache is invalid.

The approach described in this subsection requires fewer programming steps compared to the cache invalidation mechanism described in Section 19.3.2. It is also more efficient in the multi-casting version of OrbixTalk, because a single multi-cast message is used instead of requiring an individual call-back message for each smart proxy.

20 Loaders: support for persistent objects

When an operation invocation arrives at a process, Orbix searches for the target object in the process's object table. By default, if the object is not found, Orbix returns an exception to the caller. However, if one or more **loader** objects are installed in the process, these will be informed about the **object fault** and provided with an opportunity to load the target object and resume the invocation transparently to the caller. The loaders are maintained in a chain, and are tried in turn until one can load the object; if no loader can load the object, an exception is returned to the caller.

Loaders can provide support for persistent objects – long-lived objects stored on disk in the file system or in a database. (The notion of persistent objects should not be confused with the term 'persistent server.' The latter is the CORBA term for a server that is launched manually (or otherwise – in some way other than by the Orbix daemon). In Orbix, persistent objects can be supported by both automatically and persistently (manually) launched servers.) These loaders may be written by the application writer, and frequently one simple loader will be written for each IDL interface that has persistent instances. Alternatively, a sophisticated loader may handle all of the objects managed by a particular Database Management System (DBMS). This second model of loader forms part of what are known as **database adapters**, which are discussed in more detail in Section 22.2 (p.362).

Loaders are not part of the CORBA standard. In fact, they should be viewed as a way of extending an ORB, rather than as an application-level facility. For example, the CORBA standard allows for the replacement of a component called the Object Adapter with one designed to provide some specialist functionality; for example, to integrate the ORB with a DBMS. This extension, or adapter, can be written using a loader to load a target object when a request arrives in a server's address space. Typically, the adapter also contains a filter (see Chapter 18) that starts a database transaction when each request, or sequence of requests, starts.

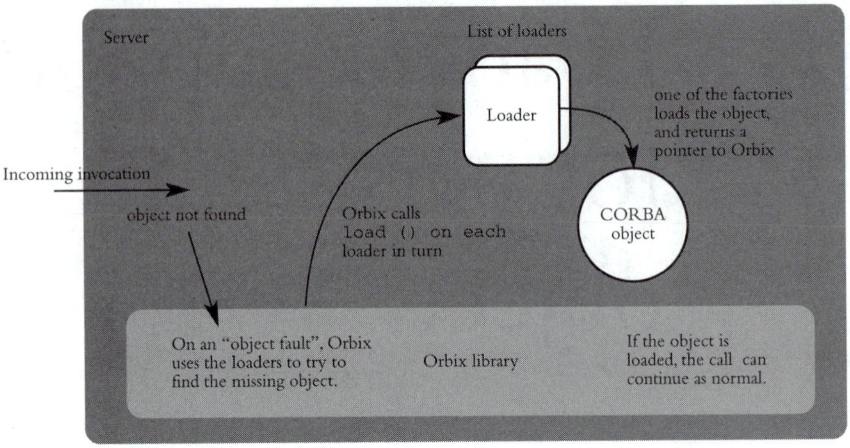

Figure 20.1 *Loading an object.*

Overview

Loaders are coded by defining a derived class of `CORBA::LoaderClass`, and they are installed by creating a (dynamic) instance of that new class. `CORBA::LoaderClass` provides the following four functions:

- `load()`: Orbix uses this function to inform a loader of an object fault. The loader is given the interface name and marker of the missing object so that it can identify which object to load. Figure 20.1 illustrates this. `load()` is also called when an object reference enters an address space, say as a parameter and not just when a 'missing object' is the target of a request.
- `save()`: when a process terminates, each object can be saved by its loader. To allow this, Orbix makes an individual call to `save()` for each object managed by that loader. The `save()` function is also called when an object is destroyed; and it can be explicitly called through the `CORBA::Object::_save()` function, defined on all Orbix objects.
- `record()` and `rename()`: these functions are used to control the naming of objects, and they are explained in Section 20.2.

Overview of `CORBA::LoaderClass`

`CORBA::LoaderClass` is declared as follows:

```
// C++ , in CORBA::
```

```
enum saveReason {
      processTermination, explicitCall, objectDeletion
};

class LoaderClass {
protected:
      LoaderClass(unsigned char registerMe = 0);
public:
      virtual ~LoaderClass();

      virtual Object_ptr load (const char* interface,
                               const char* marker,
                               Boolean isLocal,
                               Environment&)
            throw (CORBA::SystemException);

      virtual void save (Object_ptr obj,
                         saveReason reason,
                         Environment&)
            throw (CORBA::SystemException);

      virtual void record(Object_ptr obj,
                          char*& marker,
                          Environment&)
            throw (CORBA::SystemException);

      virtual Boolean rename(Object_ptr obj,
                             char*& marker,
                             Environment&)
            throw (CORBA::SystemException);
};
```

The `CORBA::Environment` parameters are used for raising exceptions when the C++ compiler does not support native exceptions.

Section 20.6 (p.336) shows an example loader, but first the preceding sections explain the different aspects of the loader mechanism in more detail.

20.1 Specifying a loader for an object

Each object in memory is associated with a loader object, which is informed when the object is named or renamed (Section 20.2) and when the object is to be saved (Section 20.4). If no loader is explicitly specified for an object, then it is associated with a default loader, implemented by Orbix.

An object's loader can be specified as the object is being created, using either the TIE or the BOAImpl approach. In the TIE approach, this can be done by passing a pointer to the loader as the third parameter to the TIE constructor. For example,

```
// C++
// myLoader is a pointer to a loader object.
FrontOffice_i* p = new FrontOffice_i ( "Savoy", /* . . . . */ );
FrontOffice_ptr FOptr;
FOptr = new TIE_FrontOffice(FrontOffice_i) (
                      p,              // Object pointer.
                      "Savoy",        // Marker.
                      myLoader );     // Loader pointer.
```

In the BOAImpl approach, this can be done by passing a pointer to a loader as the second parameter to the constructor of the BOAImpl class. For example:

```
// C++
class FrontOffice_i : public virtual FrontOfficeBOAImpl {
     . . . .
public:
     FrontOffice_i(char *name,

                    /* . . see Section 6.4, p.136 . . . */,

                    CORBA::LoaderClass*);
};


FrontOffice_i::FrontOffice_i(char *name,
     /* . . . . */,
     CORBA::LoaderClass* pl)
     // Set marker (to name) and loader (to pl).
     : FrontOfficeBOAImpl(name,pl)
{
     // Rest of constructor.
}
```

Each BOAImpl class's constructor takes a marker name as its first parameter, defined as `char*=""`; this is explained in Chapter 7. Its second parameter is a pointer to a loader object, defined as `CORBA::LoaderClass*=0`.

Each object is associated with a simple default loader if no loader is specified for it. That loader does not support persistence.

20.2 Connection between loaders and object naming

When supporting persistent objects, it is often important to control the markers that are assigned to them. For example, it is frequently a requirement to set an object's marker to be a key to search for its persistent data; and the format of these keys will depend on how the persistence is implemented by the loader. Therefore, it is common for loaders to choose object markers, or at least to be given the chance to accept or reject markers chosen by application-level code.

Recall from Section 7.1 (p.159) that an object can be assigned the marker `"Savoy"` in a number of ways:

- By passing a marker name to the TIE constructor; for example:

```
FrontOffice_i* p = new FrontOffice ("Savoy",
                                    /* .... */);
FrontOffice_var foVar;
foVar = new TIE_FrontOffice(FrontOffice_i) (p,
                                       "Savoy"
                                       myLoader );
```

- By passing the marker name to the BOAImpl constructor; for example:

```
class FrontOffice_i : public virtual
                          FrontOfficeBOAImpl {
public:
   FrontOffice_i(char* name,
                 /* . . . . */,
                 CORBA::LoaderClass* loader);
        /* . . . . */
};

FrontOffice_i::FrontOffice_i(char* name,
                         /* . . . . */
                         CORBA::LoaderClass* loader)
   : FrontOfficeBOAImpl(name, loader)
{}

FrontOffice_ptr fo = new FrontOffice_i ("Savoy",
                                       /* . . . . */,
                                       myLoader);
```

- By calling `CORBA::Object::_marker(const char*)`; for example:

```
b->_marker("Savoy");
```

In all cases, Orbix calls the object's loader to confirm the chosen name, thus giving the loader a chance to override the choice. In the first two cases above, Orbix calls `record()`; in the last case it calls `rename()` because the object already exists. If no marker is specified by the application, then `record()` or `rename()` is given an empty string.

20.3 Loading objects: `load()`

When an **object fault** occurs, the `load()` function is called on each loader in turn until one of them successfully returns the address of the object, or until they have all returned zero. It is not possible for Orbix to call the correct loader directly, because the object does not yet exist in the address space at the time of the object fault.

The responsibilities of the `load()` function are:

- To determine if the required object is to be loaded by the current loader.
- If so, to recreate the object and assign the correct marker to it.

The `load()` function is given the following information to carry out its responsibilities:

- The target object's marker and interface name.
- ✚ A `CORBA::Boolean` value, set to True if the object fault occurred because of actions by the server itself (for example, because of a call to `_bind()` within the server); and set to False otherwise. This parameter is usually ignored.
- An `Environment` parameter (to allow `load()` to raise an exception if C++ native exceptions are not supported). ✚

20.4 Saving objects: `save()`

When a process terminates, Orbix iterates through all of the objects in the object table of the process and calls the `save()` function on the loader associated with each object. A loader may save the object to persistent storage (either by calling a function on the object, or by accessing the object's data and writing this data itself).

The `save()` function is also called on the loader associated with an object when that object is destroyed; and a programmer can also explicitly cause it to be called by calling an object's `_save()` function. The `_save()` function simply calls the `save()` function on the object's loader.

These three reasons are distinguished by the second parameter (of type `CORBA::saveReason`) to `save()`, as follows:

- `processTermination`: the process is about to exit.
- `explicitCall`: the object's `_save()` function has been called.

- `objectDeletion`: `CORBA::release()` has been called on the object, which previously had a reference count of `1`.

It is common to write a loader's `save()` function so that it deletes the persistent representation of the object if the reason is `objectDeletion`.

Orbix does not delete the objects themselves as it iterates through its object table on process termination; it simply calls `save()` on each object's loader. It does, however, destroy the loader objects afterwards.

Section 20.5 further discusses how `save()` should be used, especially in a database adapter.

20.5 Aspects of writing a loader

If a loader is being written for a specific interface, then the following actions are normally carried out:

- The `load()` function should be redefined to do the main work of the loader, that is, to load an object on demand. The object's marker is normally used to find the object in the persistent store.
- The `save()` function should be redefined so that it saves the loader's objects on process termination, and also if `_save()` is called. It normally deletes an object's persistent storage if the save reason is `objectDeletion`.
- The `record()` and `rename()` functions are normally redefined. Often, `record()` chooses the marker for a new object; and `rename()` is sometimes written to simply prevent objects' markers being changed. However, `record()` and `rename()` are sometimes not redefined in a simple application, where the code that chooses markers at the application level can be trusted to choose correct values.

If a loader is written as part of a database adapter between CORBA and an OODBMS (see the introduction to this chapter, and also Section 22.2) then the following are common:

- `load()` should use the supplied marker to find the required object using the OODBMS facilities, and return a pointer to Orbix.
- `save()` should not need to carry out any work, because the OODBMS will look after the saving of objects (often at the end of a transaction), and also the deletion of their persistent state.

- `record()` should choose a marker for the object (perhaps using a low-level facility of the OODBMS to get a string form of the object's persistent object reference); and `rename()` frequently prevents changes to the markers of objects stored by the OODBMS.

20.6 Example loader

This section presents a simple loader for one interface. Recall the IDL definitions:

```
// IDL
interface Booking {
      readonly attribute Date when;
      readonly attribute Places seats;
      void cancel();
};

interface FrontOffice{
      /* rest not shown here */

      Booking makeBooking (
                 in Places chosenPlaces,
                 in Date when,
                 in CreditCard payment)
           raises ( /* . . . . */ );
};
```

Interfaces `Booking` and `FrontOffice` are implemented by classes `Booking_i` and `FrontOffice_i`, respectively. For variety, this chapter uses the TIE approach to implement some of the interfaces implemented using the BOAImpl approach in Chapter 6. Some function parameters, in particular those to C++ class constructors, have been omitted here, and replaced with comments. Code has been added to manage persistence and markers.

Instances of class `Booking_i` are made persistent using a loader (of class `Loader`). The persistence mechanism used is very primitive: it uses one file per `Booking` object. Nevertheless, the example acts as a simple introduction to loaders. The `FrontOffice` objects are not associated with an application-level loader, so they are implicitly associated with the Orbix default loader.

The implementation of class `Loader` is shown later, but first the implementations of classes `Booking_i` and `FrontOffice_i` are shown. Class `Booking_i` is implemented as follows:

```
// C++
class Booking_i {
protected:
      Date m_when;      // Format DD.MM.YYYY.
      Places_var m_seats;
      FrontOffice_i* m_office;
public:
      Booking_i( FrontOffice_i* office,
                 const Places& where,
                 const char* when)
            : m_office (office)
      {
            m_when = CORBA::string_dup(when);
            m_seats = new Places(where); // Copy the sequence.
      }
      virtual ~Booking_i() {
            CORBA::string_free(m_when); // Would not be needed if
                                  // m_when where CORBA::String_var.
            // m_seats de-allocates itself.
      }

      // Functions to implement IDL operations and
      // attributes. Not shown here.

      // Two Non-IDL functions to support persistence:
      static Booking_ptr loadMe (const char *file_name,
                                 CORBA::LoaderClass *);
      virtual void saveMe(const char* file_name);
};

DEF_TIE_Booking(Booking_i);
```

Two functions have been added to the implementation. The function `loadMe()` is called from the `load()` function of the loader, and it is given the name of the file from which to load the `Booking` object. The function `saveMe()` writes the member variables of a `Booking` to a specified file. These functions can be coded as follows:

```
Booking_ptr Booking_i::loadMe (const char *file_name,
                               CORBA::LoaderClass *pl) {
      ifstream from(file_name); // Open to read.
      if (from) { // if opened ok:
            char aDate[11];
            Places aSeqOfPlaces; // Empty initially.

            from >> aDate;
            // Then read the sequence of places, placing it in
            // aSeqOfPlaces. Code not shown here.
```

```
            // Now create the object and TIE:
            Booking_i* p = new Booking_i( /* . . . . */,†
                                        aSeqOfPlaces, aDate);
            char* marker = file_name; // Just to reflect two usages.
            Booking_ptr bPtr = new TIE_Booking(Booking_i)
                                              (p,marker,pl);
            return bPtr;
      }
      else return 0; // Cannot load
}


void Booking_i::saveMe(const char* file_name) {
      // Error handling not shown in this case.
      ofstream dump(file_name);
      dump << m_when << endl;
      // Write the sequence of places in m_seats.
      // Code not shown here.
}
```

The statement:

```
Booking_ptr bPtr = new TIE_Booking(Booking_i) (p, marker, pl);
```

in `Booking_i::loadMe()` creates a new TIE for the object pointed to by `p`, and specifies its marker to be `marker` and its loader to be the loader pointed to by the parameter `pl`. (Actually, this example creates only a single loader object, as we will see.)

Class `FrontOffice_i` can be implemented as follows:

```
// C++
class FrontOffice_i {
protected:
      CORBA::Loader* m_loader;
      unsigned long m_nextNum;
      // Other member variables not shown here.
public:

      FrontOffice_i(const char *name, /* . . . . */,
                    CORBA::LoaderClass* loaderPtr);
      virtual ~FrontOffice_i()

      // Functions for IDL operations.
      virtual Booking_ptr makeBooking (
                        const Places& chosenPlaces,
```

† There is probably only one `FrontOffice_i` object in this server: pass a pointer to it.

```
                         const char* when,
                         const CreditCard& payment)
                 throw (CORBA::SystemException);

      /* rest of class not shown here */
};

DEF_TIE_FrontOffice(FrontOffice_i)


FrontOffice_i::FrontOffice_i(const char *name,
                             /* . . . . */,
                             CORBA::LoaderClass* loaderPtr):
      m_loader(loaderPtr)
{ // Read the value of m_nextNum from a
  // configuration file. Code not shown here.
  /* . . . . . */
}

FrontOffice_i::~FrontOffice_i()
{ /* . . . . . */ }


Booking_ptr FrontOffice_i::makeBooking(
                 const Places& chosenPlaces,
                 const char* when,
                 const CreditCard& payment)
            throw (CORBA::SystemException)    {
      char marker[25];
      sprintf(marker, "booking-%d", m_nextNum++);
      Booking_i* b_p = new Booking_i( this, chosenPlaces, when);
      Booking_ptr newBooking = new TIE_Booking(Booking_i)
                                  (b_p, marker, m_loader);
      // Add the new Booking object into a local list:
      // code not shown here.
      // Duplicate so that the new Booking object is not deleted:
      Booking::_duplicate(newBooking);
      return newBooking;
}
```

The statement:

```
Booking_ptr newBooking = new TIE_Booking(Booking_i)
                                  (b_p, marker, m_loader);
```

creates a new TIE for the object pointed to by `b_p`, assigning it the marker `marker` and the loader pointed to by `m_loader`.

Each `FrontOffice_i` object holds a pointer (`m_loader`) to the loader object to associate with each `Booking` object as it is created. Each booking is assigned a unique booking number, constructed from the string '`booking-`' and a unique counter value. This ability to choose markers is an important feature for persistence. In a real implementation, the marker would be a key into the underlying database. In the case of a relational database, the marker would be a key that could be be used in an SQL statement to find the object's data; and in the case of an object database, it could be a similar key, or, more commonly, it can be a stringified version of the object reference assigned by the DBMS.

The server mainline must create a loader and a `FrontOffice`, for example:

```
// C++
// Loaders must be dynamically created:
Loader* myLoader = new Loader;
FrontOffice_i* fo_p = new FrontOffice_i( "Savoy",
                                        /* . . . . */,
                                        myLoader);
FrontOffice_ptr foPtr = new TIE_FrontOffice(FrontOffice_i)
                                               (fo_p,"Savoy");
```

Coding the loader

Class `Loader` can be implemented as follows:

```
// C++
class Loader : public CORBA::LoaderClass {
      // No private data in this case.
public:
      Loader();
      virtual ~Loader() {}

      // Redefine load() and save(),
      // (inherit rename() and record()).

      virtual CORBA::Object_ptr load(
                        const char* interface,
                        const char* marker,
                        CORBA::Boolean isLocal,
                        CORBA::Environment&)
                  throw (CORBA::SystemException);

      // Save object referenced by r:
      virtual void save(CORBA::Object_ptr r,
                         CORBA::saveReason reason,
                         CORBA::Environment&)
                  throw (CORBA::SystemException);
};
```

These functions can be defined as follows:

```
// Note that the constructor of a loader must specify whether or
// not Orbix should directly call its load() function.
```

```
// In this case (and most cases), specify that Orbix should:
Loader::Loader()
      : CORBA::LoaderClass(1)   // 1 for true.
{}


CORBA::Object_ptr Loader::load(
                        const char* interface,
                        const char* marker,
                        CORBA::Boolean isLocal,
                        CORBA::Environment&)
                  throw (CORBA::SystemException) {
      if ( strcmp(interface,"Booking")==0 ) {
            char* fileName = marker;
            return Booking_i::loadMe(fileName,this);
      }
      else        // Not recognized:
        return 0;
}


void Loader::save(CORBA::Object_ptr obj,
                  CORBA::saveReason reason,
                  CORBA::Environment&)
                  throw (CORBA::SystemException) {
      if (reason != CORBA::objectDeletion) {
            char* filename= obj->_marker();
            // Want to call the saveMe() function on the
            // object. But first must traverse the TIE to
            // find the implementation object (note that
            // saveMe() is not a valid function on the
            // TIE because it is not defined in the IDL.)
            Booking_i* ap = (Booking_i*)obj->_deref();
            ap->saveMe(filename); // Save to file filename.
      }
      else {
            // Could delete the object's persistent state here.
      }
}
```

The `_deref()` member function can be called on a TIE: it returns a pointer to the object (in this case of type `Booking_i`) that the TIE contains a pointer to.

Note that the constructor of `CORBA::LoaderClass` takes a parameter to indicate whether or not the loader being created should be included in the list of loaders that are tried when an object fault occurs. By default, this value is false; so our loader class's constructor passes a value of `1` to the `CORBA::LoaderClass` constructor to indicate that instances of `Loader` should be added to this list.

✚ Note also that the `Booking_i::loadMe()` function assigns the correct marker to the newly created object. If it failed to do this, subsequent calls on the same object would result in further object faults and calls to the `Loader::load()` function.

Adding `loadMe()` and `saveMe()`

Extending `Booking_i` with `loadMe()` and `saveMe()` made the coding of the loader significantly easier. It is a common technique to add functions such as these when persistence is implemented without the aid of a DBMS.

It would have been possible for the `Loader::load()` function itself to read the object's persistent data, rather than calling the static function `Booking_i::loadMe()`. However, to construct the object, `load()` would be dependent on there being a constructor on class `Booking_i` that takes all of a `Booking`'s state as parameters. Since this will not be the case for all classes, it is safer to introduce a function such as `loadMe()`. Equally, `Loader::save()` could have accessed the `Booking` object's data and written it out, rather than calling `Booking_i::saveMe()`. However, it would then be dependent on `Booking_i` providing some means to access all of its state.

In any case, having `loadMe()` and `saveMe()` within class `Booking_i` provides a sensible division of functionality between the application-level class, `Booking_i`, and the loader class, `Loader`. ✚

Loaders are transparent to clients

Of course, the loader class in the server is not visible to the client code. A client can make an invocation on a `Booking` object without concern for whether or not it is currently in the server's memory. If it is not, then the loader will be involved, transparently to the client.

20.7 Summary

Loaders are a low-level facility for supporting persistent objects. Their main design criterion is to give system-level code a great deal of freedom in how persistence is provided, rather than to make loaders easy to use. Some applications may write their own loaders, either because their persistence requirements are easily supported and they therefore do not need the sophistication of a DBMS, or because they wish to implement some application-specific support. Other applications may use loaders provided as part of a database adapter (Section 22.2, p.362; and Section 25.4, p.446) that hides any complexity from them.

The simple example we have seen in Section 20.6 used a separate file for each `Booking` object. However, it would also be easy to implement a version of this that uses a single record of a file or database per object. If that database is managed by a relational DBMS, then the loader (or some function such as `Booking_i::loadMe()`)

will need to make SQL statements on the database (or use some database middleware to do this).

The example also used one loader class for a single application-level interface, `Booking`. If several interfaces in a server require loaders, then it is easier to have an application-specific loader class per interface, rather than to have one overly-complex loader that handles multiple classes. Of course, if the implementer of a database adapter can provide a single loader that is independent of the types of objects being loaded, then this is the best approach.

✚ The one disadvantage of having one application-specific loader per interface is that, in some applications, it may be costly to iterate through a long list of loaders. If each loader has to perform some disk I/O to determine whether the missing object is its responsibility, then the overall efficiency of the application may suffer. This is easily addressed using a **master loader**. In this approach, Orbix is informed about a single loader object, which will receive all `load()` requests. In addition, there is one **slave loader** per interface, but instead of having their `load()` function called directly by Orbix, these loaders register themselves with the master loader. They give the master a pattern (such as an interface name) that it can use to determine which slave loader to pass each `load()` call to. The master can use some efficient structure, such as a hash table, to determine which slave to use.

This chapter has not dealt with the issues that arise because of interface hierarchies. The only difficulty is that a client can use the `_bind()` function to bind to an object of a derived interface; for example, it can use `Booking::_bind()` to bind to a `GroupBooking` object. The interface name available in the server will then be "Booking" rather than "GroupBooking." The standard way to address this is to store an indication of an object's type with its data. The master loader, if this approach is being used, will normally locate the object, determine its type, and then call the correct slave loader. Most OODBMSs implicitly or explicitly store some indicator of an object's type with its data, and this fact can be used by a loader that is part of a database adapter.

This difficulty does not arise if object references are passed to a client using the Naming Service, or as parameters or return values. The correct interface name will then be passed to the `load()` function in the server when such object references are used. It is only if the `_bind()` call is used to obtain object references that the server need worry about the interface name being a base interface of the actual interface of the object that is to be loaded. ✚

Finally, although loaders provide a useful low-level facility for supporting persistent objects, most applications that use a loader will increasingly use one that is incorporated into a database adapter.

21 Multi-threaded servers

This chapter explains the benefits of multi-threaded clients and servers, and the mechanisms available for programming them. Normally, Orbix client and server programs contain one thread that starts executing at the beginning of the program (executing `main()`) and continues until the program terminates. Many modern operating systems allow a process to create lightweight threads, with each thread having its own set of CPU registers and its own stack. In particular, each thread is independently scheduled by the operating system, so that it can run in parallel with the other threads in its process. The mechanisms for creating and controlling threads differ between operating systems (although the POSIX standard is supported by most systems), but the underlying concepts are common.

The programming steps required to create threads in Orbix are particularly simple, and, in addition, many different models of thread support can be programmed.

The remainder of this chapter is organized as follows. In Section 21.1, we begin by looking at the advantages of multi-threaded clients and servers. In Section 21.2, we discuss the mechanism for supporting them. Finally, in Section 21.3, we look at some of the server-side threading models that can be chosen.

21.1 Benefits of multi-threaded clients and servers

We begin by looking at the benefits of multi-threaded servers, because these are stronger and easier to explain than the benefits of multi-threaded clients.

It is satisfactory for some servers to accept one request at a time: to process each request to completion before accepting the next. Where parallelism is not required by an application, there is little point in making such servers multi-threaded. However, some servers would offer a better service to their clients if they could process a number of requests in parallel. Parallelism of such requests may be possible because a set of clients can concurrently use different objects in the same server, or because some of the objects in the server can be used concurrently by a number of clients.

Some operations can take a significant amount of time to execute, because they are compute bound, because they perform a large number of I/O operations, or because they make invocations on remote objects. If a server can execute only one such operation at a time, then clients will suffer because of long latencies before their requests can be started. The benefits of multi-threading are that the latency of requests can be reduced, and the number of requests that a server can handle over a given period of time (that is, the server's throughput) can be higher. Multi-threading also allows advantage to be taken of multiprocessor machines.

The simplest threading model is where a thread is created *automatically* for each incoming operation/attribute request. Each thread executes the code for the operation/attribute being called, executes the low-level code that sends the reply to the caller, and then terminates. Any number of such threads can be running concurrently in a server, and they can use normal concurrency control techniques (such as mutex or semaphore variables) to prevent corruption of the server's data. This protection must be programmed at two levels: the underlying ORB library must be thread-safe so that concurrent threads do not corrupt internal variables and tables; and the application level must be made thread-safe by the application programmer.

Threads are not without their costs, however. Firstly, it may be more efficient to avoid creating a thread to execute a very simple operation. The overhead of creating a thread may be greater than the potential benefit of parallelism. Secondly, application programmers must ensure that their code is thread-safe. In particular, Solaris, Windows NT, HP/UX, SGI and POSIX threads are pre-emptive; that is, they can be interrupted at any time and delayed while other threads execute. Nevertheless, the benefits frequently outweigh the costs, and multi-threaded servers are considered essential for many applications.

A benefit of CORBA is that the actual creation of threads in a server is very simple, and therefore this adds little or no cost for application programmers. We will see in Section 21.3 that CORBA can support many different threading models, giving applications a great deal of flexibility in how and when threads are created.

Multi-threaded clients can also be useful. In particular, a client can create a thread and have it make a remote operation call, rather than making that remote call directly. The result is that the thread that makes the call will block until the operation call has completed, but the rest of the client will be able to continue in parallel. A later subsection will compare this approach with the use of non-blocking calls made by single-threaded clients. Another advantage of a multi-threaded client is that it can receive incoming operation requests to its objects (for example, a call-back from a server to inform the client about some matter) without having to poll for communication events. (Communication events can be awaited or polled for using `processNextEvent()`, `isEventPending()`, and `ProcessEvents()`.)

Clients must create threads explicitly, using the threading facilities of the underlying operating system, but this is not difficult to do. Naturally, multi-threaded clients must also be coded to ensure that they are thread-safe, using some concurrency control mechanism. As for servers, the difficulty of doing this depends on the complexity of the data, the complexity of the concurrency control rules, and the form of concurrency control mechanism being used.

Threads can also be created explicitly in servers. This can be done for the same reason as for clients: so that a remote call can be made without blocking the server. It can also be done within the code that implements an operation or attribute so that some complex algorithm can be parallelized and carried out by a number of threads. These threads can be in addition to those created automatically to handle each request.

Comparison with non-blocking calls

Some of the benefits of using multiple threads can also be gained by making operation calls that do not block the caller. IDL `oneway` calls do not block their caller, (unless the communication system and CORBA level buffering are swamped by burst mode activity), and normal calls can be made without blocking by using the DII function `send_deferred()` on a `Request` (these are explained in Section 15.6, p.253). Such calls may be made within a client or a server.

However, use of threads is both easier and more powerful than use of non-blocking calls, which means that there is little to be recommended in non-blocking calls:

- Easier: threads are an easier way to gain concurrency: "Threads are for concurrency; messages are for communication." Consider a client that wishes to carry out a number of actions, each action requiring a number of two-way operation requests. One way to achieve this is to make the first two-way operation call associated with each action without blocking, and to process the results in whatever order they arrive. In this way, at any time, there will be one outstanding (non-blocking) operation call for each action. Once a reply arrives for the current operation call for an action, the next call for that action can be made. The difficulty is that the client must loop to accept each reply, and it must maintain a table to indicate the next request to make for each action. This is complex and error-prone. In contrast, the equivalent coding using threads is very simple. A thread can be created for each action, and that action can make normal blocking calls for each request that is to be made in turn.

- More powerful: the real benefits of multi-threaded servers cannot be gained using non-blocking calls; that is, the ability to handle calls from a number of clients concurrently. Consider an attempt to do so. A single-threaded server can accept an incoming operation request, and during the processing of this it can use a non-blocking call to make a request on a remote object. Naturally, the server will not block while the remote object is processing the call, but it cannot accept another incoming operation request from the same or another client. The only way that it can accept another operation call is to complete the first one (by exiting the C++ member function that implements the operation): the one on whose behalf it has made the non-blocking remote call. Hence, the server cannot accept another call until it has completed the current one.

✚ Some older communication facilities could be used to allow a server to handle multiple requests concurrently when combined with non-blocking calls. These were not based on remote procedure calls, but instead on message exchange between clients and servers. A client constructed a message and sent it using a *send* primitive; and servers accepted incoming messages by waiting on a *receive* call. Typically, the server's main function looped on this receive call; but it could also call it at any other time.

Therefore, during the processing of one message, a server could make a non-blocking remote call, and then call the receive primitive to handle another client's request. The difficulty, of course, was that the flow of control within such a server was very difficult to manage: it might be handling one particular incoming message, make a non-blocking remote call, and then be expected to handle a different type of incoming message. In addition, it had to track each outstanding non-blocking call, so that it could (within a single thread) continue in the correct way when one of them completed. ✚

In contrast, the benefit of handling multiple clients concurrently is simple to achieve using a multi-threaded server. In addition, multi-threaded servers also allow parallelism of compute bound and I/O bound operation calls.

Notwithstanding this, non-blocking calls can sometimes be useful. Firstly, some operating systems do not support threads; and secondly, although threads may be available, it might not be possible to use them because an application is using some library that is not thread-safe. Finally, for very simple uses of non-blocking calls in clients, the complexity of using non-blocking calls is no greater than that of using threads. Nevertheless, the real benefits of multi-threaded servers (the ability to handle calls from different clients concurrently) cannot be gained using non-blocking calls.

21.2 How to start threads in servers and clients

Orbix-MT provides a thread-safe version of the Orbix libraries for use with the underlying operating system's threads package. At appropriate points within the Orbix libraries, locking code has been added to ensure that Orbix's internal data structures are correctly managed in a pre-emptive threading environment.

Nevertheless, by default there is only one thread created to handle incoming requests: in particular, a server will only handle one call at a time. To create a thread per incoming request, the programmer must install a filter (see Chapter 18) that creates these threads. This code is supplied, and it can be used without modification. It should be viewed as code that extends the ORB, rather than as application-level code.

It may seem to be better to have built the thread-creation code into Orbix. This has not been done because it would make it significantly more difficult to use different threading models, other than the default thread per request model. This issue is discussed in Section 21.3. In addition, exposing the code via a filter allows a server programmer to make subtle changes to the thread per request model, such as creating a thread only for some objects or only for some operations, or only if the load on the machine is below a threshold.

Operating system support for creating threads

Before discussing the filter code that creates threads, this subsection shows the functions that are required to create a thread on different operating systems. These calls will be used in a later subsection that shows the filter code.

For Solaris:

```
#include <thread.h>
thr_create (void* stack_base, size_t stack_size,
            void*(start_routine)(void*), void* arg,
            long flags, thread_t* new_thread);
```

For Windows NT:

```
#include <process.h>
HANDLE CreateThread(
                LPSECURITY_ATTRIBUTES lpsa,
                DWORD cbStack,
                LPTHREAD_START_ROUTINE lpStartAddr,
                LPVOID lpbThreadParm,
                DWORD fdwCreate,
                LPDWORD lpIDThread);
```

For POSIX compliant threading facilities:

```
#include <pthread.h>
int pthread_create(pthread_t* tid,
                   pthread_attr_t*,
                   void*(start_routine)(void*),
                   void* arg);
```

If a client or server creates a thread to make a remote request, it can wait for that thread to terminate, using one of the following calls (in Solaris, NT, and POSIX, respectively):

- `thr_join()`
- `WaitForSingleObject()`
- `pthread_join()`

21.2.1 Creating a thread to handle a request

As mentioned in Chapter 18, a per-process filter's `inRequestPreMarshal()` function can create a thread to handle an incoming request. The `inRequestPreMarshal()` function should use an underlying threads package – for example the Solaris threads package – to create a thread, and the thread should then handle the request, usually by instructing Orbix to send the invocation to the target object.

Note that `inRequestPreMarshal()` should return `-1` to Orbix to indicate that it has created a thread that will handle the call. Unlike the other filter points, `inRequestPreMarshal()` has a return type `int`. This allows it to return `1` to indicate that the request is accepted and should be processed as normal; return `0` to indicate that the request should be rejected (normally a C++ exception is raised instead); or return `-1` to indicate that the call is being handled by a separate thread.

The new filter class should inherit from `CORBA::ThreadFilter`, which in turn derives from `CORBA::Filter`. The code below is the example thread filter than creates a thread per request. The version shown uses the Solaris threading facility:

```
// C++
class CreatesThread : public CORBA::ThreadFilter {
public:
      // Only consider one monitor point here:
      virtual int inRequestPreMarshal (CORBA::Request&,
                                       CORBA::Environment&)
                      throw (CORBA::SystemException);
};

// Create the required single instance:
CreatesThread threadDispatcher;
```

```
// Define start function for new threads:
static void* startThread(void* vp) {
      // Tell Orbix to resume processing a request:
      CORBA::Orbix.continueThreadDispatch (*(CORBA::Request*)vp);
      return 0;
}

// Implementation of inRequestPreMarshal():
int CreatesThread::inRequestPreMarshal (CORBA::Request& r,
                                        CORBA::Environment&)
                        throw (CORBA::SystemException) {
      // Create a thread using the threads-package:
      // The thread entry point is startThread()
      thread_t tid;
      thr_create(NULL, 0, startThread, (void*)&r,
                  THR_DETATCHED, &tid);
      // Indicate to Orbix that we created a thread:
      return -1;
}
```

Figure 21.1 shows the function calls and threads.

`CreatesThread::inRequestPreMarshal()` is the first part of this code to execute. It uses the Solaris function `thr_create()` to create the new thread, specifying that the new thread is to execute the function `startThread()`. The value `-1` is then returned to inform Orbix that a new thread has been created.

The role of `startThread()` is to instruct Orbix to continue to process the operation or attribute request (of course, within the new thread it is running in). It does this by calling the low level Orbix function `continueThreadDispatch()`, passing the `Request` that represents the request being made. The request is passed to `startThread()` as parameter `vp`, which although declared to be of type `void*`, is actually of type `CORBA::Request*`. The rules of the Solaris threading package dictate

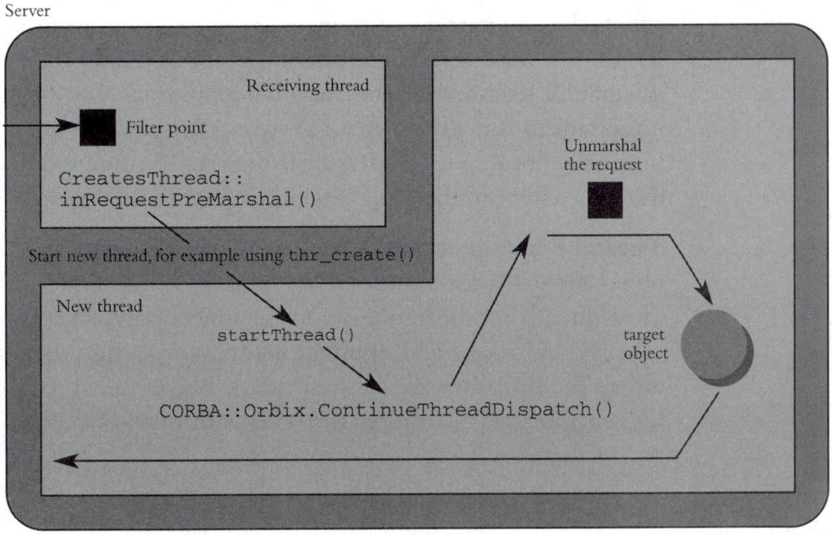

Figure 21.1 *Thread creation.*

that the function that a thread is to execute (`startThread()` in this case) must take a `void*` parameter, which is passed as the fourth parameter to `thr_create()`.

Although Orbix contains sufficient locks to ensure the thread safety of its internal variables and tables, and the low-level variables associated with each Orbix object, application programmers are responsible for ensuring the thread safety of their code and variables, including the safety of application-level member variables of Orbix objects.

21.3 Models of thread support

As well as the 'thread per request' model described in Section 21.2, a derived class of `ThreadFilter` can be used to program other models, such as the following (Schmidt and Vinoski, 1996a, b, c):

- **Pool of threads**: in this model, a pool of threads is created in the server to handle incoming requests. The size of the pool puts some limit on the server's use of resources, and in some cases this is better than the unbounded nature of the 'thread per request' model. Each thread waits for an incoming request, and handles it before looping to repeat this sequence.
- **Thread per client**: in this model, a thread is created for each client process that is currently connected to the server. Each thread handles the requests from one client process, and ignores other requests. This may be useful if thread creation is too expensive to have a thread created for each request; but of course it does give the potential of having idle threads corresponding to clients that are currently not making requests to objects in the server. One particularly important use of this model is for DBMS integration (Section 22.2, p.362), where in some cases it is important to run all of a client's requests in the same thread (normally because it is necessary to run consecutive requests from the same client in the same transaction).
- **Thread per object**: in this model, a thread is created for each object (actually, for a subset of the objects in the server). Each of these threads accepts requests for one object only, and ignores all others. This can be an important model in real-time processing, where the threads associated with some objects need to be given higher priorities that those associated with others.

✚ The remainder of this section gives a brief outline of how these models can be implemented.

- **Pool of threads**: to implement this model, a pool of threads should be created, and each thread should wait on a shared semaphore. When a request arrives, the `inRequestPreMarshal()` function of the `ThreadFilter` should place a pointer to the `Request` in an agreed variable (or a queue can be used), and signal the semaphore. One of the threads will awaken, and should call `continueThreadDispatch()` before looping to repeat the sequence.

- **Thread per client**: there are two variations on how this should be implemented, depending on whether or not a single client can make concurrent calls on objects in a server. If a client can only make one call at a time, then the `inRequestPreMarshal()` function should determine the identity of the caller (perhaps finding the file descriptor on the server that the call was made through), and use this to locate the corresponding thread. To be more exact, a synchronization variable (a mutex or semaphore) is located; and this is signaled so that the thread associated with the client will awaken. `inRequestPreMarshal()` should pass (a pointer to) the `Request` object to the thread, so that it can call `continueThreadDispatch()`.

  If a client can make concurrent calls to the objects in the server, then `inRequestPreMarshal()` should use a queue to communicate with the chosen thread: it should add the `Request` to the correct thread's queue, and signal a semaphore to mark the fact that there is one more entry in the queue. There should be one semaphore and one queue per thread, and each thread should wait on its own semaphore.

- **Thread per object**: to implement this model, a thread should be created for each of (or a subset of) the objects in the server. Each thread should have its own semaphore and queue of requests, and it should wait on its own semaphore. `inRequestPreMarshal()` should add (a pointer to) the `Request` to the correct queue of requests, and signal the correct semaphore. When the thread awakens, it should call `continueThreadDispatch()` to process the topmost request, and then loop to await the next one.

In addition to being able to change the threading model, a programmer can also change the type of threads used internally by Orbix. Although this issue is not discussed here, the code to create these threads is exposed and can be replaced. ✚

22 Technology integration

One of the important features of CORBA is that it can be combined with other technologies to improve the development platform available to programmers. CORBA addresses the needs of programmers of distributed software and of architects integrating systems from existing and new components. If provides the interfacing and messaging technologies required for this. However, it is not the aim of CORBA to address all of the needs of programmers, architects, and administrators. For example, CORBA does not aim to be a database management system (DBMS) or a tool for generating graphical user interfaces, nor does it define a threading package. Instead, these facilities should be provided as independent software systems that are either constructed using CORBA or integrated with it; or they should be provided within the chosen operating system.

This approach allows a specialist software company to produce an implementation of CORBA and to integrate it with the other software systems that programmers and administrators need to use – allowing purchasers to decide on what other 'best of breed' components they need. Some of these integrations can be implemented jointly by the two vendors involved, while others can be implemented by one vendor using the published interfaces of the other system.

Of course, there is nothing preventing an ORB vendor from attempting to provide many other software components. The danger is that the result will be a monolithic software system, rather than an integration of efficient components. This approach will also inevitably restrict the choice offered to software purchasers.

A number of integrations are described in this chapter:

- Orbix+OLE: the integration between Orbix and Microsoft's OLE is discussed in more depth in Chapter 11. Many of the tools and programming languages on Windows use OLE to communicate with each other; for example, between a word processor and a spreadsheet. Languages such as Visual Basic and systems such as Delphi can provide front-ends to systems as long as these have OLE interfaces.The Orbix+OLE integration allows any language or tool that can invoke on an OLE interface to invoke on a CORBA object anywhere on the network. The caller need not be aware that it is invoking a CORBA object, and the CORBA object will not be aware that the call came from the OLE world. In addition, the integration is based upon Window's OCX support so that an IDL interface can be implemented by OLE code. This allows transparent calls from a CORBA object to OLE code; for example, a call to notify a user interface that a particular event has occurred on a server.

- Talk and Listen (Section 22.1): some clients need to communicate the same information to a set of objects in the system. This can be tedious and error prone to program, and inefficient to execute. In some cases, a client may have no sensible way of knowing what objects to communicate with: it wishes simply to send the information to those objects that are interested in it. This communication style may arise because the application needs to be able to add new interested objects without modifying a client, and yet does not want to program the client to have to determine the interested objects at runtime. OrbixTalk is an extension to CORBA that allows a client to send a message that is sent efficiently to a set of interested objects. The client is known as a **talker** and the interested objects are known as **listeners**. Each stream of communication is related to some **topic**, and any number of talkers and listener can be active on a given topic.
- Integration with DBMSs (Section 22.2): some applications implemented using a DBMS will benefit from being able to define IDL interfaces that can be called from any CORBA client or server. Of equal importance, some CORBA servers need to store their objects in a DBMS. The integration of CORBA and DBMSs allows a CORBA server to use a DBMS, and in particular it allows an object to be both a CORBA object and a DBMS object.

22.1 Talk and Listen: OrbixTalk

IDL operation calls are an ideal mechanism for communicating between a client and a server: an object in a server can advertise its IDL interface and clients can use this interface using simple and familiar programming constructs. A C++ function call can result in the activation of an object on a different node, running on a different operating system, and written in a different programming language.

However, this direct point-to-point communication is not ideal when a client must make the same operation call on a set of objects. Having to make a sequence of operation calls is laborious to program, and inefficient to execute. Such communication is also inappropriate if a client needs to make the same operation call on a variable set of objects that the client cannot, or should not, be able to enumerate. A client may not know the objects that it needs to communicate with because this set is very variable (so it would be difficult to maintain a list of object references in the client), or because the client and the target objects should not know of each other.

To handle this form of interaction, a client should be able to communicate information simply by making an operation invocation, and the middleware should handle the passing of this operation call to the set of objects that should receive it. In a normal client to target object interaction, the target object can be decoupled from the client: the target need not know the location or nature of the client. To handle some applications, the client needs to be decoupled from the target objects that it communicates with: it simply communicates and the middleware accepts the responsibility of knowing which objects to send operation calls to.

This second form of communication is supported by the CORBA Event Service (Section 23.1, p.369). This section describes OrbixTalk, a special implementation of this style of communication. The term **message** is used to describe one unit of communication between a client, called the **talker**, and a set of target objects, called the **listeners**. The talker need not be concerned with the identity, nature, or even the number of the listeners: it can send a message simply by making an IDL operation call. Each message is sent on a stream of messages known as a **topic**. Each listener can specify the topics that it is interested in, and what it does when a message arrives concerning a given topic. There can be any number of simultaneous talkers and listeners on a given topic.

Messages are unidirectional, from the talker to a set of listeners. To reflect this, each listener has an IDL interface, consisting entirely of `oneway` calls. Each listener is an Orbix object; and a process can listen on many topics at the same time because it can contain many listeners. If a listener needs to communicate with a talker, then it can either use a normal IDL-based interaction, or a second OrbixTalk stream (again consisting entirely of `oneway` operations) in the opposite direction.

Figure 22.1 shows a set of talkers and listens for a topic, called "`switches/failures`". Topics have hierarchical names, so that they can be managed more easily in a large system.

Example usages

In a financial application, a topic may exist for the sales price of a given stock, and one of the IDL operations may announce that the stock price has risen beyond a particular threshold. The application that updates stock price may talk on this topic

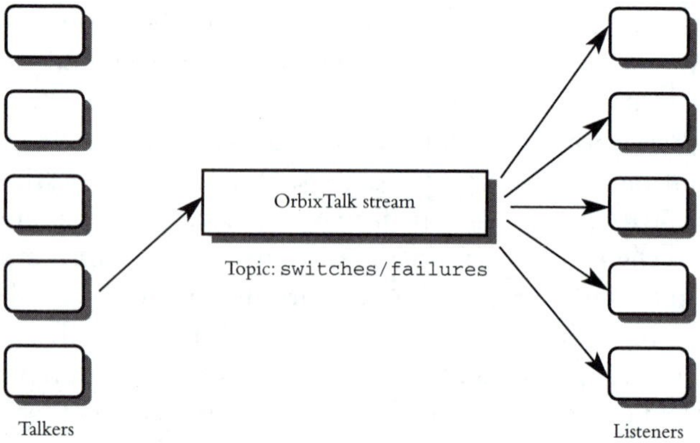

Figure 22.1 *An OrbixTalk stream.*

(by calling the IDL operation that announces that the stock prices has risen beyond the threshold). The listeners might include a government reporting department; an insider trader watchdog; and an automated purchasing and sales system. Other topics might include the fact that a stock's price is raising at a threshold rate; a stock's price is falling at a threshold rate; the stock exchange's rate of activity is above a threshold number of sales per hour; trading in any stock has been suspended; and so on. It would be inefficient to have the stock update application make a number of separate operation calls; and it is more flexible to keep the talkers and listeners decoupled so that new listeners and talkers can be added. If a new application component needs to watch stock prices, then it can create a listener (an object that supports the correct IDL interface) and register it as a listener on the topic.

In a manufacturing application, a talker may announce that a particular piece of plant is available again after repair. The listeners may include the staffing supervisor, the automated scheduling system, and the inventory system.

In a telecommunications application, a talker may announce the failure of a switch. The listeners may include the supervisor, the repair department, and the automated routing systems. Figure 22.1 shows the topic name `switches/failures` being used between a set of talkers and listeners. (If a protocol mode were specified, see Section 22.1.2, the full topic name might be `otrmp//switches/failures`).

A number of general themes run through these examples. The sender of a message is interested in informing the listeners of an event, but is not interested in waiting until the listeners have processed that event. Further, the sender wishes to continue even if one or all of the listeners are currently unavailable. Finally, the caller is not required to know all of the potential listeners.

Section 19.3.3 (p.327) describes how OrbixTalk can be used in our cinema application. In particular, it can be used to send seat price changes to interested clients. The ease and efficiency of this approach is contrasted with explicit call-back operation calls, which were used in Section 19.3.2 (p.320).

Implementation outline

OrbixTalk can be implemented in a number of different ways, depending on the underlying network technology. In one of these implementations, an OrbixTalk message is sent to its listeners by UDP multi-casting a single message to their machines. (A multi-cast packet is sent to a set of nodes on the network in a single step. In contrast, point to point messages are sent to a single node; and broadcast messages are sent to all nodes on the network. A multi-cast address represents the set of nodes that a multi-cast packet will be sent to. Naturally, multi-cast can be mimicked by sending multiple point to point packets, but this can be inefficient.)

The message is not broadcast because this is both inefficient (every machine would receive it, and the protocol layer on each machine would have to discard many unwanted messages), and broadcasts often cannot be sent across network routers. The message is not sent multiple times because this would simply move the inefficiency (and the requirement to track the listeners) from the application to the OrbixTalk level. Instead, just one network message is sent, and this is received only by those machines with listeners for that message (that is, for that topic).

To manage this, each OrbixTalk topic name is translated into a UDP multi-cast address. This translation is carried out by the OrbixTalk Directory Enquiries Daemon. Therefore, OrbixTalk on each client and server must find the multi-cast address for a topic by communicating with this daemon, but subsequent communication between a talker and its listeners does not involve this server.

Since multi-casting is by itself unreliable, OrbixTalk in the talkers and listeners uses a Reliable Multi-cast Protocol to ensure that each listener receives all of the messages sent by a particular talker and in the correct order.

Other versions of OrbixTalk use normal IIOP, or proprietary messaging such as MQ series or Pipes.

22.1.1 Example of using OrbixTalk

This section illustrates OrbixTalk with a simple telecommunications application that monitors the availability of switches. The relevant IDL interface is:

```
typedef long SwitchId;

interface SwitchReports {
      oneway void reportFailure (in SwitchId id);
      // Other operations not shown here.
};
```

This interface can be implemented as usual by C++ class `SwitchReports_i`. However, it is likely to be implemented more than once: for example, once each in the supervisor's server, the repair department's server and the automated routing system's server. Each implementation will carry out its own actions – for example, the supervisor's implementation will report the failure and record it graphically on the screen; the repair department's implementation will schedule the repair and print a job description; and the automated routing system's implementation will decide how best to maintain service for the telephone users by re-routing calls via different switches.

Each of these three servers would have one object of type `SwitchReports`, and would need to register it as a listener on the `switches/failures` topic. Objects can be created and registered as follows:

```
#include <OrbixTalk.h>

main () {
      OrbixTalk_var OrbixTalkMgr;

      SwitchReport_var switchListener;
      try {
            OrbixTalkMgr = OrbixTalk::initialize();

            switchListener = new SwitchReport_i ("switches/
                                                   failures");
            OrbixTalkMgr->registerListener(switchListener);

            // If this is an Orbix server (that is, registered with
            // putit), now call CORBA::Orbix.impl_is_ready().
            // Otherwise call CORBA::Orbix.processEvents():
      }
      catch (CORBA::SystemException &e) {
            // Handle the exception.
      }
      catch (...)
            // Handle the exception.
      }
}
```

A talker can be coded as follows:

```
#include <OrbixTalk.h>

main () {
      OrbixTalk_var OrbixTalkMgr;

      SwitchReport_var switchTalker;

      try {
            OrbixTalkMgr = OrbixTalk::initialize();

            // Create a proxy for the topic:
            CORBA::Object_ptr obj;
            obj = OrbixTalkMgr->registerTalker("SwitchReport",
                                                "switches/failures");
```

```
            // Narrow this proxy to be of the right type:
            (switchTalker = SwitchReport::_narrow(obj)
            if (!CORBA::_is_nil(SwitchTalker))
                /* all ok */
            else
                /* . . handle the error .. */ ;

            // Can now talk by calling operations; for example:
            switchTalker->reportFailure( /* . . . . */ );

            // Do any other actions, internal or related to Orbix
            // or OrbixTalk. Call impl_is_ready() if this is
            // an Orbix server.

        }
        catch (CORBA::SystemException &e) {
            // Handle the exception.
        }
        catch (...)
            // Handle the exception.
        }
}
```

At any time, after initializing OrbixTalk, this code can report a switch failure by calling:

```
switchTalker->reportFailure( /* . . . . */ );
```

Note that both talkers and listeners must process incoming Orbix events (by calling `impl_is_ready()` or `processEvents()`).

22.1.2 OrbixTalk MessageStore

The messages sent between the talkers and listeners on any chosen topics can be stored by OrbixTalk in a **MessageStore**. This allows a talker to reliably send messages when there are no listeners, and it allows a failed listener to re-start execution by receiving messages that it has missed. A message store is also useful as an audit log, and for debugging and testing.

Two message delivery modes are supported. In the first, **store-and-forward**, a talker's messages are first sent to the MessageStore, which distributes them to the listeners. In the second, **store-only**, the OrbixTalk layer of a talker distributes messages to all listeners and to the MessageStore, which acts like another listener. In both cases, a reliable protocol is used to ensure that listeners receive all messages, in the correct order. The MessageStore is responsible for re-transmitting messages, not the OrbixTalk layer of the talkers.

To use the MessageStore, the topic name being used by the talkers and listeners must indicate the chosen protocol mode: either `otsfp` (OrbixTalk store-and-forward protocol) or `otsop` (OrbixTalk store-only protocol). A topic name contains the chosen protocol mode and the hierarchical topic name, for example:

```
otsfp//switches/new_switches
```

The default mode is `otrmp` (OrbixTalk reliable message protocol), which indicates that the OrbixTalk MessageStore is not to be used.

22.2 Orbix and DBMSs

Many CORBA applications must support persistent objects. In some applications, the CORBA objects themselves need not be persistent, but instead they can act as **front-end** objects that manipulate the persistent data on behalf of the clients. In other applications, the CORBA objects themselves must be persistent. Both approaches are valid, and some of the issues involved in each will be discussed in this section, which covers the integration of CORBA and DBMSs.

Front-ending

A server's data can be managed by an object-oriented database management system (OODBMS), a relational DBMS (RDBMS), or by a file system. In the front-ending approach, the clients do not have direct access to this data, but instead they invoke on CORBA objects that access and manipulate the data on their behalf. The clients see only the IDL interface to these front-end objects.

The original `FrontOffice` objects introduced in Section 2.3 (p.24) are a good example of objects that can behave in this way. Recall the IDL definitions:

```
// IDL. In file front.idl.

typedef float Price;
struct Place {
      char row;
      long seat;
};

interface FrontOffice{
      readonly attribute string name;
      readonly attribute unsigned long numberOfSeats;

      Price findPrice (in Place chosenPlace);
      boolean bookSingleSeat (in Place chosenPlace,
                              in string creditCard);
};
```

A `FrontOffice` object can be used by a client without worrying about how it stores the booking and price information. In this case, there is a single object of type `FrontOffice` in a server, but other arrangements are also possible. For example, there may be one `FrontOffice` object for each cinema, and all of these may appear in one server. In another application that manages access to a sales catalog, there may be a front end object for each client currently using the server. Each such object would maintain its client's current position in the catalog that its client is browsing.

The overall requirement for using the front-end approach to persistence is that there is a manageable number of front-end objects and that these can be created without difficulty: for example, a `FrontOffice` object may be created when a server is started; and a catalog browser object can be created when a client logs in.

Common though this approach is, it does not address the requirements of all applications. In particular, some applications require that CORBA objects themselves be persistent.

Persistent CORBA objects

Section 2.12 (p.39) extends the cinema example by defining interface `Booking`:

```
interface Booking {
      readonly attribute Date when;
      readonly attribute Places seats;
      void cancel ();
};
```

The cinema application must create and manage a `Booking` object for each place or group of places booked by a customer. Clients can invoke on `Booking` objects to check details of a booking or cancel a booking. In addition, the operation to book some seats is changed to return a reference to a `Booking` object:

```
Booking makeBooking (in Places chosenPlaces,
                     in Date when,
                     in CreditCard payment)
           raises (NoSuchPlace,
                   PlaceAlreadyBooked,
                   InvalidCreditCard,
                   InvalidDate);
```

With these changes, a different approach to persistence is likely within the cinema application. In particular, the `Booking` objects need to be persistent, and there will be too many objects to keep in memory at the one time. However, when an invocation is made on one of these objects, it must be loaded from the persistent store and reinstated as a CORBA object. The clients need not be aware of the type of persistent store chosen or the details of how it is used.

If an OODBMS is used then the application can be more easily written if a single object can be both a CORBA object and an object stored in the database. A **database adapter** needs to be written between the CORBA system and the

OODBMS to load objects automatically when they are invoked and to allow control over transactions. In Orbix, a database adapter consists of a loader (see Chapter 20) and other low-level components that manage object loading, the OODBMS's transaction system, and the mapping of CORBA object references to and from OODBMS object references.

If an RDBMS is used, then the following four steps must be carried out (Baker, 1996):

(1) Decide on the object-oriented to relational mapping (or, in some cases, the opposite mapping). This may use a relational table for each object type, with a column for each member variable.

(2) Code this mapping.

(3) Write or import a loader that will create a C++ object for each `Booking` object that is invoked by clients.

(4) Ensure that the RDBMS is updated at the end of a transaction and that `Booking` objects are removed from memory. In some cases, it is better to write to the database immediately a change is made to the data, rather than just updating transient data. In fact, in some cases, transient data is not used at all, and instead the database is manipulated directly by each object.

The object-oriented to relational mapping, including the generation of the required code, can be automated by tools such as Persistence (www.persistence.com) and Ontos (www.ontos.com), or the coding step can be aided by tools such as RogueWave (www.roguewave.com). DB Component (I-Kinetics, 1995) automates the last two steps, without addressing the first two. Some OODBMSs and related tools, in particular ObjectStore (www.odi.com), O_2 (www.o2tech.com; O_2 Technology, Versailles, France), Ontos, and Persistence, allow their objects to be stored in an RDBMS, so if a database adapter is available for one of these then all four steps may be automated.

Three-tiered architecture

In the remainder of this section, we will concentrate on OODBMSs. Before focusing on this, it is worth looking at the nature of the three-tiered architecture that results from CORBA and DBMS integrations. In Figure 22.2, the database servers are shown at the bottom. The CORBA servers make direct access to this data, and, in many DBMSs, this results in this data being loaded into the CORBA servers. The CORBA clients are shown in the upper layer. Of course, a single process can be both a server and a client.

Orbix and ObjectStore

To illustrate the integration of CORBA and DBMS, this section gives an outline of how the cinema `Booking` objects can be implemented as C++ objects that are both

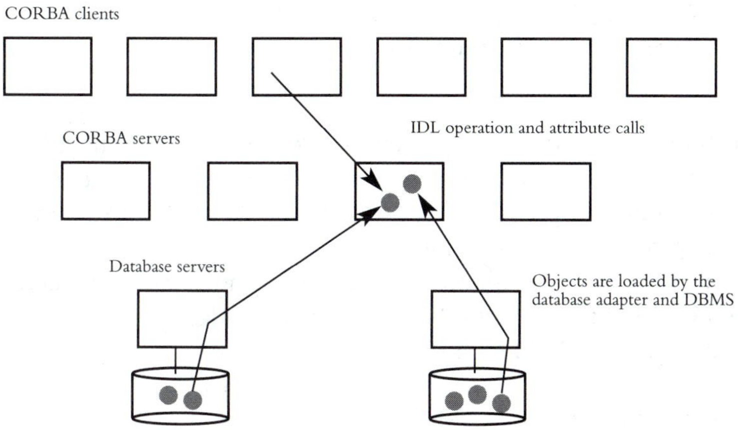

Figure 22.2 *Three-tiered architecture.*

Orbix and ObjectStore objects. DBMSs such as Versant, Poet, Objectivity, and Ontos could also have been used to illustrate the steps.

The programming steps are a combination of the normal steps required when using Orbix, and those required when using ObjectStore. For the Orbix programming steps, the IDL definitions are written as before, and either the BOAImpl or the TIE approach can be used to implement each interface. For the ObjectStore programming steps, the C++ classes that implement the IDL interfaces must be scanned by the schema analyser (this is a common step when using an OODBMS; the schema analyser records the definition of each class and how it is laid out in memory, which allows the OODBMS to store and retrieve objects of those types); and each persistent object must be created with ObjectStore's overloaded operator `new()`.

Interface `Booking` may be implemented as shown in the following outline:

```
#include <oosa.h>

class Booking_i : public virtual BookingBOAImpl {
      Places chosenPlaces;
      char* when;
      char* creditCardNumber;
      char* creditCardExpiryDate;
public:

      // Constructor and destructor as usual.
      Booking_i();
      virtual ~Booking_i();

      // Function to implement the two attributes: when, seats;
      // and the operation cancel(). Code not shown here.

      // For ObjectStore:
      static os_typespec* get_os_typespec();
```

```
        // For the adapter:
        void* _deref() { return this; }
};
```

`_deref()` is defined as a virtual function by class `CORBA::Object`, and it is redefined by class `Booking_i` so that the database adapter can get a pointer to the `Booking_i` aspect of an object given a pointer of type `CORBA::Object_ptr`. A runtime warning is output if the programmer forgets this step.

As well as initializing ObjectStore and opening a database, the server's main function must initialize the adapter (OOSA) and call the adapter's `initDB()` function on each database that can hold persistent CORBA objects:

```
#include <Booking_i.h>

int main (int argc, char** argv) {

        char* databaseName;
        os_database* db;

        // Initialize databaseName to hold the name
        // of the database to be opened. Not shown here.

        objectstore::initialize();

        db = os_database::open(databaseName);

        oosa->initDB(db);

        // Call CORBA::Orbix.impl_is_ready() as usual.
}
```

A persistent `Booking` object can be created at any time as follows:

```
Booking_ptr p = new (db) Booking_i ( /* . . . . */ );
```

When an invocation is made on a persistent `Booking` object that is not currently loaded, Orbix will pass the invocation to the **Orbix+ObjectStore Adapter**, which will cause the object to be loaded from the database, and Orbix will then pass the invocation to that object. Neither the client, nor the application-level code in the server, will be aware that this loading is taking place.

✚ Transactions

Distributed transactions, and in particular the CORBA Object Transaction Service (OTS), are discussed in Section 23.3 (p.394). The OTS provides an IDL interface through which a client can start a transaction, and eventually terminate it by committing or aborting it. All operations that a client calls are implicitly associated with its current transaction, and are made permanent or rolled back depending on the outcome of this transaction. In the implementation of the OTS, a (two-phase) distributed commit protocol is required when the client modifies data in more than one server in the system.

Even when a single server is being used, the application and/or the client must have control over the transactions. In a database adapter, the server is provided with a set of C++ functions to control transactions, but it can easily export these to its clients as IDL operations. Some of these functions determine the **style** in which the server (and/or clients) uses transactions (these are illustrated in Figure 22.3):

- **perOp**: in this style, a transaction is created for each operation call on an object in the server. This is a simple style, but it is not always appropriate. Firstly, it may be too inefficient to create many very short-lived transactions; and secondly, the overall intent of a client may span a number of operation calls and hence transactions will have to be longer than the duration of a single operation call. Nevertheless, this style is useful, especially where a single operation can carry out a complex task. Also, some applications do not wish to have a transaction continue between operation calls because this might mean that data would be locked for long periods.
- **phased**: in this style, a transaction is started if a call arrives at the server when it does not have a transaction running. This transaction is allowed to continue when this call completes, and it is terminated (committed or rolled back) only when a subsequent operation call informs the database adapter (using a server-side C++ function) that this is to happen. The interaction between a client and a server is therefore broken into phases, with each phase defining the lifetime of a transaction. The operation call that finishes a phase can be an IDL operation specially added for that purpose. Alternatively, it can be an IDL operation that is part of the

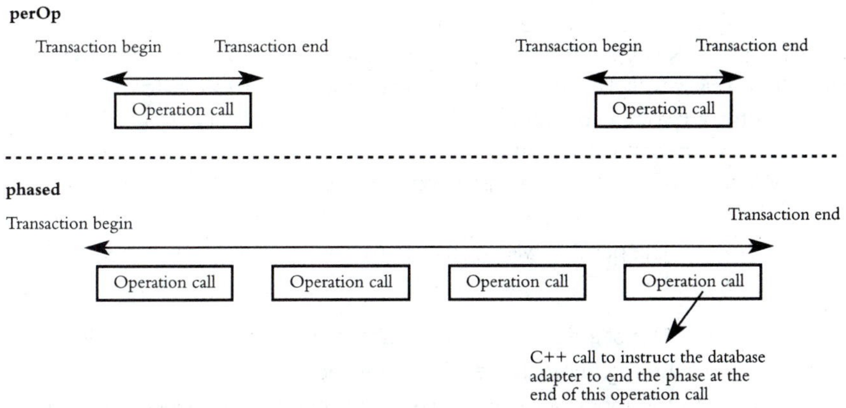

Figure 22.3 *Transaction styles.*

normal client–server interaction but is also interpreted by the server to indicate the end of a phase. For example, in the cinema application, a phase might be started when a client calls an operation to browse the availability of seats, and this phase might be ended when the `makeBooking()` operation is called.

Threads

Chapter 21 discusses the use of multiple threads in a server to improve throughput and responsiveness. Multiple threads may also be important to many servers that manage persistent data.

Most DBMSs support multiple threads, but there are some ways in which this support can be provided that make it unsuitable for a CORBA application. Consider a server that manages persistent data, using either the front-ending approach or by having some of its CORBA objects stored by a DBMS. Since this server will have multiple clients, it may wish to have multiple simultaneous transactions, one for each current client.

Assuming the phased style of using transactions, when an operation call arrives from a particular client, the server must associate that call with that client's transaction. The easier way to do this is to have a thread per client (see Section 21.3, p.352), so when a new operation call arrives from a particular client, its thread will process that call within the context of that client's current transaction. It might also be possible to have a thread created per operation call (a thread that is started to carry out just one operation call), but then it must be possible to create a new thread and associate it with the existing transaction of the calling client. (Applications differ in whether a thread per client or a thread per request is best. If a server has a large number of clients, but only a small number of these make operation calls at the same time, then it may be wasteful to have a thread per client. It is a tradeoff of the cost of thread creation versus the cost of having idle threads.)

The important question is how the DBMS handles these threads and their locks and transactions. Ideally, these threads should compete for locks – because these threads are running on behalf of different clients. Also, when one thread terminates its transaction, this should not terminate the transactions of other threads.

Many DBMSs provide the required support, but some support threads in a manner unsuitable to CORBA: threads share locks and, in effect, they all run within the same transaction. This is useful support because it allows a process to create multiple threads that cooperate to carry out a complex task. However, this is unsuitable to a CORBA server handling many independent clients.

When such a DBMS is necessary, one of three approaches can be used:

- The perOp style of using transactions can be used in a single threaded server. Each operation will run in isolation within its own transaction.
- The phased style of using transactions can be used, but the server must be registered in the per-client-process mode (see Section 8.2, p.178). In this mode, a server process is created for each client. Each such process

can run in isolation, with its own locks and transaction termination. In this way, heavyweight processes are used instead of lightweight threads.

- If a server makes only read-only access to a database, then it can create a transaction before it accepts any operation calls, and if it runs in the phased style then no further transactions will be created. The server can have multiple threads, and it is acceptable that these share locks because the database is only being read. ✚

Part five

CORBAservices

The OMG has defined a set of standard services, known as CORBAservices, that can be provided as options above the core CORBA system. These make it easier to develop applications because each provides a service that would have to be developed afresh for a wide range of applications. The CORBAservices define some of the most commonly required assistance that application programmers need for their systems, and without them, many application programmers would have to re-invent similar definitions and then use valuable time implementing them.

Currently the following services have been defined:

(1) **Naming** (Section 7.3, p.162): this service allows a client or server to easily find the objects it requires. A name can be bound to an object, and later that name can be resolved to acquire a reference to the object. The Naming Service is described in Chapter 7.

(2) **Events** (Section 23.1, p.377): rather than communicating directly with one or more objects by invoking operations on them, an application can send an event to a 'middle-man' (a so-called Event Channel) and have it distribute the event to the objects interested in that event. This form of communication has advantages for some applications.

(3) **Security** (Section 23.2, p.386): when CORBA objects can be accessed across an open network, there is a strong need to restrict access to authorized clients, and to restrict each client in the set of objects, and sometimes the set of operations, that it can use. The Security Service defines a general security framework that can be implemented in many ways, including through the use of access control lists or capabilities.

(4) **Transactions** (Section 23.3, p.394): if the actions of an application (or a group of applications working closely together) result in the updating of more than one database in the system, then this CORBAservice provides the support necessary to atomically (all or nothing) commit or roll back all of the changes. Individually committing or rolling back the changes made in each individual database would not provide the data integrity guarantees required in a complex system.

(5) **Trading** (Section 23.4, p.405): as an alternative to using the Naming Service to find a reference to a desired object, an

application can use the Trading Service. Instead of specifying the desired object by name, a constraint is given that chooses among the set of objects of a given type. A set of objects is returned to the caller, each one of which satisfies the constraint. The trader, therefore, consists of a set of offers, with each offer containing a reference to an object and a set of properties for that object. When a lookup is made, the trader matches constraints and properties to find the set of objects that match.

(6) **Life Cycle** (Section 24.1, p.413): CORBA objects can be created very easily, especially where the chosen programming language supports objects. For example, a CORBA object can be created as easily as creating a C++ object. If a server wishes to allow its clients to create objects in the server's address space, then it is very easy for it to provide a set of operations to do this. The `FrontOffice::makeBooking()` operation is a good example – it creates objects of type `Booking`.

The Life Cycle Service defines a general framework for creating, moving, and copying objects. There is no requirement to use the IDL interfaces defined in this server, and, in many cases, it is better to use application-level interfaces, such as `FrontOffice`.

(7) **Externalization** (Section 24.2, p.416): using the Externalization Service, the internal values of an object can be written to a stream of bytes and later read to construct a new object with the same values. A stream can be written to a file or other storage system.

(8) **Licensing** (Section 24.3, p.420): an application writer can use the Licensing Service to control the use of the application at an installed site. Many different models of licensing are supported that can be used to restrict the usage to specified individuals or computers, or to a specified level of usage on a network of machines.

(9) **Time** (Section 24.4, p.422): the Time Service provides a set of interfaces that provide applications with the current time, and allow time and time interval values to be manipulated. An optional extension to this service, the Timer Event Service, allows an application to receive an operation call to notify it that a specified duration has elapsed, or to receive a series of such notifications at a specified interval.

(10) **Property** (Section 25.1, p.429): some of the properties that an application needs to apply to an object can be applied using the object's attributes and operations. However, not all of the required properties might be captured in this way by the IDL definitions.

For example, a travel agency application might need to apply a rating property to each `FrontOffice` object, but might not be able to modify the `FrontOffice` IDL definition.

The Property Service supports the notion of a property set, and any object can be associated with an object of this type. A property set holds a set of property values: each with a name and a value. If an application that must associate a property with an object cannot change the IDL definitions, then it should associate a property set with the object and add the required property to this set.

(11) **Relationships** (Section 25.2, p.435): relationships between objects can be defined in IDL, using IDL definitions introduced by the Relationship Service. Using this service, two types of objects can be related without changing either of their IDL definitions; but of course it is sometimes better to relate two objects by having an attribute in one that gives an object reference to the other (or an operation could be used to achieve this).

(12) **Concurrency Control** (Section 25.3, p.442): access by concurrent threads or transactions to a CORBA object must be controlled to prevent its state becoming corrupted. The Concurrency Control Service provides a number of IDL interfaces to a locking facility that an object can use to control concurrent access. These interfaces are normally not visible to clients because objects normally encapsulate their concurrency control, allowing clients to be simple and independent of implementation decisions.

(13) **Persistent Objects** (Section 25.4, p.446): some CORBA objects must be stored in a persistent storage system, such as a database or a file system. The Persistent Object Service defines a general framework in which this can be achieved. It defines a set of interfaces that can be implemented on top of any storage system, and a set of interfaces that an object may support in order to allow the service to store it. Section 25.4 presents this service and also the Object Adapter approach to persistence that is also supported by CORBA.

(14) **Query** (Section 25.5, p.451): this service defines a simple collection type and a framework for making queries over the objects in such a collection. It does not define a new query language, but instead it allows for languages such as SQL and OQL. A query is passed as a string, along with an indication of which query language it is written in.

It can be seen from these simple descriptions that the CORBAservices are not designed for use by end users, but instead they help designers and programmers by providing off-the-shelf solutions to common problems. They are not specialized to any particular application domain. Like the core CORBA specification itself, these specifications are applicable across many domains, although specialized implementations may be required to cater for domains such as telecommunications, manufacturing, and finance.

The CORBAservices are not of equal importance, nor of equal quality. The Naming Service, for example, is a simple, clear specification that is easily implemented on a standard CORBA system and then used in many applications. Some of the CORBAservices have a much more narrow focus, and some of the specifications are complex. The Object Transaction Service, for example, is sophisticated and difficult to implement, but, thankfully, it is easy, and indeed almost transparent, for applications to use.

The CORBAservices should be used only when they are appropriate, and it should always be remembered that, by itself, a core CORBA implementation provides a framework for application integration and construction. Some application domains, such as realtime or embedded systems, may not be able to, or may not need to, use any of the CORBAservices. The needs of such systems may not require the sophistication of some of the CORBAservices, and the footprint and performance requirements may prevent the use of others.

This part describes each of the CORBAservices in turn (except Naming), in each case giving a general overview without attempting to cover all of the details. Those in Chapter 23 are the most important.

23 CORBAservices 1

23.1 Event Service

The Event Service allows decoupled communication between objects: instead of a client directly invoking an operation on a target object, it can send an event that can be received by any number of objects. The sender of an event is called the **supplier**, and the receivers are called the **consumers**. Suppliers and consumers are decoupled because they do not need to know each other's identities, and the number of consumers and suppliers of events relating to some high-level issue can change with ease.

The Event Service specification introduces the notion of an **Event Channel**. Suppliers send events to an Event Channel, and consumers receive these events. Each channel can have multiple consumers and suppliers, and all events sent by a supplier are made available to all consumers of that channel.

There are obvious similarities between the Event Service and OrbixTalk (Section 22.1, p.356). As we will see, the Event Service is specified in two parts, one of which has a very similar nature to OrbixTalk.

In the first part of the Event Service, events are in fact values of type `any` that are sent by a supplier to an Event Channel, and from the Event Channel to the consumers. Use of `any` in this way is a low-level approach, of course, and one that results in runtime, rather than compile-time, type checking.

In the second part of the Event Service, suppliers makes IDL application-specific operation calls to raise events, and these calls are passed, through an Event Channel, to the consumers. As with OrbixTalk, these operations must be unidirectional operations, but of course they can have arbitrarily complex (`in`) parameters. This is the aspect of the Event Service that has most in common with OrbixTalk.

The standard only specifies functional aspects, and in particular it is left as an implementation decision whether or not the Event Service stores messages if consumers are not available, and if it does store messages whether it uses persistent or transient storage for this.

We will explain the two parts of the Event Service in turn, starting with the version that passes values of type `any` between the suppliers and consumers.

Introduction using directly connected suppliers and consumers

To help introduce the programming model for suppliers and consumers, this subsection shows the interfaces that are used by a *directly* connected client and server that communicate with each other using the Event Service rules. This usage of the Event Service is unlikely to be common, but it acts as a good introduction when learning about the Event Service.

To send an event to the consumer, the supplier can call an IDL operation specified by the standard. Alternatively, the consumer can call an IDL operation on the supplier. These two modes are referred to as the push and pull models, respectively:

- Push model: the supplier *pushes* each event to the consumer by calling an IDL operation on it.
- Pull model: the consumer *pulls* each event from the supplier by calling an IDL operation on it.

Both are illustrated in Figure 23.1.

Within the push model, the consumer must support the following interface, of which the `push()` operation is the more important of the two operations:

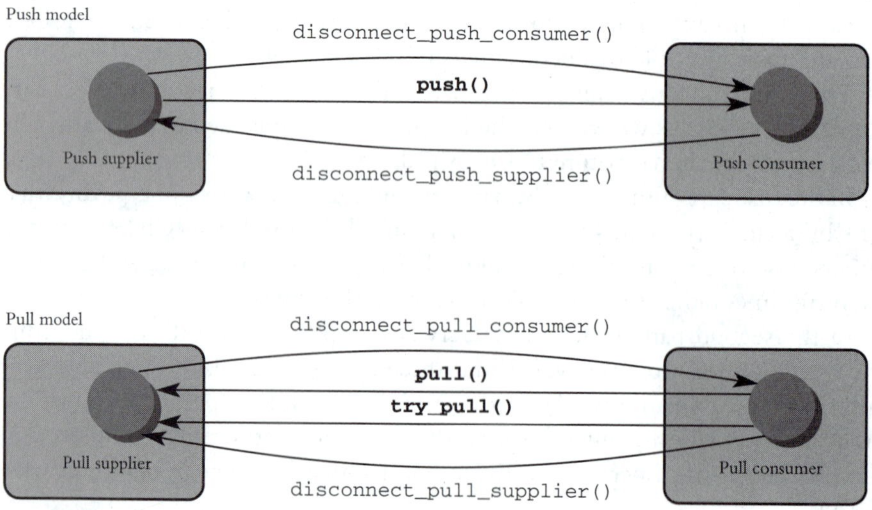

Figure 23.1 *Push and pull models.*

```
exception Disconnected {};

interface PushConsumer { // Consumer of push calls:
      void push (in any data) raises (Disconnected);
      void disconnect_push_consumer();
};
```

All of these definitions appear within the `CosEventComm` module, which is shown in Appendix A, Section A.1.1.

The supplier calls the `push()` operation when it wishes to send the consumer an event; and it passes the event's data as a parameter of type `any`. This can raise the `Disconnected` exception if the consumer has broken the connection between the supplier and the consumer (the consumer should have called the `PushSupplier::disconnect_push_supplier()` operation described in the next paragraph).

✚ In the model, the supplier can also support an IDL interface prescribed by the standard, but this is not used for event transfer, but simply to give the consumer a way of informing the supplier that the connection between them is to be broken. This interface is as follows:

```
interface PushSupplier { // Supplier (maker) of push calls
      void disconnect_push_supplier();
};
```

Alternatively, the supplier can be the one to decide to disconnect, in which case it should call `PushConsumer::disconnect_push_consumer()` on the consumer. ✚

The coding of a supplier of an event is simply a matter of constructing an `any` with the desired value and calling `PushConsumer::push()` to communicate with the consumer:

```
try {
      CosEventComm::PushConsumer_var con = /* . . . . */ ;

      CORBA::Any a;
      CORBA::Long x;
      x = /* . . . . */ ;
      a <<= x;

      con->push(a);
}
/* catch clauses not shown here. */
```

The consumer must implement the `PushConsumer` interface as it would any other IDL interface. In the push model, the supplier is a client and the consumer is a server. In this, we are referring to the supplier's and consumer's *roles* and not necessarily to their status as Orbix clients and servers. It it certain that the supplier makes IDL calls and the consumer receives them. However, the supplier may also accept calls (for example, the `pushSupplier::disconnect_push_supplier()` operation), and hence it can be a server, or alternatively it can be a client that accepts call-backs. Similarly, the consumer can make calls; and it can be a server, or a client that accepts call-backs.

The pull model defines two similar interfaces, `PullSupplier` and `PullConsumer`:

```
interface PullSupplier { // Supplier for pull calls:
      any pull () raises (Disconnected);
      any try_pull( out boolean has_event ) raises (Disconnected);
      void disconnect_pull_supplier();
};

interface PullConsumer {
      void disconnect_pull_consumer();
};
```

The supplier must support the `pull()` operation – which the consumer calls when it is ready to process an event. The consumer can alternatively call the `try_pull()` operation, which does not block the consumer if the supplier has no event to give it currently. The `has_event` parameter will be true or false depending on whether or not the call to `pull()` returns an event (as the value of the `any` return value). In the pull model, the consumer is a client and the supplier is a server.

✚ The pull consumer can break the connection by calling `PullSupplier::disconnect_pull_supplier()`; or alternatively the pull supplier can call `PullConsumer::disconnect_pull_consumer()` to indicate to the consumer the decision to disconnect. ✚

Note that in the case of directly connected suppliers and consumers, the Event Service itself provides no functionality; it simply defines a number of IDL interfaces.

✚ Although we do not expect directly connected suppliers and consumers to be commonly used, this simple configuration does have its uses. For example, the Time Service (see Section 24.4, p.422) has an optional extension, the Timer Event Service, which allows an application to receive an operation call to notify it that a specified duration has elapsed, or to receive a series of such notifications at a specified interval. When the specified time duration has elapsed, the Timer Event Service makes a `push()` operation call to a `CosEventComm::PushConsumer` object in the application. In this case, the Timer Event Service (the supplier) and the application (the consumer) can be directly connected, or an Event Channel can be used to connect them. ✚

Event Channels

There are a number of advantages in placing an Event Channel between the suppliers and consumers (see Figure 23.2):

Figure 23.2 *Proxy suppliers and consumers in an Event Channel.*

- Any number of suppliers and consumers can communicate in connection with a given type of event, and the Event Service can be used to deliver each event to each consumer.
- The events can be buffered by the Event Channel to allow for consumers of different speeds.
- The events can be persistently stored by the Event Channel to ensure that events are not lost on system failures. In addition, the event store could be transactional: that is, its update could depend on whether a distributed transaction commits or aborts (see Section 23.3, p.394).
- As we will see, the communication of push consumers and push suppliers can be supported; and also pull consumers and pull suppliers.

Examples of this form of communication have been given for OrbixTalk in Section 22.1 (p.356). It is important to note the wide range of potential usages.

As with directly connected suppliers and consumers, different push and pull models are supported. However, in this case, there are four combinations: the supplier can be a pull or push supplier, and the consumer can be a pull or push consumer. In more detail:

- Push suppliers, push consumers: the supplier(s) push events to the Event Channel, which in turn pushes them to the consumer(s).
- Push suppliers, pull consumers: the supplier(s) push events to the Event Channel, and each pull consumer pulls an event when it is ready to process it.
- Pull supplier, push consumer: the Event Channel pulls events from the supplier(s), and then it pushes these to the consumer(s).
- Pull supplier, pull consumer: the consumer(s) pull events from the Event Channel, which in turn pulls them from the supplier(s).

An Event Channel can, in theory, have any mix of suppliers and consumers at any time.

Despite the introduction of an Event Channel, the suppliers and consumers have the same view of passing events. For example, a push supplier expects to make calls to `push()` on a `PushConsumer` object, despite the facts that the supplier does not directly communicate with the consumer(s) and that there may or may not be any push consumers. This problem is easily resolved because the Event Channel itself provides the `PushConsumer` object for the push supplier to call.

Therefore, for a push supplier:

- A push supplier expects to make calls to `push()` on a `PushConsumer` object: this object is provided within the Event Channel, and is referred to as a **proxy push consumer**.

For a pull consumer:

- A pull consumer expects to make calls to the `pull()` and `try_pull()` operations on a pull supplier object: this object is provided within the Event Channel, and is referred to as a **proxy pull supplier**.

(Note that this is a different use of the term 'proxy' to that in other chapters. Other than in this section, the term 'proxy' refers to a representative of a target object within a client. Here, the term means the representative of a supplier or consumer within an Event Channel.)

Figure 23.3 shows the resulting architecture. Later we will show how a supplier or consumer can gain access to the proxy push consumer or proxy pull supplier within the Event Channel.

The figure also shows two other proxy objects: **a proxy pull consumer** and a **proxy push supplier**. A pull supplier expects to have a pull consumer make calls to its `pull()` operation: the Event Channel provides this object, a proxy pull consumer, to make these calls. A push consumer expects to have a push supplier make calls to its

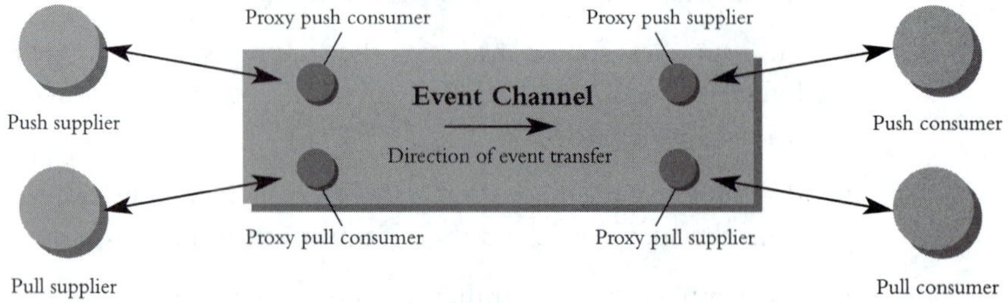

Figure 23.3 *Proxy suppliers and consumers in an Event Channel, showing proxies.*

`push()` operation: the Event Channel provides this object, a proxy push supplier, to make these calls.

Obviously, none of these *proxy* objects needs to exist physically; as long as the Event Channel behaves as expected, its implementation details are not of concern.

Event Channels: setting up suppliers and consumers

A supplier or consumer can bind to an Event Channel in any of the normal ways (for example, using the Naming Service or the `_bind()` call). The relevant IDL interface is:

```
interface EventChannel {
      ConsumerAdmin for_consumers();
      SupplierAdmin for_suppliers();

      /* . . . . */
};
```

To connect a supplier to an Event Channel, an application must first obtain an object reference for the Event Channel's `SupplierAdmin` object. It can find this in any of the normal ways, or it can call the `for_suppliers()` operation on an `EventChannel` object. The same applies to consumers and the `ConsumerAdmin` interface of an Event Channel.

The two 'administration' interfaces provide the following operations:

```
interface ConsumerAdmin { // Used by consumers.
      ProxyPushSupplier obtain_push_supplier();
      ProxyPullSupplier obtain_pull_supplier();
};

interface SupplierAdmin { // Used by suppliers.
      ProxyPushConsumer obtain_push_consumer();
      ProxyPullConsumer obtain_pull_consumer();
};
```

Using these operations, a supplier or consumer can find the 'proxy' objects internal to the Event Channel.

For example, a push supplier would use the `SupplierAdmin::obtain_push_consumer()` operation to find the proxy push consumer object in the Event Channel. Once it has obtained a reference to the proxy push consumer, it should call `ProxyPushConsumer::connect_push_supplier()` to make a proper connection to it:

```
module CosEventChannelAdmin {
      exception AlreadyConnected {};
      exception TypeError {};

      interface ProxyPushConsumer :
                        CosEventComm::PushConsumer {
```

```
        void connect_push_supplier(
                in CosEventComm::PushSupplier push_supplier)
                        raises (AlreadyConnected);
    };

    /* rest not shown here */
};
```

Similarly,

- A push consumer should call `ConsumerAdmin::obtain_push_supplier()`, followed by `ProxyPushSupplier::connect_push_consumer()`.
- A pull supplier should call `SupplierAdmin::obtain_pull_consumer()`, followed by `ProxyPullConsumer::connect_pull_supplier()`.
- A pull consumer should call `ConsumerAdmin::obtain_pull_supplier()`, followed by `ProxyPullSupplier::connect_pull_consumer()`.

✚

Typed events

In the second way to use the Event Service, callers can use an application-specific IDL interface, rather than using operations such as `PushConsumer::push()`. In particular, this allows applications to decide on the data that is to be passed on each event, rather than always passing a value of type `any`.

In the push model, the consumer supports an interface of type `TypedPushConsumer`:

```
module CosTypedEventComm {
    interface TypedPushConsumer : CosEventComm::PushConsumer {
        Object get_typed_consumer();
    }
};
```

The supplier calls `get_typed_consumer()` to obtain a reference to an object in the consumer; and it uses this object to send events to the consumer. This object's interface is application-specific (therefore, the supplier and consumer must have prior knowledge of the nature of this interface), but it must consist entirely of `oneway` operations. To be exact, the operations do not need to be marked as `oneway`, but they must obey the same restrictions (that is, no return value, no `out` or `inout` parameters, and no `raises` clause). The supplier will narrow the object reference returned by `get_typed_consumer()` to a reference of the agreed type.

✚ The connection between the supplier and the consumer can be closed in the same way as for untyped events. The supplier can call the `PushConsumer::disconnect_push_consumer()` operation on the consumer; or the consumer can call `PushSupplier::disconnect_push_supplier()` on the supplier.

Note that `TypedPushConsumer` inherits from `PushConsumer`, and so it must provide the `push()` operation. However, if a consumer wishes, it can provide a null implementation for this operation, by raising the `NO_IMPLEMENT` standard exception. ✚

The pull model is a little more complex. The consumer calls `get_typed_supplier()` on the supplier to obtain an object reference to the object in the supplier that it must pull the events from:

```
module CosTypedEventComm {
      interface TypedPullSupplier : CosEventComm::PullSupplier {
            Object get_typed_supplier();
      };
};
```

The complexity is that the IDL interface that the supplier defines is automatically modified so that the consumer can use it to pull events. An application specific interface of the form

```
interface SwitchReports {
      oneway void reportFailure (in SwitchId id);
      // Other operations not shown here.
};
```

will be changed to

```
interface SwitchReports {
      void pull_reportFailure (out SwitchId id);
      boolean try_reportFailure(out SwitchId id);
      // Other operations not shown here.
};
```

`pull_reportFailure()` blocks the consumer until there is an event to pull. Note that the parameter has been changed to an `out` parameter. `try_reportFailure()` will not block: if there is an event to pull then it behaves like `pull_reportFailure()` and returns true; otherwise it returns false and the parameters have undefined values.

✚ To close the connection, the supplier can call `PullConsumer::disconnect_pull_consumer()` on the consumer; or the consumer can call `PullSupplier::disconnect_pull_supplier()` on the supplier.

Note that `TypedPullSupplier` inherits from `PullSupplier`, and so it must provide operations `pull()` and `try_pull()`. However, if a consumer wishes, it can provide null implementations for these operations, by raising the `NO_IMPLEMENT` standard exception. ✚

Typed events and Event Channels

Appendix A, Section A.1.2 gives the IDL interfaces for establishing a supplier–consumer relationship using a **typed** Event Channel. These are very similar to the interfaces for untyped Event Channels; the differences are noted in the appendix.

23.2 Security Service

Security is concerned with the **confidentiality** and **integrity** of data, the **accountability** of users so that they cannot deny actions, and the **availability** of the system, despite attempts at malicious denial to authorized users. Confidentiality and integrity require that data is only accessed and modified by users who have the right to do so, and then only in the ways that they are authorized to.

All aspects of a system must be involved in making it secure, and therefore it is not sufficient simply to run the Security Service as a standalone service on top of the ORB. Instead, the ORB itself, and some CORBAservices and some applications, must cooperate with the Security Service to guard against breaches in security. For example, if a system must ensure that unauthorized users cannot obtain a log of which operations are being called on a server, then we must ensure that the server itself or any CORBAservice does not breach this by keeping an insecure log of the calls it sees.

Furthermore, an ORB must provide certain facilities to the Security Service, and cooperate with it. This can be done either by enhancing the ORB itself, or it can make a set of callouts as it does its normal work, and these callouts can be implemented by an external security layer. In addition, the IIOP standard protocol (see Chapter 1) for communicating between ORBs must be augmented to ensure security. At the time of writing the final details of this extended protocol are being agreed.

Some clients and applications can continue to use a secure system without being concerned with the Security Service. A client need logon only once to obtain security credentials, and then it can make IDL calls as normal. It receives the `CORBA::NO_PERMISSION` exception if it attempts to call an operation or attribute that it has no right to use. A server can be completely unaware of security, and rely on the Security Service to make certain checks before allowing a client to communicate with it; or it can be aware of the Security Service and perform more advanced checks on the IDL calls made to it (for example, using the parameters that are being passed), and it can also use the Security Service to secure its own internal data.

The Security Service addresses the following aspects of security:

- **Authentication of users** so they can correctly claim to be who they are. This is extended to authentication of **principals**: a principal is a human user or system entity that is registered in the system and can be authenticated by it. Two-way authentication is provided, where required, so that a server can know the identity of the caller, and the caller can be sure of the identity of the server.

- **Access control of calls** to a server, so that only authorized principals can call certain operations on an object or group of objects. These access controls can be implemented using access control lists (ACLs), labels, or capabilities, and this choice is hidden from the application level.
- **Delegation** of a principal's security credentials, so that an object that it invokes can act on its behalf when invoking on other objects. Therefore, if a client invokes on an object, that object can be allowed to use the client's (the **initiating principal's**) credentials and possibly its own to invoke on other objects.
- **Recording of a security audit** so that administrators of a system have an audit of important calls, and can use this to trace the actions of principals if there is a security breach. The Security Service provides only the facilities to record the log; it does not provide management or auditing tools.
- Currently **non-repudiation** is an optional feature. This can be used to prevent a principal (normally a human user) from falsely denying an action that it has in fact carried out. The aim is to make principals accountable for their actions, by providing irrefutable evidence about a claimed action. Among other events, non-repudiation can relate to a client making a particular call, or to a server having received and/or acted on a call.
- Encryption and other protection of messages on the network.

The Security Service defines two levels at which it can be implemented:

- Level 1 supports clients and servers that are not aware of the Security Service, and also those that make very simple uses of its facilities. This level applies to all applications running under a secure ORB, whether or not they are aware of security. It includes security of invocations between clients and target objects, message protection, some delegation, access control, and audit recording.
- Level 2 supports clients and servers that are aware of the Security Service. It includes further enforcement and delegation options, and the administration interfaces. The number of options available at this level results in the bulk of the IDL for the Security Service.

Security can be expensive, both in computer processing time and also in operational overhead. Therefore, the Security Service allows installations to be flexible in what aspects of security they wish to enforce in various parts of the system, and how strictly these should be enforced. Also, different implementations of the Security Service may be more suitable for low- and high-security installations.

Note that a number of aspects of the specification help to reduce its overhead. Access control can be specified on groups of objects, and not just on individual objects. Access control can also apply to a group of principals, and not just to an individual principal. The overall installation can be structured as a set of (possibly overlapping and nested) **security domains**, and different security policies can be applied in each domain. The security within some domains can be very lightweight, for example, within a single process there will often be no security checks at all; and more extensive security may be applied for communication over a public network than over a trusted LAN.

Before looking at the details of the security architecture in more detail, it must be noted that there are a number of different viewpoints of its facilities:

- Client: a client need not be aware of the Security Service, and, in particular, the way in which a client makes IDL calls is not changed. A principal must obtain some **security credentials** by logging on to the system, but it need only do this once.
- Application: security checks can be made exclusively outside of a server, so it need not be aware of the Security Service. Alternatively, it can augment these checks with application-specific ones; for example, checks which take into account the state of the server's data. That is, a server can extract the **privileges** of the caller and use these in local access control decisions.
- Administrator: interfaces are provided for the administration of domains, access controls, auditing, delegation, and non-repudiation (where this is supported).
- Implementer: The implementation of the Security Service hides the use of any particular security technology, whether this be a technique such as access control lists, labels, or capabilities, and whether or not a commercially available suite of security software is used. In fact, a number of commercial security systems provide a common C-based API known as GSS, and one of these systems can be used by an implementation of the Security Service without concern for the details of the underlying security technology.

The following subsections give some further details of the security architecture. In particular, concepts such as security credentials, attributes, privileges, and delegation are discussed. This is then followed by some details of the specification.

Security credentials, attributes

A principal's **credentials** determine what it is allowed to do in the system. These credentials contain the principal's **security attributes**. Currently there are two types of attributes: identity attributes (which specify who the principal is), and privilege attributes (which specify what it can do, what **groups** it is a member of, what **roles** it plays, and what **capabilities** and **clearances** it has). Privilege attributes are frequently referred to simply as **privileges**.

In this way, a credentials object acts like a software equivalent of a security pass: in a simple case, one that holds its owner's picture and, perhaps, a list of areas of a building that he or she is allowed to enter.

A principal may use a single credentials, implicitly passing this with all calls it makes; or it can create more than one credentials and use each when invoking on some subset of the objects that it uses. Figure 23.4 shows a caller that has three credentials (with the same identity attribute but with different security attributes), and how it might use two of these in separate calls to different objects. Naturally, if it created a single credentials that contained all of the security attributes of the others, then it need only use that one credentials object, but this may mean that it uses privileges that are too strong when invoking some objects. The danger in this is easily seen when delegation is considered: when delegation is allowed, the principal's credentials that are used to make a call are passed to the (intermediary) target object, which can use them to make calls to other objects. The principal may wish to use a restricted credentials in order to restrict what the intermediary target object is allowed to do. Restricted credentials can also be useful to prevent a principal accidentally carrying out some action on an object that it wishes not to.

A principal can create a credentials object by copying an existing one and then removing or adding attributes (or **features**; see later). It can then specify (using the `Current` object, introduced later) that any chosen credentials object be used for a period of time; that is, to be used for all calls, until another one is specified. Alternatively, a principal can attach a credentials to an object reference, which results in that credentials being used for all of its calls to the target object. Note that a

Figure 23.4 *Use of different credentials.*

principal can attach a credentials to an object reference, not to the target object itself. In Orbix terms, a principal can attach a credentials to a proxy in its own address space.

Delegation

When a client makes a call on an object that passes that call (or, more commonly, a call that is made to help carry out the call from a client) to another object, there are a number of choices as to how the intermediate object handles the client's security credentials:

- No delegation: the intermediate object uses its own credentials to make the second call.
- Simple: the intermediate object uses the client's credentials to make the second call.
- Composite: the intermediate object passes both sets of credentials when making the second call.
- Combined privileges: the intermediate object merges the two sets and uses the merged version to make the second call.
- Traced: with the client's permission, the intermediate object passes both sets of credentials when making the second call, and all of the other objects in the chain do the same. The final target object can see the full trace of credentials. (This is a special case of composite delegation.)

Note that the client must give its permission for its credentials to be delegated in any of these ways.

Figure 23.5 shows delegation from a user on the left-hand side via a central server that makes a call to another server on the right-hand side. Each credentials has an identity attribute (represented by the picture in the diagram) and some number of privilege attributes (represented in the diagram as lines on the credentials).

A credential is an object with an IDL interface `Credentials`, whose operations can be used to achieve these variations. For example, to implement combined privileges, the intermediate object can copy its own credentials and add privileges from the client's credentials, and then make the call using the new credentials object.

A client may also need to manipulate credentials; for example, it may need to create a credentials that contains a subset of its privileges, and pass this to an object when it makes a call. In this way, the target object will be given the least privileges it needs to do its work, and the client can prevent it abusing some powerful privilege that it possesses. The client can also restrict the duration of delegation, and in some implementations, it can restrict the number of invocations in which its credentials can be delegated by the intermediate object.

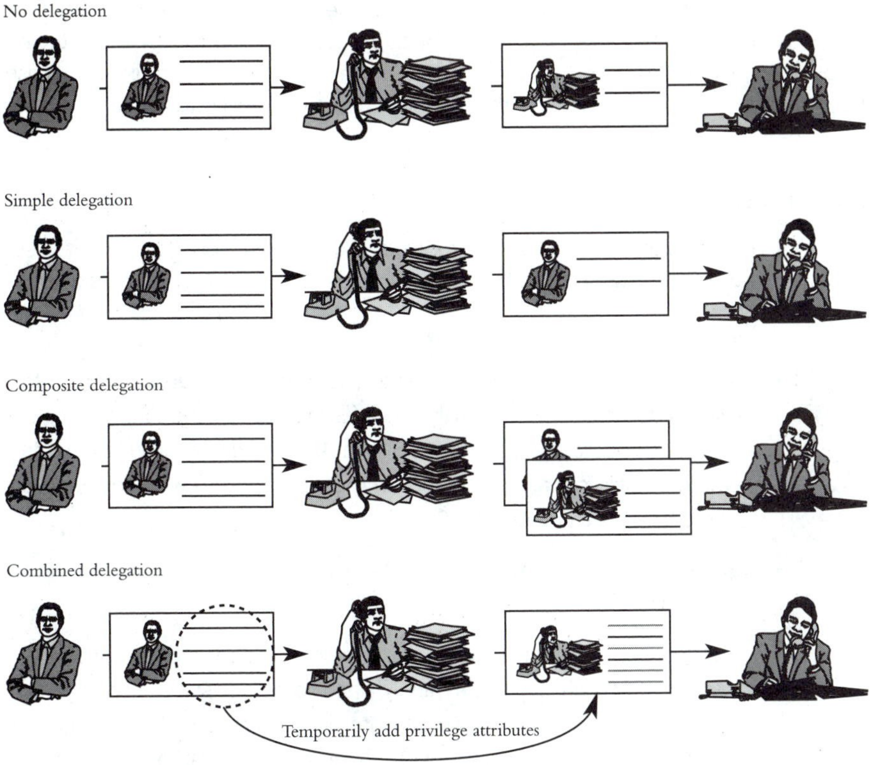

Figure 23.5 *Various forms of delegation.*

IDL interfaces

Security level 1 includes no IDL definitions that need concern us here. In fact, it defines only a single interface, with a single operation.

In contrast, security level 2 is rather complex, as it includes IDL definitions for advanced clients and servers, and for administrators. The non-repudiation option is also defined in IDL at this level. The Security Service also defines a set of interfaces that an ORB can use: the ORB can make calls to these interfaces at specified times during an operation call, and the implementation of these interfaces can implement the required security checks and facilities.

The following subsections introduce the main level 2 interfaces used by advanced clients and servers.

IDL interface: `PrincipalAuthenticator`

The main operation, `authenticate()`, defined in interface `PrincipalAuthenticator`, allows a principal to obtain a `Credentials` object, provided it can supply a name, authentication data, and a set (sequence) of requested privileges. However, many clients and servers do not need to call this operation explicitly; it is called by their environment, allowing them to be initialized with a credentials object.

The other operation defined by `PrincipalAuthenticator` is `continue_authentication()`. This is used if the authentication step requires two or more phases; for example, a call to `authenticate()` can return a **challenge** to the caller, in which case the caller must calculate the response to the challenge and call `continue_authentication()`.

IDL interface: credentials

Recall that a client or server may have one or more `Credentials` objects, which it uses to prove its rights to call operations on objects. The `Credentials` interface defines the following operations:

- `set_security_features()` sets one or more **features** on or off for calls made with this credentials. Features include whether a credentials object can be delegated, and, if so, what form of delegation is allowed; whether messages are protected on the network; and whether the replay of messages is to be detected.
- `get_security_features()` returns an on or off indication for each feature.
- `set_privileges()` allows a client or server to set individual security attributes (actually any of the family of attributes known as **privilege attributes**). Example privilege attributes include: group identifiers, the role of the caller, and its clearance level. (The other family of attributes are **identity attributes**. Three such identity attributes are supported: `AuditId`, `AccountingId`, and `NonRepudiationId`.)
- `get_attributes()` takes a set of attribute types as a parameter, and returns the values of these attributes.
- `is_valid()` returns a `boolean` to indicate whether or not the credentials is still valid.
- `refresh()` attempts to renew a credentials that has timed out, and it returns a `boolean` to indicate success or failure.

IDL interface: object references

The Security Service adds a number of operations to object references. Each of these can be called by a client or server that holds an object reference to an object, but it is important to realize that these operations affect the object reference (that is, the proxy), and not the target object. Actually, these operations are defined in interface `SecurityLevel2::Object`, which inherits from `CORBA::Object`:

- `override_default_credentials()` allows a `Credentials` object to be associated with a particular object reference; that is, a particular credentials will always be used when that object reference is used.

- `override_default_QOP()` allows a client or server to control the Quality of Protection (QOP) for messages that are sent using that object reference. QOP determines whether there is no protection, just integrity, just confidentiality, or both integrity and confidentiality. Note that a request for a particular QOP can be overridden by the **security policy** enforced by the system administrators.
- `get_security_features()` returns an on or off indicator for each security feature of the credentials object that applies to the object reference (either the default credentials or one explicitly assigned using `override_default_credentials()`).
- `get_active_credentials()` returns a reference to the credentials object that applies to the object reference.

Some other operations are also supported, but these need not concern us here.

IDL interface: **`Current`**

Each client and server has a `Current` object that it can use to determine security aspects of the current operation call (in a multi-threaded server, there is a `Current` object per thread). Its operations include:

- `get_credentials()` allows the caller to obtain the credentials object associated with the `Current` object; that is, the credentials that are used with object references on which `override_default_credentials()` has not been called.
- `set_credentials()` allows the caller to specify the default credentials object to be used with object references on which `override_default_credentials()` has not been called.
- `readonly attribute received_credentials`. This is called by a server to find the `Credentials` object used by the client to make the current call. The credentials object can then be used to determine whether or not the call should be allowed to continue. In fact, a sequence of credentials objects is returned because composite or traced delegation could be used. The credentials object at the start of the sequence is always that of the initiating principal.
- `readonly attribute received_security_features`: This returns a list of security features for the current call.
- `get_attributes()` allows a server to get security attributes (identity and privilege attributes) of the `Credentials` object used by the client (actually the initiating principal) to make the call. This operation is provided at security level 1, so that clients do not need to use the `Credentials` interface, which is defined at security level 2.

(In fact, there are two `Current` interfaces. `SecurityLevel1::Current` defines operation `get_attributes()`, and the other operations are defined in `SecurityLevel2::Current`, which inherits from the `SecurityLevel1::Current`.)

Some other operations are also supported, but these need not concern us here.

IDL interface: **`AuditChannel`**

This defines a single operation, `audit_write()`, which allows a client or server to write event-specific data to an audit log.

IDL interface: **`AuditDecision`**

This defines a single operation, `audit_needed()`, which returns an indication of whether or not an event should be written to an event log. It also defines a single `readonly` attribute, `audit_channel`, which returns a reference to an `AuditChannel` object.

IDL interface: **`AccessDecision`**

The Security Service defines an interface, `SecurityLevel2::AccessDecision`, which in turn defines a single operation, `access_allowed()`. This is given information about the current call (including the credentials object(s), a reference to the target object, the name of the called operation/attribute, and the name of the target object's interface). It returns an indication of whether or not the call should be allowed to continue.

This interface is intended for use by the implementer of the Security Service, not by clients or servers. However, if a server needs to do application-level checks, such as taking the operation call's parameters into account, then it is recommended that it defines an interface that extends `SecurityLevel2::AccessDecision`, and adds application-specific operations. ✚

23.3 · Transaction Service (OTS)

The Transaction Service, commonly called the Object Transaction Service (OTS), supports the notion of transaction (or 'unit of work'), common in databases, within a distributed CORBA system. A client can start a transaction, modify a number of objects, and then decide whether to commit or rollback the transaction. Committing a transaction means that all of the changes made during it will be durable. Rolling back a transaction means that the client has decided that none of the changes made during the transaction will be made durable; the effects of a transaction can also be rolled back if an error occurs during the transaction or while the OTS is trying to carry out a commit request. The now common **ACID** properties are supported by OTS transactions:

- **Atomic**: means that *all or none* of the effects of a transaction are made durable, never just a subset of these effects.

- **Consistent**: a transaction should take the data from one consistent state to another.
- **Isolated**: no client, except code within a transaction itself, can see the data that has been modified by a transaction that has not yet committed. (In fact, the OTS allows this restriction to be weakened to allow increased concurrency between transactions, but this can lead to inconsistent data if used incorrectly.)
- **Durable**: the effects of a committed transaction are persistent and are not lost (except by a catastrophic failure).

The OTS allows a client to start a transaction and then to make operation and attribute calls on objects distributed throughout the system. All of these calls will be implicitly associated with the client's transaction, without any special action of the client. In OTS terminology, the client's **transaction context** is implicitly propagated in any calls that it makes to transactional objects. When the client commits the transaction, all of the actions that it carried out during that time will be committed. Similarly, if it rolls back the transaction, all of these actions will be rolled back.

The OTS allows objects to be **non-transactional** (these are not affected by whether they are invoked from within a transaction or outside of any transaction) or **transactional** (that is, those that are affected by transactions). A client can use a mix of transactional and non-transactional objects at any time. In fact, the OTS defines the term **recoverable object** to refer to those transactional objects that have data that must be committed or rolled back when a transaction terminates. The notion of a recoverable object is central to the standard because these are the objects that are most affected by transactions.

The OTS requires no changes to be made to the IDL language, and in particular it does not introduce keywords to mark interfaces or operations as transactional. However, it does introduce an interface, `TransactionalObject`, from which any other IDL interface can inherit. When an invocation is made on an object whose interface inherits from `TransactionalObject`, the OTS will implicitly pass the caller's transaction context to the target server.

✚ A client's transaction context can also be passed explicitly as a normal parameter to an operation, in which case there is no need to inherit from `TransactionalObject`; but of course the OTS is then less transparent because the parameter list to each relevant operation must be changed. If the transaction context is passed in this way, the target object is *not* automatically added to the caller's transaction.

This is known as explicit passing of the transaction context. It may be useful for some low-level parts of the system, or to handle CORBA implementations that do not pass the transaction context implicitly; that is, ones that do not support the OTS standard. Implicit and explicit passing can both be used in the same system. ✚

`Resource` objects

Each recoverable object must have an associated `Resource` object that is informed when a client transaction terminates (commits or rolls back). A `Resource` object can be shared by many objects, but each `Resource` object is associated with exactly one transaction. Hence, in a typical usage, if a transaction uses some objects in a server then that server will have a `Resource` object associated with that transaction.

When an invocation arrives at a server, the OTS must determine whether or not there is a `Resource` object in that server for the caller's current transaction. If there is no such `Resource` object, the OTS must create one. A transaction may read or update data in a set of servers in the system, and these may store their data in different databases. Therefore, a transaction may have many `Resource` objects associated with it, distributed throughout the system.

It is the `Resource` objects that actually carry out the work of committing or rolling back their associated transaction. They may carry out this work themselves, or they may interface to some underlying transaction manager (such as Encina), DBMS, or transactional file system.

It is very important that the set of `Resource` objects for a transaction acts consistently; that is, that they all commit or all rollback a transaction when a client terminates it. The data in the system would become inconsistent if some commit and others rollback. To carry out the task of coordinating the actions of the `Resource` objects, each transaction has a single `Coordinator` object. This carries out a client's wish to commit a transaction by first asking each `Resource` object (using its `prepare()` operation) if it is willing to commit. The return value of this operation allows a `Resource` object to **vote** on whether the overall outcome is to be commit or rollback. If all of the `Resource` objects are willing to commit, the coordinator calls the `commit()` operation on each `Resource` object to confirm the decision. If any `Resource` object indicates that it cannot commit, the coordinator calls the `rollback()` operation on each `Resource` object to inform them of the actual decision to rollback.

Figure 23.6 shows a client using objects in two servers. Each server has one `Resource` object, which registers itself with the transaction's `Coordinator`.

If a client wishes to rollback a transaction, the coordinator does this simply by calling the `rollback()` operation on each `Resource` object associated with the transaction.

When attempting to commit a transaction, the rules used by the coordinator are known as the **two-phase commit protocol**. This protocol is well established in commercial databases and in transaction managers. A transaction's coordinator object drives the two-phase commit protocol, and its `Resource` objects (within the servers that it uses) actually implement the protocol. This is shown in Figure 23.7.

As we will see, each transaction has a number of OTS objects associated with it: a single `Coordinator` object, a single `Control` object, a single `Terminator` object, and (at least) one `Resource` object in each server that needs to be informed of the transaction's termination. Each of these interfaces will be explained later in this section.

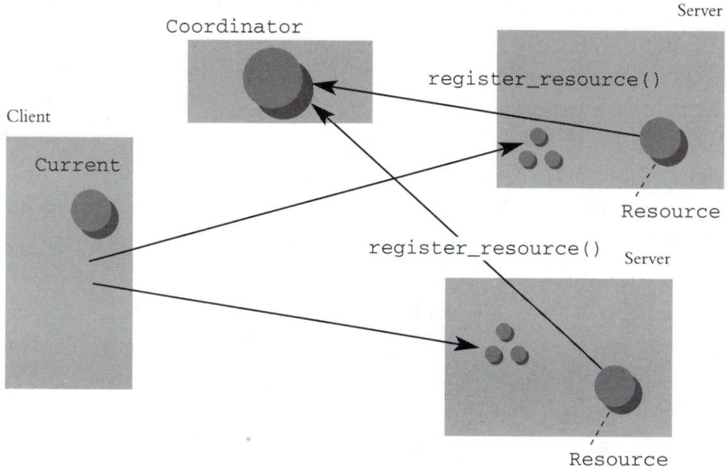

Figure 23.6 `Resource` *objects registering themselves with the coordinator.*

✚ A transaction can have more than one `Coordinator` object associated with it if communication with a single coordinator is too expensive. An implementation of the OTS may decide that it is better to have a single **root coordinator** object for a transaction and some number of **subordinate coordinators** (sometimes called interposed coordinators). The root coordinator will be informed of the client's decision to commit or rollback the transaction, and this decision will be passed by it to the subordinates, each of which will be responsible for informing the `Resource` objects that have registered with it. Rather than extending the `Coordinator` interface to allow a root coordinator to inform subordinates of the decision to commit or rollback, each subordinate should create a `Resource` object

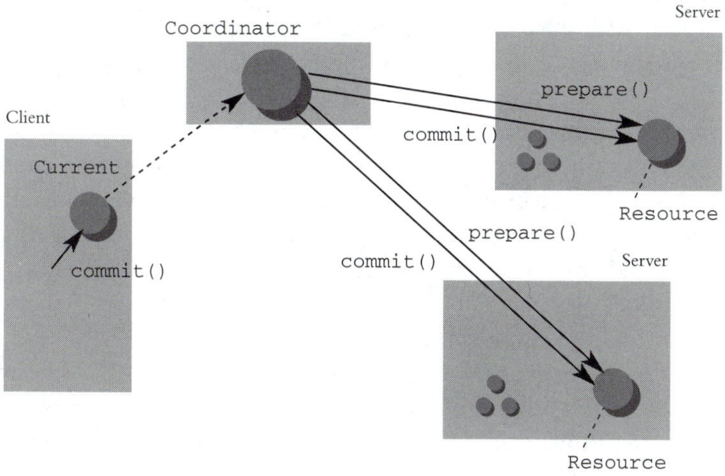

Figure 23.7 *Two-phase commit protocol.*

that it registers with its parent coordinator. The task of such `Resource` objects is to inform their associated subordinate coordinator of the commit or rollback decision. Any level of coordinator nesting (known as coordinator interposition) is allowed, but the set of coordinators associated with a transaction always forms a tree. ✚

The OTS specifies the IDL interfaces of types such as `Resource`, but of course it does not restrict how these should be implemented. Some implementations will be on the **XA Interface**, which is defined by X/Open and is supported by many DBMSs (most relational DBMSs and a growing nunber of OODBMSs). If a server stores its data in a DBMS that supports this interface, then a `Resource` object in that server can implement its `prepare()`, `commit()`, and `rollback()` operations by passing them on to the corresponding (C) functions of the XA Interface. `prepare()` would call `xa_prepare()`; `commit()` would call `xa_commit()`; and `rollback()` would call `xa_rollback()`. XA is not a requirement, of course: if a DBMS supports any suitable form of separate prepare and commit calls then it should be easy to implement the OTS's `prepare()` and `commit()` operations.

Nested transactions

The OTS includes support for nested transactions (sometimes called **subtransactions**), although this is an optional portion of the specification. If a client is currently not involved in a transaction and begins one, then a **top-level transaction** is begun. If a client is currently in a transaction and begins one then the second transaction is said to be nested in the first; however, this call will be rejected if the OTS implementation does not support nested transactions.

Some applications can benefit substantially by using nested transactions. Consider a travel agency system that is booking a vacation for a customer. The overall booking can take place within a top-level transaction, and the individual bookings (cinema, flight, car, hotel, and so on) can take place as nested transactions within the top-level one. If any individual booking cannot be carried out, its effects can be rolled back without aborting the overall booking. Nested transactions can isolate a top-level transaction from failures (for example, if the car rental company's machine fails then another company can be tried), or allow the top-level transaction to try one approach, analyze the results and try another approach if necessary.

Nesting can occur to any level, resulting in a parent–client hierarchy. The term **ancestors** is used to refer to a transaction's set of higher level transactions.

A nested transaction can abort independently of its parent (that is, without aborting its parent). However, when a nested transaction commits, its effects are not made durable until all of its ancestors have committed. If any one of them aborts, then the effects of the nested transaction are also undone.

Nested transaction support has been made optional by the OTS because it is not possible (or at least it is prohibitively expensive) to implement nested transactions on a DBMS, transaction manager, or transactional file system that does not provide native support for them.

23.3.1 IDL interfaces

The following subsections describe the IDL interfaces that make up the OTS specification. The full IDL is listed in Section A.2 (p.482). Figure 23.8 shows the types of objects introduced by the OTS.

IDL interface: `Current`

For clients, the most visible IDL interface is `Current`. Each client that can use the OTS has a pseudo-object (one whose object reference cannot be transmitted) of this type in its address space, and it uses this to begin and manage transactions. If a client creates a transaction using its `Current` object, then each subsequent operation call and attribute access that it makes will have this transaction context implicitly associated with it – and these actions will therefore be committed or rolled back by the transaction's outcome. The transaction context will contain the transaction identifier of the transaction begun using the `Current` object.

The operations defined in `Current` are:

- `begin()`: if the client is not within a transaction then begin a top-level transaction; otherwise begin a nested transaction (if the OTS does not support nested transactions, then an exception is raised).
- `commit()`: commits the current top-level or nested transaction.
- `rollback()`: rolls back the current top-level or nested transaction.
- `rollback_only()`: sets a status flag associated with the transaction to prevent it being committed. Transactions placed in this state

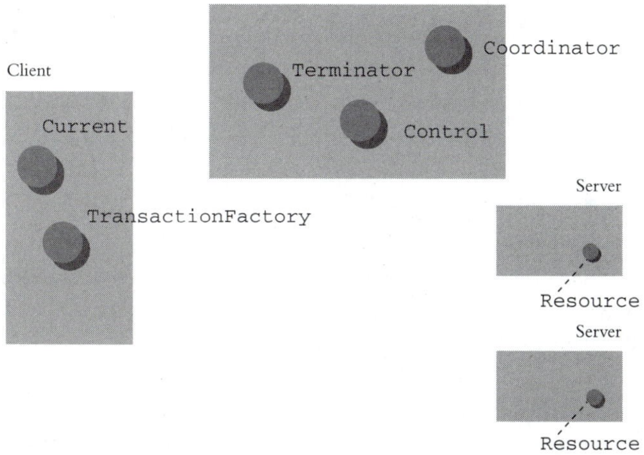

Figure 23.8 *Objects introduced by the OTS.*

are useful for "what if" investigations where the results of a transaction should not be made durable.

- `get_status()`: returns the status of the current transaction.
- `get_transaction_name()`: returns a string that may be useful for debugging.
- `set_timeout()`: sets a timeout in seconds, after which the transaction will be rolled back if it has not been explicitly committed.
- `get_control()`: returns a reference to the transaction's `Control` object. As we will see later in this section, a `Control` object can be viewed as representing a transaction to a client or a server.
- `suspend()`: acts like `get_control()` but also allows a client to retain the returned `Control` object reference and pass it to subsequent calls to `resume()`.
- `resume()`: this takes a `Control` object reference as a parameter and makes the caller become associated (that is, to work within) the specified transaction.

As can be seen from this list of operations, a client can begin and manage transactions using its `Current` object. The advantage of this approach is that such transactions are implicitly propagated (that is, their transaction context is transmitted when a client makes a remote call).

✚ Interface `TransactionalObject` is provided for the server side: if an invocation is made to an object that inherits from this interface, then the client's transaction context is made available to the target server. The target server can find the transaction context by calling `get_control()` on its `Current` object (remember that servers can act as clients, so they too must have an object of type `Current`). This returns a `Control` object, from which information about the transaction can be obtained (this is obtained indirectly, as we will see). Interface `TransactionalObject` does not define any operations or attributes, it is just a way of indicating that a target object is able to obtain the transaction context of the caller.

IDL interfaces: `TransactionFactory` and `Control`

Before considering the server side in further detail, a second way to create and manage transactions will be described. This uses interfaces `TransactionFactory` and `Control`. Each client has a `TransactionFactory` pseudo-object in its address space that it can use to begin a top-level transaction. It defines a single operation:

- `create()`: creates a top-level transaction and returns the object reference of a `Control` object that the client can use to manage that transaction. A timeout period can be specified (in case the coordinator cannot be contacted).

Transactions created in this way are not propagated implicitly by the OTS. Instead, they can be propagated explicitly by passing an object reference of type `Control` as a parameter to an IDL operation.

A `Control` object represents a transaction: by retaining a reference to the `Control` object, the creator of a transaction can manage it. In fact, a `Control` object does not directly provide the operations required for managing a transaction – instead, this management is provided by the `Coordinator` and `Terminator` interfaces. The `Control` interface provides two operations, `get_terminator()` and `get_coordinator()`.

IDL interface: `Terminator`

A client or server can use a transaction's `Terminator` object to commit or rollback a transaction. Interface `Terminator` supports the following operations:

- `commit()`: commits the transaction.
- `rollback()`: rolls back the transaction.

These are the normal operations used to terminate a transaction started by `TransactionFactory`.

IDL interface: `Coordinator`

A coordinator object has two roles. Firstly, it acts as the coordinator during its transaction's termination, to ensure that all of the effects are either committed or rolled back. Secondly, it is available to clients and servers to provide the status of its transaction, allow subtransactions to be created, and so on. It provides the following operations:

- `get_status()`: returns the status of the coordinator's transaction.
- `get_parent_status()`: returns the status of the parent of the coordinator's transaction.
- `get_top_level_status()`: returns the status of the coordinator's transaction if this is a top-level transaction; otherwise returns the status of the top-level transaction that the current transaction is nested within.
- `is_same_transaction()` : returns True if the coordinator's transaction is the same as the one passed as a parameter.
- `is_related_transaction()`: returns True if the coordinator's transaction has a common ancestor with the one passed as a parameter.

- `is_ancestor_transaction()`: returns True if the coordinator's transaction is the same or is an ancestor of the one passed as a parameter.
- `is_descendant_transaction()`: returns True if the coordinator's transaction is the same or is a descendant of the one passed as a parameter.
- `is_top_level_transaction()`: returns True if the coordinator's transaction is a top-level transaction.
- `hash_transaction()`: returns an `unsigned long` hash value (that is not guaranteed to be unique). This is useful if a set of transactions (actually, `Resource` objects) is entered into a hash table. This may be done in a server that has many outstanding transactions, each with a `Resource` object in the server. When an operation call arrives at the server, the OTS runtime should determine if the operation's transaction is known to the server already; that is, if it has a `Resource` object for that transaction. For efficiency, the server's `Resource` objects can be in a table hashed on the result of calling `hash_transaction()` or `hash_top_level_tran()`.
- `hash_top_level_tran()`: returns a hash value for the top-level transaction of the coordinator's current transaction.

- `register_resource()`: is called by a `Resource` object as it is created to inform the coordinator that the `Resource` object should be asked to vote on whether the coordinator's transaction can commit, and also be informed of the final commit or rollback decision. The parameter is the object reference of the `Resource` object calling the operation.

- `register_subtran_aware()` is used to inform the coordinator that the `Resource` is interested in the outcome of a subtransaction (`register_resource()` is used to inform the coordinator of interest in a top-level transaction). The parameter is of type `SubtransactionAwareResource`, which is a derived interface of `Resource`. This interface has two operations: `commit_subtransaction()` and `rollback_subtransaction()`, which are called by the coordinator when the subtransaction terminates. Unlike `Resource`, `SubtransactionAwareResource` does not have a `prepare()` operation: a subtransaction is simply committed (but, of course, the commitment of its changes is ultimately determined by whether its ancestors commit or abort). The two-phase commit protocol is run when a top-level transaction is committed.

- `rollback_only()`: sets a status flag associated with the transaction to prevent it being committed. Transactions placed in this state are useful for "what if" investigations where the results of a transaction should not be made durable.

- `get_transaction_name()`: returns a string that may be useful for debugging.

- `create_subtransaction()`: creates a subtransaction nested within the coordinator's current transaction, and returns a `Control` object for the subtransaction.

Note that interface `Coordinator` does not have operations to commit or rollback a transaction. A client or server can use operations on a `Current` object or a transaction's `Terminator` object to specify the desired outcome of a transaction, and the implementation of the OTS must determine how best to inform the transaction's coordinator (so that it can assume responsibility for informing the transaction's `Resource` objects, and assume responsibility for the atomic outcome of top-level transactions). ✚

IDL interface: `Resource`

Interface `Resource` provides the operations required by a coordinator to inform each `Resource` of the desired outcome of a transaction, to gather votes, and then to tell the `Resource` objects of the final outcome decision. The `Resource` operations are called by a transaction's coordinator:

- `prepare()`: is called by a transaction's coordinator when the desired outcome is to commit the transaction. `prepare()` returns a vote (enum value `VoteCommit`, `VoteRollback`, or `VoteReadOnly`) to indicate whether or not a `Resource` object can actually commit the effects of the transaction.

  When `VoteCommit` is returned, the implementation of `prepare()` should place the transaction in a state from which it can be committed (without error) if the coordinator receives all `VoteCommit` votes from the other `Resource` objects; or from which the `Resource` object can rollback the transaction if the coordinator receives one or more `VoteRollback` votes. In the former case, the coordinator will call `Resource::commit()` after `Resource::prepare()`; in the latter case, the coordinator will call `Resource::rollback()` after `Resource::prepare()`.

The return value `VoteReadOnly` can be used by a `Resource` object to indicate that no changes have been made to its objects; it can therefore commit without difficulty and does not need to be informed of the overall decision after the other votes have been gathered.

- `commit()`: is called after `prepare()` to tell the `Resource` object that the final outcome is to commit the effects of the transaction (all of the `Resource` objects voted `VoteCommit`, or `VoteReadOnly`). This operation raises an exception if `prepare()` has not been called. Once `commit()` is called, the `Resource` object can be deleted.
- `rollback()`: is called by the coordinator to instruct the `Resource` object to undo the effects of the transaction. This operation will be called if the client has chosen to rollback the transaction; or if the client has chosen to commit it but one of the transaction's `Resource` objects has voted `VoteRollback`. In the latter case, `prepare()` will have been called beforehand. Once `rollback()` is called, the `Resource` object can be deleted.

✚

- `commit_one_phase()`: if the coordinator decides to commit the transaction in one phase, then it will call this operation on each `Resource` object – without calling `prepare()`.
- `forget()`: if the `Resource` object indicates a heuristic outcome (by raising a heuristic exception to `commit()`; see p.405), then it may have been holding information about the transaction for a prolonged period of time. The coordinator can call `forget()` to tell the `Resource` object to forget about the transaction (in fact, this `Resource` can then cease to exist). ✚

Indirect, direct/implicit, explicit

Transactions begun using the `Current` pseudo-object (so-called indirect creation) are propagated implicitly (that is, the transaction context is sent to servers without having to add any extra parameters to the IDL operations called). Transactions begun using the `TransactionFactory` (so-called direct creation) are normally propagated explicitly using a `Control` object reference parameter to the IDL operations called.

✚ It is possible to explicitly propagate indirectly created transactions (using `Control::get_control()` to obtain the `Control` object, which is then passed as a parameter); and to implicitly propagate directly created transactions (by passing the `Control` object to `Current::resume()`).

New standard exceptions

The OTS specifies three new standard exceptions that can be raised by any IDL operation or attribute access (and, of course, these cannot appear in an IDL `raises` clause). They are defined in module `CosTransactions` with the following names: `Transaction Required` (indicates that the caller is not within a transaction but is required to be); `TransactionRollback()` (indicates that the transaction associated with the client has already been rolled back; some other client or server will have terminated the transaction. For example, an implementation of the OTS can allow a client or server other than the initiator of a transaction to terminate that transaction, and if this is supported, the initiator will be associated with a transaction that may have been rolled back); and `Invalid Transaction` (indicates that the transaction associated with the caller is invalid and not known to the OTS). These three exceptions have been added to Orbix.

Heuristic reporting

If the coordinator of a transaction has not completed the two-phase commit in a reasonable period of time (that is, if the period between the `prepare()` and `commit()`/ `rollback()` calls to a `Resource` object is too long), then a `Resource` object may decide to commit or rollback its prepared transaction without waiting any longer for the decision of the coordinator. This may lead to errors, and particularly to non-atomic commit or rollback (that is, different `Resource` objects may decide differently). When a client calls `commit()`, it passes a `boolean` parameter to specify whether or not such errors should be reported to it (as an exception). ✚

23.4 Trading Service

The Naming Service (Chapter 7) plays a central role in aiding applications to obtain references to an initial set of the objects that they need to use. Objects are registered and looked up by name. The Trading Service provides an alternative – indeed, an enhancement – to this, in which objects can be registered with a set of properties and then searched for by specifying a **constraint** over these properties.

An entry, termed an **offer**, is made in the trader by specifying the following information:

- a **service type**
- a **set of properties** (the appropriate properties depend on the service type)
- an object reference to the object that is being registered

When an application searches for an object, it specifies a constraint in a **constraint language**: a constraint is a string that is made up of property names, literals (for example, of integer and string types), and operators to connect them (for example, comparison and logical operators). The application can also specify a **preference**: a string that is used to determine the **order** in which the set of matching offers is returned by the trader. The application that registers an offer is said to **export** it. An application that uses a trader to search for a set of offers is said to **import** those offers.

The Naming Service has a very simple task in comparison with that of the trader, and this simplicity is reflected in the Naming Service's IDL specification. It is likely also to be reflected in its performance. The complexity of the Trader is justified when an application needs to search for an object among a large set of similar objects, rather than simply to obtain an object reference to an object that it already knows about. For example, if an application knows the name of a given cinema, then it should use the Naming Service to obtain an object reference to it. The Naming Service is therefore used to determine the object's location and set up a connection to it. On the other hand, if an application wishes to find what cinemas are showing interesting movies; that is, ones that fulfill some constraint, then it should use the trader.

Further comments on the difference between the Naming Service and the Trading Service are given at the end of this section.

Trader operations

This following subsections describe the operations supported by the trader.

Trader operations: lookup

Table 23.1 describes the `query()` operation, which is used to search a trader.

Table 23.1 *Trader operations: lookup.*

Operation name	Meaning
`query()`	Searches for a set of offers that match a specified constraint. It takes the following `in` parameters: – service type name – constraint – preference – policy sequence – `how_many (unsigned long)`† It has the following `out` parameters: – sequence of offers (maximum length is `how_many`) – offer iterator – policy name sequence

† The `how_many` parameter specifies the maximum size of the sequence of offers that is returned as an `out` parameter. If there are further offers, these can be accessed using the offer iterator (see Section 7.3.6, p.170, for an explanation of iterators).

- **Service type name**: a query can specify the type of object it is searching for by specifying the service type name. Service types are registered with the trader, and each service type consists of the following information:

  - a service type name
  - an IDL interface name
  - a set of property names and types (each property also has a mode; that is, whether it is a mandatory and/or a readonly property)
  - a set of names of base service types

  An example service type may be cinema, which would have an interface type `FrontOffice` and the following set of properties (as examples):

  - title of type `string`
  - duration of type `long`
  - category of type `string`

  A service type `entertainment` could also be defined, and **cinema** could have `entertainment` as its base service type. The Trading Service defines an IDL interface `CosTradingRepos::Service TypeRepository`, which has operations to define, remove, and list service types.

- **Constraints**: the Trading Service specifies a constraint language that is used by applications to specify the desired set of objects when calling `query()`. Each constraint is a string that conforms to this simple language.

  ✚ In fact, other constraint languages can also be supported by a trader, but a constraint specified in a different language must begin with the name of that (proprietary) constraint language, enclosed in double angle brackets ('<<....>>'). ✚

- **Properties**: the type of a property that can appear in a constraint is restricted to one of: integer types, floating point types, `boolean`, `string`, `char`, and sequences of these. The operators that are supported are comparison (`==, !=, >, >=, <, <=, ~` (substring match), `in` (test if an element is in a sequence)), boolean connectives (`and`, `or`, `not`), property existence (`exist`; `exist Name` determines whether or not the offer being tested has a property called `Name`), and mathematical operators (`+`, `*`, `-`, `/`). Literals must be numeric, string, character, or booleans.

- **Preferences**: a preference can be specified when calling `query()` to indicate the order in which the set of matching offers should be returned by the trader. A preference string consists of one of the following: `max`, `min`, `with`, `random`, or `first`. `max` and `min` must be followed by a property name: this results in the offers being ordered by that property name (and offers without the specified property are listed last). `with` must also be followed by a property: offers with this property are listed first. `random` results in the returned sequence being randomly ordered; `first` results in the returned sequence being returned in the order that the offers happened to be found to match the constraint.

- **Policies**: the actions of a trader can be controlled by specifying a set of policies that that trader should obey. These control whether or not the trader supports some of the advanced trading features (such as **proxy offers**, described later), and also what maximum values it applies to limit the size of a search or the size of the returned sequence of offers. Policy values that affect an individual query (such as the maximum number of offers that can be returned, or how **links** are to be followed; see later) can be specified as a parameter to that query.

Trader operations: register

Offers are managed using the operations described in Table 23.2.

Table 23.2 *Trader operations: register.*

Operation name	Meaning
`export()`	This creates an offer within the trader. The following are passed as `in` parameters: – an object reference to the object being – offered – a service type name – a set of properties (names and values) This returns an **offer id**, which is used in the next three operations in this section to uniquely identify an offer
`withdraw()`	Removes an offer, specified by an offer id
`describe()`	Returns a description of an offer, specified by an offer id
`modify()`	Modifies a given offer by specifying a set of properties to delete, and a set of properties to modify

`withdraw_using_constraint()`	Given a server type name and a constraint (as used in `query()`), this removes all offers which match that constraint
`resolve()`	This is used when traders are federated and an application wishes to find a trader by specifying a name known to the target trader

Trader operations: admin

Table 23.3 describes two operations that are used to list the contents of a trader.

Table 23.3 *Trader operations: admin.*

Operation name	Meaning
`list_offers()`	Lists the offers in the trader.
`list_proxies()`	Lists the **proxy offers** (see later) in the trader

Trader operations: link

A trader is not expected to know of all of the objects that may be registered and searched for. Instead, one trader can be **linked** to any number of other traders; and a query on a trader can be forwarded to some or all of its linked traders to search for other offers that match the query's constraint. In this way, a set of traders can be **federated** to form a **trading graph**. Table 23.4 shows the operations for managing links.

Table 23.4 *Trader operations: link.*

Operation name	Meaning
`add_link()`	Adds a link, with a specified name, to the target trader. A reference to the linked trader is specified (actually a reference to a `Lookup` interface; see later), and also indicators of whether or not to follow the new link when a search is being made
`remove_link()`	Removes the link of a given name
`describe_link()`	Returns information to describe the link of a specified name
`list_links()`	Lists the links within the target trader
`modify_link()`	Modifies a link (actually its **follow rules**; see later) with the given name

Traders can be linked in an arbitrarily complex trading network, and, therefore, in complex installations, it is important that the system controls the passing of searches along the links connecting traders. Each link can be labeled with one of the three **follow rules**:

- `local_only`: the link is followed only by explicit navigation (using the `resolve()` operation introduced earlier.
- `if_no_local`: the link is followed only if there are no local offers that satisfy the query.
- `always`: the link is always followed.

In addition, a maximum number of hops can be specified for each query (so if one trader passes the query to another, and the latter passes it to another, and so on, then there is a limit to the length of any one of these chains). A maximum number of hops can also be specified for each link; this limits the length of any chain involving that link.

The traders involved in a system can label each query they send over a link, so that they can recognise it if it arrives back again via another link. This is used to avoid infinite loops.

✚ *Trader operations: proxy*

Some of the offers within a trader can be **proxy offers**. Like normal offers, they have a service type name, a set of properties, and a registered object reference, but they behave differently when they match a given query. Instead of the trader simply adding the object reference to the matching set, as it does with a normal offer, it makes a `query()` call on it and adds the sequence of object references that are returned to the matching set. A proxy offer is an object of type `Lookup`, which will be explained shortly.

In response to the `query()` call, a proxy offer can perform its own search of its "database." In this way, a proxy offer behaves much like a link: the difference is that a link does not have a service type name and a set of properties, which must be matched before it is followed. In addition, a link has a **follow rule**.

Table 23.5 describes operations provided for proxy offers.

Table 23.5 *Trader operations: proxy.*

Operation name	Meaning
`export_proxy()`	Creates a proxy offer in the target trader. An `OfferId` is returned
`withdraw_proxy()`	Removes a proxy offer with a given `OfferId`
`describe_proxy()`	Returns information about a proxy offer with a given `OfferId`

Structure of the Trading Service IDL

Rather than the trader's operations being specified within a single IDL interface, they have been grouped in the way shown in the previous subsections, into lookup, register, admin, link, and proxy sections. Each of these sections is specified as an IDL interface (`Lookup`, `Register`, `Admin`, `Link`, and `Proxy`). A trader can support any number of these five interfaces.

There is no single interface that inherits from these five interfaces. Instead, given a reference to an object of any one of these interfaces, the references to any of the other four objects can be obtained. This is supported because each of the five IDL interfaces inherits from `TraderComponents`:

```
interface TraderComponents {
      readonly attribute Lookup lookup_if;       // Get Lookup
                                                 // object.
      readonly attribute Register register_if;   // Get Register
                                                 // object.
      readonly attribute Link link_if;          // Get Link object.
      readonly attribute Proxy proxy_if;        // Get Proxy object.
      readonly attribute Admin admin_if;        // Get Admin object.
};
```

Because a trader can support a subset of these five interfaces, there can be many different combinations. The trader specification discusses six of these:

- Query trader: supports only the `Lookup` interface.
- Simple trader: supports `Lookup` and `Register`.
- Standalone trader: supports `Lookup`, `Register`, and `Admin`.
- Linked trader: supports `Lookup`, `Register`, `Admin`, and `Link`.
- Proxy trader: supports `Lookup`, `Register`, `Admin`, and `Proxy`.
- Full trader: supports all five interfaces.

The trader specification defines three other interfaces, each of which defines a number of `readonly` attributes that indicate how the trader is configured:

- `SupportAttributes`: tells whether the trader supports features such as proxy offers. It also has an attribute to obtain a reference to the type repository interface of the trader, through which **service types** can be added or removed. `SupportAttributes` is inherited by interfaces `Lookup`, `Register`, `Link`, and `Admin`.
- `ImportAttributes`: gives information about certain default and maximum counters; for example, the default and maximum upper bound of the number of offers that can be returned from a search. (The default

upper bound is used if the query does not specify a **policy** that gives a different upper bound; and the maximum upper bound gives a value that cannot be exceeded even if a query specifies a higher value as a policy.) This interface is inherited by interfaces `Lookup` and `Admin`.

- `LinkAttributes`: has a single attribute which specifies the 'maximum' follow rule for that link: `local_only` is considered less than `if_no_local`, which in turn is less than `always`. No query can specify a larger follow rule as a policy. This interface is inherited by interfaces `Link`, `Proxy`, and `Admin`.

The IDL definition of the trader is rather large, and therefore only the definition of interface `Lookup`, and any associated types, has been given in Appendix A (Section A.3). ✚

Finding the Trading Service

A reference to the Trading Service itself can be obtained by passing the string "`TradingService`" to the `resolve_initial_references()` function (Section 7.3.3, p.165) on the ORB. This returns a reference to a `CosTrading::Lookup` object.

24 CORBAservices 2

24.1 Life Cycle Service

The Life Cycle Service defines support and conventions for creating, deleting, copying, and moving objects. Unlike the other CORBAservices, a large portion of the Life Cycle Service can be written by application writers and not by the ORB vendor or the CORBAservice provider.

The central notion is that of a factory — an object that creates other objects. There is nothing special about factory objects; they have IDL interfaces, as do all other CORBA objects. One or more of a factory s operations create objects, and normally an object reference to a created object is returned to the caller. The `FrontOffice` object of Chapter 6 is a factory object.

CORBA IDL does not provide any constructor notation, nor is it sensible to allow a client to create an object unilaterally in a server or in another client. Instead, a server can expose a factory object to its clients if it wishes to allow them to create objects in the server. The parameters to the various creation operations can supply the server with the information needed to decide whether or not to create the new object, and, if so, how to initialize it.

The Life Cycle Service encourages application designers to determine their own, application-specific, factory interfaces, following naturally from the analysis of the application. However, the Life Cycle Service provides an interface, `GenericFactory`, that can be used when no natural application-specific factory interfaces can be identified. Use of the Life Cycle Service gives uniformity of object creation and simple aspects of management across applications, but this must be weighed against the major advantages of using application-specific interfaces (such as `FrontOffice`).

Another important interface defined by the Life Cycle Service is `LifeCycleObject`. Application-level interfaces can inherit from this to provide three standard operations: `copy()`, `move()`, and `remove()`. An application that needs this functionality can decide to adopt these three operations, or to provide this functionality in some application-specific way.

Interface `GenericFactory`

The IDL definition of `GenericFactory` (in module `CosLifeCycle`) is as follows (the full IDL for the Life Cycle Service is given in Section A.4, p.486):

```
interface GenericFactory {
     boolean supports (in Key k);
     Object create_object (in Key k,
                           in Criteria the_criteria)
          raises (NoFactory,InvalidCriteria,CannotMeetCriteria);
};
```

`create_object()` takes a `Key` to specify the type of object to be created. The `Key` is a name (it is a `typedef` to `CosNaming::Name`, which is defined by the Naming Service; see Chapter 7). Such names have two internal strings: a `kind` member and an `id` member. The Life Cycle Service does not specify how these (dual) names are to be interpreted, but it does give some examples:

(1) The `kind` could be the string object interface, in which case the `id` string is interpreted as the name of the interface that the new object is to support.

(2) The `kind` could be the string object implementation, in which case the `id` is interpreted as the name of the implementation (in C++, the name of the class) that the new object is to support.

The `the_criteria` parameter allows any number of optional parameters to be passed. Some or all of these can be passed to the new object to initialize it. A `Criteria` is an IDL sequence of name—value pairs:

```
typedef struct NVP {
     CosNaming::Istring name; // Just a string.
     any value;
} NameValuePair;
typedef sequence <NameValuePair> Criteria;
```

✚ The Life Cycle Service does not specify how the `Criteria` are to be interpreted, or even how to identify the subset of values to be passed to the new object. However, it does give an example interpretation, in which each `name` of a name–value pair can be one of the following:

(1) "initialization," in which case the `value` is expected to be of type `sequence<NameValuePair>`, and this value is passed to the new object to initialize it.

(2) "filter," in which case the `value` is expected to be of type `string`, and is used by the `GenericFactory` to decide where or how to create the new object. For example, the string may specify that the new object is to be created on a machine running a specified operating system, or in a specified programming language. The Life Cycle Service includes an appendix that specifies a filter language, but this is not part of the service itself. ✚

The result of `create_object()` is of type `Object`. Typically, the caller will have to narrow the returned object reference to get an object reference it can use.

When using the Life Cycle Service, applications are often required to specify *where* to create a new object or *where* to move or copy an existing object. This is done by telling the Life Cycle Service which factory to choose; this factory then creates the new object or the copy local to itself.

The `LifeCycleObject` interface

As explained earlier, application-level IDL interfaces can inherit from interface `LifeCycleObject` in order to support a standard way to copy, move, and remove their instances. Before explaining this in detail, the notion of a `FactoryFinder` must be understood:

```
typedef Object Factory;
typedef sequence<Factory> Factories;

interface FactoryFinder {
      Factories find_factories (in Key factory_key)
                  raises (NoFactory);
};
```

Given a `Key` (a name with a `kind` and an `id` string), a factory finder attempts to find a factory object that supports the specified key. A factory finder does not interpret the key; it simply matches it with the keys of the factories that it knows of. It can use the `GenericFactory::supports()` operation to do this matching (see previous page). Since more that one factory can match a given key, `find_factories()` returns a sequence of factory object references.

The `LifeCycleObject` interface is defined as follows:

```
interface LifeCycleObject {
      LifeCycleObject copy (in FactoryFinder there,
                            in Criteria the_criteria)
            raises (NoFactory, NotCopyable,
```

```
                InvalidCriteria, CannotMeetCriteria);
    void move (in FactoryFinder there,
                in Criteria the_criteria)
          raises (NoFactory, NotMovable,
                   InvalidCriteria, CannotMeetCriteria);
    void remove ()
          raises (NotRemovable);
};
```

The `copy()` operation requests a factory object to create a copy of the target object. The `there` parameter specifies which factory finder object to use to find the factory which is to create the copy. (The choice of the factory is important since it determines *where* the copy is made.)

The `move()` operation requests that an object be moved from its current position and recreated by a factory object elsewhere. The `there` parameter specifies which factory finder object to use to find the factory which is to recreate the object. The `remove()` operation deletes the target object.

✚ The implementation of `copy()` and `move()` must use the supplied `FactoryFinder` to decide which factory to use to create the new copy of the object. To allow the `FactoryFinder` object to make this decision, `copy()` and `move()` must pass a key value to the `FactoryFinder::find_factory()` operation; they must determine the key value to pass from some internal details of the target object. For example, the key could be a private member variable of the target object, or it could be determined using the target object's interface. From the sequence of factories returned by the `FactoryFinder`, the implementation of `copy()` or `move()` must select a factory to use, and request it to create the new object. The `Criteria` parameter is passed to the chosen factory. ✚

The Life Cycle Service also discusses the copying and moving of **compound objects**; that is, groups of objects related by relationships defined by the Relationship Service.

24.2 Externalization Service

The Externalization Service defines the interfaces needed to store an object to a **stream of bytes**, and later to reconstruct the object from the data in the stream. The term **externalization** is used to refer to the actions required to write an object to a stream; and the term **internalization** is used to refer to the actions required to reconstruct an object.

The contents of a stream can be stored to a file or transmitted to another machine in some way (for example, by storing the stream on a tape and loading the tape on another machine). Different storage formats are allowed, but one standard format is defined by the service. An important point to note is that streams exist external to the ORB.

The Externalization Service is dependent on the Life Cycle Service (see Section 24.1) (in particular, it uses factories and the `FactoryFinder` interface), and advanced features are dependent on the Relationship Service (see Section 25.2). The IDL definitions are given in Section A.5 (p.487).

Externalizing an object

Figure 24.1 shows the actions carried out when an object is externalized.

The `externalize()` call is made to a `Stream` object, giving it a reference to the object to be externalized. The stream passes the call to the object using the `Streamable::externalize_to_stream()` operation, passing it a reference to a `StreamIO` object. Each object that can be externalized/internalized must inherit from interface `Streamable`.

The object then makes a sequence of calls to the `StreamIO` object, to write its internal state. The `StreamIO` interface supports operations to write each of the IDL basic types (for example, `write_char()` and `write_long()`). Operation `write_object()` is called where the object holds an object reference and it wishes to have that object externalized along with itself (the Externalization Service will then follow the same steps as shown in Figure 24.1).

Finally, the `flush()` call must be made to the stream to force the object's data to the storage media.

A client or server can create a `Stream` object using the `create()` operation on a `StreamFactory` object. This creates and returns a reference for a stream (without specifying any special storage media). The `create()` operation on a

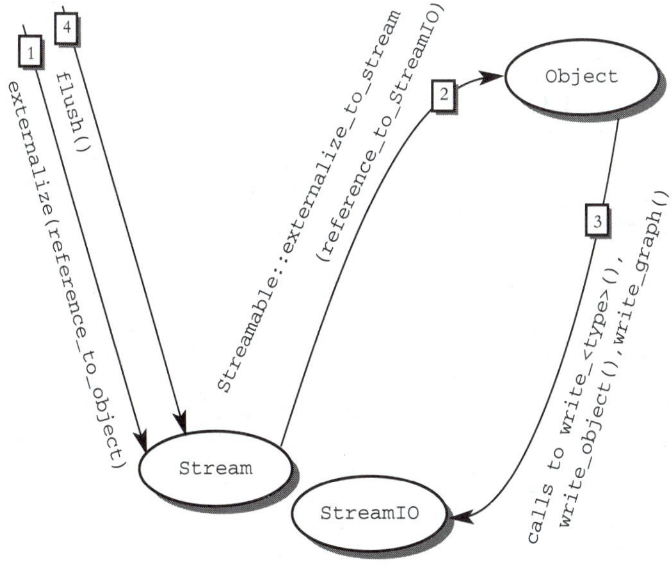

Figure 24.1 *Actions carried out to externalize an object.*

`FileStreamFactory` object takes a file name as its parameter, and creates and returns a reference for a stream that uses the specified file as the storage media.

The `Stream` and the `StreamIO` objects can be the same object (by combining their interfaces using multiple inheritance, and then implementing that interface), or the `Stream` object can hold a reference to a separate `StreamIO` object. The choice is an implementation detail.

Internalizing an object

Figure 24.2 shows the actions carried out when an object is internalized. It is more complex than the previous figure because the object does not exist at the time of the call to `internalize()`. The stream must arrange to have the object recreated by first finding a `StreamableFactory` and then asking it to recreate the object in an uninitialized state.

The `internalize()` operation creates a new object with state identical to what was externalized, and it returns a reference to the new object. Note that a new object is created, with a different object reference to the one externalized.

✚ The `StreamableFactory` is found using the factory finder (see the Life Cycle Service; Section 24.1) passed as a parameter to the call to `internalize()`. The factory finder must find the `StreamableFactory` using the key that the `Stream` passes to it: the stream must have recorded this key when the object was externalized. Once the

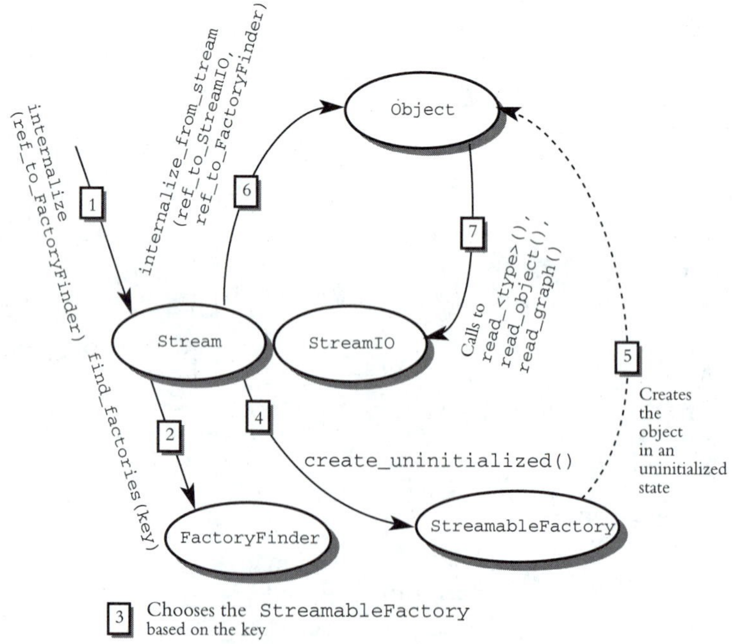

Figure 24.2 *Actions carried out when an object is internalized.*

`StreamableFactory` is found, the stream calls `create_uninitialized()` on it to create an uninitialized object with the correct interface and implementation. It then calls `internalize_from_stream()` on the object, passing it a reference to a `StreamIO` object. The object then makes a sequence of read calls on the `StreamIO` object, in the same order as the stream was written to during the `externalize_to_stream()` operation call (see Figure 24.1).

As can be seen, the creation of the object is rather complex. The `StreamableFactory` object must exist to create the object of the correct interface and implementation (the Externalization Service itself cannot do this because it will not be aware of all of the interfaces and implementations it has to deal with). The factory finder object must exist to find the `StreamableFactory` object.

Each object of type `Streamable` has an attribute, `external_form_id`, that gives its key. A key can be viewed as an indicator of an object's type. The necessity to store the type of an object with its persistent state is a common requirement of object databases. An Object Database Management System can implicitly store an object's type (by storing all objects of a given type in the same table), or an object's type can be stored explicitly with its data.

Contexts and object references

If a client or server wishes to externalize a set of objects that refer to each other, then it is likely that it will want to specify that these references be maintained when these objects are internalized. Hence, if object A and object B both refer to object C, then when these are externalized and subsequently internalized, the new objects A and B should refer to the new object C.

The client can do this simply by bracketing the externalization of these objects with calls to `Stream::begin_context()` and `Steam::end_context()`. Each object will then be stored only once in the stream (in the time between the begin and end calls) and object references will be maintained correctly. A call to `begin_context()` cannot be made if it has been called already without a matching call to `end_context()`.

Storing objects outside of a context breaks object references; for example, if objects A and B both refer to object C, and if these are externalized outside of a context and then internalized, the new object A will refer to one copy of object C and the new object B will refer to a different copy.

Graphs of objects

Although not detailed here, the Externalization Service also defines the support and interfaces needed to store a graph of objects supported by the Relationship Service (see Section 25.2, p.435).

Standard stream data format

Any suitable data format can be used to store an object's externalized data. However, the Externalization Service specifies one such format, which can be used between different CORBA implementations and different CPU hardware. The format for each data type is specified, and if this is not the native format of a particular hardware then the data should be converted to and from that format when an object is externalized and internalized.

The details of the standard format are given here because this helps to clarify the nature of the Externalization Service.

Each object is stored as a list of bytes, beginning with a byte with value hex 'F0.' This is followed by the object's key, which gives its type information. This is stored as a length (stored in one byte), followed by that number of null-terminated strings. The key is followed by the object's data: a list of tag and value pairs.

Each tag specifies the type of data stored, and implicitly indicates the number of bytes required to store the value. The tags (and implicit lengths of the values) are shown in Table 24.1.

Table 24.1 *Standard stream data format.*

Tag	Basic type	Data format and length
hex F1	`char`	One byte (ASCII)
hex F2	`octet`	One byte
hex F3	`unsigned long`	Four bytes, big endian format
hex F4	`unsigned short`	Two bytes, big endian format
hex F5	`long`	Four bytes, big endian format
hex F6	`short`	Two bytes, big endian format
hex F7	`float`	Four bytes, IEEE 754 single precision format, sign bit in first byte
hex F8	`double`	Eight bytes, IEEE 754 double precision format, sign bit in first byte
hex F9	`boolean`	One byte, True=1, False=0
hex FA	`string`	Null-terminated list of bytes

24.3 Licensing Service

Many software vendors need to control the use of their software at end-user sites, to ensure that the software is not used by unlicensed users or on unlicensed machines. Alternatively, a network model may be used, in which a specified number of users on the network can use the software simultaneously, but further usages will be delayed or denied.

The Licensing Service specifies the interface that a vendor s software can use to interact with the licensing system. A vendor s software can be a CORBA application that uses the Licensing Service as one of the useful services in the system; or it can be an application whose only use of CORBA is to interact with the Licensing Service. The licensing system itself can be implemented specifically for the CORBA environment, or it can be layered on top of an existing commercial licensing package for distributed systems.

The interface to the Licensing Service needs to be very flexible because of the large number of licensing models that are used by different software vendors, and because of the large number of variations to these that may be required by particular end users or by particular usage patterns. The following are some of the approaches that are possible in isolation or in combination:

- Licensing a copy of the vendor's software to work on a specified node or set of nodes.
- Licensing the vendor's software to a set of named users.
- Allowing a maximum number of users to use the software simultaneously; each user would automatically acquire a license on using the software and release it when finished.
- Allowing a maximum number of usages of the software; in this scheme, licenses would be 'consumed' as they were used, without the possibility of being released later.
- Licensing the software for a particular period of time, possibly with a mixture of the other licensing restrictions.

When a license cannot be granted, the vendor's software must be free to decide how to continue, including termination of the program being used, notification to the user that there is a problem but continuing, and notification to the user, presenting him or her with a dialogue box with a number of choices on how to continue.

The Licensing Service is used by the vendor's software as follows:

- It communicates with a `LicenseServiceManager` to acquire an object reference to a `ProducerSpecificLicenseService` object. All further interactions are with the latter object, which provides three operations: `start_use()`, `check_use()`, and `end_use()`.
- The vendor's software calls `start_use()` when it is started up, or when a separately controlled part of it is used, or when a new user uses it. The parameters to this operation include the identity of the user on whose behalf the license is being sought; the name of the licensed software and its version number; a list (of type `Property::Property`, see Section 25.1) of details about the user, the host operating system; the node name, and so on; a call-back object reference (see later); and a **challenge**. The challenge is a simple form of authentication that the vendor's software can use to ensure that it is communicating with a bona fide `ProducerSpecificLicenseService`, and not a rogue one that is installed by the end user to grant licenses when they should not be granted. The challenge must be processed by the

`ProducerSpecificLicenseService` object, and the correct values returned; otherwise, the vendor's software should not trust the licensing system. The specification clearly states that this challenge system should in future be replaced with use of the Security CORBAservice (which was specified after the Licensing Service).

- Depending on the licensing rules being obeyed, the licensing system may expect the vendor's software to contact it periodically while a granted license is being used. This may be done because the license has been granted for only a specific period of time; or because the licensing system does not want to have the license lost if the vendor's software crashes. This periodic re-checking is done using the `check_use()` operation. One of the `out` parameters to this operation specifies the re-check interval, so if the vendor's software is aware that re-checking may be required, then it should call this operation once to find the re-checking interval, and then it should call this operation at least that frequently. The Licensing Service can be requested (by passing a non-nil call-back object reference to the `start_use()` operation call) to make periodic calls to the vendor's software to remind it that a call to `check_use()` is required.
- Finally, when the vendor's software wishes to release a license, it should call `end_use()`.

24.4 Time Service

The Time Service defines a set of interfaces that provide applications with the current time, and allow time and time interval values to be manipulated. An optional extension to this service, the Timer Event Service, allows an application to receive an operation call to notify it that a specified duration has elapsed, or to receive a series of such notifications at a specified interval.

The Time Service defines three important interfaces: `TimeService`, `UTO`, and `TIO`:

- A `UTO` (Universal Time Object) represents a fixed point in time. It defines attributes that allow its components to be viewed, and it provides an operation to compare itself with another `UTO`. Its components are its time value, an estimate of its accuracy, and its time zone (the difference from Greenwich Time Zone).

- A TIO (Time Interval Object) represents a duration of time; that is, the interval between two time values. It provides operations to determine if and how two time intervals overlap.
- Interface TimeService defines the operations required to create UTO and TIO objects. Each TimeService object is therefore a factory.

There are many low-level representations for time values; at least as many as there are operating systems. Of these, Time Service has chosen the Universal Time Coordinate (UTC) representation from the X/Open DCE Time Service. This represents time values as 64-bit quantities: the number of nanoseconds since 15th October 1582 00:00:00. A UTC always refers to time in the Greenwich Time Zone.

The types specific to the Time Services are defined in module Time:

- TimeT: this is a 64-bit UTC value.
- InaccuracyT: this is a 48-bit value that gives an estimate of the inaccuracy of a time value.
- TdfT: this is a 16-bit value that gives the time displacement in seconds from the Greenwich Time Zone.
- UtcT: this is a struct that contains a TimeT value (that is, a UTC), an inaccuracy, and a TdfT value. The members of this struct are not available for use outside of the implementation of the Time Service. In fact a UtcT is a 16-byte value that holds all three important data elements of a time value (it is defined as a struct in the standard simply for convenience).
- IntervalT: this is a struct that represents a time interval; it holds a lower_bound and an upper_bound member, both of type TimeT.

Figure 24.3 shows that the Time Service supports three different data types for time, all based ultimately on the (64-bit) UTC representation of time. (The details are given in Section A.6, p.490) Interface UTO defines the type of CORBA object that represents time; TimeT is exactly the UTC representation of time (64-bit values); and UtcT is a struct type that holds a time as a TimeT value, and an inaccuracy and time zone. The Time Service defines two different data types for time intervals. Interface TIO defines the type of CORBA object that represents time intervals; IntervalT is a struct type that holds an interval as a pair of lower and upper TimeT values.

✚ Interfaces TimeService, UTO, and TIO are defined in module CosTime. In addition, this module defines three enumerated types (ComparisonType,

CORBA object for time

```
UTO
-------------------------------------
Time::TimeT time;
Time::InaccuracyT inaccuracy;
Time::TdfT tdf;
Time::UtcT utc_time;
-------------------------------------
absolute_time();
compar_time ();
time_to_interval ();
interval ();
```

CORBA object for interval

```
TIO
-------------------------------------
Time::IntervalT time_interval;
-------------------------------------
span ();
overlap ();
UTO time();
```

`TimeT`

```
64-bit UTC value
```

`UtcT`

```
struct UtcT {
          TimeT time;  // 64 bits
          unsigned long inacclo;   //
          unsigned short inacchi;  // 48 bits
};  // Total 16 bytes.
```

`IntervalT`

```
struct IntervalT {
        TimeT lower_bound;
        TimeT upper_bound;
};
```

Figure 24.3 *Time and interval types.*

`TimeComparison`, and `OverlapType`) that are useful for comparing times and time intervals.

Interface `UTO` defines the following attributes and operations (in module `CosTime`):

- Attribute `time`: this is of type `TimeT`, and it gives the universal time (a UTC) that the `UTO` holds. A `UTO` is immutable, and hence always represents the same time value.
- Attribute `inaccuracy`: this is of type `InaccuracyT`, and it gives an estimate of the inaccuracy of the time value.
- Attribute `tdf`: this is of type `TdfT`, and it gives the time zone information (the displacement from the Greenwich Time Zone).
- Attribute `utc_time`: this is a struct of type `UtcT`. It gives the same information as the other three attributes, but as a struct whose members are not designed for use by applications.
- `absolute_time()`: as will be seen when the Timer Event Service is discussed on p.426, some `UTO` objects represent times relative to some other time. This operation takes such an object and returns a `UTO` object that represents an absolute time.

- `compare_time()`: this compares the time held by the target `UTO` with the time passed as a parameter (also of type `UTO`). The return value indicates whether the target was equal to, less than, or greater than the parameter. The result can also be indeterminate, if the inaccuracies of the two time values are large enough that they overlap. There is a second parameter to this operation, to indicate whether the inaccuracies should be taken into account or ignored.
- `time_to_interval()`: this takes a `UTO` as a parameter and it returns a time interval (a reference to a `TIO` object) that represents the difference in time between the parameter and the target `UTO`. The result is meaningless if the time zones of the two time values are different. Again, there is a second parameter to this operation, to indicate whether the inaccuracies should be taken into account or ignored.
- `interval()`: this uses the inaccuracy associated with the target `UTO` to generate a time interval, and returns a reference to a `TIO` object that represents this time interval.

Interface `TIO` defines the following attributes and operations (in module `CosTime`):

- Attribute `time_interval`: this converts the time interval into a struct of type `Time::IntervalT`. The `lower_bound` and `upper_bound` values can then be used (both are 64-bit UTC values).
- `span()`: returns an enumerated value to indicate whether the target `TIO` contains, is contained by, overlaps with, or has no overlap with the `TIO` value passed as a parameter. This operation also has an `out` parameter that returns a `TIO` that spans the two other `TIO` values (from the earliest time of the two to the latest time of the two).
- `overlap()`: returns an enumerated value to indicate whether the target `TIO` contains, is contained by, overlaps with, or has no overlap with the `TIO` value passed as a parameter. This operation also has an `out` parameter, of type `TIO`, which gives the amount of overlap (it should be ignored if the return value indicates that the two `TIO` values do not overlap).
- `time()`: transforms the values in the target `TIO` into a `UTO` object. This is done by making the time in the `UTO` be the midpoint of the interval; and making its inaccuracy equal to the duration of the time interval.

Interface TimeService defines the following operations (in module CosTime):

- `universal_time()`: returns the current time, as a reference to a `UTO` object.
- ✚ `secure_universal_time()`: returns the current time, as a reference to a `UTO` object, but only if the time can be guaranteed to have been obtained securely (see p.428),
- `new_universal_time()`: this takes three parameters (a `TimeT`, an `InaccuracyT`, and a `TdfT`) and returns a reference to a `UTO` object.
- `uto_from_utc()`: this takes a parameter of type `UtcT` (which holds a time, an inaccuracy, and a time zone) and returns a reference to a `UTO` object constructed from these.
- `new_interval()`: this takes a lower and an upper time (both of type `TimeT`) and returns a reference to a `TIO` object. ✚

The Timer Event Service

The Timer Event Service is an optional extension to the Time Service. It allows an application to receive an operation call to notify it that a specified duration has elapsed, or to receive a series of such notifications at a specified interval. When the specified time duration has elapsed, the Timer Event Service makes a call to a `CosEventComm::PushConsumer` (see Section 23.1, p.377) object in the application.

The Timer Event Service supports two interfaces:

- `TimerEventHandler`: each `TimerEventHandler` object represents an alarm clock – a timer that can be requested to trigger at a specified time. When it triggers it makes an invocation on a `PushConsumer` object in an application, passing it a value of type `any`. This value, known as the **event data**, is set when the `TimerEventHandler` is created (but it can be changed subsequently).
- `TimerEventService`: this acts as a factory for `TimerEventHandler` objects – its `register()` operation creates a `TimerEventHandler` object and returns a reference to it. To create a `TimerEventHandler` object, an object reference to a `PushConsumer` object and the event data (a value of type `any`) must be provided. The created `TimerEventHandler` object is not *set*; that is, the application has not requested that it trigger at some future time. It can be set by calling the `TimerEventHandler::set_timer()` operation.

The types and interfaces associated with the Timer Event Service are defined in module `CosTimerEvent`. These types are:

- `TimeType`: this is an enumerated type. When a `TimerEvent Handler` is set, the time can be specified to be an `Absolute` time, a time `Relative` to the current time, or a `Periodic` time (in the last case, the timer will be set to trigger at a time relative to the current time, and then reset with that same relative time immediately after it triggers each time).
- `EventStatus`: this is an enumerated type that gives the status of a `TimerEventHandler`. This will be one of `TimeSet` (the timer has been set and will trigger some time in the future), `TimeCleared` (the timer is not set to trigger: either it was never set, or it was set and was subsequently cleared), `Triggered` (the timer was set and has triggered), or `FailedTrigger` (the timer was set, but the operation call could not be made to the `PushConsumer` object in the application).
- `TimerEventT`: this is a struct that holds a `Time::UtcT` value (this holds a time, an estimate of inaccuracy, and a time zone) and event data (a value of type `any`).

Interface `TimerEventService` (in module `CosTimerEvent`) defines the following operations:

- `register()`: given an object reference of type `PushConsumer` and event data (of type `any`), this creates and returns a reference to a `TimerEventHandler` object. The `TimerEventHandler` object is not set to trigger (this must be done by calling an operation on the `TimerEventHandler` itself).
- `unregister()`: this deletes the `TimerEventHandler` object passed as a parameter.
- ✚ `event_time()`: this takes a `TimerEventT` struct as a parameter (a time and event data) and returns the time (an object reference to a `CosTime::UTO` object) at which the associated event was triggered. To implement this operation, the `TimerEventService` object must record the time at which each `TimerEventHander` object has triggered in the past, and the event data associated with it when it triggered. ✚

Interface `TimerEventHandler` (in module `CosTimerEvent`) defines the following attributes and operations:

- Attribute `status`: gives an enumerated value of type `EventStatus`.

- `time_set()`: returns a `boolean` to indicate whether or not the timer is set. If set, it returns the set time as an `out` parameter of type `CosTime::UTO`.
- `set_timer()`: sets the timer to trigger at some future time. The time type (absolute, relative, or periodic) and a value of type `CosTime::UTO` are passed as parameters.
- `cancel_timer()`: cancels the triggering of the timer; returns a `boolean` to indicate whether or not the timer is actually canceled.
- `set_data()`: changes the event data to the value (of type `any`) passed as a parameter.

✚ Secure time values

Operation `CosTime::TimeService::secure_univeral_time()` returns an object reference to a `UTO` object, but only if the Time Service can guarantee that the time has been read and transmitted securely; otherwise it raises the `CosTime::TimeUnavailable` exception. To return a secure time value, a Time Service must ensure that the time source that it reads cannot be manipulated by unauthorized users, and that any time values it transmits cannot be tampered with. ✚

Transmission of time values

Two important issues arise regarding the transmission of time values over a network. Firstly, the estimate of the inaccuracy of a time value may be valid on the machine that calculated that time value, but the inaccuracy estimate may no longer be valid when this value has been transmitted over a network that does not guarantee its transmission delays. This problem can be addressed by giving each machine its own time source, maintained sufficiently accurate for its own needs; or by modifying the inaccuracy of a time value when it is transmitted (if the network delay can be bounded).

Secondly, when an object of type `UTO` is passed as a parameter or return value to an operation, an object reference to an object is transmitted and not a value that can be directly used on the receiving side. If a value is preferred, then the parameter or return type should be `Time::UtcT`, rather than `CosTime::UTO`. The same applies to intervals: if a value is required, then a parameter or return type of `Time::IntervalT` should be used, rather than `CosTime::TIO`.

25 CORBAservices 3

25.1 Property Service

The Property Service allows properties to be associated with objects. Each property is a name—value pair: a string name and a value of type `any`. These properties, unlike attributes, are not part of the type system; in fact, they are the dynamic equivalent of attributes. Unless there is a constraint to the contrary, a property of any type can be added to any object.

Consider an application which defines a type `Document`, with attributes such as `title` and `length`. It is important to realize that these attributes cannot cater for all users of documents. For example, users may need to associate an importance with each document they own. Although it is possible for users to define a derived interface of `Document` and add attributes to this new interface, they may not be able to ensure that all documents they use are of this new type. Also, there will be occasions when it is not appropriate to change the type system to cater for the needs of an individual user. Instead, the Property Service can be used to construct a property with name importance, and some integer or enumerated value. (As we will see, all property values are represented as values of type `any`). Other examples of properties for a document might be its library classification and library unique identifier.

The central interface in the Property Service is `PropertySet`. Instances of this type can contain any number of properties, each with a different name. `PropertySet` defines operations to find the value of a property given its name, to add new properties, to modify the value of an existing property, to list the property names that have been added to the `PropertySet`, and to determine whether or not a `PropertySet` has a property with a specified name. See Section A.7 (p.493) for details of the IDL definitions.

Each object can be associated with zero or more `PropertySet` objects. The Property Service does not define how this association is to be made, and leaves this as an implementation and usage detail. An object can have an attribute of type `PropertySet`, or the Relationship Service (see Section 25.1) could be used to associate an object and its `PropertySet`. Alternatively, some of an application s interfaces may inherit from `PropertySet`. Whatever way is chosen, once an object s `PropertySet` object can be located, property values can be obtained and properties can be added or removed. Each object in an application can have its own `PropertySet`, and it is only convention that determines the set of property names that should appear in the `PropertySet` objects associated with objects of a given type. Each such `PropertySet` object may have a set of mandatory and a set of optional properties, but the Property Service does not enforce these conventions.

✚ If a `PropertySet` contains a property of a given name, it is possible to modify that property value, but only to another value of the same type (that is, an `any` with the same `TypeCode`; see Chapter 14). To change the type, the existing property must be removed and a new one added. ✚

As well as defining operations that allow individual properties to be looked up, added, or removed, `PropertySet` also defines operations to look up, add, or remove a sequence of properties in one step. These operations are straightforward to define, except for defining the exceptions that can arise. The Property Service defines a number of exceptions (`InvalidPropertyName`, `ConflictingProperty`, `PropertyNotFound`, `UnsupportedTypeCode`, `UnsupportedProperty`, `UnsupportedMode`, `FixedProperty`, and `ReadOnlyProperty`) that can be raised by the operations that manipulate a single property. It also defines an exception (`MultipleExceptions`) that can be raised by operations that do batch lookup or modifications. This exception contains a sequence of structures, with each structure containing the name of a property that there was difficulty looking up or modifying, and an indication (an enumerated value) of which exception would have been raised if that property had been looked up or modified individually.

Therefore, if an application calls one of the operations that does a batch look up or modification, it should catch the `MultipleExceptions` exception, and iterate through the sequence of structures to determine which properties could not be looked up or modified, and why.

This complex mechanism for reporting errors is not used for all batch operations that look up or modify a set of properties. Instead, a `boolean` value is returned by the simple batch operations to indicate whether or not all of the batch lookup or modification was successful. If the return value is false, the application can only know which property or properties the operation call failed for by trying to manipulate each property individually.

Property modes

The Property Service also defines interface PropertySetDef, which inherits from Property. Each property in a PropertySetDef can have a mode, which can be one of the following (these are enumerated constants of type PropertyModeType):

- normal: means that there is no restriction on a given property. An application can change its value and also delete it.
- read_only: means that the value of the property cannot be changed, although the property can be deleted.
- fixed_normal: means that the value of the property can be changed, but the property cannot be deleted.
- fixed_readonly: means that the value of the property cannot be changed, nor the property deleted.
- undefined: a property cannot have this mode. Instead, it is used in one of the batch operations, PropertySetDef::get_property_modes(). This operation takes a sequence of property names as an in parameter, and returns a sequence of modes. If one of the specified names is not of a defined property (that is, one that has actually been added to the set), then mode undefined will be returned for that property.

An attempt to modify a read_only or fixed_readonly property raises the ReadOnlyProperty exception. An attempt to delete a read_only or fixed_readonly property raises the FixedProperty exception.

Modes are primarily for use by PropertySetDef and not PropertySet. In particular, the mode of a property cannot be set or read using the operations defined by PropertySet. However, an implementation of the Property Service may define a set of default properties for some or all of the PropertySet objects created, and some of these properties can have modes other than normal. In addition, a set of properties can be specified for a PropertySet when it is being created, and an implementation of the Property Service is allowed to give these a mode other than normal.

Creating PropertySet and PropertySetDef objects

The Property Services defines two factory interfaces, PropertySetFactory and PropertySetDefFactory, which create PropertySet and PropertySetDef objects, respectively. Once created, a PropertySet or PropertySetDef object must be associated with some application-level object, in whatever way the application chooses.

IDL types

The following IDL types are defined by the Property Service (see Section A.7, p.493 for details).

A `Property` contains a name and a value:

```
typedef string PropertyName;
struct Property {
      PropertyName property_name;
      any property_value;
};
```

The modes are defined as:

```
enum PropertyModeType {
      normal, read_only, fixed_normal,
      fixed_readonly, undefined
};
```

Instead of using type `Property`, interface `PropertySetDef` uses an extended structure that contains the mode of the property:

```
struct PropertyDef {
      PropertyName property_name;
      any property_value;
      PropertyModeType property_mode;
};
```

When just the property name and mode are being referred to, interface `PropertySetDef` uses the following structure:

```
struct PropertyMode {
      PropertyName property_name;
      PropertyModeType property_mode;
};
```

In addition, the following sequence types are defined:

```
typedef sequence<PropertyName> PropertyNames;
typedef sequence<Property> Properties;
typedef sequence<PropertyDef> PropertyDefs;
typedef sequence<PropertyMode> PropertyModes;
typedef sequence<TypeCode> PropertyTypes;
```

All of these definitions appear within module `CosPropertyService`.

Interface `PropertySet`

Interface `PropertySet` defines the following operations:

- `define_property()`: defining a property means adding it to a `PropertySet`. This operation takes both a name and a value (of type `any`) and defines a new property; it can be used to change the value of an existing property in the target `PropertySet`, as long as the types of the old and new values are the same.
- `define_properties()`: adds or modifies a sequence of properties to the target `PropertySet`. This raises the `MultipleExceptions` exception if there is any error.
- `get_number_of_properties()`: returns the number of properties in the target `PropertySet`.
- `get_all_property_names()`: this operation has an `out` parameter of type `PropertyNames` (a sequence of property names).

  ✚ The maximum length of sequence that the caller is willing to accept is specified by the `how_many` parameter; if the target `PropertySet` contains more properties, their names are made available through the third parameter, which is of type `PropertyNamesIterator`. The `next_one()` operation can be called on the iterator to retrieve, in turn, each of the remaining property names. ✚

- `get_property_value()`: this operation returns (as an `any`) the value of a property whose name is passed as a parameter.
- `get_properties()`: this operation takes as an `in` parameter a sequence of property names (`PropertyNames`), and has an `out` parameter of type `Properties`, which gives the name and value of each requested property. If all of the requested properties can be returned, the operation returns true; otherwise it returns false.
- `get_all_properties()`: this operation has an `out` parameter of type `Properties` (a sequence of `Property`).

  ✚ The maximum length of sequence that the caller is willing to accept is specified by the `how_many` parameter; if the target `PropertySet` contains more properties, their names and values are made available through the third parameter, which is of type `PropertiesIterator`. The `next_one()` operation can be called on the iterator to retrieve, in turn, each of the remaining properties (values of type `Property`). ✚

- `delete_property()`: this deletes a specified property from the target `PropertySet`.
- `delete_properties()`: this deletes the specified properties (a sequence of property names) from the target `PropertySet`. It raises the `MultipleExceptions` exception if there is any error.
- `delete_all_properties()`: this deletes all properties from the target `PropertySet`. If returns true if all of the properties could be removed; and returns false otherwise.
- `is_property_defined()`: returns true if the specified property is defined; and returns false otherwise.

Interface `PropertiesIterator` defines the following three operations:

- `next_one()`: returns, as an `out` parameter, the next `Property` in the iterator. Returns true if there is such a property; and returns false otherwise.
- `next_n()`: this takes an `in` parameter of `how_many` that indicates the number of properties to return; these are returned in an `out` parameter of type `Properties`. Returns true if any property can be returned; and returns false otherwise.
- `reset()`: sets the iterator to point once again at its first property.

Interface `PropertyNamesIterator` defines the same operations, except that property names are returned instead of `Property` structures.

Interface `PropertySetDef`

Interface `PropertySetDef` defines the following operations, in addition to those defined in interface `PropertySet`:

- `get_allowed_property_types()`: returns, as an `out` parameter, a sequence of property value types that the target `PropertySetDef` object can handle. The set of types can be constrained when a `PropertySetDef` object is created: its factory takes a sequence of types as one of its parameters. If this sequence is empty then the creator chooses to place no such constraints on the types of values. In addition to restrictions made when a `PropertySetDef` is created, the implementer of the Property Service may restrict the set of types, to make the service easier to implement.
- `get_allowed_properties()`: returns, as an `out` parameter, a sequence of property names, value types, and modes (this is a sequence of structures of type `PropertyDef`).

- `define_property_with_mode()`: adds a property with a specified mode; or it can change the value and/or mode of an existing property in the target `PropertySetDef` as long as the types of the old and new values are the same.
- `define_properties_with_modes()`: adds or modifies a sequence of properties, giving each a specified value and mode.
- `get_property_mode()`: returns the mode of the specified property.
- `get_property_modes()`: returns the mode of each of the specified properties. This returns true if the mode of each of the specified properties can be obtained; or it returns false if any error occurs.
- `set_property_mode()`: changes the mode of the specified property.
- `set_property_modes()`: changes the modes of each of the specified properties. This returns true if the mode of each of the specified properties can be changed; or it returns false if any error occurs. ✚

25.2 Relationship Service

In most applications, objects do not exist in isolation but they are related to each other in ways determined by the object-oriented analysis of the system. In some of these applications, these relationships must be visible at the CORBA level rather than being internal to a server. In such cases, these relationships must be specified in a manner that is independent of implementation features, such as the programming language, operating system, or Database Management System (DBMS), if one is being used. In other words, the relationships must be specified in IDL. It would have been possible to define a new language in which relationships could be defined, but instead the members of OMG have defined the Relationship Service to provide a set of standard IDL interfaces in which relationships can be defined. This section describes these interfaces and how they can be used to define many forms of relationships between objects.

Throughout this section, it should be remembered that many applications can use other, more concrete, facilities for defining relationships between objects in a server. In particular, a Relational Database Management System (RDBMS) or an Object Database Management System (ODBMS) can be used to store a server s data; and these define their own ways of recording relationships.

Applications therefore have a choice of whether or not to use the Relationship Service. In making this choice, the first decision for an application is whether or not it needs to make the relationships between its objects visible using IDL. If not, then the Relationship Service should not be used (instead, any internal approach, such as the use of a DBMS, should be considered). If it should, then an application has a choice between using the Relationship Service or making the relationships visible using its objects' operations and attributes. These operation and attribute definitions would be chosen following the analysis phase for the application. For example, our `Booking` objects could have an attribute that returns a reference to their `FrontOffice` object.

One of the main characteristics of the Relationship Service is that it allows relationships to be defined between objects without reflecting these relationships in the IDL definitions of these objects themselves. Objects can therefore be related in ways that were not considered when their interfaces were defined. For example, a `Booking` and a `FrontOffice` can be related without having this reflected in their IDL definitions.

It should also be remembered that this section describes the specification of the Relationship Service, and that implementers of this service have been given a great deal of freedom in how it should be implemented. Relationships defined using the Relationship Service can be implemented using CORBA objects to record individual relationships, or an underlying RDBMS or ODBMS could be used. The Relationship Service is best viewed as giving clients a consistent view of relationships, independent of whether or not a DBMS is used in the server (or what programming language or operating system is used).

To begin the explanation of the Relationship Service, consider the following types of relationships:

- A *person* Owns *cars*.
- A *document* Contains *figures*.
- A *person* Checks Out *books* from *libraries*.

Relations have a number of important properties:

(1) Type: each relationship is between specified types of objects.

(2) Role: each object in a relationship plays a particular role. For example, in the relationship shown between people and cars, a person plays the Owner role, and the car plays the Owned By role.

(3) Degree: this is the number of roles required in a relationship of a given type. The Owns relationship is of degree 2; and the Checks Out relationship is of degree 3. A relationship of degree 2 is called a binary relationship.

(4) Cardinality: this is a property of each role within a relationship and it determines the number of relationships of a given type that can be associated with a given role. A person can own one or

more cars, so the cardinality of the Owner role in the Owns relationship is minimum zero and maximum many (or more clearly, there is no maximum). Further, a car can be owned by only one person (in this example), so the cardinality of the Owned By role of the Owns relationship is minimum 1 and maximum 1.

(5) Attributes: a relationship can have attributes. For example, the Owns relationship between a person and a car can specify the year of purchase. Clearly, this attribute could be made an attribute of the car, but it is clearer to view it as an attribute of the relationship (and in any case, the relationship and its year_of_purchase attribute may have to be established without changing the IDL interface of the car). The year_of_purchase attribute cannot be moved to the person, because a person can own many cars.

Relationships and roles

The key interfaces defined by the Relationship Service are `Relationship` and `Role`. Instances of these classes are independent (first class) objects with their own IDL interfaces (but, as stated above, they might be implemented in optimized ways).

A role object contains an object reference to a single application-level object (such as a person). The object it refers to is known as its **related object**. A relationship object contains object references to the set of role objects that it relates (it does not contain references to the related objects themselves). Of course, a role object and a related object can be one and the same, because the IDL interface for the related object could inherit from `CosRelationship::Role`. Using the Owns relationship as an example, Figure 25.1 shows the graphical notation used in the standard.

Relationships are immutable: once a relationship has been established, it cannot refer to other role objects. Any degree of relationship can be supported, but the number of relationships with degrees higher than three is likely to be very small.

Applications define particular relationship types by defining interfaces that inherit from interfaces `Relationship` and `Role`; for example:

```
interface Person { /* . . . . */ };
interface Car { /* . . . . */ };

interface Owns : CosRelationship::Relationship {};
interface Owner : CosRelationship::Role {};
interface OwnedBy : CosRelationship::Role {};
```

Interfaces `Relationship` and `Role` are defined in module `CosRelationship`. The detailed IDL definitions are shown in Section A.8 (p.497).

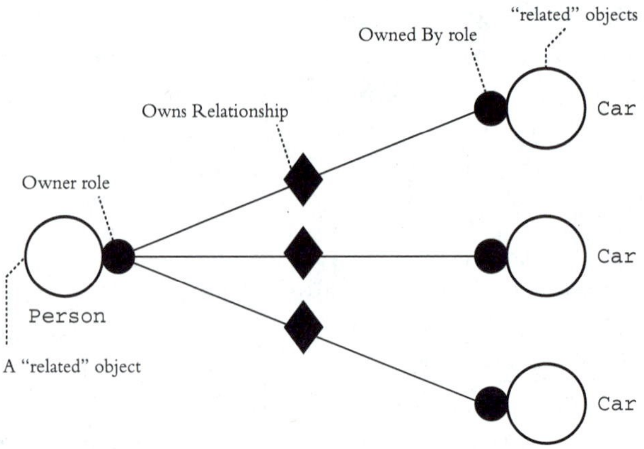

Figure 25.1 *Example relationship.*

To set up a relationship between a `Person` and a `Car`, a programmer would carry out the following actions:

(1) Create the role objects: an `Owner` object (its related object would be the `Person`), and an `OwnedBy` object (its related object would be the `Car`).

(2) Create the `Owns` relationship object, telling this about the two role objects.

A role object is initially unconnected to any relationship object (but it must always be connected to its related object). When a relationship is created, each of the roles to be related must be specified (in an IDL sequence). The newly created relationship object informs each role about the association (by calling the `Role::link()` operation on each role object). Each role object enforces its maximum cardinality constraint by raising an exception in its `link()` operation if more than the allowed number of relationship objects try to involve it in an association.

For example, if a second attempt is made to create an `Owns` relationship object involving the same `OwnedBy` role object, the role object would raise an exception when the second relationship object tried to involve it in the relationship, and the relationship object would propagate this to the application. There is no difficulty in involving the `Owner` role in other `Owns` relationships.

The minimum cardinality cannot be enforced in the same way. For example, if the minimum cardinality is not zero then it will be violated when a role is created (because it will not be associated with any relationship). Therefore, the minimum cardinality must be checked explicitly by calling an operation on a role (`Role::check_minimum_cardinality()`); this returns false if the minimum cardinality is not fulfilled.

Type safety is ensured in two ways. Firstly, a relationship knows the type of role objects that it must relate. Secondly, each role type has a set (actually, a sequence) of related object types that its instances can reference.

Attributes on relationships are handled by adding attributes to the derived interfaces of `Relationship`; for example:

```
interface Owns : CosRelationship::Relationship {
     readonly attribute string date_of_purchase;
};
```

Attributes can also be added to role objects.

Interfaces: overall definitions

The types defined in the Relationship Service are defined within module `CosRelationship`:

```
module CosRelationships {

      interface RelationshipFactory;
      interface Relationship;

      interface RoleFactory;
      interface Role;

      interface RelationshipIterator;

      // A number of typedefs and struct definitions
      // not shown here.
};
```

Creating a relationship

Each relationship type (that is, each derived interface of `Relationship`) must have an associated factory object of type `RelationshipFactory`. The `create()` operation on a particular factory is used to create relationships of a particular type. Each factory object knows the important properties of the type of relationships it creates, including:

- The type identifier of the derived interface of `Relationship` that it creates.
- The degree of the relationship (the number of roles involved).
- The name of each role (as a string) and the type of the derived interface of interface `Role` involved. This information is kept as a sequence of structs, with each struct holding a string and a type identifier. For the `Owns` relationship, this sequence would hold

the string "Owner" and the type identifier of the `Owner` role, followed by the string "OwnedBy" and the type identifier of the `OwnedBy` role.

These properties are available as `readonly` attributes of each relationship factory. Once a relationship type is defined, an instance of `RelationshipFactory` should be created and given this property information. Relationships are then created using the `create()` operation on the factory.

Creating a role

The creation of a role follows a similar pattern. Each role type (that is, each derived interface of `Role`) must have an associated factory object of type `RoleFactory`. The `create_role()` operation on a particular factory is used to create roles of a particular type. Each factory object knows the important properties of the type of role it creates, including:

- The type identifier of the derived interface of `Role` that it creates.
- The minimum and maximum cardinalities.
- The legal types of related object (the related object of a role must be of one of these types).

These properties are available as `readonly` attributes of each factory. Once a role type is defined, an instance of `RoleFactory` should be created and given this property information. Roles are then created using the `create_role()` operation on the factory.

✚ Interfaces: `RelationshipFactory` and `Relationship`

The attributes of a `RelationshipFactory` object reflect the important properties of the relationships that it creates: type of relationship created, degree, and name and type information for each role. Its single operation (`create()`) takes a sequence of role objects and returns a new relationship object that relates each of these. The sequence of role objects is specified as a sequence of structs, with each struct giving the name of the role and an object reference to the role object that plays that role (the role names must match those that the factory expects).

The `Relationship` interface has one attribute, `NamedRoles`, which gives the roles that a `Relationship` relates. This attribute is a sequence of structs, each struct giving a role name and an object reference to a role object. Its single operation, `destroy()`, allows a relationship to be deleted.

Interfaces: `RoleFactory` and `Roles`

A `RoleFactory` object has four attributes that record the important properties of the `Role` objects it creates: the type identifier of the role type that it creates, the minimum and maximum cardinalities, and the allowed types for the related object of a role of this type (the allowed types are recorded as a sequence of type identifiers). Its single operation, `create_role()`, allows a role to be created by specifying its related object.

The `Role` interface has a single attribute, `related_object`, that records the object reference of a role's related object. Interface `Role` has eight operations:

(1) `get_other_related_object()` returns the related object pointed to by one of the other role objects involved in the relationship. The parameters are the relationship that is being used and the name of the role whose related object is being sought.

(2) `get_other_role()` returns the object reference of a role object involved in the relationship. The parameters are the relationship that is being used and the name of the role that is being sought. Operation `get_other_related_object()` is similar to this operation except that it returns the related object rather than the role object.

(3) `get_relationships()` returns all of the relationships that the target role is involved in. This takes one `in` and two `out` parameters. References to the relationship objects are returned in a sequence `out` parameter, and the only `in` parameter specifies the maximum allowed length of this sequence. If there are more relationships beyond this maximum then the second `out` parameter will refer to a `RelationshipIterator` object that can be used to iterate through the remaining references to relationships.

(4) `destroy_relationships()` calls the `destroy()` operation on each of the relationships that the target role is involved in.

(5) `destroy()` deletes the role, but this is only valid if the role is currently not involved in any relationships.

(6) `check_minimum_cardinality()` returns true if the target role's minimum cardinality restriction is currently fulfilled; returns false otherwise.

(7) `link()`: this operation is for use by a relationship object, not by an application. It is called when a relationship involving this role object is created. It is given a reference to the relationship and the name and identity of each of the roles. It can reject its involvement in the new relationship if, for example, the maximum cardinality constraints would be violated; and if this happens then the relationship cannot be constructed.

(8) `unlink()`: this operation is for use by a relationship object, not by an application. It is called when a relationship involving this role is deleted.

A `RelationshipIterator` object can be returned (as an `out` parameter) by the `Role::get_relationships()` operation. It supports three operations. `next_one()` returns (as an `out` parameter) the next relationship in the set that involves the role; it returns true if there is a next one and false otherwise. `next_n()` returns (as an `out` parameter) a sequence of such relationships. The maximum allowed length of this sequence is specified as an `in` parameter. This operation returns true if there is at least one relationship to return, and false otherwise. `destroy()` deletes the target `Relationship Iterator`.

Levels of support

In fact, the Relationship Service defines three levels of service that can be provided by an implementation, each level extending the previous one with services that are useful for a subset of applications. Each implementation of the server must implement the Base level; the other two levels are optional:

(1) Base: defines interfaces `Relationship`, `Role`, `RelationshipFactory`, `RoleFactory`, and `RelationshipIterator`. This level is mandatory for any implementation of the Relationship Service.

(2) Graph: defines nodes and traversal objects.

(3) Specific: defines two particular relationship types: contains and contained. These can be used to define relationships such as those between a document and a figure that is contained within it.

The Graph level allows the relationships that an object is involved in to be determined and traversed. It defines an interface `CosGraphs::Node` that a related object can inherit from, and this interface allows the roles and relationships that an object is involved in to be determined. Alternatively, an instance of `CosGraphs::Node` can be interposed between a role and a related object, so that the related object itself does not need to be modified to inherit from `CosGraphs::Node`.

The Specific level defines interfaces `CosContainment::Relationship`, `CosContainment::ContainsRole`, and `CostContainment::ContainedInRole`. These can be used to define a relationship between two objects where one contains or owns the other. Of course, these relationship types could be defined at the application level, but they are included in the Relationship Service because they are commonly used. ✚

25.3 Concurrency Control Service

Access to an object by concurrent threads or transactions must be controlled to prevent its state becoming corrupted. The Concurrency Control Service provides a number of IDL interfaces that an object can use to achieve this. These interfaces are normally not visible to clients, because objects usually encapsulate their concurrency control for similar reasons that they encapsulate their state (to allow clients to be simple, and to isolate them from any changes to the policy or implementation details). Therefore, when an operation is called on an object, that operation s implementation may apply concurrency control rules during its execution. The Concurrency Control Service must coordinate with the Object Transaction Service if both are being used for the same objects.

Not all objects need to control concurrent access; and not all objects that require such control need to use the Concurrency Control Service (instead, a more advanced facility can be used, such as Scheduling Predicates (McHale, 1994) or Guards (Atkinson, 1990), or the normal concurrency control provided by a DBMS in the case of persistent objects).

Locks are used as the concurrency control facility in the Concurrency Control Service. An operation s implementation may request a lock of a particular type at the start or during its code, and this request will be blocked if the requested lock would conflict with one already held. The normal read (`R`) and write (`W`) locks are supported, as well as three more sophisticated locks.

There is one unusual feature: locks can be associated with threads or with transactions. In the former case, an object explicitly releases the locks that a thread holds when those locks are no longer needed. In the latter case, locks are associated with a transaction, and normally these locks are automatically released when that transaction commits or rolls back. Locks can also be released early by a transaction, but it is well known that this breaks the serializability guarantees required by many applications. The standard allows the mixing of the two types of clients (thread clients and transaction clients) for one object.

If one client (a thread or transaction) has a lock on an object, then an attempt by another client to acquire a conflicting lock on that object will block until sufficient locks are released to allow the attempt to continue. To record the set of locks held on an object, it can have an associated `LockSet` object. The `LockSet` object records the currently held set of locks, and supports operations to acquire and release locks. Concurrency control is actually achieved because the operation (on `Lockset`) to acquire a lock blocks the caller until the requested lock can be granted.

In fact, associating a `LockSet` object with an application-level object is just one possible level of granularity. Instead, an object may have more than one `LockSet` object associated with it, or a group of objects may share a `LockSet` object. The standard states that each protected **resource** must have one associated `LockSet` object: where a resource can be an object, part of an object, or a group of objects. (This use of the term resource is different from that used in the Transaction Service; Section 23.3)

The standard does not dictate that an object must encapsulate its concurrency control from its clients. In fact, the `LockSet` object or objects associated with an object can be made visible to clients, which can call the operations to acquire and release locks. However, this approach has the normal disadvantages of breaking the encapsulation of an object. It is particularly dangerous in this case because the operations on a `LockSet` object are very flexible, and serializability can be easily broken by misuse of the interface.

Lock modes

In addition to the Read (`R`) and Write (`W`) lock modes, the Concurrency Control Service supports the lock modes Update (`U`), Intention Read (`IR`), and Intention Write (`IW`). `IR` and `IW` allow for variable granularity locking, especially for objects nested within each other. A `U` lock should be acquired when the object is only to be read at this time but with the likelihood that it will have to be written in the future by the same thread or transaction. Each of these lock types has been used by many other concurrency control facilities and studied in depth in the literature (Bernstein *et al.*, 1987; Gray and Reuter, 1993).

The lock table for these lock modes is shown in Table 25.1.

Table 25.1 *Lock compatibility.*

Granted mode	**Requested mode**				
	Intention read (`IR`)	Read (`R`)	Upgrade (`U`)	Intention write (`IW`)	Write (`W`)
Intention read (`IR`)					★
Read (`R`)				★	★
Upgrade (`U`)			★	★	★
Intention write (`IW`)		★	★		★
Write (`W`)	★	★	★	★	★

The ★ character indicates a conflict.

✚ The intention modes are provided to improve concurrency and reduce the overhead when locks are acquired on objects that are nested. Consider a book, made up of chapters and sections, being written by a number of authors. Authors can acquire a lock on the whole book, a chapter, or a section. Acquiring a read or write lock on the book provides the corresponding access to all of the chapters and sections. Acquiring a read or write lock on a chapter provides the corresponding access to all of the sections in that chapter. Therefore, some simple mechanism is required to prevent one author acquiring a lock on an entity when a higher or lower entity is locked in a conflicting mode: acquiring a lock on a chapter when the book is locked in a conflicting mode; acquiring a lock on the book when a chapter is locked in a conflicting mode; acquiring a lock on a section when that section's chapter or the book are locked in a conflicting mode; acquiring a lock on the book or a chapter when some contained section is locked in a conflicting mode. The `IR` and `IW` locks work as follows to prevent such concurrent access.

Before a section can be locked in `R` mode (similarly, `W` mode), an `IR` (respectively, `IW`) lock must be acquired firstly on the book and then on the section's chapter. If another client has a conflicting lock on the book or the chapter, the eventual granting of the `R` mode lock will be delayed. Once it is granted, no client can acquire a conflicting lock on the section's chapter or on the book. Two different authors can acquire locks on different sections in the same chapter, or one can acquire a lock on a chapter and the other a lock on a section in a different chapter.

Similarly, before a chapter can be locked in `R` mode (similarly, `W` mode), an `IR` (respectively, `IW`) lock must first be acquired on the book.

Multiple possession semantics

Unlike some other concurrency control systems, the Concurrency Control Service allows a client to hold many locks on the same resource at the same time. The alternative is to allow a client to hold one lock at a time, and if that client requests another lock on the same resource, the two locks are combined into one (the lock mode that is at least as strong as the new and the old locks). In the Concurrency Control Service, a client can also hold more than one lock of the same mode: a reference count is maintained for each lock mode.

Transactions

The Concurrency Control Service must be coordinated with the Object Transaction Service where both are supported. In particular, the Concurrency Control Service must be aware of when a lock is being requested by a transaction (rather than a non-transactional thread), and be able to release all locks held by a transaction when it commits or rolls back. It does this by associating a `LockCoordinator` object with each transaction: each `LockCoordinator` object knows which `LockSet` objects its transaction holds locks on, and it releases these locks when its transaction commits or rolls back.

Nested transactions are supported: a lock request made by a nested transaction does not conflict with any locks held by any of its parent transactions. If a child transaction commits, then the locks it held must be retained until all of its parent transactions commit or rollback. ✚

Interfaces

The central interface in the Concurrency Control Service is `LockSet`, which defines the following operations:

- `lock()` is used to request a lock in a specified mode.
- `try_lock()` is used to poll whether a lock of a specified mode can be acquired. It returns a `boolean`.
- ✚ `unlock()` is used to release a lock in a specified mode (the reference count is decremented if the lock is held more than once by the caller). This operation is normally not required when the Concurrency Control Service is used in conjunction with the Transaction Service. In particular, for transaction clients, all locks are normally released at transaction termination and not before.
- `change_mode()` requests that a lock of a given mode be changed to another specified mode. The reference count of the first is decremented

and the second incremented. Simple uses of the Concurrency Control Service do not require this operation.

- `get_coordinator()` returns the object reference of the `LockCoordinator` of a specified transaction. This lock coordinator will be informed of the transaction's termination, so that it can release all of its locks.

Typically, this interface is used by a resource, rather than by clients. The details are shown in Section A.9 (p.501).

25.4 Persistent Object Service

The Persistent Object Service defines interfaces that can be used to encapsulate the mechanisms for making objects persistent. The actual mechanisms are not specified; instead, this CORBAservice allows for a very wide range of mechanisms, including Relational Database Management Systems (RDBMSs), Object Database Management Systems (ODBMSs), and flat files. Therefore, the Persistent Object Service provides a framework for persistence, rather than offering a detailed specification.

Persistent objects are considered to have **dynamic state** and **persistent state**. An object s dynamic state represents its value in transient storage and is directly manipulated by the code that implements its operations/attributes. Its persistent state is stored in non-volatile storage and survives from one server run to another, and it survives machine crashes. (Nevertheless, the Persistent Object Service does not address transaction issues; instead, these are addressed by the Object Transaction Service; Section 23.3.)

Before continuing with the explanation of the Persistent Object Service, it must be remembered that there is no requirement for a persistent CORBA object to use the Persistent Object Service to implement its persistence. The Persistent Object Service is just one standardized approach, and any other facility can be used. In particular, the CORBA standard specifies a second approach: one of its central components, the Basic Object Adapter, to be replaced or augmented to provide persistence. The Basic Object Adapter is a component of the core CORBA system on the server side, and it is responsible for communicating between the ORB and the objects being invoked by clients. Its roles include finding the target object of an invocation (and handling any object references passed as parameters), determining what operation/attribute to call, and actually making the call on the target object.

The Basic Object Adapter can be replaced or augmented to give a Database Adapter that handles the fact that the target object (or one of the objects whose references are passed as parameters) may be in a database. Figure 25.2 shows how a Database Adapter can load a target object from the database when it is required, and hide this step from the client making the operation call.

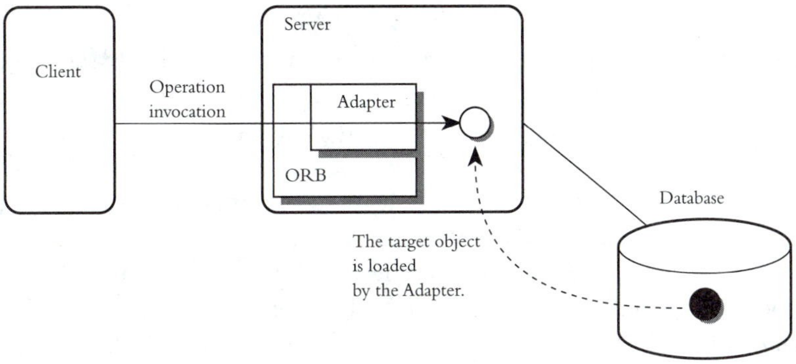

Figure 25.2 *Actions of a Database Adapter.*

As we will see, the Database Adapter approach has a much simpler architecture than that of the Persistent Object Service. Chapter 22 discusses Database Adapters in more detail. The Persistent Object Service is currently being redefined by the members of the OMG – to increase the importance of Database Adapters and the ODMG standard. The new standard will address the weaknesses discussed here, and provide much needed improvements.

Architecture of the Persistent Object Service

The architecture of the Persistent Object Service is shown in Figure 25.3.

Each object has an associated persistent identifier (PID). In contrast to an normal object identifier (which identifies an object itself), an object's PID identifies its persistent state within its chosen Datastore. Each PID holds the identity of the chosen Datastore and of the object within that Datastore. An object and its PID can be associated in any way – this is an implementation decision within the Persistent Object Service. For example, the state of an object can include its PID.

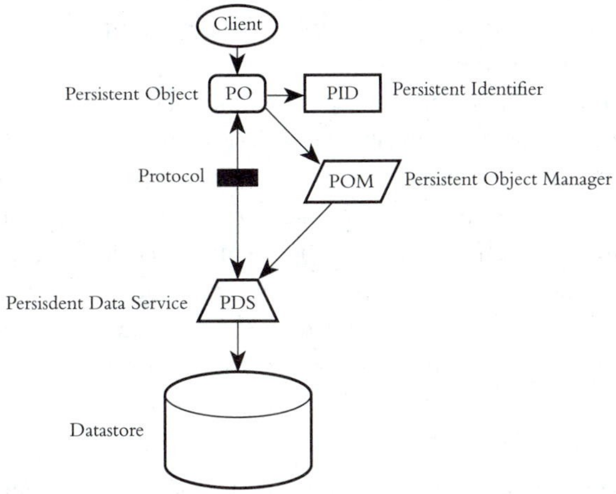

Figure 25.3 *Architecture of the Persistent Object Service.*

The role of the Persistent Data Service (PDS) is to interface between an object and its associated Datastore to actually store or restore the persistent state to or from the Datastore. Any number of PDSs can coexist in the system, each managing a different Datastore or providing a different way to use a common Datastore.

It is the interaction between the PDS and a persistent object which allows an object s dynamic state to be stored or restored to or from its persistent state. The rules under which this interaction occurs are known as a **protocol**. Three protocols are suggested (in different degrees of completeness) by the Persistent Object Service specification, but others are allowed. Standardized or new protocols can take many forms, including an IDL interface that the PDS must support in order for a persistent object to store/restore its data; an IDL interface that a persistent object must support in order for the PDS to extract the data from the persistent object and write data to it; and virtual memory control by the PDS to allow it to write/read pages of virtual memory to and from the Datastore.

In the Persistent Object Service, either the client of a persistent object or the object itself can decide when to store or restore the persistent state. (The benefits of each approach will be explained shortly.) When either decides to store or restore the persistent state, the persistent object passes the request to the Persistent Object Manager (POM), which decides which PDS to choose. Note that the persistent object itself does not make this choice. The indirection allows an object to move to another PDS without changing its own code or state, thereby providing some of the flexibility required in order to move an object from one Datastore to another.

The main potential advantage of the Persistent Object Service is that it defines a flexible framework that caters for many of the ways that can be envisaged for storing and restoring persistent objects. It also allows objects to migrate from one Datastore to another without changing the code of clients that use them. It is important to note, however, that arbitrary migration of objects between Datastores is not possible. To move from one PDS to another, an object must support the protocol supported by the new PDS (or at least one of the protocols if more than one is supported by the new PDS). Typically, a persistent object supported by the Persistent Object Service will be explicitly coded to support one protocol.

The Database Adapter mechanism for supporting persistence has no inherent notion of migration between Datastores, but it does isolate a client from all details of the Datastore chosen to store a persistent object. The real difference is that a Database Adapter makes no attempt to hide the chosen Datastore from a persistent object itself. Instead, there is normally a tight connection between the code for a persistent object and a DBMS. The disadvantage of this is that migration is difficult; the advantages are simplicity and the ability to take advantage of the details of commercial DBMSs. The Database Adapter approach appears to be more commercially viable.

Client or object control of persistence

The Persistent Object Service allows a client to control when a persistent object stores and restores its data to and from its persistent state in its chosen Datastore. It defines an IDL interface, `CosPersistencePO::PO`, which provides the operations (and, in particular, operations `store()` and `restore()`) that the client can call to achieve this. (The full interface is shown in Section A.9, p.501.) A persistent object s IDL interface can inherit from `CosPersistencePO::PO` in order to allows its clients to call these operations; and a client can use the Interface Repository to determine whether or not a given object supports the `CosPersistencePO::PO` interface (or, more simply, it can try to narrow an object reference to this type; see Section 4.4.3, p.100). A persistent object is not obliged to support this interface: if it does not, then it is expected to make its own decisions about when to store and restore its state.

Providing these operations increases the flexibility of clients in using a persistent object, but it also substantially increases their complexity. Rather than supporting the `CosPersistencePO::PO` interface, it will frequently be better for the designer of an interface to a persistent object to provide (higher level) application-specific operations that trigger the storing or restoring of the object. Another useful high-level approach is to rely on the integration of the Persistent Object Service and the Object Transaction Service, so that objects are stored at the end of a transaction, and restored when they are next required in a future transaction.

Interface `CosPersistencePO::PO` provides three other operations: `connect()` establishes a connection between a persistent object and its underlying PDS and Datastore; `disconnect()` ends this connection; `delete()` removes the object s persistent state from the Datastore.

Interfaces to POM and PDS

The five operations, `store()`, `restore()`, `connect()`, `disconnect()` and `delete()`, also make up the interfaces to the POM and the PDS. If the client calls one of these operations on a persistent object, or if a persistent object decides itself that this action is required, then the persistent object will call the corresponding operation on the POM, which will locate the chosen PDS and pass the corresponding operation call to it. The PDS carries out (possibly in conjunction with the persistent object itself) the work required to store or restore the persistent object to the Datastore.

The role of the POM is simply to decide which PDS to pass each call to. It must know what PDSs exist, what protocol(s) each supports and what Datastore(s) each provides access to. For each persistent object, the POM must be able to determine the protocol and Datastore it is using, and hence determine the PDS to route calls to. The identity of an object s Datastore is easily found: it must be encoded in its PID. The Persistent Object Service specification does not state how an object s Protocol can be determined: for example, it could be encoded in the object s PID, or simply determined from the object s type.

The Persistent Object Service specification does not say how the POM is to be told what PDSs exist, or how to know which protocol(s) and Datastore(s) each supports. This information might be given to the POM by providing it with a configuration file, or by giving it an IDL interface that can be called by each available PDS to register its protocol(s) and Datastore(s).

Protocols

The Persistent Object Service specifies three Protocols: Direct Access (PDS_DA) protocol, ODMG-93 protocol, and Dynamic Data Object protocol. The first and last are defined in detail, but the ODMG-93 protocol is only mentioned as a possibility, without any details. Other protocols can be added in private or public standards.

✚ In the `PDS_DA` protocol, the PDS is of type `PDS_DA` (which inherits from `CosPersistencePDS::PDS`). Each persistent object is stored using one or more **data objects** (maybe as a rooted graph) held by the PDS, which allows them to be read or written. Each data object has an application interface defined in a language known as DDL (Data Definition Language), which is a simple subset of IDL in which all interfaces consist only of attributes (inheritance can also be used). (A data object's interface can also inherit from interface `CosPersistencePDS_DA::DAObject`, shown in Section A.9, p.501.) Once a persistent object has located its data object(s), it can use the attributes to read or write its persistent state.

The following example DDL might be used for part of a cinema application:

```
// DDL
interface CinemaDataObject {
          readonly attribute string name;
          readonly attribute char lastRow;
          readonly attribute long seatsPerRow;
};
```

Remember that this definition is part of the implementation of the persistence required in the application, and not part of the interfaces visible to the clients. Whereas IDL is used to define an object's external interface, DDL is used to define its storage, which is not visible to clients.

A persistent cinema object can locate its `CinemaDataObject` data object and use the attributes of this to read or update its persistent state. In this case, it is likely that the cinema object will be coded with explicit knowledge of the attributes of the `CinemaDataObject` interface. Alternatively, it could use the Interface Repository and DII to understand and use the DDL interface. The Interface Repository and DII are in fact overly flexible in this case. Therefore, the Persistent Object Service also defines an interface, `DynamicAttributeAccess`, that a data object can optionally inherit from. If it does then it has three extra operations: `attribute_names()` returns a sequence of attribute names in a DDL interface; `attribute_get()` takes the name of one of these attributes and returns a CORBA `any` value (giving the type and value of the attribute); and `attribute_set()` takes the name of an attribute and a CORBA `any` value.

Note that the protocol between the persistent object and the Datastore is partly defined by fixed IDL interfaces (such as that of the `PDS_DA` interface), and partly by the DDL definitions of data objects. Note also that a persistent object is the active player in this protocol: it calls the `PDS_DA` interface and reads and writes the DDL attributes.

The ODMG-93 protocol extends the PDS_DA protocol by allowing the interfaces to data objects to be defined in the ODMG-93 definition language, ODL (Object Definition Language). Like IDL, ODL allows interfaces with attributes and operations to be defined, but it has some special database facilities such as allowing keys and inverse relationships to be defined. As mentioned earlier, this protocol is not defined in detail.

The final protocol currently defined by the Persistent Object Service is the Dynamic Data Object protocol. It is also based on the notion of data objects, but each dynamic data object has a very flexible structure, consisting of a PID, an object type, and a set of data items. Each data item has a name, a value, and a set of properties. Each property has a property name and a value. The IDL interface (`DDO`) of a Dynamic Data Object provides operations to allow any chosen property to be read or written.

25.5 Query Service

The Query Service defines a very general facility for querying collections of objects. Given a collection (an object of type `CosQueryCollection::Collection`), an application can issue a query against this object, and then process the results of the query. Collections contain objects (or in some cases, records), and a query can refer to all aspects of such objects, in particular to their attributes and operations, when searching a collection. The Query Service cannot allow a client to bypass object encapsulation, by allowing it to view the implementation of an object rather than just its interface.

Nevertheless, the Query Service itself can be given special knowledge of how a collection of objects is implemented. In particular, the Query Service allows queries on large collections of structured data to be efficient. In other words, it allows a collection to maintain whatever indices it requires, and to store its objects in whatever format is best suited to it. For example, a collection might just store references to its objects, and have to iterate through each object to process a query. Alternatively, it can store some or all of the objects data in efficient indices. Such decisions are not dictated by the Query Service. It is also important that the collections and queries defined by the Query Service can be implemented using an underlying DBMS — in particular, an RDBMS or an OODBMS.

The Query Service defines a simple `Collection` data type. This allows objects to be added and removed in various ways. To allow a collection to be iterated over, the Query Service defines interface `Iterator`. Among other operations, this interface defines operation `next()`, which can be used to retrieve each member of a collection exactly once. Collections are not limited to type extents (a type extent is a collection that holds all instances of a given type). Instead, an application can create a collection and add whatever members it wishes.

The Query Service does not define a new query language. This is an important decision, one that reflects the fact that there are a number of such languages to choose from at present, and that the standards bodies and DBMS vendors are actively extending, and even merging, these languages. In these circumstances, it would not have been sensible for the Query Service to introduce a new language that would have to be related to the others and also kept up to date with continued research.

A query is passed as a string to the Query Service, which in turn passes this string to the underlying query evaluator, either to a specially written one or to the query facility of an underlying DBMS. The Query Service does not dictate how such strings are constructed: for example, this might be done using a graphical query system, or might be statically built into an application.

Although the query language is not dictated by the Query Service, each compliant implementation must support at least one of the following two languages:

- The SQL-92 query language. This is defined in ANSI (1993) and is supported by many RDBMSs.
- OQL-93. This is defined in Cattell (1994) and is supported or will be supported by many OODBMSs. (In fact, it is legal for an implementation of the Query Service to support just the subset known as the OQL-93 Basic Query Language.)

Future versions of the Query Service may be able to mandate a single non-optional language that can cater properly for RDBMSs and OODBMSs.

Collections and iterators

The Query Service defines only a single top-level `Collection` interface. Because of its simplicity, it is straightforward to map other collection types to interface `Collection`, or to derive richer types from it.

Interface `Iterator` is defined to allow an application to iterate through the members of a collection. For an ordered collection, the members will be iterated over in a defined order. In an unordered collection, the members will be iterated through in any order, but each member will be visited only once. If a member is removed from, or added to, a collection, some or all of its iterators at that time can be invalidated. Once an iterator is made invalid, it must be reset before being used again; resetting an iterator has a side effect of starting it at the first object in its collection.

An `Iterator` is created by calling an operation (`create_iterator()`) on a `Collection`, and it provides the following operations (see Section A.11, p.506 for details):

- `next()`: this returns, as a value of type `any`, the next member of a collection. An exception is raised if the iterator is invalid (if a member has been added to or removed from the collection), or if there is no next member.
- `reset()`: restarts the iterator to the start of the collection, and makes the iterator valid if it was previously invalid.
- `more()`: returns True if and only if the iterator has not returned the last member of the collection.

Note that an `Iterator` is tied to one collection for its lifetime.

Interface `Collection` defines the following attribute and operations (for all of the operations that modify the target collection, the implementation of the collection may decide not to make the specified change and instead raise the `ElementInvalid` exception; this can be done if the target collection is an intermediate result of a query that the implementation of the Query Service does not allow modifications to):

- Attribute `cardinality`: returns the number of members in the collection.
- `add_element()`: adds the specified value (of type `any`) to the target collection. If the element is added, all iterators on the target collection are marked as invalid.
- `add_all_elements()`: the parameter to this operation is a collection, and all of its elements are added to the target collection. If any elements are added, all iterators on the target collection are marked as invalid.
- `insert_element_at()`: this operation takes an element (of type `any`) and also an `Iterator` over the target collection. The element is added at the position pointed to by the iterator. If the element is added, all iterators, except the one specified as a parameter, on the target collection are marked as invalid.
- `replace_element_at()`: this operation takes an element (of type `any`) and also an `Iterator` over the target collection. The element at the position pointed to by the iterator is replaced with the one passed as a parameter.
- `remove_element_at()`: this operation takes an `Iterator` over the target collection. The element at the position pointed to by the iterator is removed from the target collection. If the element is removed, all iterators on the target collection are marked as invalid.
- `remove_all_elements()`: all of the elements are removed from the target collection. If the elements are removed, all iterators on the target collection are marked as invalid.
- `retrieve_element_at()`: this operation takes an `Iterator` over the target collection. The element at that position is returned as a value of type `any`. The iterator is not modified.
- `create_iterator()`: a new iterator is created and initialized to point to the start of the target collection.

The Query Service also defines a number of types (such as `Value` and `ValueType`) and also a collection factory. These are shown in Section A.11 (p.506).

Query framework

The remainder of the Query Service specification specifies the interfaces required to make a query on a collection. A query can be made on any object of type `QueryEvaluator`, and also on any object of type `QueryableCollection` (this inherits from both `QueryEvaluator` and `Collection`; see Figure 25.4). An application that wishes to construct a collection that it can issue queries on should construct a `QueryableCollection` object, rather than just a `Collection` object. Objects of type `QueryableCollection` can also be returned by the Query Service; that is, the result of a query could be a collection on which further queries can be issued. Interface `QueryEvaluator` is supported because some objects other than collections may have queries issued against them: in particular, in some systems, a query may be issued against a DBMS. Such objects should inherit from `QueryEvaluator` rather than `QueryableCollection`.

Interface `QueryEvaluator` defines the following attributes and operation (see Section A.11, p.506):

- Attribute `ql_types`: this returns the sequence of query language types that the target object supports. Rather than being returned as strings, these are returned as IDL interface definitions – references to objects of type `CORBA::InterfaceDef`. Such references refer to interface definition objects in the Interface Repository (Section 16.1, p.256). Therefore, the Query Service defines the following interfaces: `QueryLanguageType`, `SQL92_Query` (which inherits from `QueryLanguageType`), `OQL_93` (which inherits from `QueryLanguageType`), and `OQL_93Basic` (which inherits from `OQL_93`).
  None of these interfaces defines any attributes or operations. Use of object references to interface definitions is more complex that simply using strings, but it has the advantage that a hierarchy of language types can be supported; and in particular it shows that `OQL_93Basic` is a subset of `OQL_93`. In this hierarchy, derived types are sub-languages of their base types.

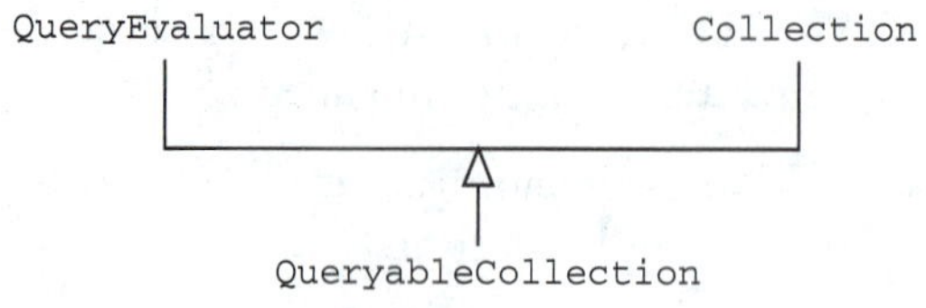

Figure 25.4 *Query framework.*

- Attribute `default_ql_type`: specifies the default language type (again as an object reference to an interface object) of the target `QueryEvaluator`.

- `evaluate()`: this operation takes a query string, a query language type and a sequence of parameters. If the query language type is specified to be a null object reference, then the default query language for the target `QueryEvaluator` is used. Each parameter is a name–value pair: each name can be used in one or more places in the query string and is replaced with the corresponding value before the query is executed. A value of type `any` is returned as the result of executing the query.

Interface `QueryableCollection` defines no further attributes or operations: it simply inherits from `QueryEvaluator` and `Collection`.

In addition, the Query Service allows an object of type `Query` to be constructed by specifying a query string and for this query object later to be prepared for execution or actually to be executed. This is an alternative to using `QueryEvaluator::evaluate()`.

The `QueryManager` interface is defined to allow `Query` objects to be constructed; it defines one operation:

- `create()`: this takes a query string, a query language type, and a parameter list, and returns a reference to a `Query` object. It does not execute the query.

A `Query` object can be prepared for execution by calling its `prepare()` operation. This may perform query optimization and set up the query path to be followed. To evaluate a query its `execute()` operation must be called. This operation need not block until the query has been evaluated. The status of the evaluation can be found by calling `get_status()` on the `Query` object; and when the status indicates that the query has been evaluated, the result (of type `any`) can be obtained by calling `get_result()`.

Part six

Point of sale example and Conclusions

Chapter 26, **Point of sale example**, explains an example introduced by the OMG to demonstrate the features of CORBA. The IDL definitions have been made simpler here, and the choices available during the implementation are discussed. No code is shown for this example.

Chapter 27, **Conclusions**, summarizes the advantages of CORBA.

26 Point of sale example

The book *CORBA Fundamentals and Programming* was written by Jon Siegel and representatives of many of the companies that have implemented the CORBA standard (Siegel, 1996). Besides giving an overview of the core standard and each of the CORBAservices defined at the time of writing, it gives a short summary of the features of each ORB, and shows how a single example — the **point of sale** system — can be coded in each. Orbix was illustrated using C++.

This chapter discusses the implementation of a simplified version of the point of sale system. No code is shown because the programming techniques have been covered already in other chapters. Instead, the implementation options are outlined. The IDL definitions have been simplified here to give cleaner interfaces and to reduce the space required to explain the base implementation.

26.1 Introduction to the example

A chain of stores has a number of point of sale terminals. Each is operated by a sales assistant and has a keypad, a barcode reader, a display, and a receipt printer. The barcode reader is used to input the unique product identifier of each item being purchased by scanning the barcode on its packet, can, or bag. The keypad can be used to input details such as the number of each item being purchased (so that each individual barcode does not need to be scanned multiple times).

The point of sale terminals in a single store share a facility from which they find the prices of items and to which they report sales. This facility is referred to as the **store**. The store in turn finds prices from the central **depot**, and orders larger quantities of goods from it.

As well as allowing sales to be recorded, any point of sale terminal can also be used by a store s management to monitor the total sales made to date in the store, and also the total sales made by each point of sale terminal in the store.

To reduce complexity, the ordering of goods by the store has not been addressed fully. The interfaces and implementation assume that the store will hold a stock of each item type that it sells and that it will order a suitable quantity of an item type when its stock falls below a certain threshold. A single operation has been added to the depot to allow a store to order goods, but other details of the ordering system have not been addressed.

26.2 IDL type definitions

The type definitions for this point of sale example are given in module `POSSystem` (in file `POSSystem.idl`):

```
module POSSystem {

      typedef string Barcode;
      typedef float Price;
      typedef unsigned long Quantity;

      typedef long POSIdType;
      typedef long StoreIdType;

      enum ItemTypes { food, clothes, other };

      struct ItemInfo {
            Barcode item;
            ItemTypes itemType;
            Price itemPrice;
            string description;
      };

      exception BarcodeNotFound { Barcode item; };
      exception InsufficientStock {
            Barcode item;
            Quantity quantityRequested;
            Quantity quantityRemaining;
      };
};
```

The types have the following meanings and usages:

- `Barcode`: unique identifier associated with each type of item.
- `Price`: price of a single unit of the item.
- `Quantity`: represents quantities of items.
- `POSIdType`: since we can deal with more than one point of sale terminal, each one needs its own identifier, of type `POSIdType`.
- `StoreIdType`: since we can deal with more than one store, each one needs its own identifier, of type `StoreIdType`.
- `ItemTypes`: this is a general classification of each item type; for example, a can of fruit would have an `ItemTypes` of `food`.
- `ItemInfo`: a structure that holds all of the information we need for each item type. `description` is a short string.
- `BarcodeNotFound`: this exception is raised if an invalid barcode is passed to an operation.
- `InsufficientStock`: this exception is raised if the store or depot does not have sufficient stock of a given item type to satisfy a request.

26.3 The IDL for the depot component

The depot component of the system is represented by an object of type `Depot`, and one object of type `DepotAccess` per store that is using the depot at any time. `Depot` is a singleton type: only one instance of it exists in a single installation. Its only operation, `login()`, allows a store to begin its use of the depot, and to acquire a reference to a `DepotAccess` object, through which it accesses the functionality of the depot. A `DepotAccess` object is created for each session; that is, for each period of time that a store is communicating with its depot – for example, one `DepotAccess` object per store per day.

This split in functionality between the `Depot` object and `DepotAccess` objects allows each `DepotAccess` object to know the identity of its caller: the object reference to a `DepotAccess` object becomes a capability (the markers of the `DepotAccess` objects can be made suitably large and random to achieve security), and the `DepotAccess` object itself becomes a **security context**. It is also a good example of using CORBA's ability to support many lightweight objects of different types in a single process.

These IDL definitions are given within the `CentralOffice` module:

```
#include "POSSystem.idl"

module CentralOffice {

      interface DepotAccess;

      interface Depot {
            DepotAccess login (in POSSystem::StoreIdType id );
      };

      interface DepotAccess {
            POSSystem::ItemInfo findItemInfo (
                                    in POSSystem::Barcode item )
            raises (POSSystem::BarcodeNotFound);

            // Submit an order to the Depot.
            POSSystem::Quantity orderItems (
                                    in POSSystem::Barcode item,
                                    in POSSystem::Quantity quantity,
                                    in boolean bestEffort)
            raises (POSSystem::BarcodeNotFound,
                        POSSystem::InsufficientStock );
      };

};
```

The operation provided by interface `Depot` is as follows:

- `login()`: allows a store to begin its usage of the depot, and returns a reference to a `DepotAccess` object. The only parameter is the store's identifier, but a full system could include security parameters (or the security information could be acquired from the application's security framework).

The operations provided by interface `DepotAccess` are as follows:

- `findItemInfo()`: given a barcode, this returns the `POSSystem::ItemInfo` structure that contains all of the information for that type of item.
- `orderItems()`: given a barcode and a quantity, this operation arranges to dispatch those goods to the requesting store. The `bestEffort` parameter indicates whether or not the depot is allowed to dispatch a smaller amount of goods if the full request cannot be satisfied: true indicates that a smaller amount is acceptable. The return value indicates the actual amount dispatched.

26.4 The IDL of the store component

The store component is used directly by the point of sale terminals; that is, by the user interfaces. As with the depot component (Section 26.3), the store component is constructed from two CORBA objects: a `Store` object, which is shared by all of the point of sale terminals in a store, and a `StoreAccess` object per point of sale terminal. These two interfaces are defined within the `StoreSubSystem` module:

```
#include "POSSystem.idl"

module StoreSubSystem {

      struct StoreInfo {
            POSSystem::StoreIdType id;
            POSSystem::Price totalSales;
            POSSystem::Price totalTaxes;
      };

      struct POSInfo {
            POSSystem::POSIdType id;
            POSSystem::Price totalSales;
            POSSystem::Price totalTaxes;
      };

      typedef sequence<POSInfo> POSInfoList;
      interface StoreAccess;

      interface Store {
            readonly attribute POSSystem::StoreIdType storeId;

            StoreAccess login (in POSSystem::POSIdType id );
      };

      interface StoreAccess {

            StoreInfo getStoreTotal();
            POSInfoList getPOSTotals();

            // Given a barcode, return store's price for the item,
            // tax to be charged, and a description.
            POSSystem::Price findPrice (
                  in  POSSystem::Barcode item,
                  out POSSystem::Price taxOnItem,
                  out string description )
            raises ( POSSystem::BarcodeNotFound );

            // Report sale of a quantity of item to the store
            void reportSale (
                  in POSSystem::Barcode item,
```

```
                in POSSystem::Quantity quantity )
            raises ( POSSystem::BarcodeNotFound );
    };

};
```

The new data types defined in this module are as follows:

- `StoreInfo`: an instance of this struct contains information about a single store, giving its identifier, the total sales made today, and the total tax incurred because of these sales.
- `PosInfo`: an instance of this struct contains information about a single point of sale terminal: its identifier, the total sales made by it today, and the total tax incurred because of these sales.
- `POSInfoList`: this represents a sequence of `PosInfo` structs.

The attributes and operations of the `Store` have the following uses:

- attribute `storeId`: each store in an installation has a unique identifier.
- `login()`: to use the services of a store, a point of sale terminal must first use this operation. It receives a reference to a `StoreAccess` object created for this session.

The operations of the `StoreAccess` interface are as follows:

- `getStoreTotal()`: this returns information about the target store (a struct of type `StoreInfo`).
- `getPOSTotals()`: this returns information about all of the point of sale terminals connected to the target store (this is a sequence of type `POSInfoList`).
- `findPrice()`: given a barcode, this returns the price of a unit of this item type. There are two `out` parameters: `taxOnItem` gives the tax on a unit of the item type (the American tax model is assumed here: the price quoted for an item excludes the tax amount); and `description` gives a short string to describe the item type.
- `reportSale()`: this is called by a point of sale terminal to inform the store that a given amount of an item type (specified by a barcode) has been sold. The store can then update its inventory records.

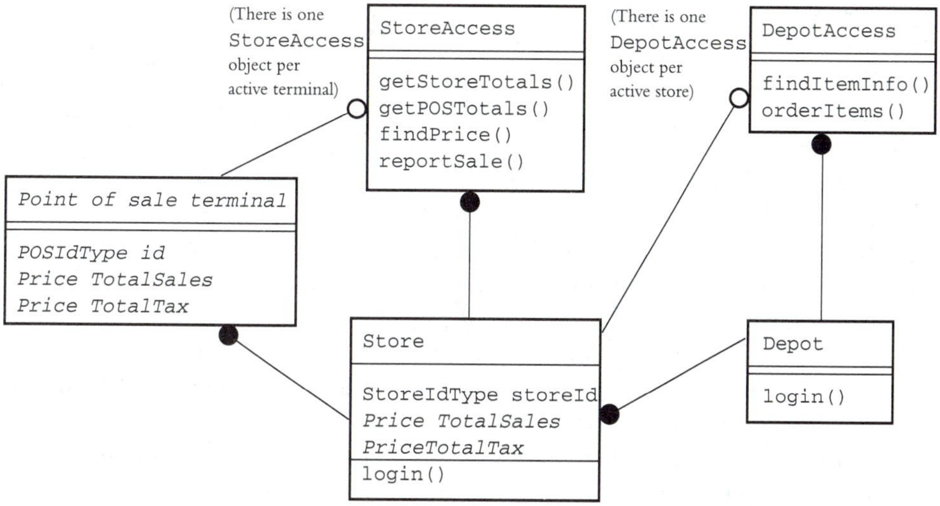

Figure 26.1 *Object model diagram of the CORBA aspects of the system.*

26.5 OMT diagram

An OMT (Rumbaugh *et al.*, 1991) object module diagram for the CORBA aspects of the system is shown in Figure 26.1. The features that do not carry through directly to the IDL definitions are shown in italic.

26.6 Implementation of the point of sale terminal

Handling the runtime environment and the specialized peripherals of the point of sales terminals may require low-level systems programming. However, the IDL attribute and operation calls are easy to make, and therefore it is easy to integrate this real-time component into the system.

If a prototype of the terminals is required then it could be implemented in Visual Basic, using the CORBA–OLE integration (see Chapter 11) to allow IDL operation and attribute calls to be made. A Java prototype would allow the latest front-end code to be loaded over the internet, perhaps for demonstration at a customer's site.

26.7 Implementation of the store

The store can be implemented as a single CORBA server that contains a `Store` object, and a `StoreAccess` object per active point of sale terminal. Interfaces `Store` and `StoreAccess` can be implemented by C++ classes `Store_i` and `StoreAccess_i`, respectively. The `Store` object can be registered with the Naming Service (Section 7.3, p.162) to allow the point of sale terminals to find it. The `Store::login()` operation should create a `StoreAccess` object, and return a reference to it (after first duplicating this reference).

The implementation of `findPrice()` need only pass the call to the `DepotAccess::findItemInfo()` operation, and extract the required data (the price and the description) from the returned `POSSystem::ItemInfo` struct. `findPrice()` also returns the tax on the item; and this can be determined from the item s type (`ItemTypes`), which is also contained in the `POSSystem::ItemInfo` struct.

The implementation of `reportSale()` must update the store s stock inventory records. At some later time, this record can be used by the store s management to order new stock from the depot. This introduces the need for a new IDL interface to the store, to allow management tools or agents to access the inventory records. It is certainly possible to implement the store without such an IDL interface, in fact providing a user interface for inventory control as an integral part of the store itself. However, this would close this aspect of the store from access from different user interfaces and agents. It would mean that different operating systems could not be used to support the store and the user interfaces; and it would mean that other systems, such as an accounting system, could not interact with the inventory management component. It is worth remembering the dictum: today s applications should be designed to be tomorrow s components — not monolithic applications.

The inventory records must be stored persistently, but this does not require the store to manage persistent CORBA objects. The implementation of `reportSale()` and the inventory management interface must access and update a database, and this can be done in a straightforward way by the member functions that implement these operations. There is no need to have a loader (see Chapter 20) to bring a CORBA object into memory when it is invoked. Instead, the store server can create its single instance of `Store` in its `main()` function, and it can create an instance of `StoreAccess` when each point of sale terminal logs in. (The example can be changed to require the store server to manage persistent CORBA objects. If the inventory records are modeled as objects with IDL interfaces, then these will be stored in the database, and a record will need to be loaded on demand when an invocation is made on it. The easiest approach to implement this is for the store server to use a Database Adapter between CORBA and the chosen DBMS. See Section 22.2, p.362, for a discussion of database access and adapters.)

The store must also track total sales and tax, in order to respond to calls to `getStoreTotal()` and `getPOSTotals()`.

The store server should be multi-threaded to allow it to handle requests from a number of point of sale terminals in parallel. The 'thread per request' model is suitable, unless the number of threads needs to be capped through the use of a thread pool.

26.8 Implementation of the depot

The depot can be implemented as a single CORBA server that contains a `Depot` object, and a `DepotAccess` object per active store. Interfaces `Depot` and `DepotAccess` can be implemented by C++ classes `Depot_i` and `DepotAccess_i`, respectively. The `Depot` object can be registered with the Naming Service (Section 7.3, p.162) to allow the stores to find it. The `Depot::login()` operation should create a `DepotAccess` object, and return a reference to it (after first duplicating this reference).

The depot server needs to maintain a database of item barcodes, prices, types, and descriptions. Whereas simple file storage may suffice in some installations, there are many advantages to using a DBMS. This data needs a management interface, and once again this should be defined in IDL and then the user interface should be implemented to use this (see Section 26.7).

As with the store server, there may be benefits in making the depot server multi-threaded. For the store server, we did not discuss the interaction between the use of multiple threads and a DBMS, but we will do so for the depot. The depot server handles a set of operation calls for a set of independent clients (the stores), and the actions of these concurrent operations must be coordinated. Some DBMSs allow a process to run a number of threads, with each thread running in its own transaction; and these transactions compete for locks and commit/abort independently of each other. This support makes it very easy for the store server to use multiple threads to support its clients; and the simplest threading model to use is 'thread per client' (see Section 21.3, p.352: in 'thread per client' each current client has one thread associated with it in the server, and this thread handles all of its calls. It is therefore easy to associate that thread with the client's transaction).

✚ The 'thread per request' model may also be used with some DBMSs: if a new thread can be attached to a currently running transaction. ✚

This issue is discussed in more depth in Section 22.2 (p.362).

Some other DBMSs support threads but the set of threads in a process share locks – they are in effect running in the same transaction. This can cause problems in some servers because the concurrency of the actions of independent clients cannot be managed using database locks. The store server may therefore have to be a single threaded server, or it can be registered as a 'shared per-client-process' server (see Section 8.2, p.179).

Some DBMSs do not support threading, in which case the store server must be single threaded; and a single process or a process per client can be used.

26.9 Extending the example

This section describes a number of enhancements that can be made to the system by using advanced CORBA and Orbix features.

26.9.1 Reducing the number of calls to the store

For economy we want to allow a small machine to host the store server, and therefore we do not want the point of sale terminals making unnecessary calls to objects in the store. One way to reduce the number of calls is to address the fact that two calls are made for each group of items of the same type: one each to `findPrice()` and `reportSale()`. A reduction in the number of calls is very easy to achieve in this case: an operation `findPriceAndReportSale()` can be added to the `StoreAccess` interface, and the terminal can be recoded to use this new operation:

```
interface StoreAccess {
      // As before, but with the following:
      POSSystem::Price findPriceAndReportSale(
                              in POSSystem::Barcode item,
                              in POSSystem::Quantity quantity,
                              out POSSystem::Price taxOnItem,
                              out string description )
                  raises ( POSSystem::BarcodeNotFound );
};
```

The interface provides the following operation:

- `FindPriceAndReportSale()`: this operation combines the functionality of the operations `findPrice()` and `reportSale()`. Such combinations are useful in a distributed system because they reduce the number of remote calls, in this case across the store's local area network.

Of course, `findPriceAndReportSale()` could have been added to an interface that derives from `StoreAccess`, rather than changing the `StoreAccess` interface itself. This is discussed in Section 26.9.4.

The implementation of `findPriceAndReportSale()` is simple: it need only call the `findPrice()` and `reportSale()` member functions of `StoreAccess_i`.

26.9.2 Smart proxies: caching

Another way to reduce the number of remote calls to the store is for the point of sale terminal to cache prices that it has recently asked the store for, and to use this cache to look up prices (see Chapter 19 for a discussion of caching). Since most purchases are likely to be concentrated on a relatively small number of popular goods, a high hit rate can be expected on this cache. Rather than changing the code for the terminal itself to use and maintain this cache, a smart proxy for the `StoreAccess` interface can be written and linked into each terminal. This smart proxy can look up its cache for prices before resorting to asking the store. This means that the rest of the client's code can continue to call `findPrice()` or `findPriceAndReportSale()` as before.

The danger of caching prices in a point of sale terminal is, of course, that we must ensure that a terminal is not using out of date prices. One way to cater for this is for the management of the store to consider it acceptable that an old price is used for a short period, say 10 minutes, after it has been changed. The individual entries in the terminal's cache of prices (maintained by its smart proxy for the store access object) can each be time stamped on entry, and old entries can be expired as an attempt is made to use them. It may also be possible to restrict price changes to a few specific times each day – at which times the point of sale terminals can discard their cache.

Another approach is for the store to make a call-back to an object in each of its terminals, informing it that the price of an individual item has changed or simply informing it that *some* price change has occurred. The latter would mean that the whole of the cache of prices would be flushed, but this may be acceptable since prices will only change a few times each day. These call-backs can be made with normal operation calls, or OrbixTalk can be used (see Section 22.1, p.356; Section 19.3.3, p.327).

Finally, each store can also be changed to cache the depot's prices for items. This can lead to significant performance gains because the store and depot are likely to communicate over a wide area network. Again, this caching can be done within a smart proxy for the depot access object, and the same call-back facility can be used to advise of prices changes. However, in this case, it is acceptable to restrict price changes to certain times each day (perhaps just once at midnight), and so cache management can be done locally within each store (for example, within its smart proxy for the depot access object).

26.9.3 Overlap between call reductions and caching

There is, of course, an overlap between the optimizations described in Sections 26.9.1 and 26.9.2. In particular, at least one call between the point of sale terminal and the store is required for each set of the same good purchased by a customer, because the store must record each sale so that it can manage its stocks. Removing the need to request the price from the store does not remove a terminal's responsibility to report the sale. However, it does mean that a terminal can find the price itself without requiring the store to do this, thus moving some processing from the store to the terminal. In many applications, reducing the processing load on a server is an important factor in allowing it to handle a larger number of clients.

The smart proxy for `StoreAccess` (running within the terminal) can respond to a call to `findPriceAndReportSale()` with either a cache look-up success followed by a call to `reportSale()` on the store, or a cache look-up failure followed by a call to `findPriceAndReportSale()` on the store.

26.9.4 Smart proxies: extended interface

In Section 26.9.1, operation `findPriceAndReportSale()` was introduced by modifying the `StoreAccess` interface. Alternatively, a new interface, say `StoreAccessEnhanced`, could be defined:

```
interface StoreAccessEnhanced : StoreAccess {
     POSSystem::Price findPriceAndReportSale(
                           in POSSystem::Barcode item,
                           in POSSystem::Quantity quantity,
                           out POSSystem::Price taxOnItem,
                           out string description )
                raises ( POSSystem::BarcodeNotFound );
};
```

This section discusses the fact that there is a choice of whether or not `findPriceAndReportSale()` is made visible to the application-level code in the point of sale terminals. Since this operation is easy to use, and since it does not interact in any complex way with other usages of the store, there is no great difficulty in making it visible to the application-level code. That is, the point of sale terminals could use interface `StoreAccessEnhanced`. However, in many cases, operations that are added to improve performance or in other ways to handle the distribution of the system are not designed for use by application code. In some cases, the operations themselves are suitable for application-level code, but the application has already been written using the base-level operations.

In the last two cases, smart proxies can be used to hide the additional operations. The smart proxy used by the application-level client code can be an instance of the derived proxy class (`StoreAccessEnhanced` in this case), but the client itself may only know about the base interface. Because the proxy is an instance of the derived proxy class, it can make calls to the additional operations on the real object (which is an instance of the derived interface).

To arrange for this, the client will normally need a smart proxy factory for both the base and the derived interfaces (`StoreAccess` and `StoreAccessEnhanced`). The `New()` function of both of these factories should create a smart proxy for the derived interface, but the application-level code in the client should only see a pointer to the base interface.

26.9.5 Filters: activity of each point of sale terminal

One of the management functions that a store may need to carry out is the recording of the requests arriving from each point of sale terminal. This recording may be required only for a short duration of each day while the system administration gathers performance statistics, or it may be required during a training session to monitor a trainee's performance.

From a system architecture viewpoint, it is important that the store and store access objects themselves are not changed to record its usage patterns – such recording is not the responsibility of the business objects in the system. In particular, the implementation of interfaces `Store` and `StoreAccess` should not be changed to record this information. This would become even more important if the store server contained objects of many other interfaces. Instead, the recording should be done at the system level, using a per-process filter (see Chapter 18). A filter class should be defined, and an instance created. Besides implementing the standard filtering member functions, the filter class can provide functions to request the beginning and ending of recording.

27 Conclusions

The promise of CORBA is that applications will no longer be implemented as closed systems, with user interface, logic, and database all within monolithic vertical slices. Instead, a high-level business layer of each application will be exposed using IDL, and the upper layers of an application will be implemented on top of this. This allows an application itself to provide alternative upper layers (for example, alternative user interfaces on different operating systems, or for different types of users) and it allows others to use the results of one project to build larger systems. By designing and implementing our systems in this way, we will build up a set of **components** that reduce the long-term cost of software development and maintenance. Integration of components will not have the high cost it does today. Decomposition of our software into components is a natural step, one that is followed in all system analysis. CORBA allows us to take advantage of this in the design and implementation phases. The surprise is that this can be done easily and without extra costs.

The resulting components are of a different nature to what we are familiar with from graphics and user interfaces. There, the components are small pieces of software that are reused in different projects. CORBA does help this level of componentization, because the components can be language independent and used on remote machines, but the form that it addresses more directly uses components that are the main architectural building blocks of our current and future systems.

When integration is not a concern, CORBA offers a single project the ability to work across boundaries (the network, operating systems, and programming languages).

Nevertheless, CORBA is not a revolution in our software approach. It capitalizes on the benefits of transparency and object-orientation, and makes these applicable to large systems. It does not force new programming models or styles on designers and implementers, and it allows for non-object-oriented programming languages and for legacy systems. Object-orientation is not used in CORBA because it is new or a silver bullet, but because it offers real benefits for defining interfaces.

Designers and implementers who believe in this form of software development require an object system that is easy to use and that scales to handle large systems. CORBA offers these properties.

CORBA is certainly easy to learn. Firstly, IDL is a very simple language to learn, and it allows the most important interfaces in a system to be defined in a clear object-oriented notation that is independent of the programming languages used to implement and use these interfaces. Secondly, it is easy to implement an IDL interface in any object-oriented programming language, or even in a non-object-oriented language. For example, in C++, a programmer must define a C++ class that implements each of the attributes and operations of an interface. Using an IDL interface from C++ is as simple as using any C++ class.

The most difficult aspect of using C++ to implement or be a client of a complex interface is to obey the memory management rules to prevent memory leakage. An understanding of these rules is important if a programmer wishes to make intuitive use of CORBA. Understanding the rules for strings and object references is the key to this.

Scaling to large systems

There are a number of factors that allow CORBA to scale to handle distributed enterprise systems. Firstly, at the design level, IDL definitions are the key to allowing CORBA to bridge boundaries such as the network, different operating systems, different programming languages, and different object systems. Some of the IDL definitions in a system define interfaces for use by client systems, such as user interfaces or applications written by other companies, departments, or projects. These definitions can be derived from the analysis of the system, because they define interfaces to the **business objects** – the objects that define the high-level view of the system. Other IDL definitions can be used to define internal interfaces, between subsystems that the system designer introduced or existing ones that must be used. For example, a designer may define an IDL definition to abstract a database that must be used in the implementation, allowing the rest of the system to use this interface rather than making direct use of the database.

The fact that IDL can be used in both of these ways is very important for its use in large enterprise systems. Use of CORBA at both levels gives uniformity to the architecture of these systems, because the same interfacing and programming techniques can be used throughout.

Secondly, one of the essential aspects of enterprise computing is to allow different departments and projects to make their own computing decisions, including different operating systems and different programming languages, and even different object systems. CORBA directly addresses the issues that these **administrative boundaries** raise.

Thirdly, an invocation on a CORBA object can be made directly from the caller to the object. This means that there is no communication bottleneck introduced within CORBA itself. Further, different forms of communication (blocking, non-blocking, object-based/group-based, decoupled, store-and-forward, publish-and-subscribe, and so on) can be used, using application-level IDL interfaces that hide the communication details from the high-level code.

Fourthly, all objects do not need to be registered centrally. Only a subset of the objects need be registered in the Naming Service, and only servers (not the many objects they contain) need to be registered with the Implementation Repository.

CORBA as the middleware

For all of these reasons, middleware has become a critical part of software development – companies no longer want to rely on low-level communication facilities to integrate their present and future software. CORBA leads this market, for a number of reasons:

- IDL bridges programming languages, operating systems, networks, and object systems.
- It is easy to define, implement, and use interfaces. These interfaces are object-oriented, making them easier to maintain.
- It is lightweight: each server can contain many objects; communication is direct from caller to target object; objects can be of any size.
- It interworks well with different middleware, including OLE. Scripting languages such as Visual Basic can both use and implement interfaces.
- The CORBAservices provide a set of optional extensions that address areas that the core itself could not address; for example, transactions, naming, events, and trading.
- It is integrated with other technologies, such as databases, reliable messaging systems, threads, user interface generation systems, and so on.
- It applies to many different vertical markets. The core level is applicable to all of these, and specialized implementations can be provided in areas such as realtime and embedded systems. The upper layers, both the CORBAservices and the CORBAfacilities, can be applied differently in the various vertical markets. The OMG has set up a number of active special interest groups to address these special needs.

- It supports both static and dynamic usage. The dynamic parts are more difficult to use but they need be used only by a subset of CORBA programmers.
- Web-based clients and servers are allowed, in particular through Java-based implementations of CORBA.
- IDL is mapped separately to each programming language, so usage from each language is natural; for example, in object-oriented languages the normal steps for implementing and using classes still apply. Many languages are supported, not just those that are currently in favor.
- There is an agreed protocol, IIOP, for communication between ORBs.
- It is a well-established and widely adopted standard, which is written and maintained by an open procedure.
- There are competing implementations, encouraging continued innovation and updates.

The scope of the CORBA standard is vast. The current standard addresses the core requirements for middleware, as well as a set of optional CORBAservices and CORBAfacilities. The standardization work is continuing, in particular in the following areas:

- The mapping of IDL to further programming languages. Also, the mapping between IDL and other definition languages, for example telecommunication-specific languages such as GDMO.
- Further integration into CASE tools, improving their ability to generate IDL from the analysis and design steps.
- Improvements to the core, such as allowing stream-based communication to handle voice and video, and the addition of new data types to IDL.
- Further work on standardizing the server-side code for C++ to allow servers to be ported between ORBs. This will change some of the server-side details shown here, but it will not change the overall approach.
- Significantly more work on the implementation of the CORBAservices. However, not all of the services are of equal importance. The Naming Service, Event Service, Security Service, Transaction Service, and Trading Service will remain the most important services for some time. Some areas are best

addressed by DBMSs (Persistent Object Service, Query Service, Relationship Service, Concurrency Service, and to a lesser extent the Property Service), especially for large data volumes.

- Most of the future work will build on the stable core and define standards specific to particular market segments.

Will CORBA win as the single object framework for the future? The computer industry rarely agrees on one unique standard, so historically we can conclude that there will be choices. However, there is strong motivation in this case to keep computer politics separate from the software engineering issues, and to integrate CORBA with whatever systems users need it to be integrated with. In this way, CORBA can become the superglue of the computer industry, the middleware of the middleware.

Appendix A IDL interfaces for selected CORBAservices

This appendix gives the IDL definitions for some of the CORBAservices.

A.1 Event Service

A.1.1 Untyped (generic) events

This section gives the IDL definitions for the untyped (generic) Event Service.

```
module CosEventComm {
      exception Disconnected { };

      interface PushConsumer {
            void push(in any data) raises (Disconnected);
            void disconnect_push_consumer();
      };

      interface PushSupplier {
            void disconnect_push_supplier();
      };

      interface PullSupplier {
            any pull() raises (Disconnected);
            any try_pull(out boolean has_event)
                  raises (Disconnected);
            void disconnect_pull_supplier();
      };
```

```
      interface PullConsumer {
            void disconnect_pull_consumer();
      };
};


module CosEventChannelAdmin {
      exception AlreadyConnected {};
      exception TypeError {};

      interface ProxyPushConsumer : CosEventComm::PushConsumer {
            void connect_push_supplier(
                        in CosEventComm::PushSupplier push_supplier)
                  raises (AlreadyConnected);
      };

      interface ProxyPullSupplier : CosEventComm::PullSupplier {
            void connect_pull_consumer(
                        in CosEventComm::PullConsumer pull_consumer)
                  raises (AlreadyConnected);
      };

      interface ProxyPullConsumer : CosEventComm::PullConsumer {
            void connect_pull_supplier(
                        in CosEventComm::PullSupplier pull_supplier)
                  raises (AlreadyConnected, TypeError);
      };

      interface ProxyPushSupplier : CosEventComm::PushSupplier {
            void connect_push_consumer(
                        in CosEventComm::PushConsumer push_consumer)
                  raises (AlreadyConnected, TypeError);
      };

      interface ConsumerAdmin {
            ProxyPushSupplier obtain_push_supplier();
            ProxyPullSupplier obtain_pull_supplier();
      };

      interface SupplierAdmin {
            ProxyPushConsumer obtain_push_consumer();
            ProxyPullConsumer obtain_pull_consumer();
      };

      interface EventChannel {
            ConsumerAdmin for_consumers();
            SupplierAdmin for_suppliers();
            void destroy();
      };

};
```

A.1.2 Typed events

This remainer of this section gives the IDL definitions for the **typed** Event Service.

```
module CosTypedEventComm {
      interface TypedPushConsumer : CosEventComm::PushConsumer {
            Object get_typed_consumer();
            };
      interface TypedPullSupplier : CosEventComm::PullSupplier {
            Object get_typed_supplier();
      };
};
```

The interfaces and operations for establishing typed event communication are similar to those for untyped Event Channels. The difference is that the operations `obtain_typed_push_consumer()`, `obtain_typed_pull_consumer()`, `obtain_typed_pull_supplier()`, and `obtain_typed_push_supplier()` take a `Key` as a parameter to indicate the required interface that the supplier is to push to or that the consumer is to pull from. If the interface cannot be found, exception `InterfaceNotSupported` or `NoSuchImplementation` is raised.

```
module CosTypedEventChannelAdmin {

      exception InterfaceNotSupported {};
      exception NoSuchImplementation {};
      typedef string Key;

      inteface TypedProxyPushConsumer :
                  CosEventChannelAdmin::ProxyPushConsumer,
                  CosTypedEventComm::TypedPushConsumer { };

      interface TypedProxyPullSupplier :
                  CosEventChannelAdmin::ProxyPullSupplier,
                  CosTypedEventComm::TypedPullSupplier { };

      interface TypedSupplierAdmin :
                  CosEventChannelAdmin::SupplierAdmin {
            TypedProxyPushConsumer obtain_typed_push_consumer (
                  in Key supported_interface)
                  raises (InterfaceNotSupported);
            ProxyPullConsumer obtain_typed_pull_consumer (
                  in Key uses_interfaces)
                  raises (NoSuchImplementation);
      };

      interface TypedConsumerAdmin :
                  CosEventChannelAdmin::ConsumerAdmin {
            TypedProxyPullSupplier obtain_typed_pull_supplier (
                                    in Key supported_interface)
```

```
                    raises (InterfaceNotSupported);
        ProxyPushSupplier obtain_typed_push_supplier (
                        in Key uses_interface)
                    raises (NoSuchImplementation);
    };

    interface TypedEventChannel {
        TypedConsumerAdmin for_consumers();
        TypedSupplierAdmin for_suppliers();
        void destroy();
    };
};
```

A.2 Transaction Service (OTS)

This section gives the IDL definitions for the Object Transaction Service.

```
module CosTransactions {

    enum Status {
        StatusActive,
        StatusMarkedRollback,
        StatusPrepared,
        StatusCommitted,
        StatusRolledBack,
        StatusUnknown,
        StatusNoTransaction
    };

    enum Vote {
        VoteCommit,
        VoteRollback,
        VoteReadonly
    };

    // Standard exceptions (added to the standard list):
    // exception TransactionRequired {};
    // exception TransactionRolledBack {};
    // exception InvalidTransaction {};

    // Heuristic exceptions:
    exception HeuristicRollback {};
    exception HeuristicCommit {};
    exception HeuristicMixed {};
    exception HeuristicHazard {};

// Exception from ORB transactions:
```

```
exception WrongTransaction {};

// Other transaction-specific exceptions:
exception SubtransactionsUnavailable {};
exception NotSubtransaction {};
exception Inactive {};
exception NotPrepared {};
exception NoTransaction {};
exception InvalidControl {};
exception Unavailable {};

// Forward references for interfaces defined
// later in this module:
interface Control;
interface Terminator;
interface Coordinator;
interface Resource;
interface RecoveryCoordinator;
interface SubtransactionAwareResource;
interface TransactionFactory;
interface TransactionalObject;
interface Current;

// Current transaction pseudo object (PIDL)
interface Current {
      void begin ()
            raises (SubtransactionsUnavailable);
      void commit (in boolean report_heuristics)
            raises (NoTransaction,
                    HeuristicMixed,
                    HeuristicHazard);
      void rollback ()
            raises (NoTransaction);
      void rollback_only ()
            raises (NoTransaction);

      Status get_status();
      string get_transaction_name();
      void set_timeout (in unsigned long seconds);

      Control get_control ();
      Control suspend ();
      void resume (in Control which)
            raises (InvalidControl);
};

interface TransactionFactor {
      Control create (in unsigned long time_out);
};

interface Control {
      Terminator get_terminator ()
```

```
            raises (Unavailable);
        Coordinator get_coordinator ()
            raises (Unavailable);
    };

    interface Terminator {
        void commit (in boolean report_heuristics)
            raises ( HeuristicMixed,
                     HeuristicHazard);
        void rollback();
    };

    interface Resource {
        Vote prepare();
        void rollback ()
            raises ( HeuristicCommit,
                     HeuristicMixed,
                     HeuristicHazard);
        void commit ()
            raises ( NotPrepared,
                     HeuristicRollback,
                     HeuristicMixed,
                     HeuristicHazard);
        void commit_one_phase ()
            raises ( HeuristicRollback,
                     HeuristicMixed,
                     HeuristicHazard);
        void forget();
    };

    interface SubtransactionAwareResource : Resource {
        void commit_subtransaction (in Coordinator parent);
        void rollback_subtransaction ();
    };

    interface TransactionalObject {};
};
```

A.3 Trading Service

This section gives a subset of the IDL definitions for the Trading Service, and in particular the `Lookup` interface:

```
module CosTrading {

   typedef string wstring;

   typedef Istring PropertyName;
   typedef sequence<PropertyName> PropertyNameSeq;
   typedef any PropertyValue;
   struct Property {
      PropertyName name;
      PropertyValue value;
   };
   typedef sequence<Property> PropertySeq;

   struct Offer {
      Object reference;
      PropertySeq properties;
   };
   typedef sequence<Offer> OfferSeq;

   typedef Istring ServiceTypeName;
   typedef Istring Constraint; // Constraint language.

   enum FollowOption { local_only, if_no_local, always };

   typedef string PolicyName;
   typedef sequence<PolicyName> PolicyNameSeq;
   typedef any PolicyValue;
   struct Policy {
      PolicyName name;
      PolicyValue value;
   };
   typedef sequence<Policy> PolicySeq;


   interface Lookup : TraderComponents,
                      SupportAttributes, ImportAttributes {

      typedef Istring Preference;
      enum HowManyProps { none, some, all };
      union SpecifiedProps switch (HowManyProps) {
            case some: PropertyNameSeq prop_names;
      };

      // Exceptions IllegalPreferences, IllegalPolicyName,
      //            PolicyTypeMismatch, InvalidPolicyValue.
```

```
      void query (
            in ServiceTypeName type, // Must be in Type Repository.
            in Constraint constr, // Which of those objects to find.
            in Preference pref, // Used to order the result.
            in PolicySeq policies, // Control how the Trader
                                   // behaves.†
            in SpecifiedProps desired_props,‡
            in unsigned long how_many, // Maximum size of offers.
            out OfferSeq offers, // The main result.
            out OfferIterator offer_itr, // Remaining offers.
            out PolicyNameSeq limits_applied)§
      raises ( /* . . . . */ );
   };
};
```

A.4 Life Cycle Service

This section gives the IDL definitions for the Life Cycle Service.

```
module CosLifeCycle {

      typedef CosNaming::Name Key;
      typedef Object Factory;
      typedef sequence<Factory> Factories;
      typedef struct NVP {
            CosNaming::wstring name;
            any value;
      } NameValuePair;
      typedef sequence <NameValuePair> Criteria;

      exception NoFactory {
            Key search_key;
      };
      exception NotCopyable {string reason;};
```

† For example, how it should follow links.

‡ Defines the set of properties (describing the offers) that are to be returned with the object references that match the constraint. The query can specify that none or all properties are to be returned; it can also specify that *some* are to be returned, in which case it must specify which properties it is interested in.

§ If any limits are applied by the trader to *actually* restrict the size of the returned set of offers, this `out` parameter will list those limits. Example limits include the overall number of offers that the trader is willing to search, the maximum number it is willing to sort, the maximum number it is willing to return, the maximum number of hops, the maximum size of an iterator, and the follow rule of links.

```
    exception NotMovable {string reason;};
    exception NotRemovable {string reason;};
    exception InvalidCriteria {
        Criteria invalid_criteria;
    };
    exception CannotMeetCriteria {
        Criteria unmet_criteria;
    };

    interface FactoryFinder {
        Factories find_factories (in Key factory_key)
            raises (NoFactory);
    };

    interface LifeCycleObject {
        LifeCycleObject copy (in FactoryFinder there,
                              in Criteria the_criteria)
            raises (NoFactory, NotCopyable,
                    InvalidCriteria,
                    CannotMeetCriteria);
        void move (in FactoryFinder there,
                   in Criteria the_criteria)
            raises (NoFactory, NotMovable,
                    InvalidCriteria,
                    CannotMeetCriteria);
        void remove ()
            raises (NotRemovable);
    };

    interface GenericFactory {
        boolean supports (in Key k);
        Object create_object (in Key k,
                              in Criteria the_criteria)
            raises (NoFactory,
                    InvalidCriteria,
                    CannotMeetCriteria);
    };

};
```

A.5 Externalization Service

This section gives the IDL definitions for the Externalization Service.

CosExternalization

```
module CosExternalization {

    exception InvalidFileNameError {};
```

```
      exception ContextAlreadyRegistered {};

      interface Stream :
                 CosLifeCycle::LifeCycleObject {

            void externalize (
                       in CosStream::Streamable theObject);
            CosStream::Streamable internalize (
                       in CosLifeCycle::FactoryFinder there)
            raises (CosLifeCycle::NoFactory,
                            CosStream::StreamDataFormatError);
            void begin_context()
                 raises (ContextAlreadyRegistered);
            void end_context();
            void flush();
      };

      interface StreamFactory {
            Stream create();
      };

      interface FileStreamFactory {
            Stream create (in string theFileName)
                 raises ( InvalidFileNameError );
      };
};
```

CosStream

```
module CosStream {

      exception ObjectCreationError {};
      exception StreamDataFormatError {};

      interface StreamIO;

      interface Streamable
                 : CosObjectIdentity::IdentifiableObject {
            readonly attribute CosLifeCycle::Key
                                              external_form_id;
            void externalize_to_stream (
                       in StreamIO targerStreamIO);
            void internalize_from_stream (
                       in StreamIO targetStreamIO,
                       in CosLifeCycle::FactoryFinder there)
                 raises (CosLifeCycle::NoFactory,
                         ObjectCreationError,
                         StreamDataFormatError);
      };
```

```
    interface StreamableFactory {
          Streamable create_uninitialized ();
    };

    interface StreamIO {
          void write_string (in string aString);
          void write_char (in char aChar);
          void write_octet (in octet anOctet);
          void write_unsigned_long (
                in unsigned long anUnsignedLong);
          void write_unsigned_short (
                in unsigned short anUnsignedShort);
          void write_long (in long aLong);
          void write_short (in short aShort);
          void write_float (in float aFloat);
          void write_double (in double aDouble);
          void write_boolean (in boolean aBoolean);
          void write_object (in Streamable obj);
          void write_graph (
                in CosCompoundExternalization::Node aNode);

          string read_string()
                raises (StreamDataFormatError);
          char read_char ()
                raises (StreamDataFormatError);
          octet read_octet ()
                raises (StreamDataFormatError);
          unsigned long read_unsigned_long ()
                raises (StreamDataFormatError);
          unsigned short read_unsigned_short ()
                raises (StreamDataFormatError);
          long read_long ()
                raises (StreamDataFormatError);
          short read_short ()
                raises (StreamDataFormatError);
          float read_float ()
                raises (StreamDataFormatError);
          double read_double ()
                raises (StreamDataFormatError);
          boolean read_boolean ()
                raises (StreamDataFormatError);
          Streamable read_object (
                      in CosLifeCycle::FactoryFinder there,
                      in Streamable aStreamable)
                raises (StreamDataFormatError);
          void read_graph (
                      in CosCompoundExternalization::Node start,
                      in CosLifeCycle::FactoryFinder there)
                raises (StreamDataFormatError);
    };

};
```

A.6 Time Service

This section gives the IDL definitions for the Time Service.

Module `Time`

```
module Time {

      // Replace the following with
      // unsigned longlong if it is available
      struct ulonglong {
            unsigned long low;
            unsigned long high;
      };
      typedef ulonglong TimeT;  // 64 bits
      typedef TimeT InaccuracyT;  // Only 48 bits
      typedef short TdfT;
      struct UtcT { // components not visible
            TimeT time;  // 64 bits
            unsigned long inacclo;  //
            unsigned short inacchi; // 48 bits
            TdfT tdf;
      };  // Total 16 bytes

      struct IntervalT {
            TimeT  lower_bound;
            TimeT  upper_bound;
      };
};
```

Module `CosTime`

```
module CosTime {

      enum ComparisonType {
            Interval, Mid
      };

      enum TimeComparison {
            EqualTo, LessThan, GreaterThan, Indeterminate
      };

      enum OverlapType {
            Container, Contained, Overlap, NoOverlap
      };

      exception TimeUnavailable {};
      interface TIO;  // Forward declaration.
```

```
interface UTO {
      readonly attribute Time::TimeT time;
      readonly attribute Time::InaccuracyT inaccuracy;
      readonly attribute Time::TdfT  tdf;
      readonly attribute Time::UtcT utc_time;

      UTO absolute_time()
            raises (CORBA::DATA_CONVERSION);

      TimeComparison compare_time (
                  in ComparisonType comparison_type,
                  in UTO uto)
            raises (CORBA::BAD_PARAM);

      TIO time_to_interval (
                  in ComparisonType interval_type,
                  in UTO uto)
            raises (CORBA::BAD_PARAM);

      TIO interval ()
            raises (CORBA::DATA_CONVERSION );
};


interface TIO {

      readonly attribute Time::IntervalT time_interval;

      OverlapType span (in TIO interval,
                        out TIO span)
            raises (CORBA::BAD_PARAM);

      OverlapType overlap (in TIO interval,
                           out TIO overlap)
            raises (CORBA::BAD_PARAM);

      UTO time();
};


interface TimeService {

      UTO universal_time ()
            raises (TimeUnavailable);

      UTO secure_universal_time()
            raises (TimeUnavailable);

      UTO new_universal_time (
                  in Time::TimeT time,
                  in Time::InaccuracyT inaccuracy,
```

```
                    in Time::TdfT tdf)
                raises (CORBA::BAD_PARAM);

            UTO uto_from_utc (in Time::UtcT utc);

            TIO new_interval (
                    in Time::TimeT lower,
                    in Time::TimeT upper)
                raises (CORBA::BAD_PARAM);
    };
};
```

Module `CosTimerEvent`

```
module CosTimerEvent {

    enum TimeType {
        Absolute, Relative, Periodic
    };

    enum EventStatus {
        TimeSet, TimeCleared,
        Triggered, FailedTrigger
    };

    struct TimerEventT {
        Time::UtcT utc;
        any event_data;
    };


    interface TimerEventHandler {

        readonly attribute EventStatus status;

        boolean time_set (out CosTime::UTO uto);

        void set_time (
                in TimeType time_type,
                in CosTime::UTO trigger_time)
            raises (CORBA::BAD_PARAM);

        boolean cancel_timer();

        void set_data (in any event_data);
    };


    interface TimerEventService {

        TimerEventHandler register (
```

```
                in CosEventComm::PushConsumer event_interface,
                in any event_data)
            raises (CORBA::NO_RESOURCE);

        void unregister (
                    in TimerEventHandler event_handler)
            raises (CORBA::INV_OBJREF);

        CosTime::UTO event_time (in TimerEventT timer_event);
    };
};
```

A.7 Property Service

This section gives the IDL definitions for the Property Service.

```
module CosPropertyService {

    // Data types:

    typedef string PropertyName;
    struct Property {
        PropertyName property_name;
        any property_value;
    };

    enum PropertyModeType {
        normal, read_only, fixed_normal,
        fixed_readonly, undefined
    };

    struct PropertyDef {
        PropertyName property_name;
        any property_value;
        PropertyModeType property_mode;
    };

    struct PropertyMode {
        PropertyName property_name;
        PropertyModeType property_mode;
    };

    typedef sequence<PropertyName> PropertyNames;
    typedef sequence<Property> Properties;
    typedef sequence<PropertyDef> PropertyDefs;
    typedef sequence<PropertyMode> PropertyModes;
    typedef sequence<TypeCode> PropertyTypes;
```

```
interface PropertyNamesIterator;
interface PropertiesIterator;
interface PropertySetFactory;
interface PropertySetDef;
interface PropertySet;


// Exceptions:

exception ConstraintNotSupported {};
exception InvalidPropertyName {};
exception ConflictingProperty {};
exception PropertyNotFound {};
exception UnsupportedTypeCode {};
exception UnsupportedProperty {};
exception UnsupportedMode {};
exception FixedProperty {};
exception ReadOnlyProperty {};

// Support for multiple exception reports:

enum ExceptionReason {
      invalid_property_name, conflicting_property,
      property_not_found, unsupported_type_code,
      unsupported_property, unsupported_mode,
      fixed_property, read_only_property
};

struct PropertyException {
      ExceptionReason reason;
      PropertyName failing_property_name;
};

typedef sequence<PropertyException> PropertyExceptions;

exception MultipleExceptions {
      PropertyExceptions exceptions;
};


// Interface definitions:

interface PropertySetFactory {
      PropertySet create_propertyset ();
      PropertySet create_constrained_propertyset (
                  in PropertyTypes allowed_property_types,
                  in Properties allowed_properties)
            raises (ConstraintNotSupported);
      PropertySet create_initial_propertyset (
                  in Properties initial_properties)
            raises (MultipleExceptions);
};
```

```
interface PropertySetDefFactory {
     PropertySetDef create_propertysetdef ();
     PropertySetDef create_constrained_propertysetdef (
               in PropertyTypes allowed_property_types,
               in PropertyDefs allowed_property_defs)
          raises (ConstraintNotSupported);
     PropertySetDef create_initial_propertysetdef (
               in PropertyDefs initial_property_defs)
          raises (MultipleExceptions);
};


interface PropertySet {

     void define_property (
               in PropertyName property_name,
               in any property_value)
          raises (InvalidPropertyName,
                  ConflictingProperty,
                  UnsupportedTypeCode,
                  UnsupportedProperty,
                  ReadOnlyProperty);

     void define_properties (
               in Properties nproperties)
          raises (MultipleExceptions);

     unsigned long get_number_of_properties();

     void get_all_property_names (
               in unsigned long how_many,
               out PropertyNames property_names,
               out PropertyNamesIterator rest);

     any get_property_value (
               in PropertyName property_name)
          raises (PropertyNotFound,
                  InvalidPropertyName);

     boolean get_properties (
               in PropertyNames property_names,
               out Properties nproperties);

     void get_all_properties (
               in unsigned long how_many,
               out Properties nproperties,
               out PropertiesIterator rest);

     void delete_property (
               in PropertyName property_name)
```

```
                raises (PropertyNotFound,
                        InvalidPropertyName,
                        FixedProperty);

        void delete_properties (
                    in PropertyNames property_names)
                raises (MultipleExceptions);

        boolean delete_all_properties ();

        boolean is_property_defined (
                    in PropertyName property_name)
                raises (InvalidPropertyName);
};


interface PropertySetDef : PropertySet {

        void get_allowed_property_types (
                    out PropertyTypes property_types);

        void get_allowed_properties (
                    out PropertyDefs property_defs);

        void define_property_with_mode (
                    in PropertyName property_name,
                    in any property_value,
                    in PropertyModeType property_mode)
                raises (InvalidPropertyName,
                        ConflictingProperty,
                        UnsupportedTypeCode,
                        UnsupportedProperty,
                        UnsupportedMode,
                        ReadOnlyProperty);

        void define_properties_with_modes (
                    in PropertyDefs property_defs)
                raises (MultipleExceptions);

        PropertyModeType get_property_mode (
                    in PropertyName property_name)
                raises (PropertyNotFound,
                        InvalidPropertyName);

        boolean get_property_modes (
                    in PropertyNames property_names,
                    out PropertyModes property_modes);


        void set_property_mode (
                    in PropertyName property_name,
                    out PropertyModeType property_mode)
```

```
            raises (InvalidPropertyName,
                    PropertyNotFound,
                    UnsupportedMode);

        void set_property_modes (
                in PropertyModes property_modes)
            raises (MultipleExceptions);
    };


    interface PropertyNamesIterator {
        void reset();
        boolean next_one(
                out PropertyName property_name);
        boolean next_n (
                in unsigned long how_many,
                out PropertyNames property_names);
        void destroy();
    };


    interface PropertiesIterator {
        void reset();
        boolean next_one(
                out Property aproperty);
        boolean next_n (
                in unsigned long how_many,
                out Properties nproperties);
        void destroy();
    };

};
```

A.8 Relationship Service

This section gives the IDL definitions for the Relationship Service.

A.8.1 Base level

```
module CosRelationships {

    interface RelationshipFactory;
    interface Relationship;

    interface RoleFactory;
    interface Role;
```

```
interface RelationshipIterator;

typedef Object RelatedObject;
typedef sequence<Role> Roles;

typedef string RoleName;
typedef sequence<RoleName>  RoleNames;

struct NamedRole {
     RoleName name;
     Role  aRole;
};
typedef sequence<NamedRole>  NamedRoles;

struct RelationshipHandle {
     Relationship the_relationship;
     CosObjectIdentity::ObjectIdentifier constant_random_id;
};

typedef sequence<RelationshipHandle> RelationshipHandles;



// In module CosRelationships:
interface RelationshipFactory {

     struct NamedRoleType {
          RoleName name;
          ::CORBA::InterfaceDef  named_role_type;
     };

     typedef sequence<NamedRoleType> NamedRoleTypes;

     readonly attribute  ::CORBA::InterfaceDef
                                   relationship_type;
     readonly attribute  unsigned short  degree;
     readonly attribute  NamedRoleTypes named_role_types;

     exception RoleTypeError {
                    NamedRoles culprits;
     };
     exception MaxCardinalityExceeded {
                    NamedRoles culprits;
     };
     exception DegreeError {
                    unsigned short required_degree;
     };
     exception DuplicateRoleName {
                    NamedRoles culprits;
     };
     exception UnknownRoleName {
                    NamedRoles culprits;
```

```
    };

    Relationship create
                    (in NamedRoles  named_roles)
          raises (RoleTypeError, MaxCardinalityExceeded,
                  DegreeError, DuplicateRoleName,
                  UnknownRoleName);
};



// In module CosRelationships:
interface Relationship :
                CosObjectIdentity::IdentifiableObject {

    exception CannotUnlink {
                Roles offending_roles;
    };
    readonly attribute NamedRoles  named_roles;
    void destroy ()  raises (CannotUnlink);
};



// In module CosRelationships:
interface Role {

    exception UnknownRoleName {};
    exception UnknownRelationship {};
    exception RelationshipTypeError {};
    exception CannotDestroyRelationship {
          RelationshipHandles offenders;
    };
    exception ParticipatingInRelationship {
          RelationshipHandles the_relationships;
    };

    readonly attribute RelatedObject related_object;

    RelatedObject  get_other_related_object (
                            in RelationshipHandle rel,
                            in RoleName  target_name)
          raises (UnknownRoleName,
                  UnknownRelationship);

    Role get_other_role (in RelationshipHandle rel,
                         in RoleName target_name)
          raises (UnknownRoleName,
                  UnknownRelationship);

    void get_relationships (in unsigned long how_many,
                   out RelationshipHandles rels,
```

```
                         out RelationshipIterator iterator);

        void destroy_relationships ()
             raises (CannotDestroyRelationship);

        void destroy ()
             raises (ParticipatingInRelationship);

        boolean check_minimum_cardinality ();

        void link (in RelationshipHandle rel,
                   in NamedRoles  named_roles)
           raises (RelationshipFactory::MaxCardinalityExceeded,
                   RelationshipTypeError);

        void unlink (in RelationshipHandle rel)
             raises (UnknownRelationship);
    };



    // In module CosRelationships:
    interface RoleFactory {

        exception NilRelatedObject {};
        exception RelatedObjectTypeError {};

        readonly attribute  ::CORBA::InterfaceDef role_type;
        readonly attribute  unsigned long max_cardinality;
        readonly attribute  unsigned long min_cardinality;
        // typedef for CORBA 2.x:
        tyepdef sequence<::CORBA::InterfaceDef> InterfaceDefs;
        readonly attribute InterfaceDefs related_object_types;

        Role  create_role (
                   in RelatedObject  related_object)
             raises (NilRelatedObject, RelatedObjectTypeError);
    };



    // In module CosRelationships:
    interface RelationshipIterator {

        boolean  next_one (out RelationshipHandle rel);
        boolean next_n (in unsigned long how_many,
                        out RelationshipHandles  rels);
        void destroy();
    };

};
```

A.9 Concurrency Control Service

This section gives some of the IDL definitions for the Concurrency Control service.

Further details on `LockSet`, `LockCoordinator`, and `LockSetFactory`

For transactional clients, a `LockSet` object must use the facilities of the Object Transaction Service to determine the transaction identifier of the current transaction. (For a non-transactional client, the transaction identifier will be null, and hence the `LockSet` object will know that there is no transaction involved). The transaction identifier of the current transaction need not be explicitly passed to a `LockSet` object, because it can use the facilities of the OTS to determine this (see Section 23.3 for an explanation of the `Current` interface). However, there is a variation of the `LockSet` interface, `TransactionalLockSet`, that supports the same set of operations, but each takes a transaction identifier as its first parameter.

It should be remembered that despite the names `TransactionalLockSet` and `LockSet`, interface `LockSet` can be used for transactional clients (the transaction identifier is passed implicitly).

A `LockCoordinator` object is associated with each transaction to record the locks it holds. This provides a single operation, `drop_locks()`. When a transaction commits or rolls backs, its `LockCoordinator` object is located and this operation is called; it informs each `LockSet` object that the transaction s locks are to be released.

Interface `LockSetFactory` is also provided with the following operations to create `LockSet` and `TransactionalLockSet` objects:

- `create()`: creates and returns an object reference to a new `LockSet` object.
- `create_transactional()`: creates and returns an object reference to a new `TransactionalLockSet` object.
- `create_related()`: creates and returns an object reference to a new `LockSet` object *related* to a specified one. If a transaction's locks on one `LockSet` are released using `drop_locks()` on a coordinator, the transaction's locks on all related `LockSet` objects are automatically released.
- `create_transactional_related()`: creates and returns an object reference to a new `TransactionalLockSet` object related to a specified one.

IDL definitions

```
module CosConcurrencyControl {

      enum lock_mode {
            read, write, upgrade,
            intention_read, intention_write};

      exception LockNotHeld {};

      interface LockCoordinator {
            void drop_locks ();
      };

      interface LockSet {
            void lock (in lock_mode mode);
            boolean try_lock (in lock_mode mode);

            void unlock (in lock_mode mode)
                  raises (LockNotHeld);
            void change_mode (in lock_mode held_mode,
                              in lock_mode new_mode)
                  raises (LockNotHeld);
            LockCoordinator get_coordinator (
                        in CosTransactions::Coordinator which);
      };

      interface TransactionalLockSet {
            void lock (in CosTransactions::Coordinator current,
                        in lock_mode mode);
            boolean try_lock (
                        in CosTransactions::Coordinator current,
                        in lock_mode mode);

            void unlock (in CosTransactions::Coordinator current,
                          in lock_mode mode)
                  raises (LockNotHeld);
            void change_mode (
                        in CosTransactions::Coordinator current,
                        in lock_mode held_mode,
                        in lock_mode new_mode)
                  raises (LockNotHeld);
            LockCoordinator get_coordinator (
                        in CosTransactions::Coordinator which);
      };

      interface LockSetFactory {
            LockSet create();
            LockSet create_related (in LockSet which);
            TransactionalLockSet create_transactional();
            TransactionalLockSet create_transactional_related (
```

```
                                 in TransactionalLockSet which);
      };
};
```

A.10 Persistent Object Service

This section gives some of the IDL definitions for the Persistent Object Service.

Persistent object (PO)

```
module CosPersistencePO {

      interface PO {  // Optionally for use by clients.
            attribute CosPersistencePID::PID p;
            CosPersistencePDS::PDS connect (
                                      in CosPersistencePID::PID p);
            void disconnect(in CosPersistencePID::PID p);
            void store (in CosPersistencePID::PID p);
            void restore (in CosPersistencePID::PID p);
            void delete (in CosPersistencePID::PID p);
      };

      interface SD { // For use by the POM.
            void pre_store();
            void post_restore();
      };
};
```

Persistent object manager (POM)

```
module CosPersistencePOM {

      interface POM {  // For use by persistent obj.
            CosPersistencePDS::PDS connect (in Object obj,
                                      in CosPersistencePID::PID p);
            void disconnect(in Object obj,
                                in CosPersistencePID::PID p);
            void store (in Object obj,
                            in CosPersistencePID::PID p);
            void restore (in Object obj,
                              in CosPersistencePID::PID p);
            void delete (in Object obj,
                             in CosPersistencePID::PID p);
      };

};
```

Persistent data service (PDS)

```
module CosPersistencePDS {

      interface PDS {  // For use by POM.
            PDS connect (in Object obj,
                         in CosPersistencePID::PID p);
            void disconnect(in Object obj,
                            in CosPersistencePID::PID p);
            void store (in Object obj,
                        in CosPersistencePID::PID p);
            void restore (in Object obj,
                          in CosPersistencePID::PID p);
            void delete (in Object obj,
                         in CosPersistencePID::PID p);
      };

};
```

Direct access (PDS_DA) protocol

```
module CosPersistencePDS_DA {

      typedef string DAObjectID;

      interface PID_DA : CosPersistencePID::PID {
            attribute DAObjectID oid;
      };

      interface DAObject {
            // Data objects can inherit from this.
            boolean dado_same(in DAObject d);
            DAObjectID dado_oid();
            PID_DA dado_pid();
            void dado_remove();
            void dado_free();
      };

      interface DAObjectFactory {
            // For creating data objects.
            DAObject create();
      };

      interface DAObjectFactoryFinder {
            DAObjectFactory find_factory(in string key);
      };

      interface PDS_DA : CosPersistencePDS::PDS {
            DAObject get_data ();
            void set_data (in DAObject new_data);
```

```
        DAObject lookup (in DAObjectID id);
        PID_DA get_pid();
        PID_DA get_object_pid (in DAObject dao);
        DAObjectFactoryFinder data_factories();
    };

    typedef sequence<string>  AttributeNames;
    interface DynamicAttributeAccess {
        // Data objects may inherit from this.
        AttributeNames attribute_names();
        any attribute_get (in string name);
        void attribute_set (in string name,
                            in any value);
    };

    // The PDS_ClusteredDA interface extends PDS_DA
    // with facilities to cluster data objects:
    typedef string ClusterID;
    typedef sequence<ClusterID> ClusterIDs;
    interface PDS_ClusteredDA : PDS_DA {
        ClusterID cluster_id();
        string cluster_kind();
        ClusterIDs clusters_of();
        PDS_ClusteredDA create_cluster (in string kind);
        PDS_ClusteredDA open_cluster (in ClusterID cluster);
        PDS_ClusteredDA copy_cluster (in PDS_DA source);
    };
};
```

Dynamic data object (DDO) protocol

```
module CosPersistenceDDO {

    interface DDO {
        attribute string object_type;
        attribute CosPersistencePID::PID p;

        short add_data();
        short add_data_property (in short data_id);
        short get_data_count();
        short get_data_property_count (in short data_id);

        void get_data_property (in short data_id,
                                in short property_id,
                                out string property_name,
                                out any property_value);
        void set_data_property (in short data_id,
                                in short property_id,
                                in string property_name,
                                in any property_value);
```

```
        void get_data (in short data_id,
                       out string data_name,
                       out any data_value);
        void set_data (in short data_id,
                       in string data_name,
                       in any data_value);
    };
};
```

A.11 Query Service

This section gives the IDL definitions for the Query Service. The IDL uses the identifier `element` to refer to a member of a collection.

Collection and iterator

Type `Istring` is a place holder for an international string type (which has recently been defined as type wstring); type `NVPair` and `ParameterList` are used by operation `CollectionFactory::create()`, but the standard does not define the legal values of this sequence of name–value pairs. However, it does specify that one of the name–value pairs must hold a name "initial_size" and a value of IDL type `long`. This is used as a hint to the implementation of the collection of the amount of space to allocate initially. Other name–value pairs may specify the type of collection required and the indices and caching to be used.

To support RDBMSs, type `Value` is defined as a union of all of the possible types that can be stored in a field of a record. Type `FieldValue` defines a value that can be null or any valid value.

```
module CosQueryCollection {

    exception ElementInvalid {};
    exception IteratorInvalid {};
    exception PositionInvalid {};

    enum ValueType {TypeBoolean, TypeChar,
                    TypeOctet, TypeShort, TypeUShort, TypeLong,
                    TypeULong, TypeFloat, TypeDouble,
                    TypeString, TypeObject, TypeAny,
                    TypeSmallInt, TypeInteger, TypeReal,
                    TypeDoublePrecision, TypeCharacter,
                    TypeDecimal, TypeNumeric};

    struct Decimal {long precision;
                    long scale;
                    sequence<octet> value;
    };
```

```
union Value switch (ValueType) {
      case TypeBoolean: boolean b;
      case TypeChar: char c;
      case TypeOctet: octet o;
      case TypeShort: short s;
      case TypeUShort: unsigned short us;
      case TypeLong: long l;
      case TypeULong: unsigned long ul;
      case TypeFloat: float f;
      case TypeDouble:double d;
      case TypeString: string str;
      case TypeObject: Object obj;
      case TypeAny: any a;
      case TypeSmallInt: short si;
      case TypeInteger: long i;
      case TypeReal: float r;
      case TypeDoublePrecision: double dp;
      case TypeCharacter: string ch;
      case TypeDecimal: Decimal dec;
      case TypeNumeric: Decimal n;
};

typedef boolean Null;
union FieldValue switch (Null) {
      case FALSE: Value v;
};
typedef sequence<FieldValue> Record;

typedef string wstring;
struct NVPair {wstring name; any value;};
typedef sequence<NVPair> ParameterList;

interface Collection;
interface Iterator;

interface CollectionFactory {
      Collection create (in ParameterList params);
};

interface Collection {

      readonly attribute long cardinality;

      void add_element (in any element)
               raises (ElementInvalid);

      void add_all_elements (in Collection elements)
               raises (ElementInvalid);

      void insert_element_at (in any element,
                              in Iterator where)
               raises (IteratorInvalid,
```

```
                    ElementInvalid);

        void replace_element_at (in any element,
                                 in Iterator where)
                raises (IteratorInvalid,
                        PositionInvalid,
                        ElementInvalid);

        void remove_element_at (in Iterator where)
                raises (IteratorInvalid,
                        PositionInvalid);

        void remove_all_elements();

        any retrieve_element_at (in Iterator where)
                raises (IteratorInvalid,
                        PositionInvalid);

        Iterator create_iterator();
    };


    interface Iterator {

        any next()
                raises (IteratorInvalid,
                        PositionInvalid);

        void reset();

        boolean more();
    };

};
```

Query framework

```
module CosQuery {

    exception QueryInvalid {};
    exception QueryProcessingError {string why;};
    exception QueryTypeInvalid {};

    enum QueryStatus {complete, incomplete};

    typedef CosQueryCollection::ParameterList ParameterList;
    typedef CORBA::InterfaceDef QLType;
```

```
    interface QueryLanguageType {};
    interface SQLQuery : QueryLanguageType {};
    interface SQL_92Query : SQLQuery {};
    interface OQL : QueryLanguageType {};
    interface OQLBasic : OQL {};
    interface OQL_93 : OQL {};
    interface OQL_93Basic : OQL_93, OQLBasic {};


    interface QueryEvaluator {

          readonly attribute sequence<QLType> ql_types;
          readonly attribute QLType default_ql_type;

          any evaluate (in string query,
                        in QLType ql_type,
                        in ParameterList params)
                     raises (QueryTypeInvalid, QueryInvalid,
                             QueryProcessingError);
    };


    interface QueryableCollection: QueryEvaluator,
                          CosQueryCollection::Collection {};


    interface QueryManager : QueryEvaluator {

          Query create (in string query,
                        in QLType ql_type,
                        in ParameterList params)
                     raises (QueryTypeInvalid, QueryInvalid);
    };


    interface Query {

          readonly attribute QueryManager query_mgr;

          void prepare (in ParameterList params)
                     raises (QueryProcessingError);

          void execute (in ParameterList params)
                     raises (QueryProcessingError);

          QueryStatus get_status ();
          any get_result ();

    };
};
```

References

ANSI (1993). American National Standard X3. 135-1992, Database Language – SQL, January

Atkinson C. (1990). An object-oriented language for software reuse and distribution. Department of Computing, Imperial College of Science, Technology and Medicine, University of London, February

Baker S. (1996). CORBA and databases. *Object Expert,* May

Bernstein P.A., Hadzilacos V. and Goodman N. (1987). *Concurrency Control and Recovery in Database Systems.* Reading, MA: Addison-Wesley

Cattell R.G.G. (1994). *The Object Database Standard: ODMG-93 v.1.2.* San Mateo, CA: Morgan Kaufmann

Ellis M.A. and Stroustrup B. (1990). *The Annotated C++ Reference Manual.* Reading, MA: Addison-Wesley

Gray J.N. and Reuter A. (1993). *Transaction Processing: Concepts and Techniques.* San Mateo, CA: Morgan Kaufmann

I-Kinetics (1995). *DB Component of Component Ware.* Boston, MA: I-Kinetics

McHale C. (1994). Synchronisation in concurrent, object-oriented languages: expressive power, genericity and inheritance. Department of Computer Science, Trinity College, Dublin, October

Schmidt D. and Vinoski S. (1996a). Comparing alternative programming techniques for multi-threaded servers – the thread-per-request concurrency model, C++ report. *SIGS,* **8**(2), February

Schmidt D. and Vinoski S. (1996b). Comparing alternative programming techniques for multi-threaded servers – the thread-pool concurrency model, C++ report. *SIGS,* **8**(4), April

Schmidt D. and Vinoski S. (1996c). Comparing alternative programming techniques for multi-threaded servers – the thread-per-session concurrency model, C++ report. *SIGS,* **8**(7), July

Siegel J. (1996). *CORBA Fundamentals and Programming.* New York: Wiley

Index